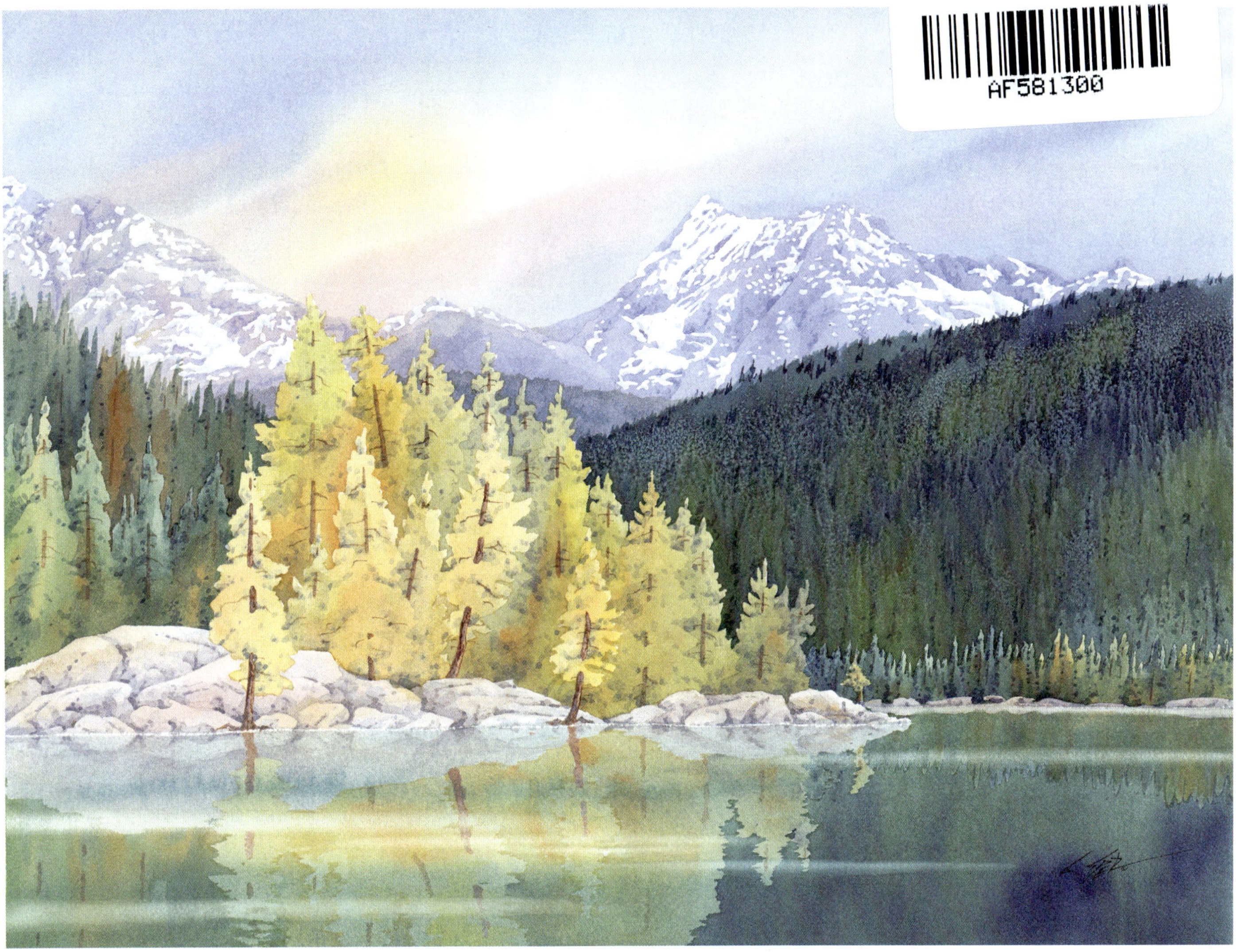

*Gary Spetz's*

# *Painting Wild Places! with Watercolors*

## "100 Series"

*Hiking the trails less traveled*
*to bring how-to-paint programming*
*to Public Television*

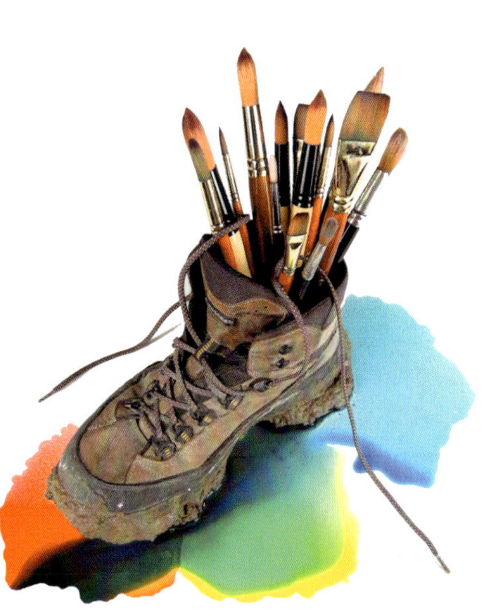

# Acknowledgments

Although she does not consider herself the editor of this book, you, as a reader, would suffer far too many commas, and worse—grammatical, spelling and other punctual errors—if it were not for the generosity of time and the diligence of **Rose Mary Bush**. Indeed, I would not likely have taken on this book project had it not been for her assurance and guidance. I would like to thank her for playing such a central role in the creation and design of this book.

I would also like to thank the well-known watercolor artist from Upper Michigan, **Nita Engle**. She, so many years ago, taught me the power of masking fluid as a painting tool—thus, influencing my painting style more than any other.

# Dedication

This book is dedicated to
**my wife, Marlene**
who has, for nearly three decades, worked tirelessly by my side.
All that I have accomplished is equally the result of her unwavering efforts,
so often hidden behind the scene.

Without a wind I cannot sail.



Published by
Gary Spetz Watercolors
PO Box 374
Lakeside, MT 59922
www.spetz.com

Printed in Canada by Friesens Corporation

Library of Congress Control Number: 2005931287
ISBN 0-9770922-0-8

10 9 8 7 6 5 4 3 2 1
Written, designed, and illustrated by Gary Spetz
Photography: Bruce & Deborah Buckmaster, Kirsten Spetz, Marlene Spetz and Gary Spetz

# Introduction

Although I have, on occasion, found it difficult to finish a painting, I have never found it difficult to begin one. I truly believe the adage, "so little time, so much to paint!" Wilderness landscapes are my inspiration and I have barely tapped this mother lode of subject matter. Mountains, rivers, lakes, oceans, rocks, trees—they are all out there, around us, waiting to be painted. Despite urban encroachment into wilderness, painting subjects still abound nearly everywhere. Granted, some places you have to look a little harder or drive a little further. But, it is out there. If you lack painting inspiration, visit a park, go on a hike—get out into nature! If you are gravitated to wilderness, you have the impulse to become a landscape painter. It is really that simple!

I paint because I want to re-live "the time and the place."

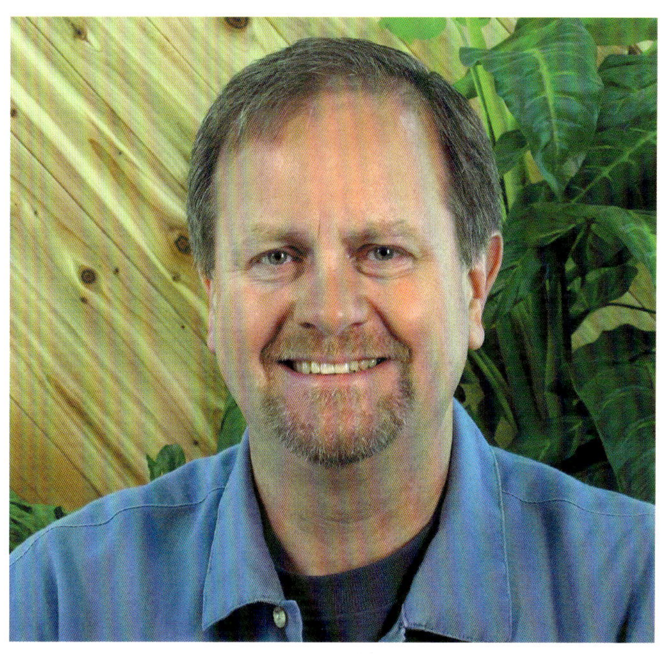

When I visit wilderness, it is a passing thing. I do not reside there. It is "of time and place," as the naturalist Sigurd Olson used to say. I come and I go, but I cannot physically go back again—not to that particular "time and place." I have tried. The interplay of variables—place, light, sound, temperature, breeze, attitude—will never intersect in the same ways again. That moment, that place, is gone from all but my memory. What I leave with and carry with me is the memory of not just the actual scene, but "the whole emotion" that it invoked. To me, painting is an avenue to reach for that feeling, again. A photograph can record a place, but creating a painting enables me to instill a bit of "the feeling." It enables me to extract those natural elements that, in some primordial way, tug at my inner-being. Perhaps it is more about the painting process than the actual output.

I cannot explain why wilderness appears beautiful to me. Such an explanation is surely beyond my mortal abilities—perhaps it is beyond everyone's. But, the impulse seems to be hard-wired within many of us, from birth. We yearn for wilderness…..

And, I contend that if we yearn, we must paint!

The following lessons will show you how *I* reach for some of these "times and places," using paint and paper. I hope that these lessons will help you reach for your "times and places," too. It is an undeniable truth that there is "so much to paint and so little time!"

So, please, don't be wasting time. Paint!

G. Speth

# Spetzisms

I will be the first to admit that I sometimes use (or misuse) words and terms in my own unique way. I have been guilty of doing this at workshops, on television and, of course, here in my book. For clarity sake, I have listed the following (all too common) "Spetzisms" with a brief interpretation.

***Mix up some (color):*** I am referring to mixing one or more of my palette "pool colors" with water, to get it to a usable consistency. Sometimes I will mix two or more colors on my palette tray, but more often than not, I will mix colors on the wet paper itself.

***Foreground trees, rocks, etc.:*** When I state "foreground," I am generally referring to the closest (to the viewer) item(s) that I am referring to. My foreground trees, for instance, may actually be in the paintings mid-ground. But, in this case, they would be the closest trees to the viewer. I name them "foreground" trees because I want to be able to differentiate them from the other trees behind them.

***Depth-Of-Field:*** While this term is generally associated with photography, I use it to explain when shading and varying color values create the illusion of depth in a painting. Naturally, if you want your viewers to be able to walk into your painting, you must provide the 2-dimensional piece of watercolor paper with some "depth."

***Thirsty Brush:*** This is not my term. But if it is unfamiliar to you, it refers to a damp brush that is used to wick up excess puddles of paint and/or water.

***Cobalt Green:*** In this book, this color is my pre-mix of Cobalt Blue and Transparent Yellow.

***Ultramarine Green:*** In this book, this color is my pre-mix of Ultramarine Blue and Transparent Yellow.

***Phthalo Green:*** In this book, this color is my pre-mix of Phthalo Blue and Transparent Yellow.

***Exacto-Knife:*** I use this term just as I do for the beverage Coke. It may be a brand name, but I have grown to use it as the item's name. Of course, I am referring to the pointed razor mounted on a pencil-sized handle.

***Masking Eraser:*** I am referring to the stiff, rubbery block, which is made to adhere, somewhat, to dry masking fluid. It makes the removal of dry masking easier.

***Rich Mix / Medium Mix / Lean Mix:*** It is difficult to quantify how much water is mixed with the various paints. A "rich mix" refers to a greater paint to water ratio. Of course, a "lean mix" refers to a lesser paint to water ratio—a watery mix.

***Paint Globs:*** When I "throw" paint, I refer to the resulting tiny puddles of paint on the paper as "globs".

***Feathered-off or Lost Edges:*** This refers to gradually diminishing an edge of paint to eliminate a hard, clearly defined edge.

***Up-light/Down-light Sides:*** The side of an object that receives direct sunlight (up-light) or its opposite side (down-light).

***Pine/Fir Tree Foliage?:*** The word "foliage" typically refers to "leaf" plants and trees. But, for lack of a better word in this book, I extend its meaning to refer also to the general greenery of pine and fir trees.

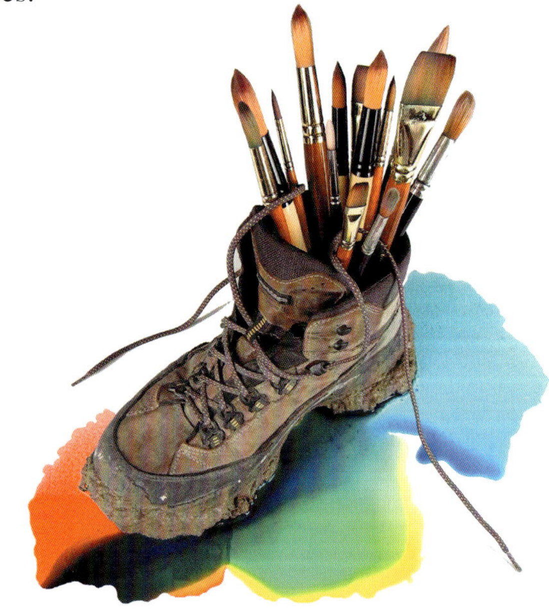

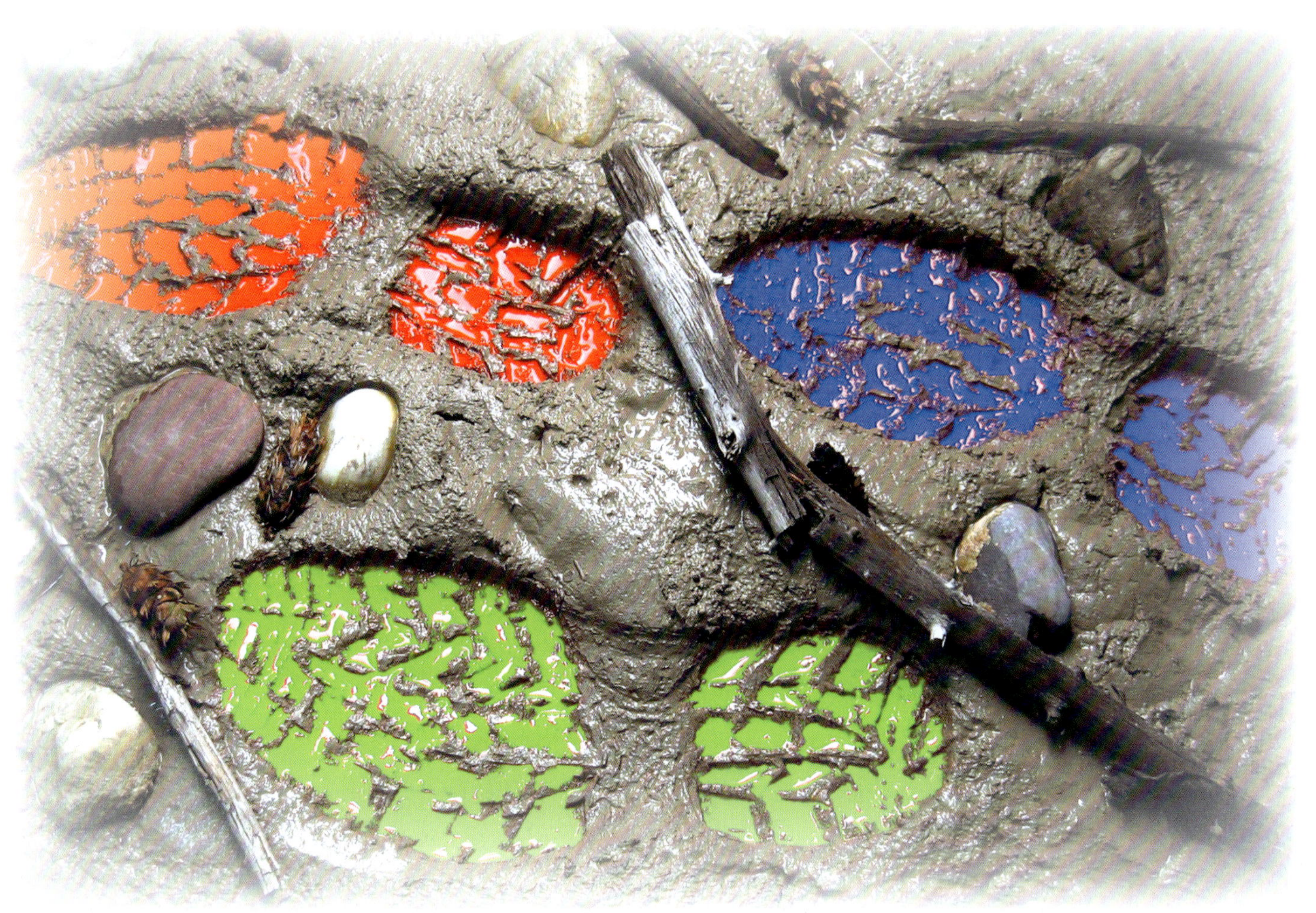

# CONTENTS

# Tools & Materials

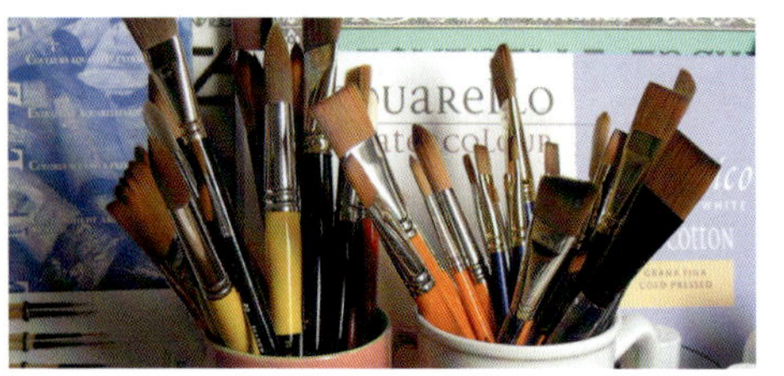

Naturally, the first step to painting is having the necessary tools and materials to work with. The following will list *my* preferences. But, this is provided to you as a guide, not necessarily as a unalterable list. In many cases, you can likely substitute paint colors, brush sizes, etc.

I do, however, strongly urge you to use both professional quality paints and professional quality paper. Yes, they do cost more than their "student grade" counterparts, but as with most things in life, you often get what you pay for. Quality paints and quality papers simply tend to behave better. And, with paints and papers that interact well together, you can more easily achieve the results that you seek. It seems to me that since they provide an easier avenue to achieve the desired end results, they are, particularly, well suited to the novice painters—who presumably need all the help that they can get! I believe that it is counter-intuitive to have a novice painter work with materials that are more difficult to paint with. Arguably, an advanced painter would, actually, be better suited to work effectively with "student grade" materials.

**BRUSHES**

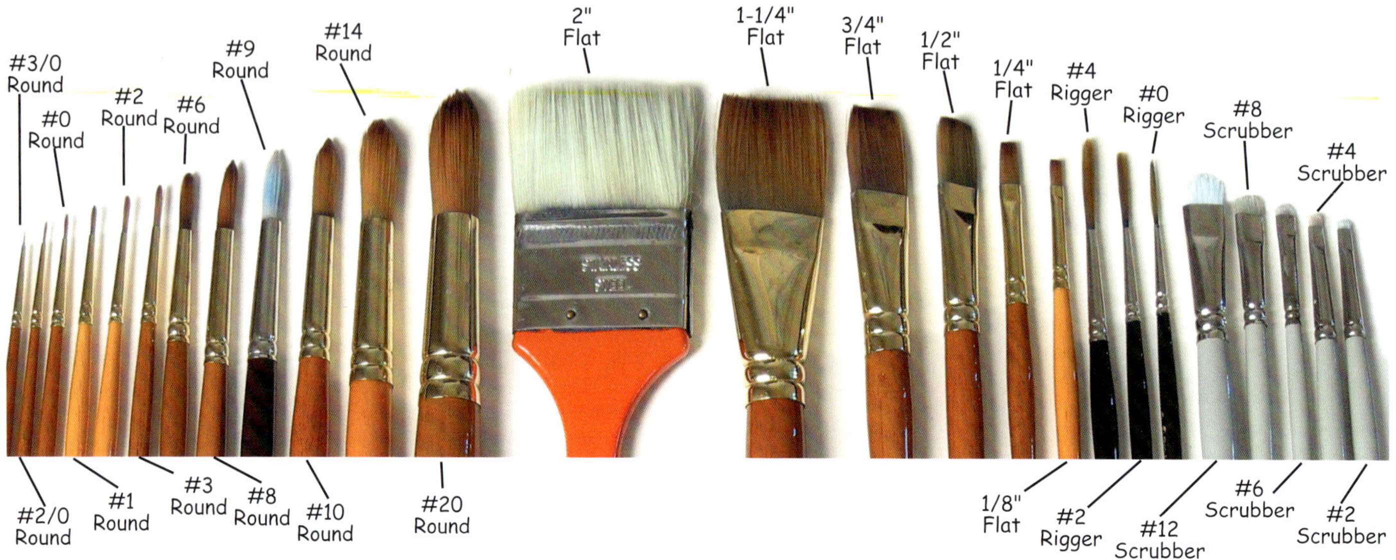


Not all of my watercolor brushes, illustrated above, are used in this book. The following is a list of those that are:

| | |
|---|---|
| **2" Flat** | **#0 Round** |
| **1 1/4" Flat** | **#2/0 Round** |
| **3/4" Flat** | **#3/0 Round** |
| **1/2" Flat** | **#4 Rigger** |
| **1/4" Flat** | **#2 Rigger** |
| **1/8" Flat** | **#12 Scrubber** |
| **#10 Round** | **#8 Scrubber** |
| **#6 Round** | **#6 Scrubber** |
| **#3 Round** | **#4 Scrubber** |
| **#2 Round** | **#2 Scrubber** |
| **#1 Round** | |

You can spend a good deal of money on natural hair brushes and you may, indeed, prefer them. Brush preference is a personal taste. But, I have been quite content with some of the recently developed synthetic watercolor brushes. As a rule, I generally purchase the top-of-the-line synthetic brushes from name brand producers. I have not been disappointed yet.

Although I have a good selection of round brushes, I actually have a strong preference for flat brushes. I probably use them three times as often as the rounds—depending on the particular painting. I simply like the ability of shifting between using the long flat end and the corners. I find flat brushes, overall, to be far more versatile and easy to work with.

## PAINTS

Shown here is my list of paints. Again these are professional grade. These paints come in squeeze tubes, similar, though smaller than toothpaste tubes. Many are non-staining, making them "scrubable/liftable" for some of my later techniques. This is not the "end-all" of paint lists, but rather is a guide. You can certainly substitute many of these colors to get the look that *you* want to achieve. Indeed, experimentation is always encouraged!

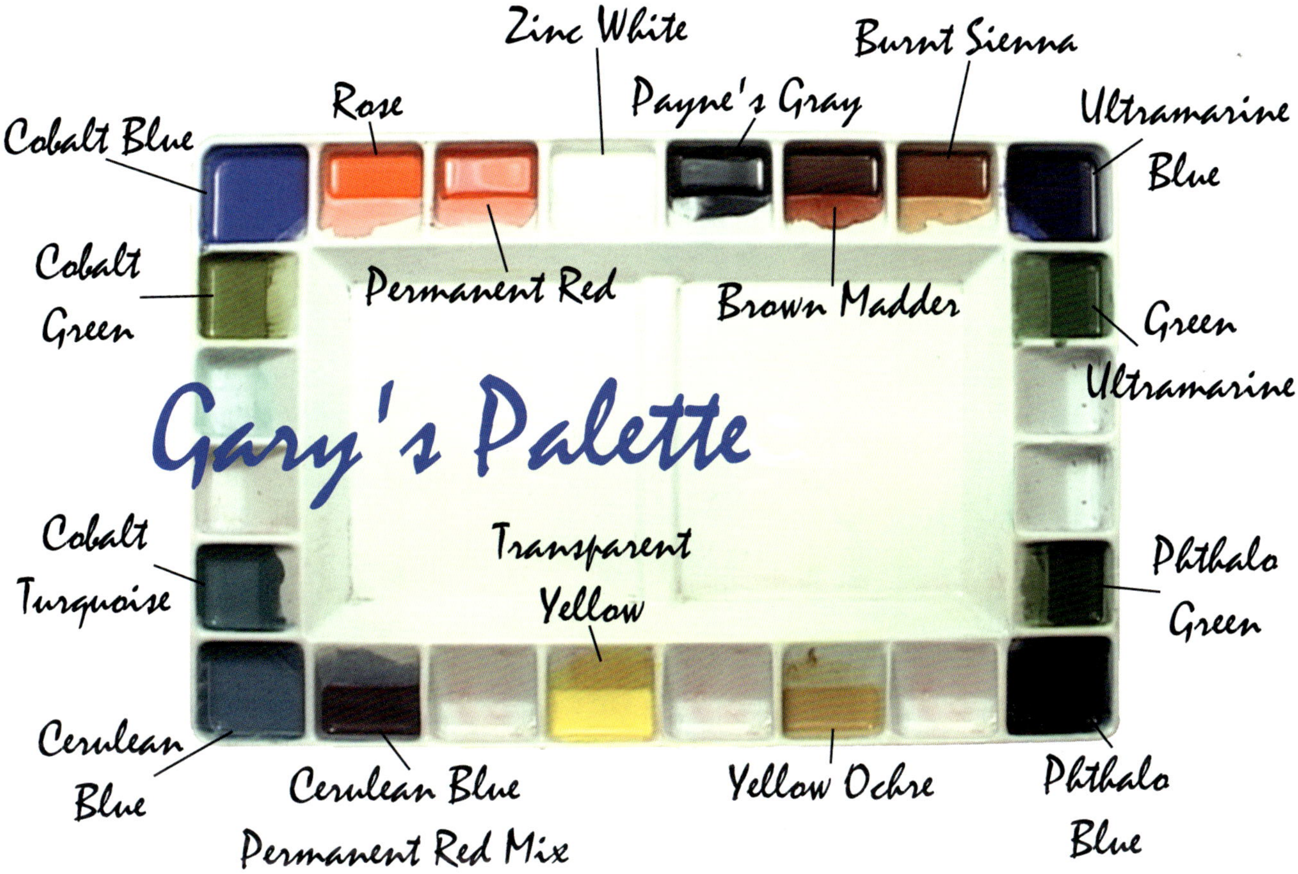

Gary's Palette

Zinc White
Burnt Sienna
Rose
Payne's Gray
Cobalt Blue
Ultramarine Blue
Cobalt Green
Permanent Red
Brown Madder
Green Ultramarine
Cobalt Turquoise
Transparent Yellow
Phthalo Green
Cerulean Blue
Cerulean Blue Permanent Red Mix
Yellow Ochre
Phthalo Blue

## PAPER

Admittedly, I have not experimented much with various paper surfaces. I nearly always paint with 140 lb. Cold Press watercolor paper. As mentioned previously, I use one of the professional grades. All of the paintings in these lessons were created on a 24" x 18" watercolor paper block. I explain this choice in the "Getting Started" section.

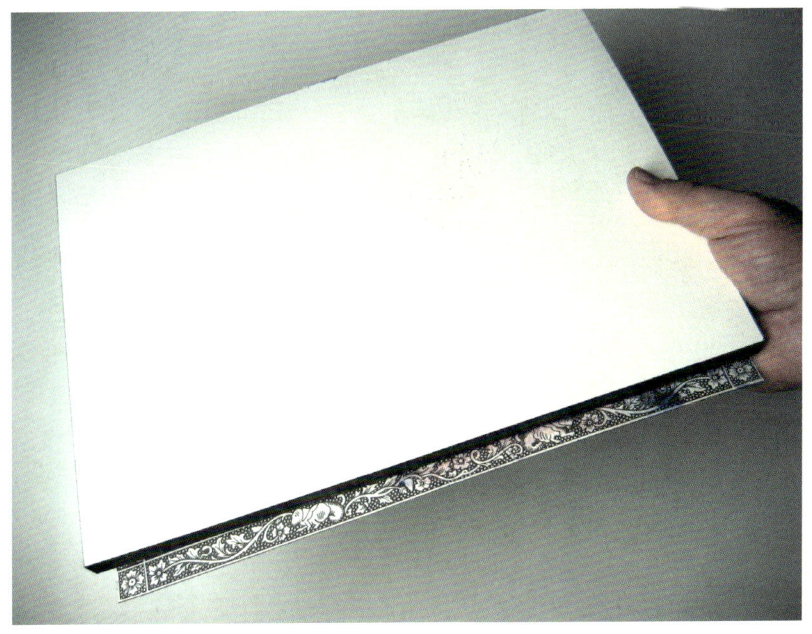

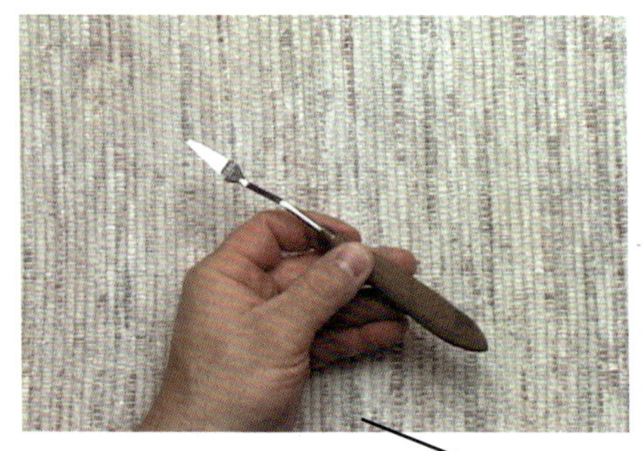

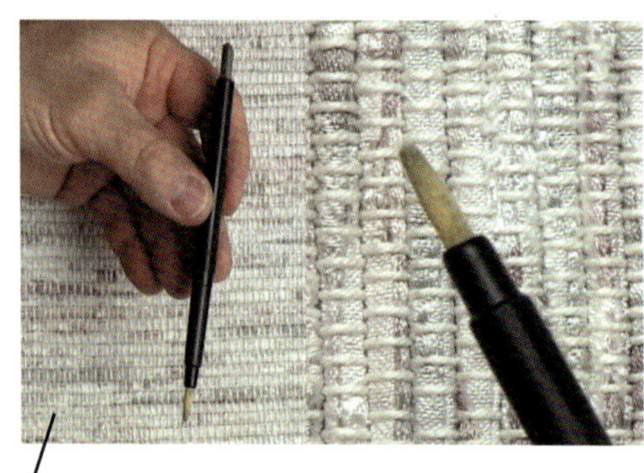

### Miscellaneous Supplies

One of the great characteristics of watercolor painting is that it is conducive to the use of alternate tools and supplies—often supplies not typically associated with art, such as table salt, syringes and toothpicks. The following is a list of these additional tools that I use:

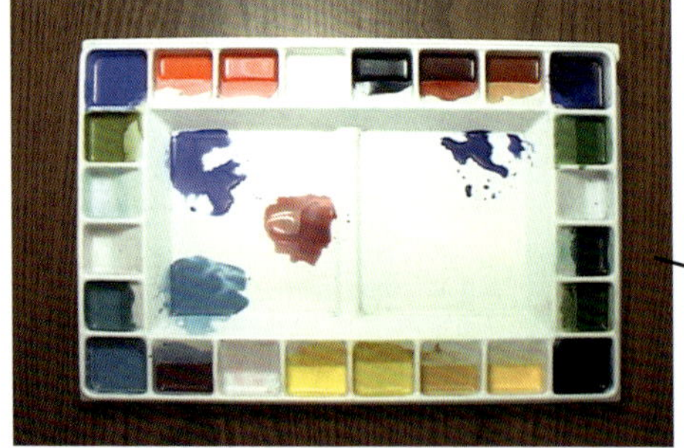

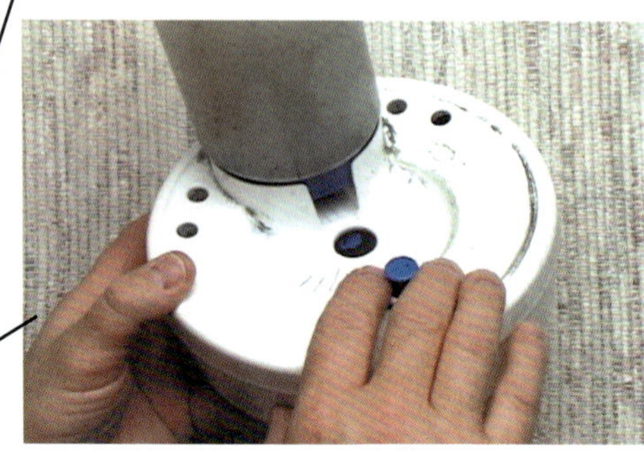

**Palette Knife**
**Felt-Tipped Nib Scrubber**
**Box of Tissues**
**Mixing Palette**
**Kneaded Eraser**
**Rinse-Well**
**"H" Lead Pencil**
**Single-Edged Razor**
**Syringe**
**Masking Tape**
**Plastic Toothpick**
**Drawing Triangles**
**Masking Fluid**
**Trigger-type Spray Bottle**
**Plunger-type Spray Bottle**
**Stiff Bristled Toothbrush**
**Children's Paintbrushes**
**Exacto Knife**
**Bamboo Brushes**

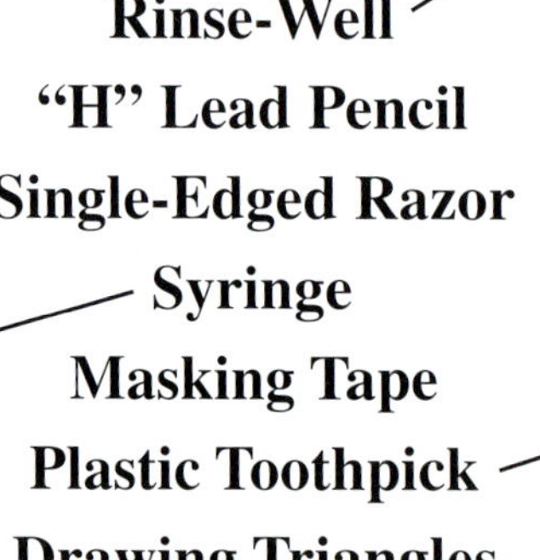

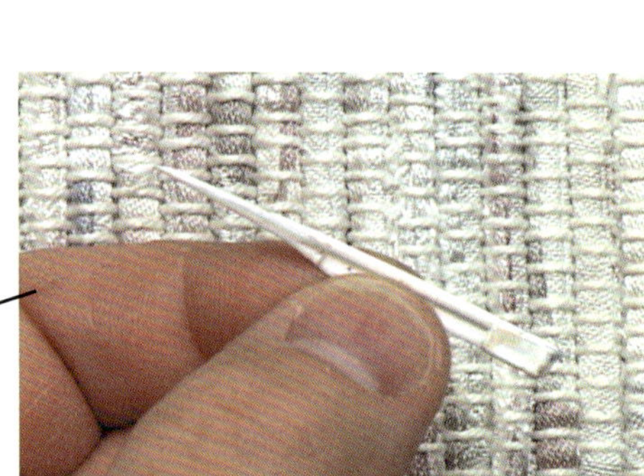

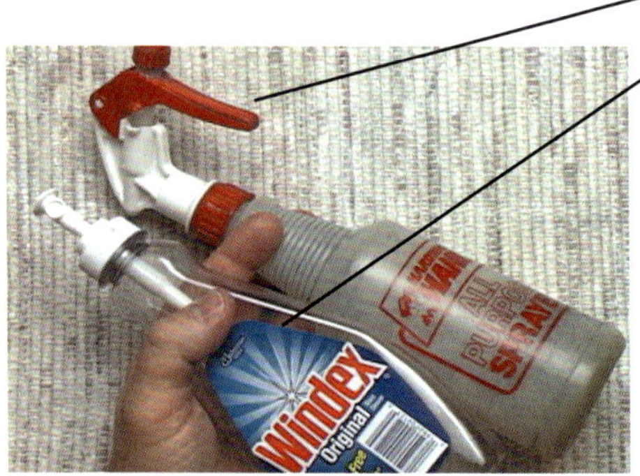


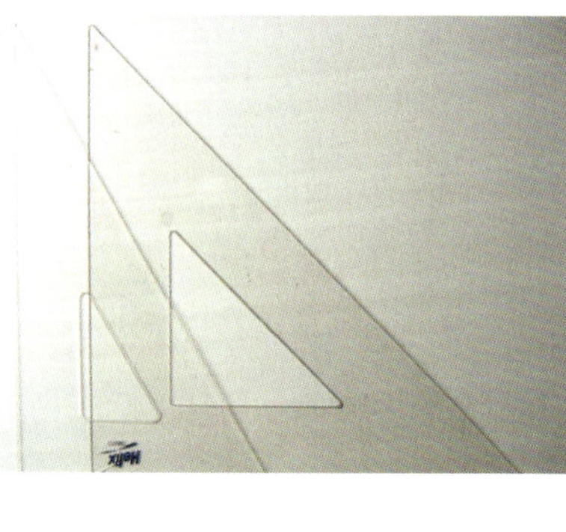

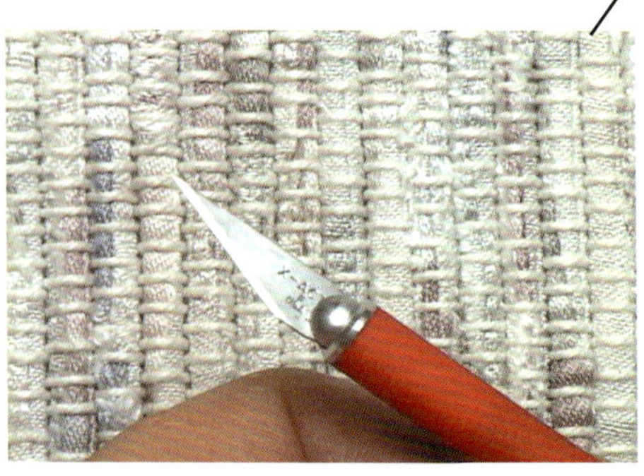

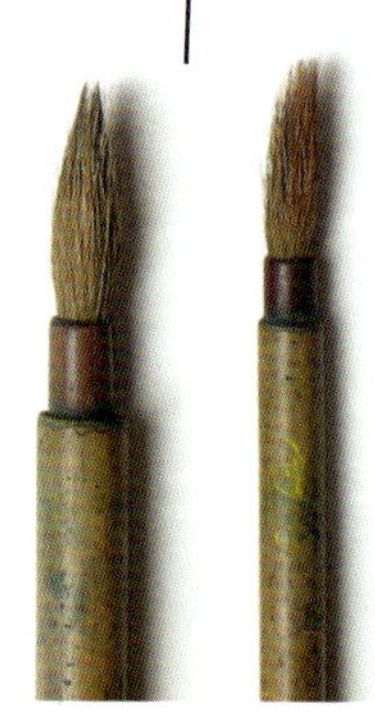

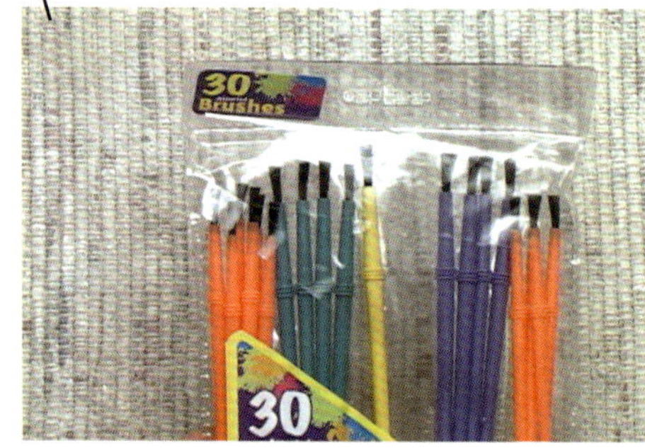

# Setting Up

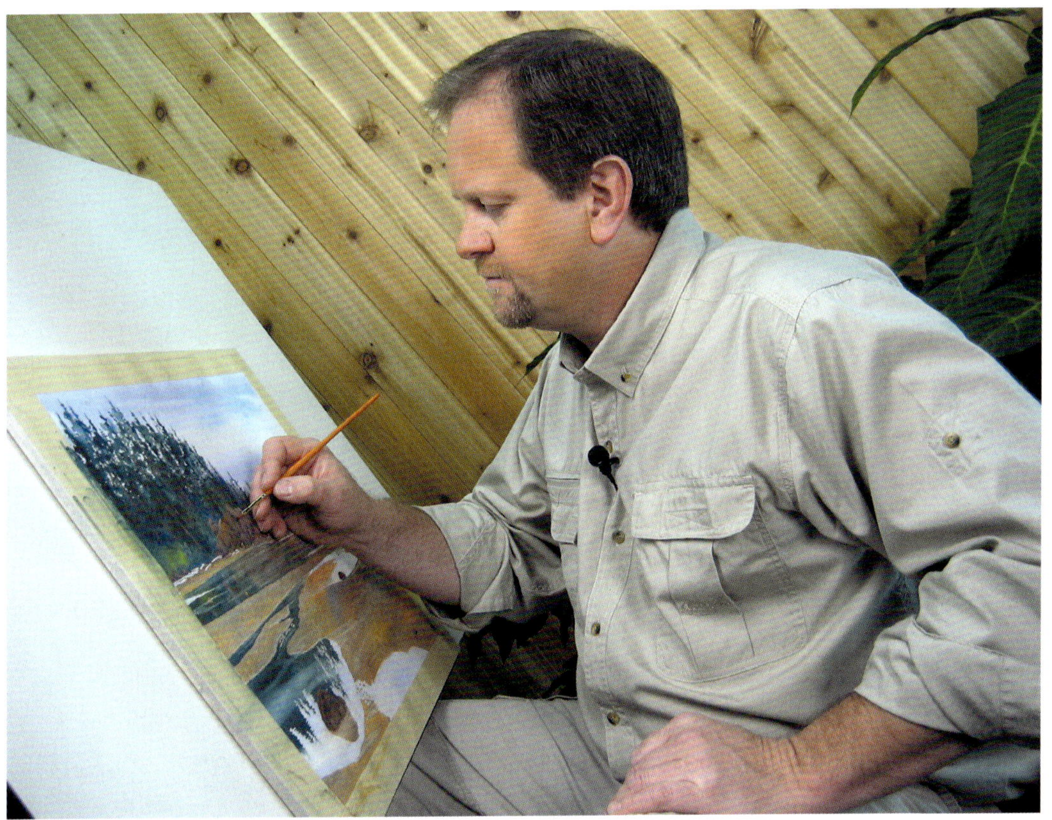

If you are a beginning painter, I recommend that you tilt your painting only slightly—perhaps 20 degrees. It will not be as good a working posture, nor will your viewing perspective be as straight-on, but the painting will be easier to manage, since gravity's force will be reduced. As you progress as a painter, however, I recommend that you gradually increase your working angle. I believe that you will find it more comfortable in the long term.

I mention this since an adjustable painting/drafting table works well for varying angles. But, it is not essential. You can achieve the same effect by simply propping your painting up on a standard flat table, with nearly any objects. When working on a flat table, I often prop my painting up with a stack of 2" masking tape cores—stacked nearly perpendicular to one another, almost like a chain.

An adjustable chair can be handy, too. This allows me to sit higher or lower, with respect to my painting, often making detail work more comfortable.

Good lighting is essential. If you do not have good natural light, consider a incandescent/fluorescent combination lamp. It is designed to provide color neutral lighting.

Since I am right handed, I prefer to work with a supply table off to my right side. On this table—positioned closest to my painting—I have my palette. Directly behind it, I locate my rinse-well, tissue box, and my most frequently used brushes (in a brush holder).

While I like to think of myself as an active person, I have never preferred to stand while painting. I like to sit. I like to be comfortable. Yes, I have heard all of the arguments about how standing permits one to better express themselves—move freely about, etc., but I, frankly, do not wholly buy into this notion. I am not opposed to standing—I simply prefer sitting. The only time that I stand while painting is when I am "throwing" paint. In this process, my painting table is near level and I need to stand so that I can position myself over the work. But, I cannot imagine working in this leaned-over position very long.

Since I do sit while I paint, I tend to have my painting table tilted upright, at a pretty steep angle—about 45 degrees. This arrangement is great posture-wise and viewing perspective-wise, but it also pits gravity against me. Some techniques, such as "throwing" paint, simply cannot be done at a steep working angle. But, nearly all other watercolor painting techniques—including applying a wet-on-wet sky wash—can, with practice, be done at steep angle. It is more difficult, however, as gravity is forcing me to try to manage more of the painting at once.

# Getting Started

## Stretch or Block

I nearly always paint on 140 lb. cold-press watercolor paper. I prefer it over the thicker papers, such as 300 lb., because it interacts more dramatically with salt (for texture effects) and it dries faster—making it easier for other texturing processes, such as "scraping bark." I usually reserve heavy-weight paper for very large-format projects—larger than 30" x 22".

But, since 140 lb. paper is relatively thin, it has a tendency to get wavy when wet. And, since watercolor is the medium of choice—"water" being the operative word, here—getting wet *is* an issue. I know of no absolute method to prevent saturated 140 lb. paper from getting wavy. But, rather than fight it, I try to work with it. There are, however, at least two avenues that may reduce this buckling effect.

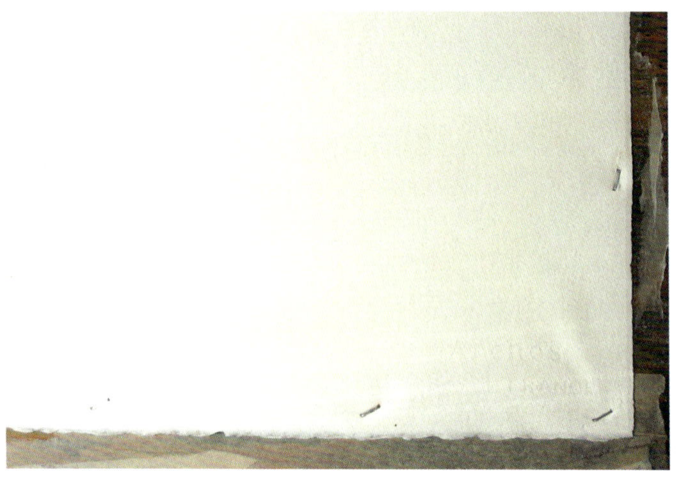

One is to cut a piece of 3/8" (or thicker) exterior grade (water proof) plywood a couple of inches wider and longer than your paper size. After soaking a sheet of watercolor paper for at least, 30 minutes in a tub of water, I carefully lay the fully saturated paper onto the cut plywood. Then, with a roofing stapler, loaded with shallow 1/4" staples, I staple the wet paper's edges to the plywood backing board. This is then laid flat and allowed to dry overnight, in a non-humid room. As the paper dries it shrinks and becomes drum-tight on its backing board.

After it has fully dried, it is ready to draw on and, of course, ready to paint. When wetted again, it will still wave a bit, but not nearly as much as it would have if it had not been stretched and stapled.

The second avenue for minimizing waves is to use a watercolor paper painting block. These still buckle a bit, but since the edges of the paper are secured to the block, they tend to not wave as excessively. Using a paper block eliminates the need to stretch the paper. But, paper blocks are typically manufactured in sizes 24" x 18" and smaller, so they are only a practical option for smaller paintings.

However, if I am creating a small painting, I will usually use a paper block. If the painting is larger than this, but smaller than 30" x 22", I will most often pre-stretch my sheet of 140 lb. cold-press watercolor paper onto a piece of plywood, as previously described. For sizes larger than this, I will usually mount the paper to plywood, but I do not pre-stretch it. As I have said, these large format sheets tend to be of a thicker paper weight—often 300 lb. Since the paper is so thick, it tends not to wave much, so I have not found it necessary to pre-stretch paper that is 300 lb. or more.

All of the paintings in these lessons were done on a 24" x 18" watercolor paper block—140 lb. cold-press.

## Nice Clean Edges

I always apply a border of masking tape to the edges of my watercolor paper, whether it is glued onto a paper block or is stapled onto a board. This does add some strength to the paper's mount, but I do this primarily

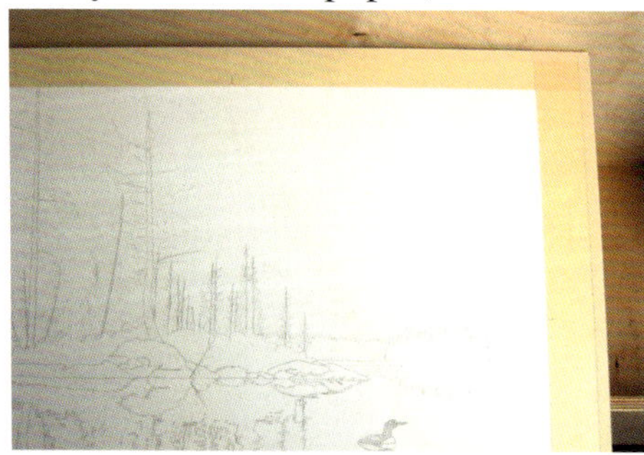

because I like the nice clean edges that it creates. Even though the painting's "clean edge" will be covered with a mat when it is framed, I just do not like paint colors running off the paper's edge.

Furthermore, I find it very handy to have tape border for capturing paint pools when applying a wash.

On stretched paper, I will typically use 2" masking tape, covering 1" of the paper and 1" of the surrounding board. For the paper blocks, I will usually use narrower tapes, covering about 1/2" of the paper, then folding the remainder down around the block's edges. While the tape borders add mounting strength in both cases, they add considerable mounting strength to the paper block edges. Without the taped borders, these edges can easily pop loose if the paper is heavily saturated with water, such as with a sky wash.

**Palette Tray**

I prefer a palette tray that has its mixing area in the center, surrounded by deep paint wells. I like the

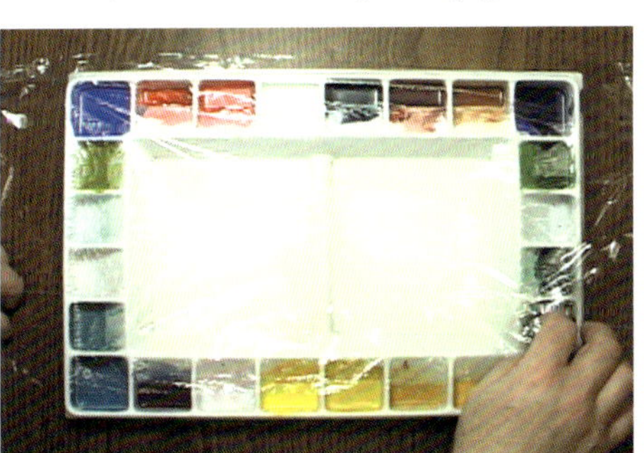

deep wells because I keep my paints wet—essentially in pools. I never allow them dry out. In fact, I add water, daily, to keep them wet. And, after I am done painting for the day—in an attempt to keep them wet—I cover my painting tray with both cling wrap

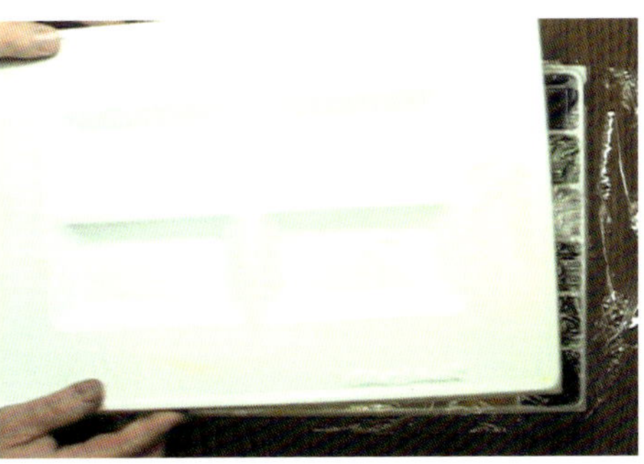

and the tray's plastic cover.

These pools of paint are kept relatively thick—a rich mix of color.

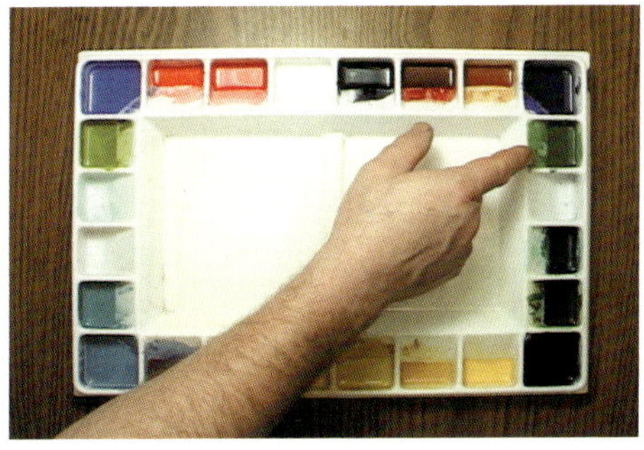

I thin them, according to the needs of my particular painting task, on the palette tray's mixing area. Just how rich is difficult to quantify, but better rich than lean, as it is easier to thin paint than it is to thicken it. Of course, as I consume the paint pools, I squeeze on more paint—mixed with more water—as needed.

**Center Not**

Perhaps the most important aspect of a painting is its composition. Once you decide *what* it is that you

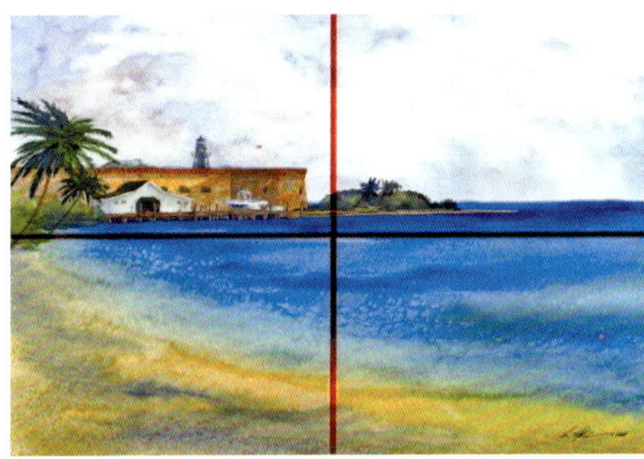

want to paint, you need to decide *how* it is that you want to depict it. Fortunately, with landscape paintings, there is often a lot of leeway in how you can design your composition.

Certainly, you want to stay true to "the place." But, you also need to keep in mind some simple composition rules—or, as I prefer to call them, tendencies.

Generally, you would not want to center prominent objects. This would create a boring, symmetrical design. You probably would not want to locate a big lone oak tree right "smack dab" in the middle of your painting. Likewise, you would not want to center the Matterhorn or the Eiffel Tower in your design. Centering prominent objects in a painting's composition almost never looks right, though it is a common error of beginning painters. Of course, there are some exceptions to this. That is why I prefer to say "tend not to center prominent objects." If you are depicting actual places in your paintings, you will encounter situations where it may be unavoidable.

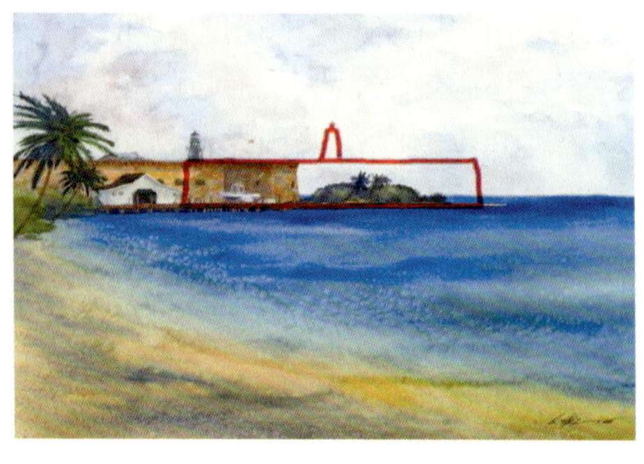

But, if the tree/mountain/waterfall/lighthouse happens to be located in the center, from your particular viewpoint, perhaps you can shift the viewpoint a bit. Often, such a compositional blunder can be easily remedied with a slight change of viewer perspective—thus shifting the prominent objects off-center.

If re-positioning your perspective places you over a cliff or into oncoming traffic, you may want to, instead, employ "artistic license." This is an area of advantage that painters have over photographers. If you prefer to have your tree/mountain/waterfall/lighthouse located a little more to the right in your composition, simply paint it there. Often, you can shift objects without compromising the integrity of the overall scene.

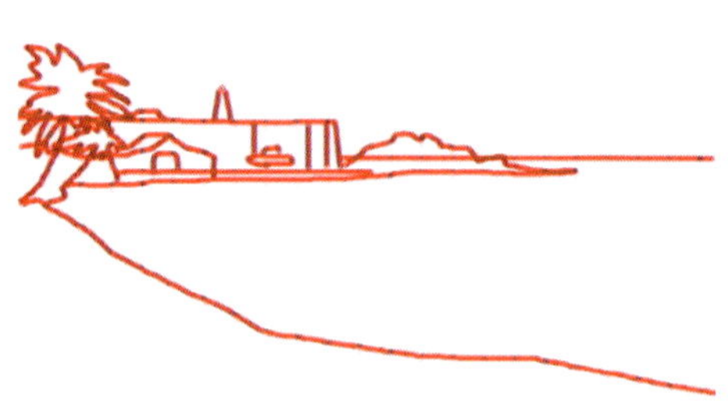

Of course, there are limits to this. You would not want to rearrange the heads of Mount Rushmore or paint a boulder on top of Old Faithful. This would unduly depreciate the recognizability of the painting's subject matter. But, often you can move a prominent rock or tree or, perhaps, even a hill, without unduly violating the subject's overall recognizability and integrity.

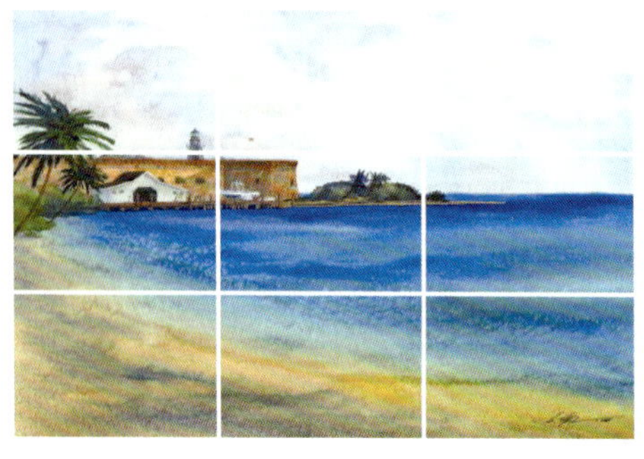

When designing your composition, you would do well to remember the simple "Rule of Thirds." In your mind—or, lightly sketched onto your watercolor paper, if you prefer— divide your painting into thirds, both horizontally and vertically. This will, essentially, create a "tick tack toe" grid.

You should try to place the main focal point—often, the main subject (tree/mountain/waterfall/lighthouse)—at the intersection of any of these horizontal and vertical lines. This keeps the prominent object off-center both horizontally and vertically.

Even a horizon line, such as the distant edge of an ocean, should be kept off-center vertically. You want to avoid symmetry in your painting. If your painting is a tiny island with a single palm tree, you do not want to vertically center your ocean's horizon line—thus equally dividing sea and sky. It simply would not look right. Rather, shift your horizon line up or down, and shift your tiny island to the right or to the left of center. There is no need to be obsessive about this asymmetrical concept, but it is something to keep in mind when designing your painting's composition. Sometimes, in nature, prominent objects must be located in the center. But, you should avoid this if you can.

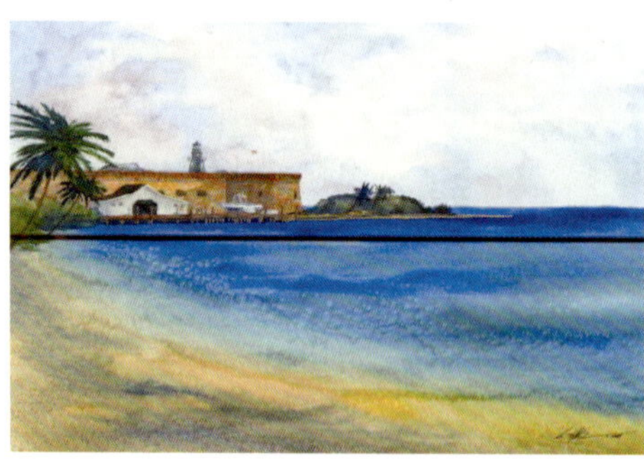

**Why Masking Fluid?**

Nearly all of my painting involves extensive masking. I simply like the ability to isolate and protect areas of light values—particularly whites. While the application of masking can be slow and tedious, it enables me to work more quickly and freely while applying my darker values. Taking the light values "off the table," gives me less to manage all at once. I far prefer focusing on how I am applying the darker values, rather than worrying

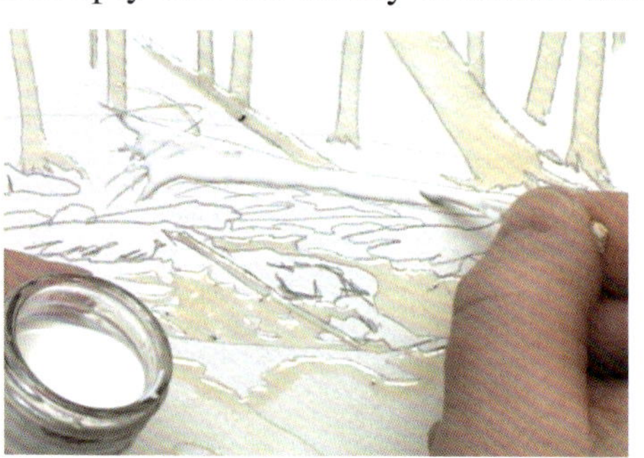

about how I am going to keep these dark values off of my intended light areas.

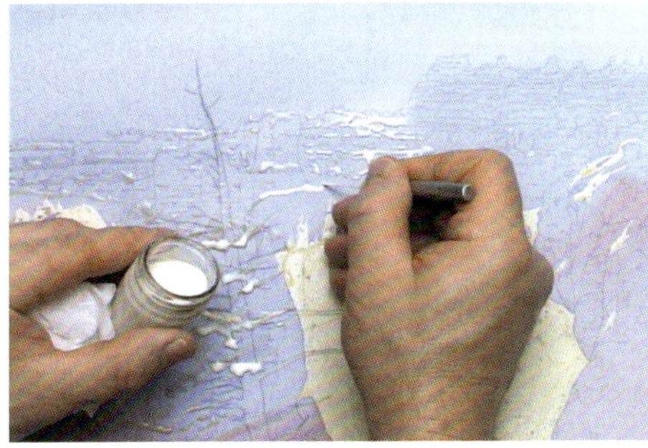

When these light areas are small intricate shapes like mountain snow, painting around them manually can be difficult, if not sometimes impossible. Remember, the watercolor paints are continuously drying as you are painting. Furthermore, good old "Murphy's Law" nearly always dictates that "if the watercolor paints *can* dry at an inopportune time, they *will* dry at an inopportune time." Masking makes life as a watercolor painter more manageable.

Pre-masking light color values also enables me to "throw" paints, such as tree foliage. I can throw

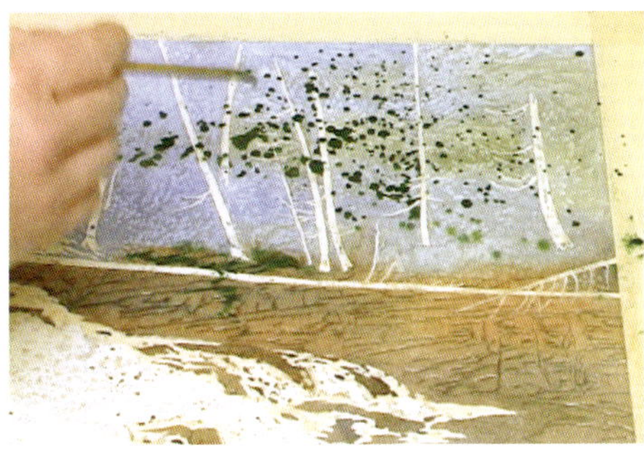

and spray paints to my heart's content, knowing that my light values are protected. Often, I will mask out recognizable shapes—such as tree trunks, rocks, boats and buildings—knowing that they will pull an otherwise, abstract painting back together again, once they are exposed. So, in this way, the tedious task of masking enables a "looser" style of painting.

But, extensive masking is not for everyone. Masking requires planning and patience. This could inhibit those who like to "paint on the fly"—those who plan their painting as they actually paint. I, personally, like a little more structure in my paintings, so I approach them much like the "third little pig," of the famed *The Three Little Pigs*, might: I plan and build a foundation of masking. It is often a lot of work in the beginning, but the payoff at the end is great!

**The Toothpick Approach**

There are those who will debate this, but I believe that if you use a good quality paintbrush to apply masking fluid, you WILL eventually ruin your brush. Yes, I have heard all of the techniques for cleaning the brush bristles and pre-soaking the brush in dish washing soap, but I am not convinced. Murphy's Law dictates that "if masking fluid *can* ruin a brush, it *will* ruin the brush"—just give it time. The phone will ring or you will accidentally knock over some paint or you will see Elvis outside of your window and you *will* forget about your brush loaded with masking fluid. Do not let this happen to you! Once

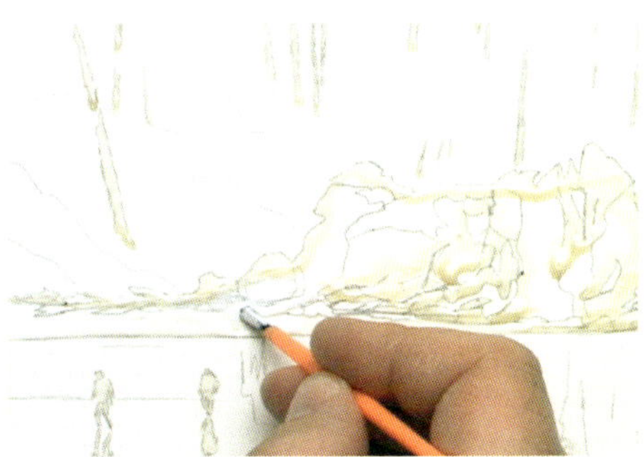

masking fluid dries in your brush's bristles it is difficult, at best, to remove. Most likely, your brush will paint no more.

There is no need to use good quality brushes for masking. The best alternative that I have found is to use toothpicks for small, intricate shapes and inexpensive (thus disposable) children's paintbrushes for simple and/or large shapes.

I prefer to use a plastic toothpick, but the "chiseled-edge-type" wood toothpicks work fine, too. The smooth rounded toothpicks do not seem to hold as much masking fluid as the chiseled edge type, but they will work in a pinch.

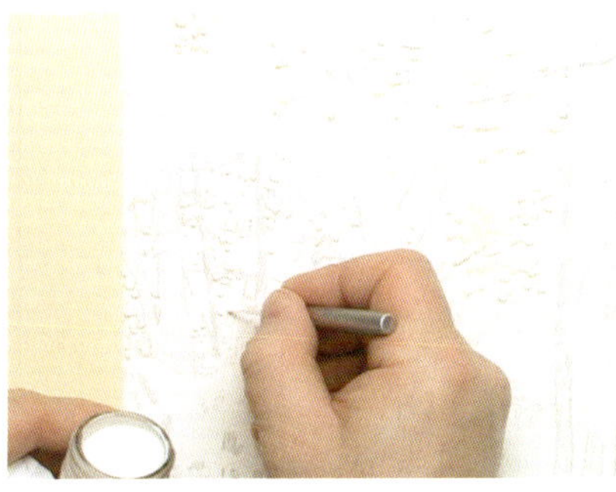

Whether plastic or wood, I dull the toothpick's tip a bit with a piece of sandpaper or an emery board. Sometimes, I will wrap masking tape on the opposite end to create a handle. If you are lucky, you may find "traveling toothpicks" on a counter display at your local hardware store. These actually have light metal handles that double as a storage case. While I cannot imagine the need to travel with such a reusable toothpick, they inadvertently make great masking tools—a plastic toothpick with a long metal tubular handle.

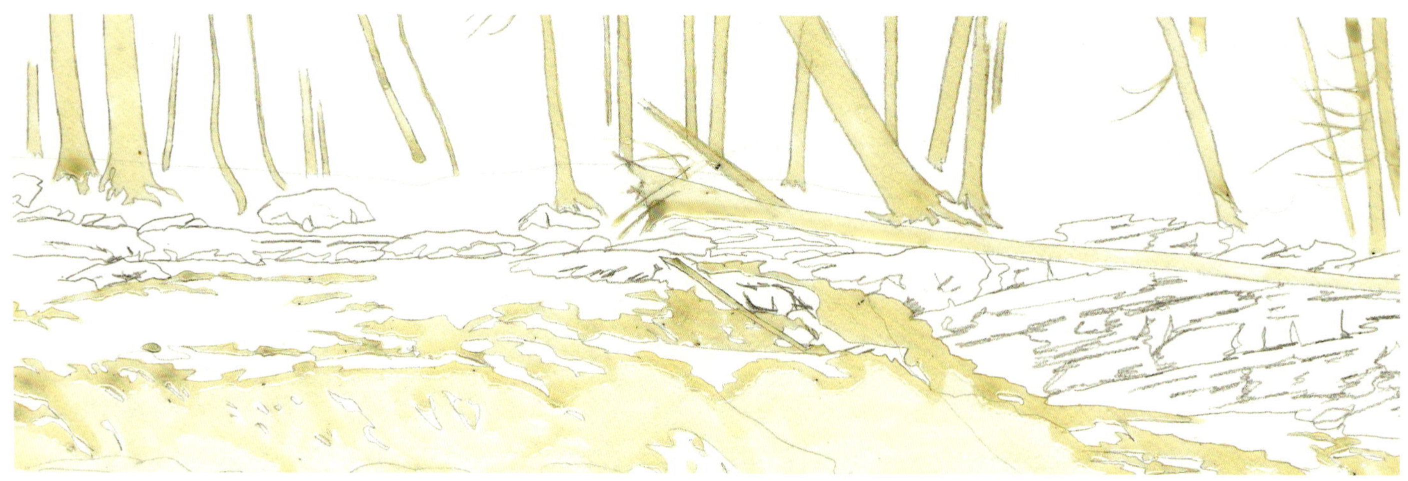

Although I have never used a quill pen with ink, I am informed that I apply masking in a similar manner. Holding a small wide-mouthed jar of masking fluid in

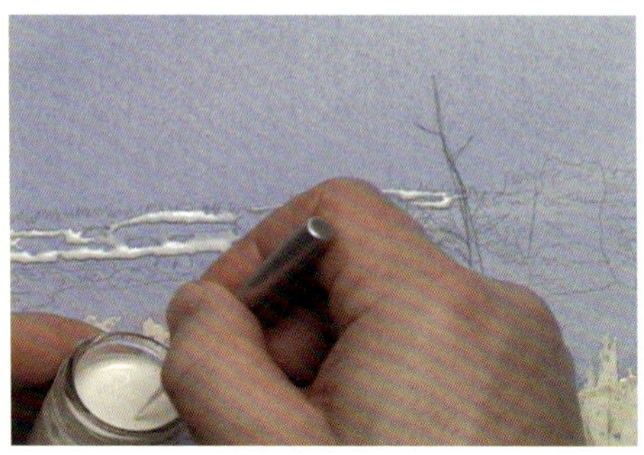

one hand, I dip my toothpick into the fluid with my other hand. This loads the pick with fluid, just like a dipped quill will load with ink. Then, I, of course, transfer this pick over to my painting where I apply the masking fluid to the small shapes that I want to protect.

The toothpick requires frequent wiping with a tissue, as the masking fluid dries quickly. At times, I also need to skim the surface of the masking jar, to remove the skin of drier masking that eventually develops. I routinely wipe the masking off of the jar's edge, as well.

I also use the toothpick to apply the masking to large shapes, when they have an intricate perimeter. Typically, I use the toothpick to accurately follow the perimeter's shape. Then, I will mark an "X" with

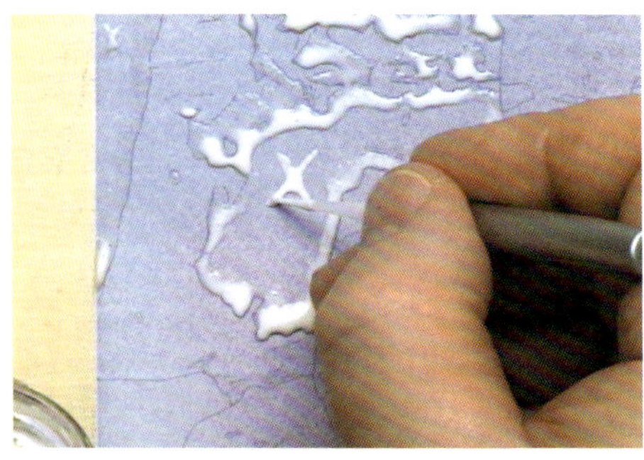

masking fluid in the center of this shape, so that I will remember to come back and fill the shape in with the larger (and faster) disposable brush. Normally, I will do all of my toothpick shapes first, and then complete the masking with the disposable brush. When I get to the final masking step, the "X's" can be easily seen by holding the painting at a low level to the light. The dried masking fluid will reflect brightly, relative to the dull surface of the paper.

**The Big Spill**

If you accidentally spill some masking fluid on your paper or if you apply the masking to the wrong shape, simply move on and mask a different area—allowing the mistaken area to dry. After it has fully dried, peel to it off and re-mask the area correctly.

Spilt masking *can* present a problem with sky areas, as the masking fluid may slightly discolor the paper. Light valued skies may be more susceptible to showing such discoloration. For this reason, I often cover my sky areas with rags. But, in other areas of the painting, slight paper discoloration can usually be disguised by the landscape colors.

**All Masking Fluids Are Not Created Equal!**

Different brands are made with different consistencies and different colors. It is important that you experiment with your particular brand on a piece of scrap paper first. Allow it to dry, then rub it off. Make sure that it does not excessively discolor the paper or, worse, tear the paper's fibers.

**Never Apply Masking To Damp Paper!**

It will soak into the paper's fibers and will likely tear the paper when you try to peel it off. This is because wet watercolor paper is like a sponge. Rather than sit on top of the paper, masking fluid will actually be wicked into wet or damp paper—effectively giving it roots, which will tear when pulled. It is essential that watercolor paper is "bone dry" before you apply masking fluid to it.

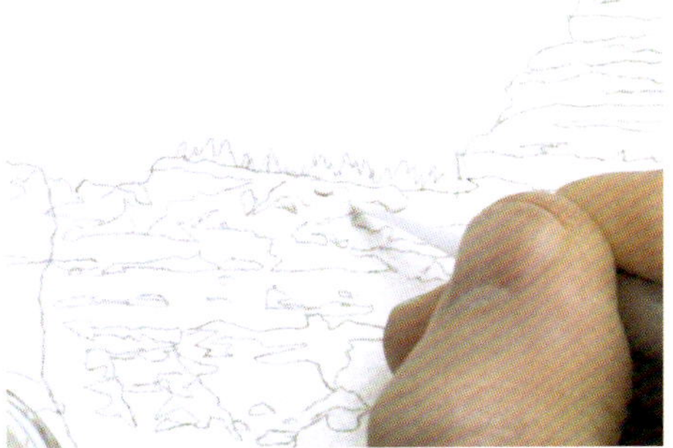

Incidentally, you do not want to wear your "Sunday best" clothing while masking, either. If you accidentally spill it on your clothes—and Murphy's Law states that you eventually will—you may find it nearly impossible to remove. Of course, the same goes for unprotected carpet. Take the same precautions that you would while working with rubber cement.

Yes, applying masking can be slow and tedious. But, put on some music or a ball game and make the process more enjoyable. Your "toils with the toothpick" will pay off in the end.

**Mask Whites First**

Typically, after my composition has been drawn out, I will mask out any white shapes. Common examples of these "white shapes" would be snow, boats, and, sometimes clouds. But, I also often mask out shapes that will eventually be painted in as light values. Examples of this would be tree trunks, sky reflections and buildings.

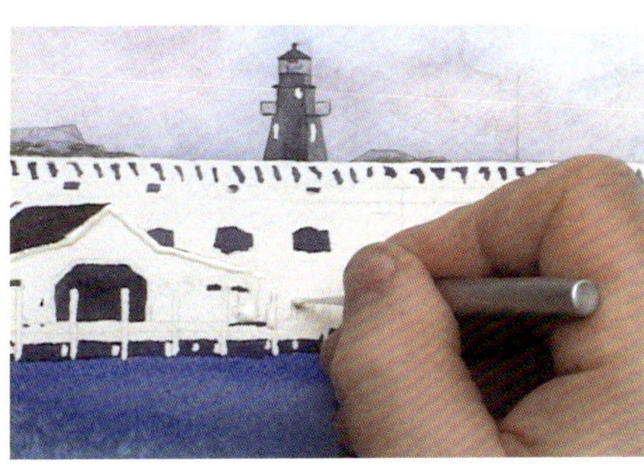

After my initial step of masking is completed and has dried, I will move on to my first step of painting—often the sky wash. As you will see in the upcoming lessons, sometimes I will mask over light values of dry paint. I sometimes do this with rock shapes. But, I prepare the rocks by first applying their base colors a bit darker than what I am aiming for. When the masking is peeled off of these rock shapes, it will remove a shade of rock color—thus making them slightly lighter than they would have been otherwise.

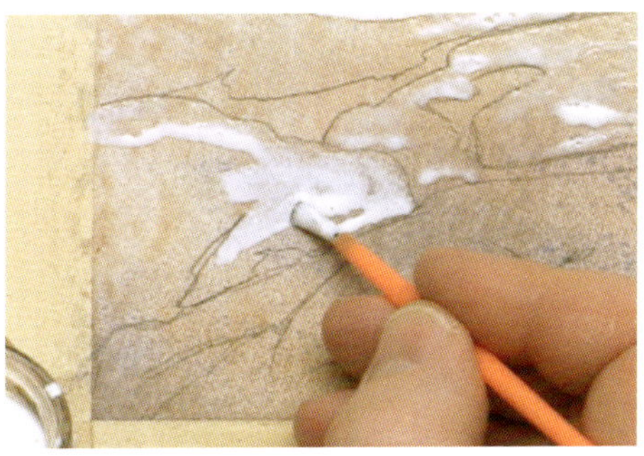

**Blow Dry Masking?**

I am often asked if it is O.K. to blow-dry masking to encourage drying. I do. But, I believe that this answer may be dependent upon the particular brand of masking fluid used. I have heard reports that blow-drying masking fluid can induce tearing when the masking is finally removed. I have never personally experienced this problem and I have always suspected that these reports were actually cases where the masking had been inadvertently applied to damp paper—which would, predictably, result in torn paper. Of course, the safest answer is to experiment with your brand of masking fluid on some scrap watercolor paper. It is better to be safe than sorry!

**Go Forth And Mask!**

Since masking represents such a major portion of my painting process, I wanted to devote some words in this section to explain why. And, of course, I wanted to cover some of the basics of the masking process itself. In the following lessons, I will clearly state what shapes I apply masking to. And, I will cite which masking tool I am using for the particular masking step that I am working on.

As I have stated previously, your "toils with the toothpick" (and masking fluid) will pay off in the end!

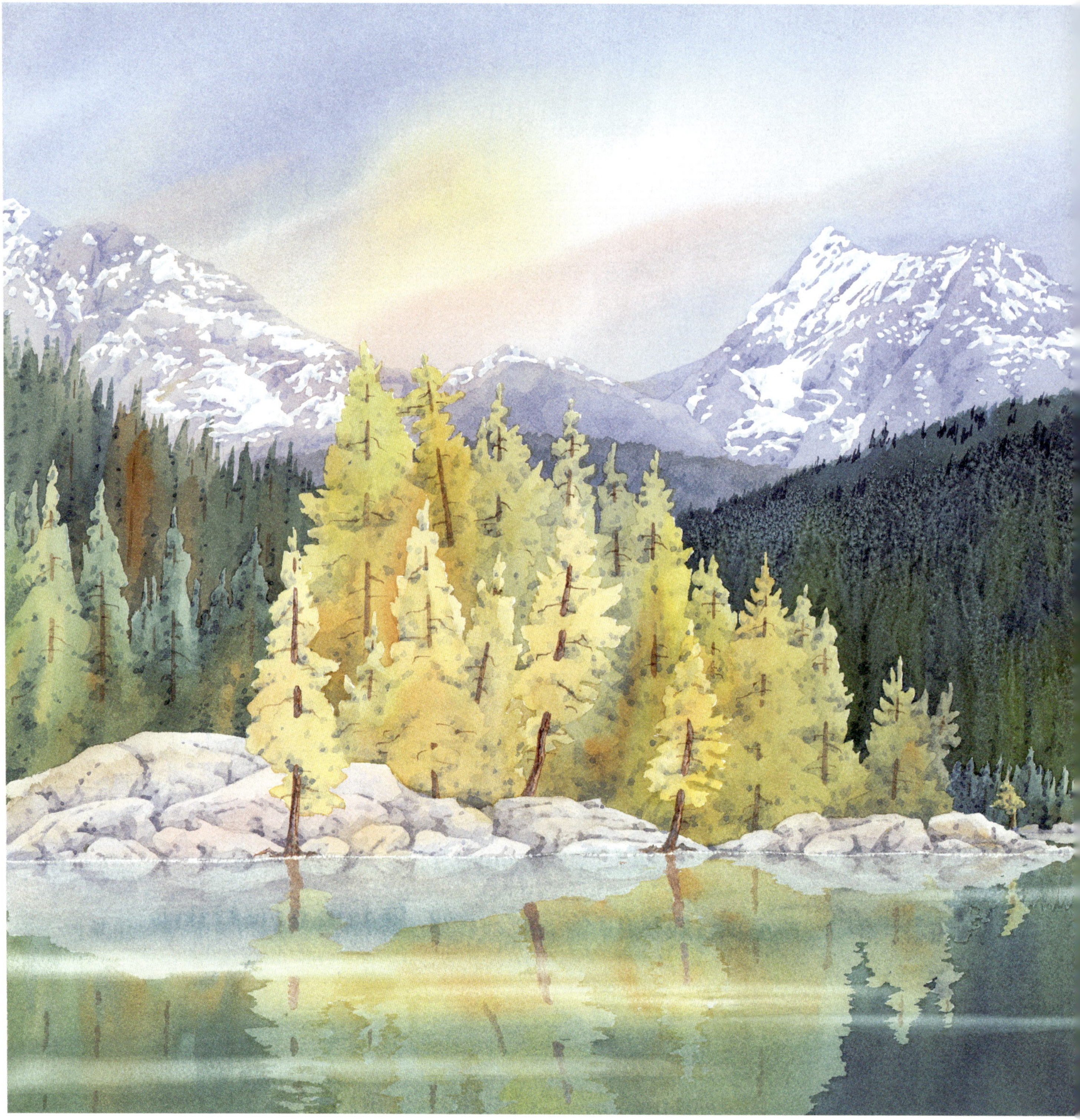

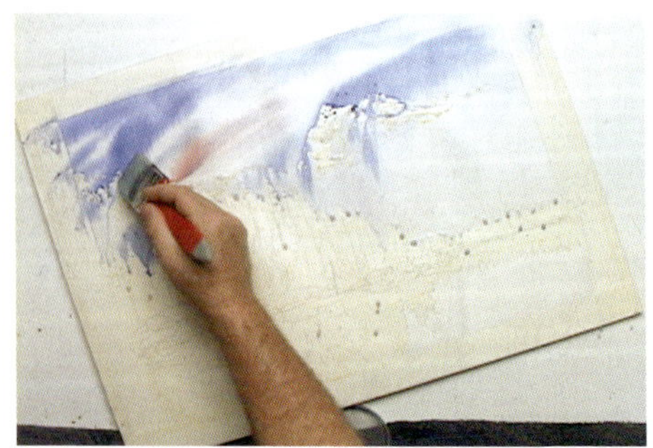

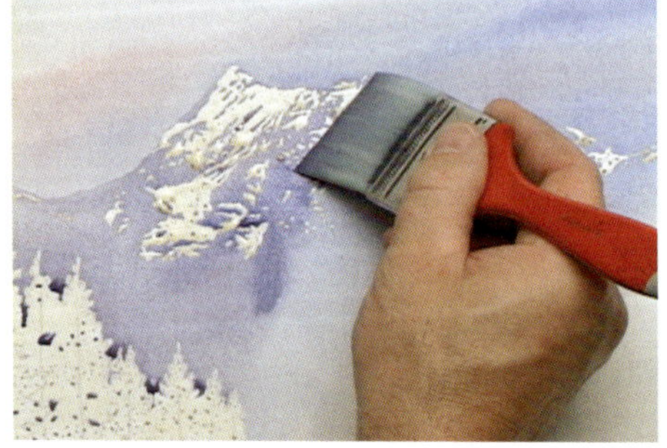

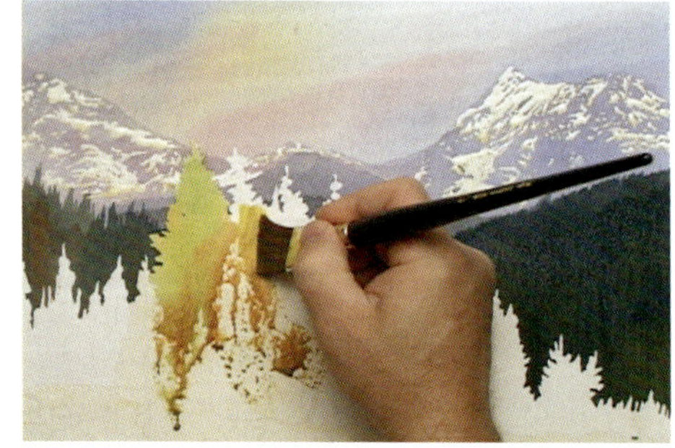

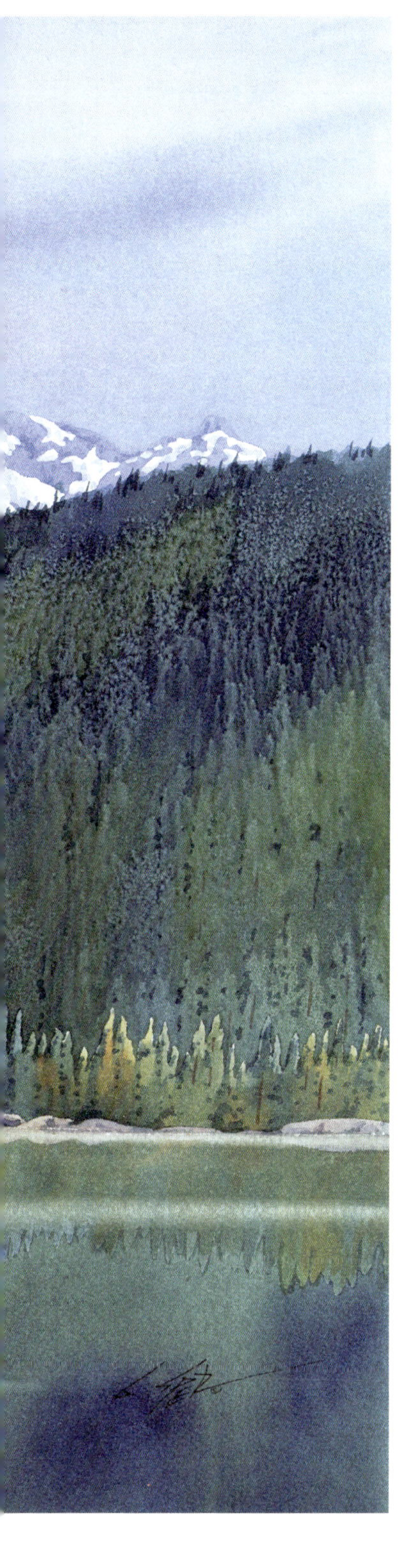

# LAKE MCDONALD

On my frequent visits to Glacier National Park, I nearly always drive by Lake McDonald. I've seen it in all of its moods. But, its early morning "serene mood" is definitely my favorite. You have got to get up pretty early to see and feel it, but it is well worth the effort!

As an artist, I find reflective mountain lakes to be irresistible! They possess a magnetism that tugs hard at my paint brush! If you are a painter and you have been to Lake McDonald on an early, calm morning, you know just what I'm talking about.

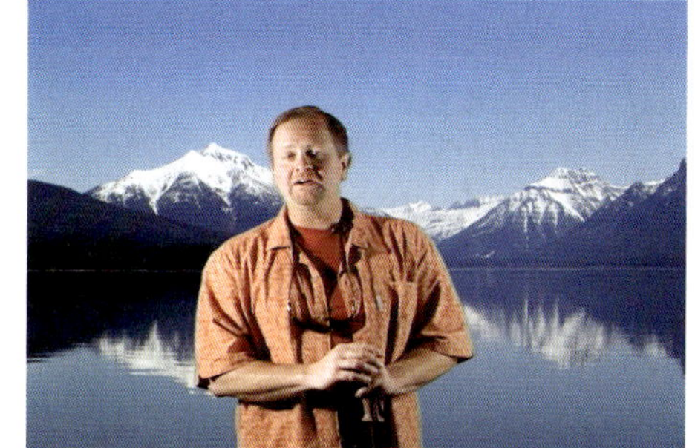

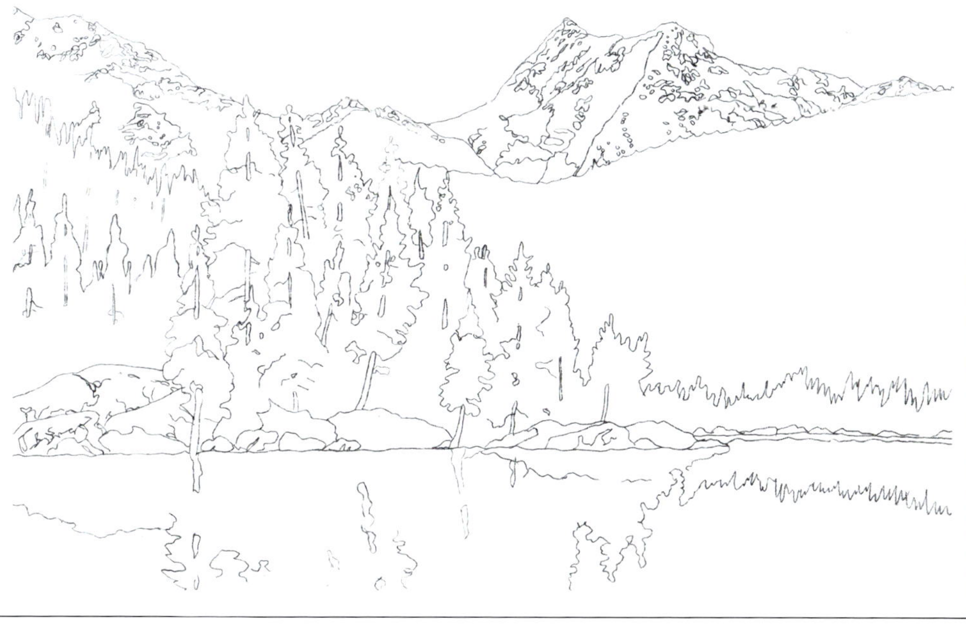

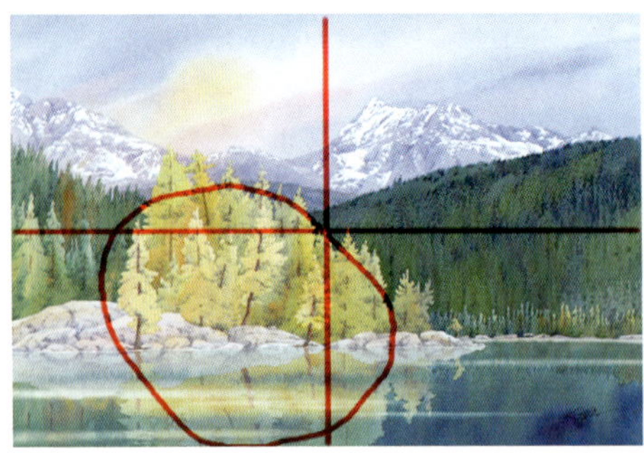

**Step 1:** I drew out my composition on the watercolor paper, using care to not center prominent objects. To help remind me of this, I marked both my vertical and horizontal center points on the sides of the painting. You can see that the foreground trees are both below and to the left of the painting's center.

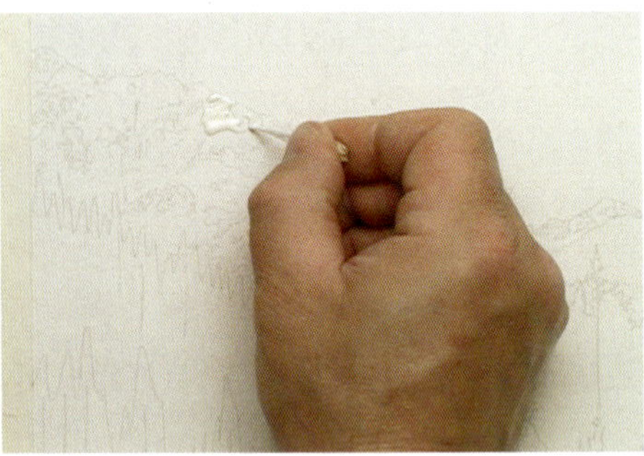

**Step 2:** Next, using liquid masking fluid and a plastic toothpick, I masked out the small intricate snow shapes in the distant mountains. Then with a disposable paintbrush, I masked out the larger, less intricate, foreground tree shapes and shoreline rocks. I also masked out their reflected shapes in the lake.

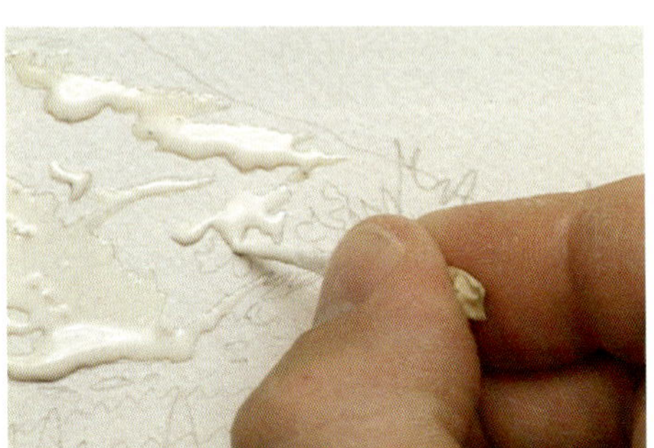

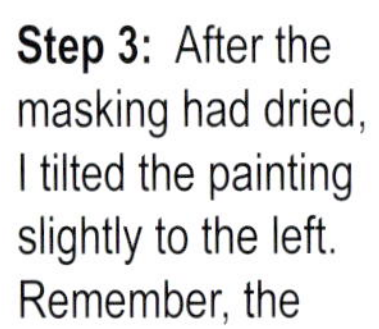

**Step 3:** After the masking had dried, I tilted the painting slightly to the left. Remember, the

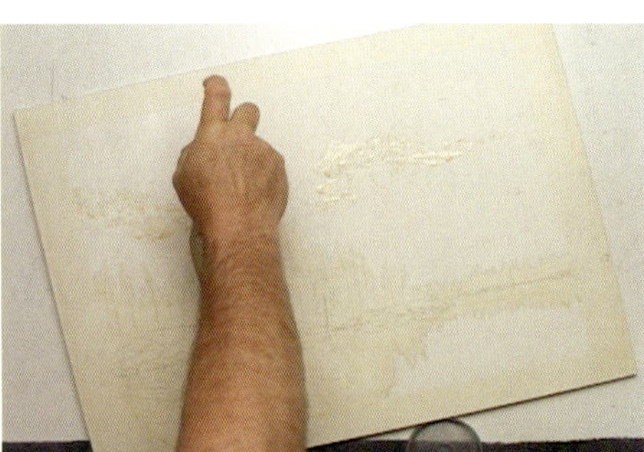

(Step 13 continued)

painting is already tilted forward on my inclined painting table. Next, I saturated the entire painting with water, using a spray bottle. With a 2" flat brush, I began quickly working in stripes of Cobalt Blue, with accents of Rose and Transparent Yellow. I did not cover the entire sky area with paint—preferring to leave areas of the white paper visible.

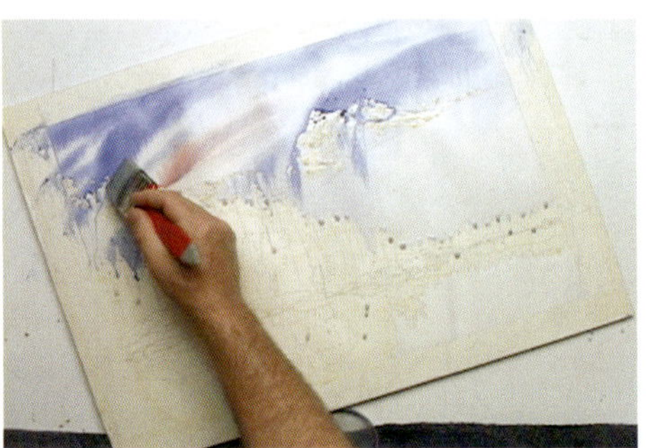

As these colors began to dry, I tipped the painting nearly 180 degrees to promote blending. But, I used care here, as a little blending can go a long way! Blending can easily be overdone.

With a tissue, I wicked up excess puddles of paint along the tape's edge.

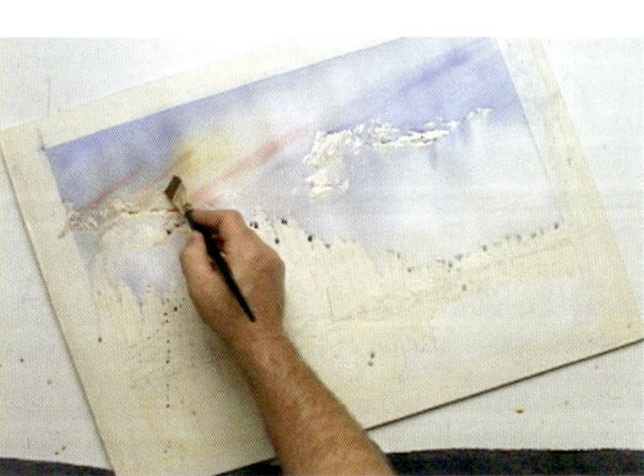

Before the sky colors had dried, I added a few more accents of Rose and Transparent Yellow with a 3/4" brush. After I achieved the look that I wanted, I locked the colors in by drying them with a blow drier.

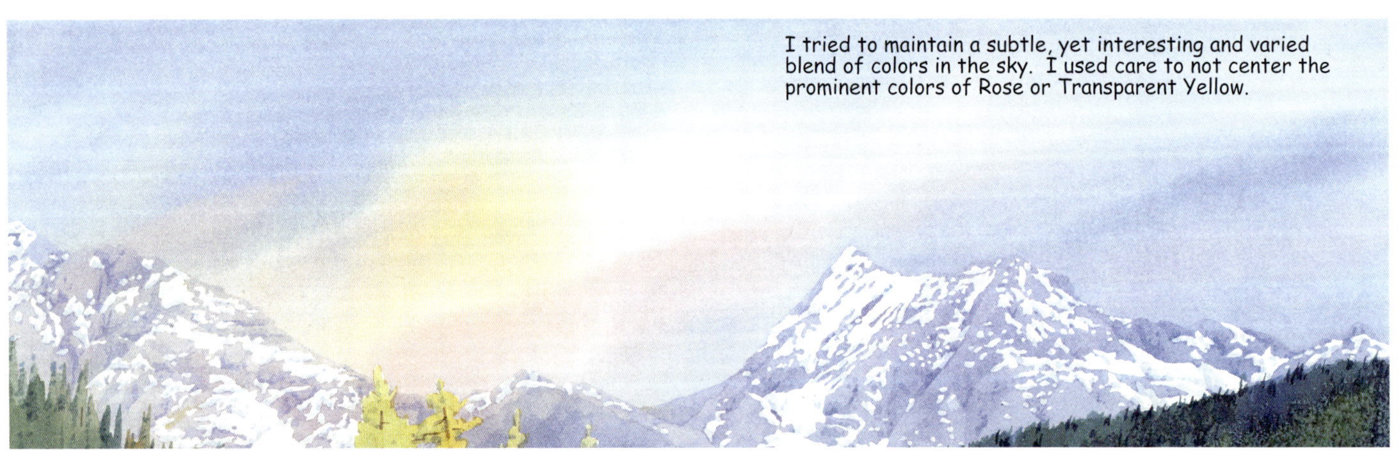

I tried to maintain a subtle, yet interesting and varied blend of colors in the sky. I used care to not center the prominent colors of Rose or Transparent Yellow.

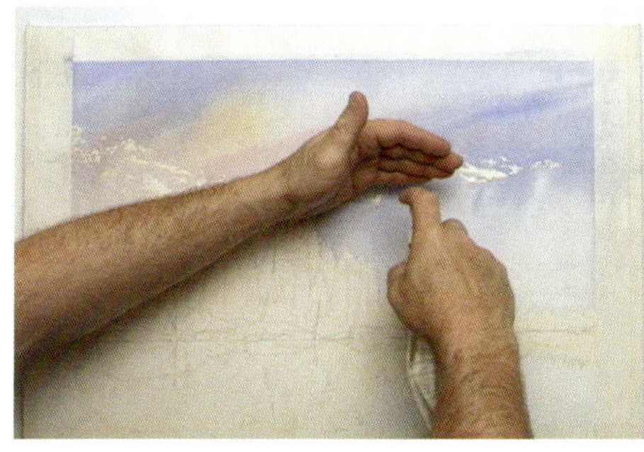

**Step 4:** After the sky colors had thoroughly dried, I re-wetted the painting below the upper edge of the mountains. Then, with the same sky color mix of Cobalt Blue and Rose, I carefully followed the mountaintop edges with a 2" brush.

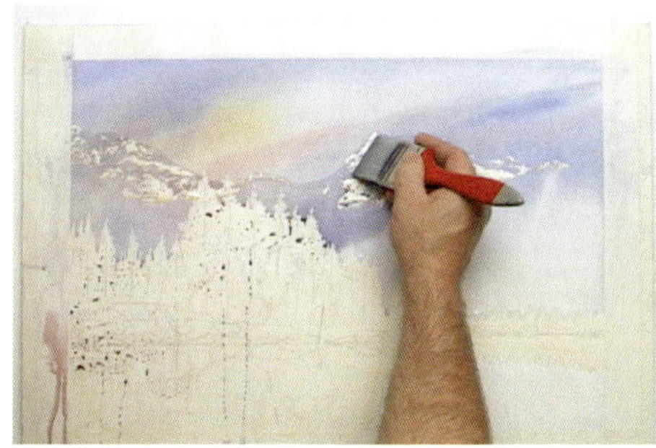

As I moved across the mountains, I varied between the two colors, being careful not to center either of them or to create any obvious pattern. I also continuously tended to the lower paint edge, below the brush, making sure that this edge blended into the previously wetted area—thus preventing an unwanted hard edge from forming.

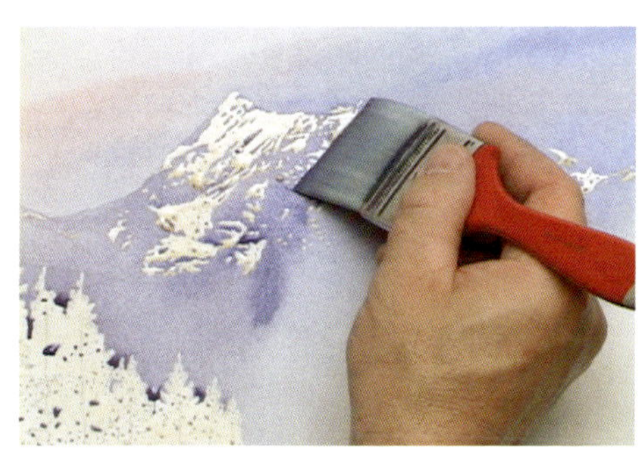

**Step 5:** After the most distant row of mountains had dried, I applied the same colors to the next closest ridge with a 1" flat brush. Since transparent watercolors are cumulative, these colors appeared darker when placed over the previously applied colors.

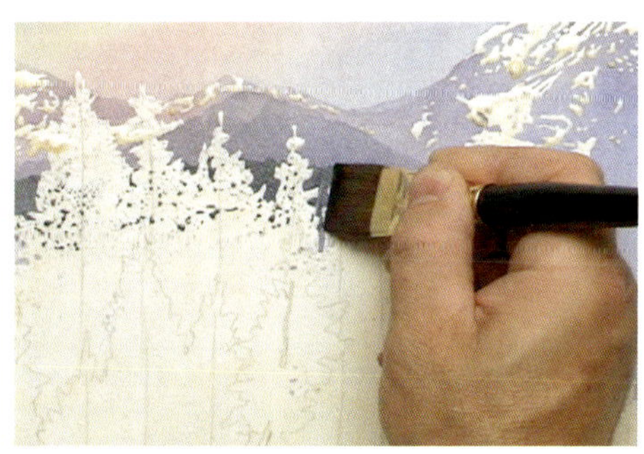

**Step 6**: After that ridge had dried, I added some Cobalt Green to the Cobalt Blue for yet the next closest ridge.

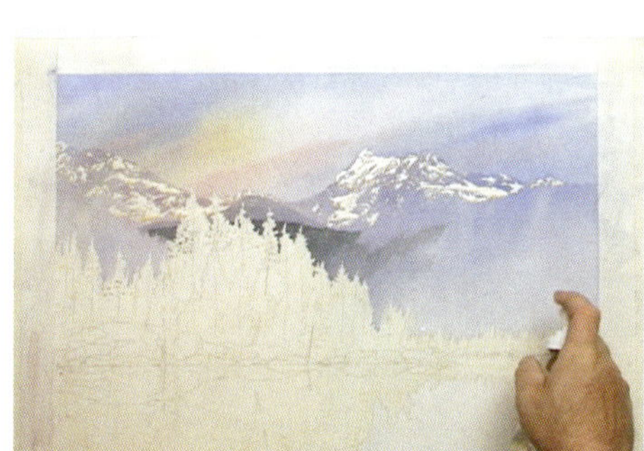

To obtain a distinct upper edge on the mountaintops, it was essential to first thoroughly dry the underlying sky colors.

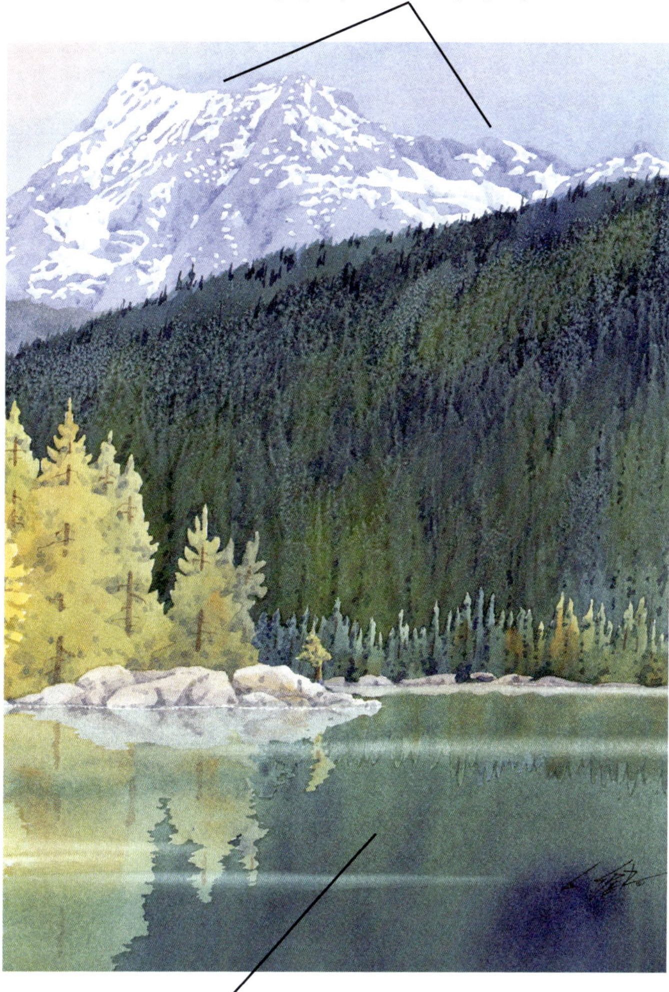

I mimicked the wooded hill colors in its reflection below.

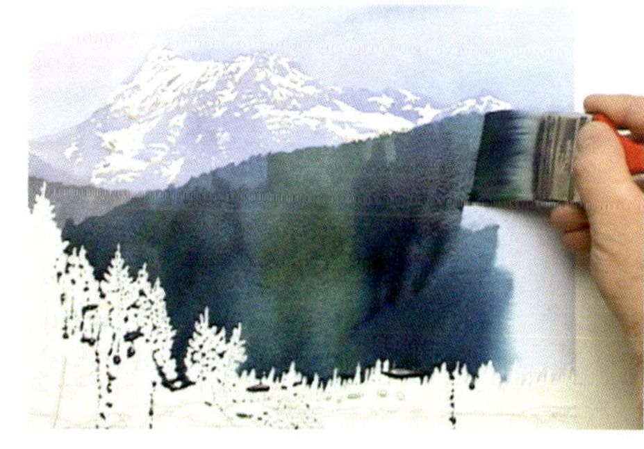

**Step 7:** Continuing to work forward with the mountains/hills, I mixed up some Phthalo Blue and Phthalo Green. Since it was a larger area I switched back to my 2" flat brush. Again, I varied between the two colors. As they dried, I added salt to promote a texturing effect. Then, with a 1" flat brush, I added rich strokes of Transparent Yellow and Phthalo Blue to simulate treetops and depth.

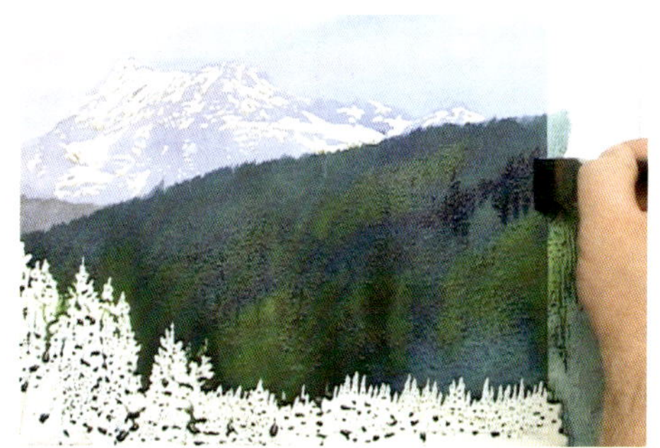

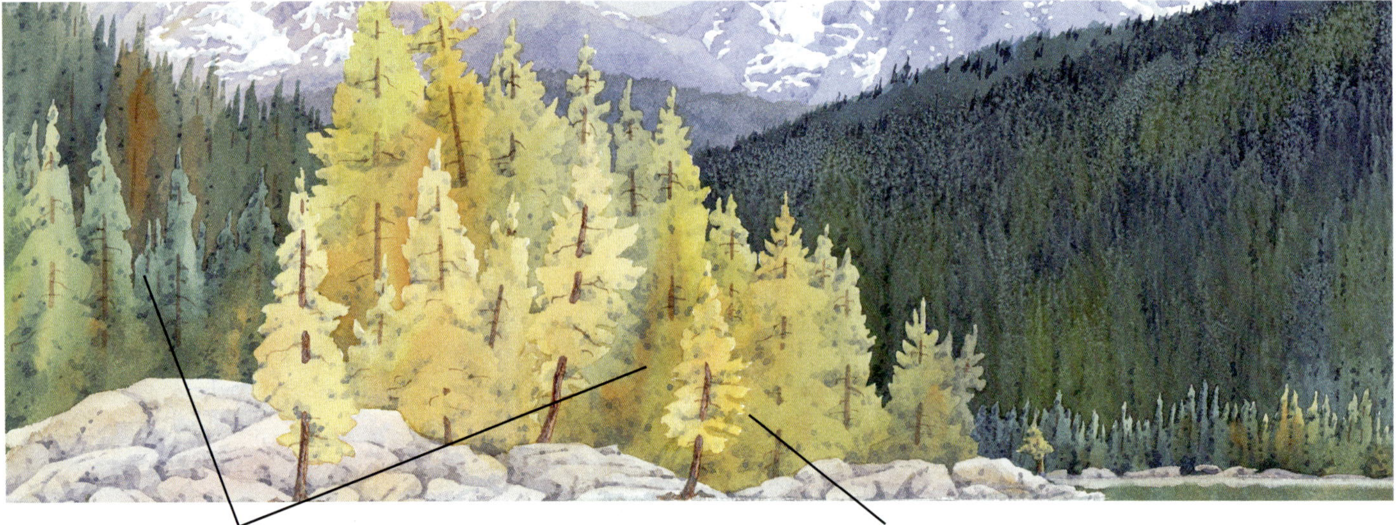

To promote the illusion of depth, I varied the color values of the rows of trees—progressively making them lighter as they approached the foreground.

For dramatic effect and to draw the attention of the viewer, I often exaggerate colors—not necessarily depicting them as they are in nature.

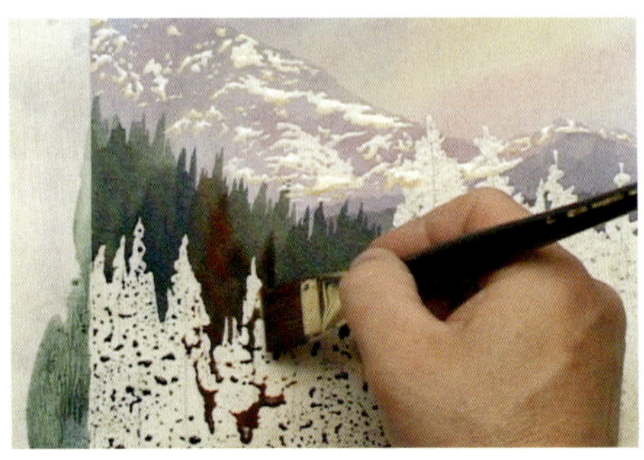

**Step 8:** Next, using a 1" flat brush and the same, but lighter, mix of Phthalo Blue and Phthalo Green, I painted in my midground trees. These were given a somewhat jagged sawtooth appearance, as their distance did not require much detail. Before these colors had dried, I added Burnt Sienna accents.

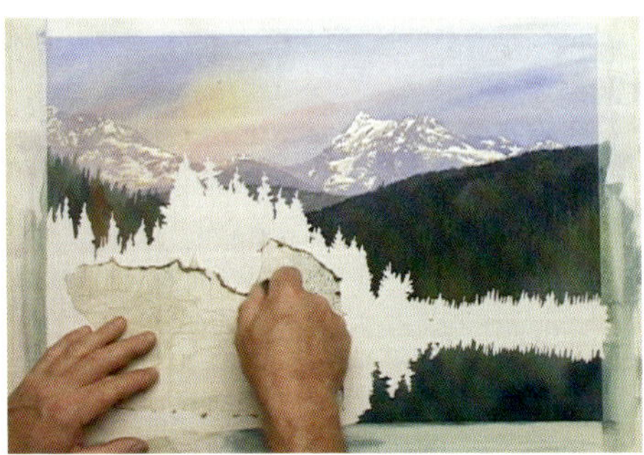

**Step 9:** After all of the painting's colors had thoroughly dried, I peeled the masking from the foreground trees and the shoreline rocks—leaving the mountain snow masking in place.

**Step 10:** But, once the masking was removed, I re-masked the closest subset of trees and the shoreline rocks. Although this may seem like needless extra work, it enabled me to easily and effectively separate the values of the rocks and the various tree groups.

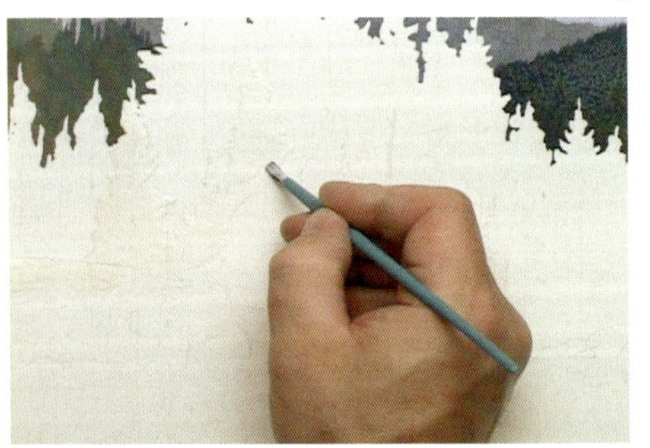

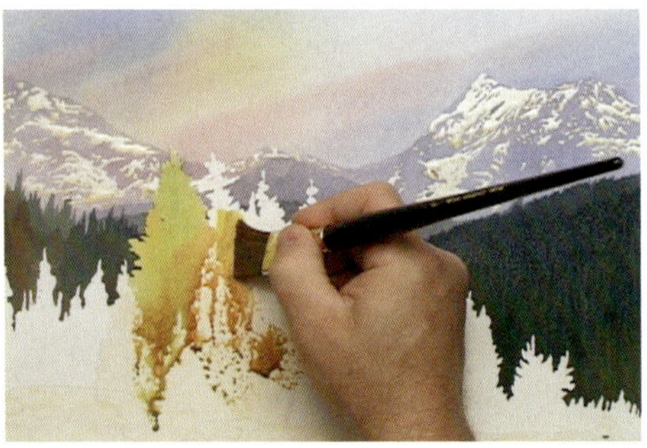

**Step 11:** Once this masking had dried, I applied a mix of Ultramarine Blue, Ultramarine Green, Burnt Sienna and Transparent Yellow to the exposed foreground trees with a 1" flat brush. I varied this mix, but weighted it towards the yellow. I also made sure that these colors were applied lighter than the tree colors behind them.

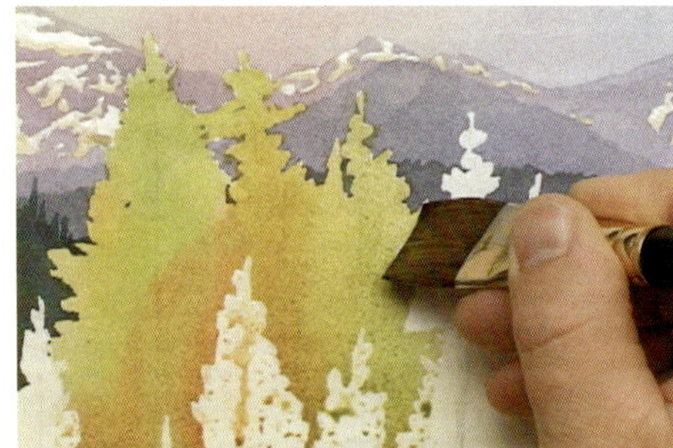

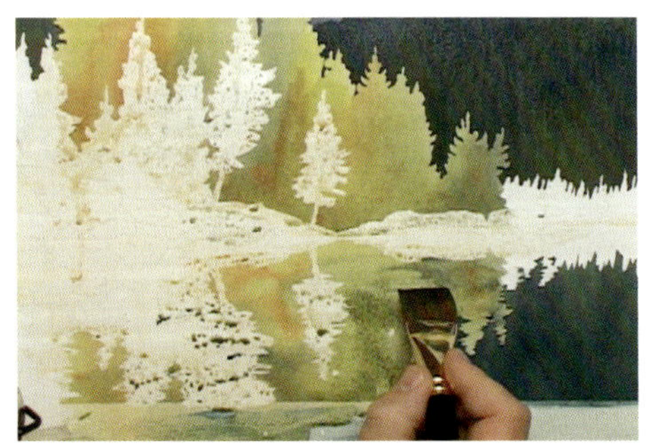

Again, I mimicked the colors above in their reflection below.

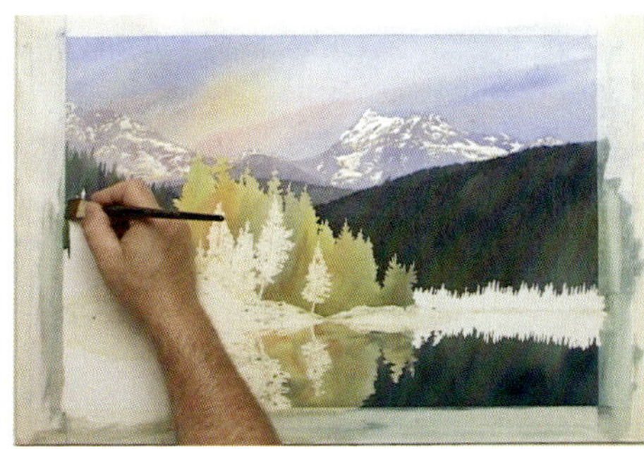

**Step 12:** Next, I painted in the group of trees to the left and behind the previously painted group. I used a 3/4" flat brush and the trees' same base colors—Phthalo Blue, Phthalo Green, Burnt Sienna and Transparent Yellow—but this time a bit darker.

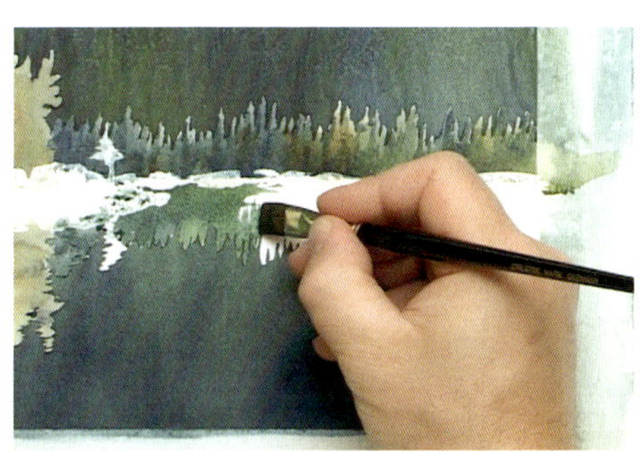

**Step 13:** And darker yet, I painted in the most distant shoreline trees on the right side. For these I used the same colors and a 1/2" flat brush.

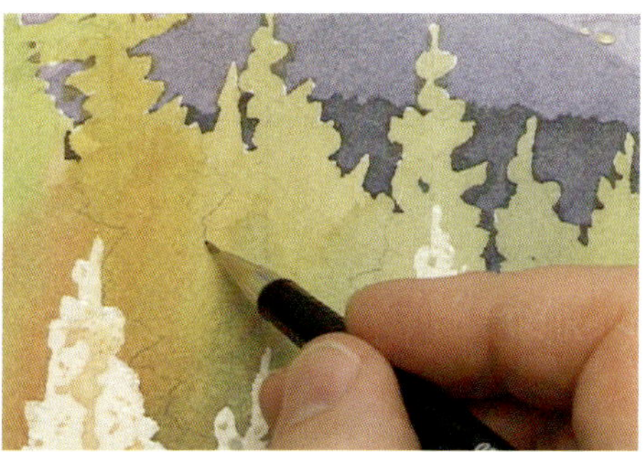

**Step 14:** Moving back to the foreground trees, I lightly sketched in some of the tree shapes—providing me with a guide for shading and sorting individual trees. With a 1/2" flat brush and a lean mix of the tree's base colors—Ultramarine Blue and Ultramarine Green—I subtly defined some of the tree edges. I would generally make one edge of the shade shape hard—effectively separating one shape from its adjacent shape. Then I would lose the other edge by dabbing it with a tissue or by diluting it with water.

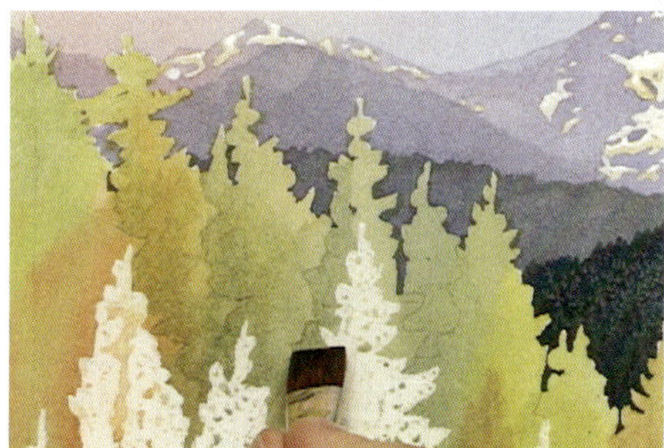

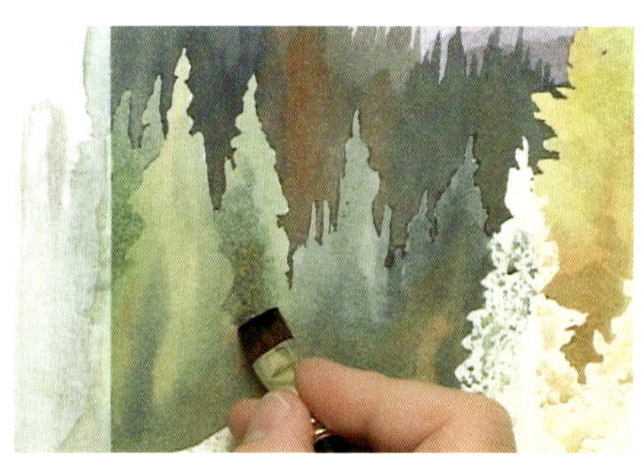

I sorted the individual trees in the next most distant group in the same manner. But, for these I used a watery version of their same base colors: Phthalo Blue and Phthalo Green.

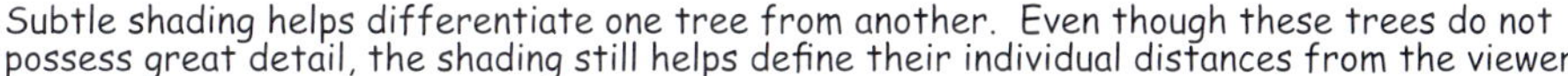


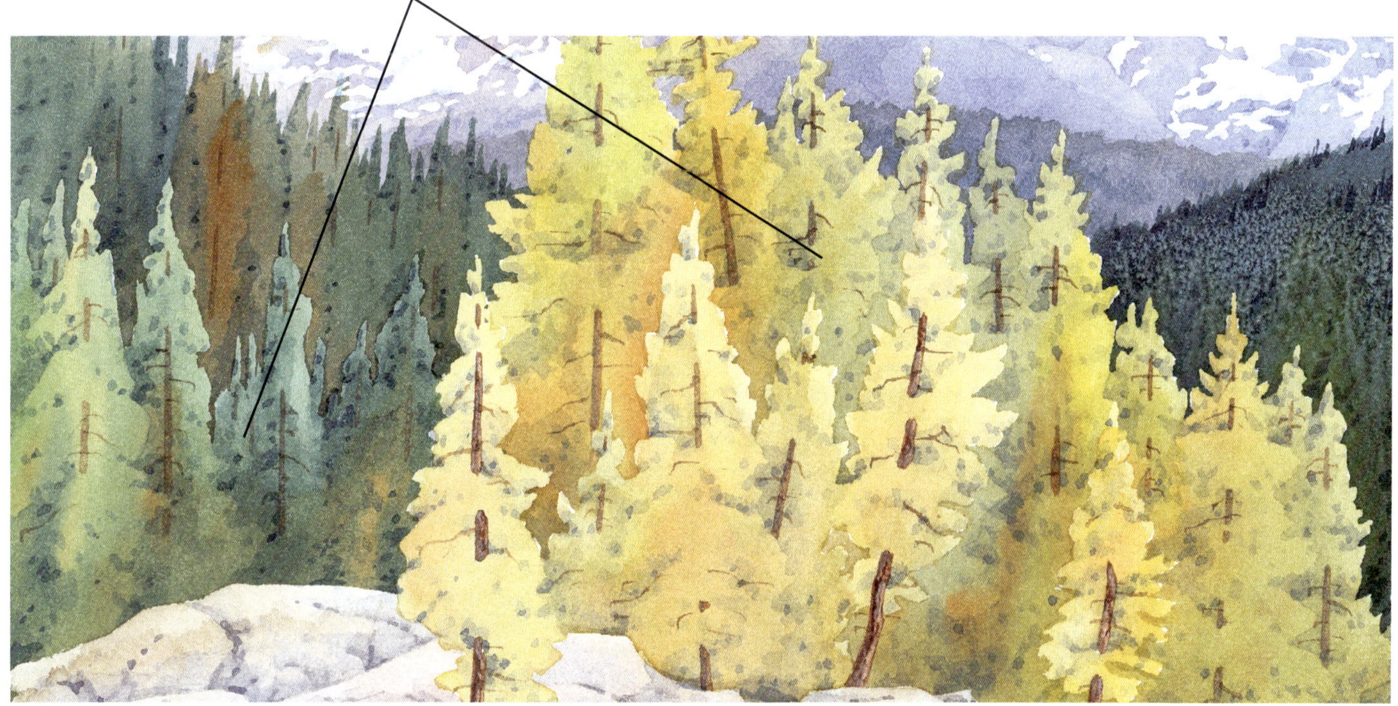

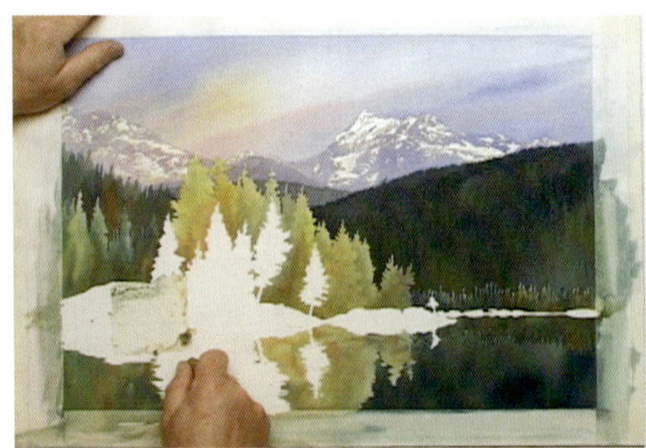

**Step 15:** Once again, I removed the masking from the remaining foreground trees and the shoreline rocks. And, once again, I did some re-masking. This time I masked the lower edge of the unpainted foreground trees—where they intersected the shoreline rocks—to protect them from the rock colors.

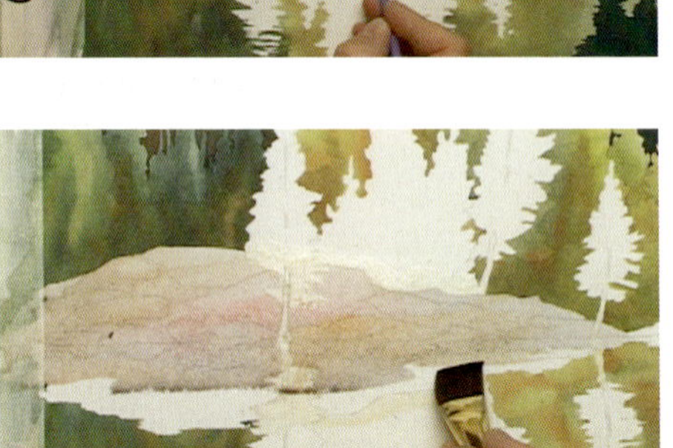

**Step 16:** Now, with a 3/4" flat brush and some Ultramarine Blue, Burnt Sienna and Rose, I painted in my base rock colors. I did not want to produce boring solid brown rocks, so I varied the colors and used care to not blend them too much.

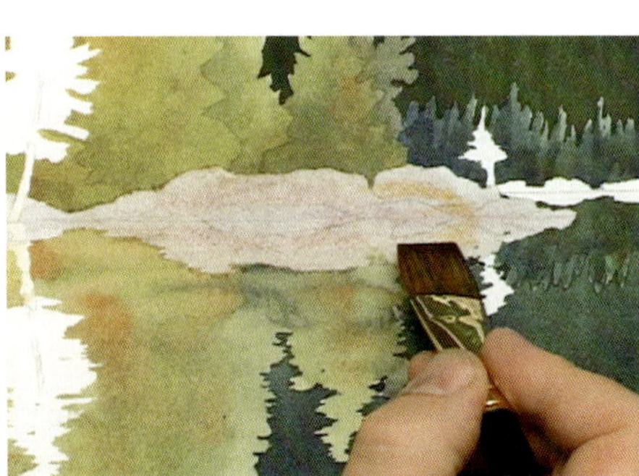

It is easy to overdo cracks and crevices on rocks. I refrained from covering too much of the underlying base rock colors.

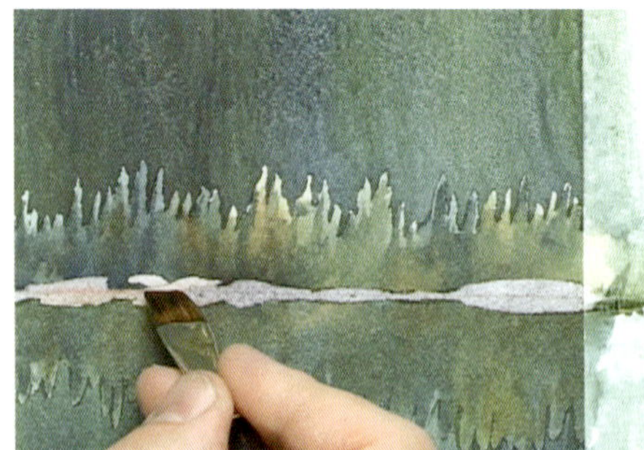

(Step 16 continued)

As I worked into the smaller rocks on the right side, I switched to a 1/2" flat brush.

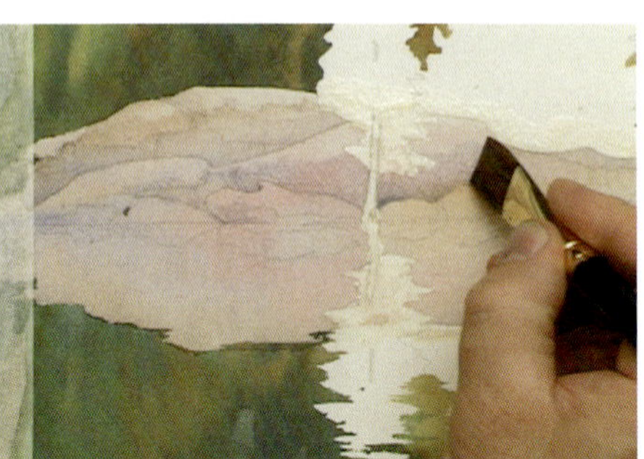

**Step 17:** After these base colors dried, I returned to them with a leaner mix of their same base colors: Ultramarine Blue and Burnt Sienna. With a 3/4" flat brush, I separated one section of rock from another, just like I had done with the trees above. Since the purpose of this step was to sort sections of rock, I refrained from painting in details like cracks. Just as with the trees, I generally made one edge of the shade shape hard to differentiate from its adjacent shape. Then I would tend to lose the other shade edge by dabbing, diluting or flaring it into other shade areas.

I mimicked some of these shade colors in their reflection below—particularly those shades close to the lake's edge.

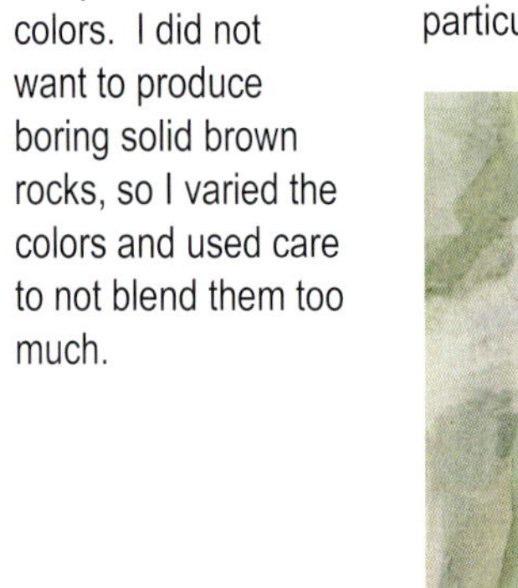

**Step 18:** After those shades had dried, I switched to a 1/2" flat brush and returned to paint in more rock shade details. This time I shaded smaller shapes within the previously shaded areas. I did not want to entirely cover and distort the underlying rock base colors. Rather, I wanted to provide minimal shading—just enough for the viewer to recognize what is represented.

Transparent watercolors are cumulative, so applying shade of the same lean value over the previous shade, creates a darker shade value. This may seem obvious, but without this knowledge it is easy to make the shade detail too dark.

I mimicked the shade details, vaguely, in the reflection below—particularly near the lake's edge.

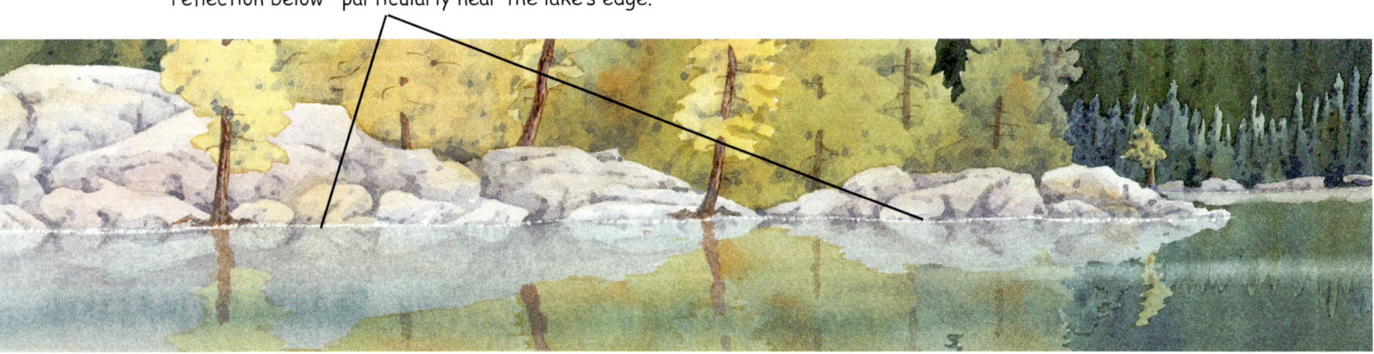

I used a very lean mix of Cobalt Blue to shade and sort sections of snow. A little Cobalt Blue goes a long way! Snow shading should be subtle, so I was careful to not apply the Cobalt Blue too dark.

Dividing sections of mountain gives them more dimension and the illusion of depth.

Individually, the snow shades appear crude and simple, but their aggregate impact provides the snow with much needed dimension.

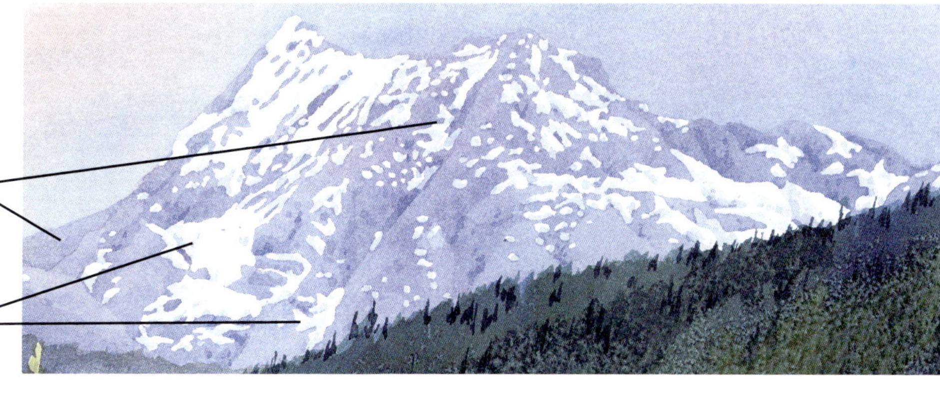

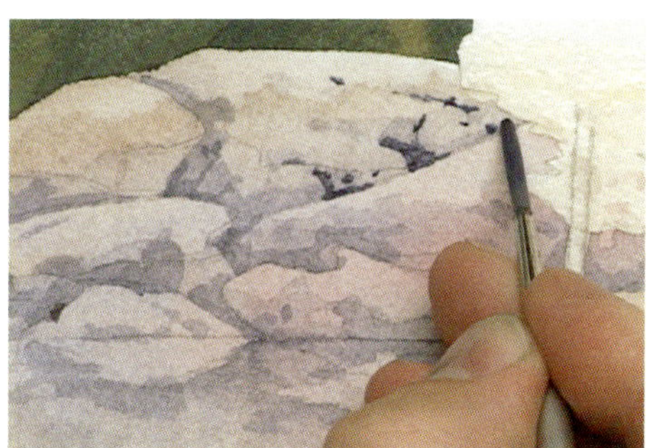

**Step 19:** To apply even more shade details, I switched to a #4 rigger brush. Again, I tended to shade within the previously shaded areas. This time, however, I would occasionally leave these shaded areas when painting a crack. I used the same colors—Ultramarine Blue and Burnt Sienna—but mixed a bit richer.

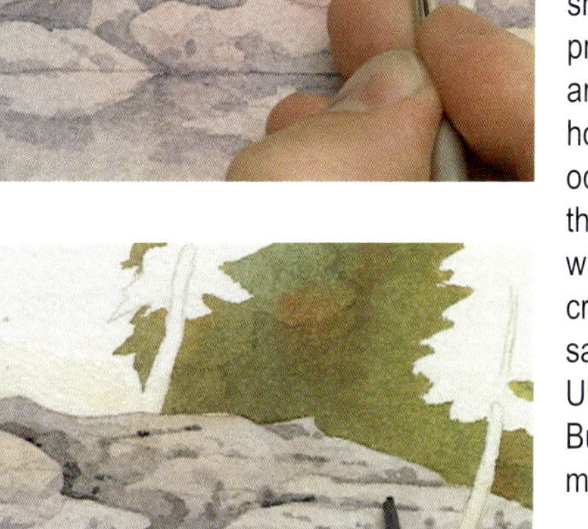

**Step 20:** Next, I peeled off the masking that was protecting the foreground tree edge. With a plastic toothpick, I remasked some of the visible tree trunk sections on these remaining unpainted trees.

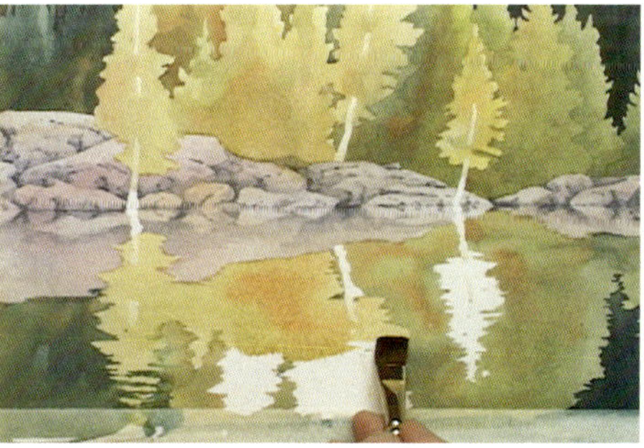

**Step 21:** With Ultramarine Blue, Ultramarine Green, Transparent Yellow, Burnt Sienna and a 1/2" flat brush, I painted in the base colors of the remaining foreground trees. To make them stand out against the other foreground trees, I painted them in a bit lighter. Again, I varied between these colors and mimicked them in the reflection below.

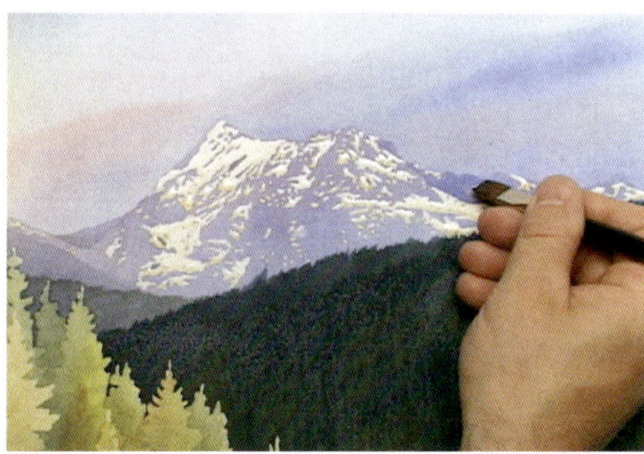

**Step 22:** Moving up to sort the sections of mountain, I used a thin mix of Cobalt Blue and Rose and a 1/2" flat brush. These mountains

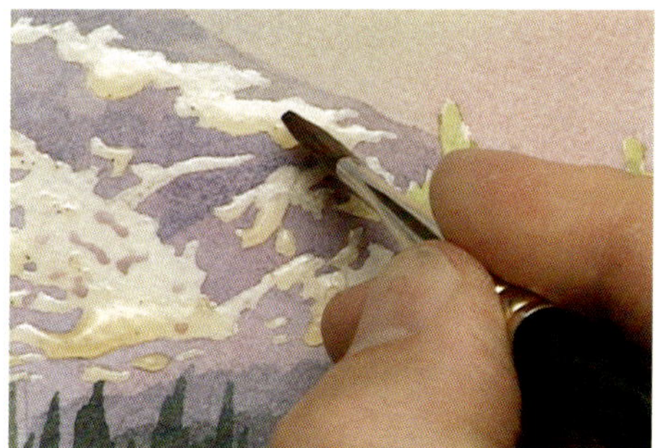

(Step 22 continued)

were quite distant from the viewer so they did not require much detail. As with the rocks and foreground trees, I sorted sections by creating one hard edge of the shade shape, while softening or losing the other edges.

**Step 23:** Once the mountains had been given some dimension by shading, I peeled the masking off of the snow shapes.

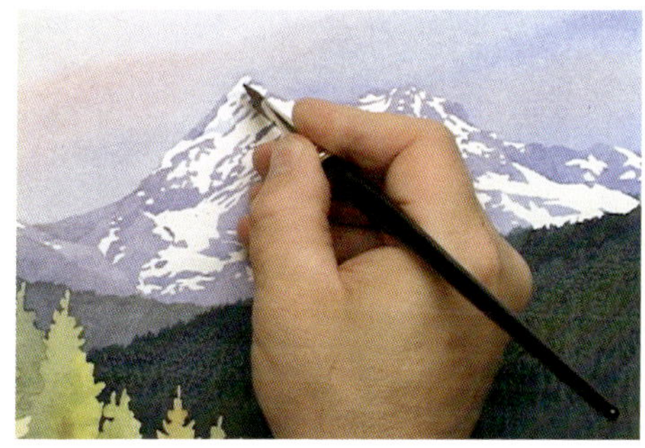

**Step 24:** Using a lean mix of Cobalt Blue and a 1/2" flat brush, I sorted sections of snow—dividing one area of snow from another. Again, this was the same basic sorting procedure that was used on the mountains, rocks, and foreground trees—a combination of hard and soft shade edges.

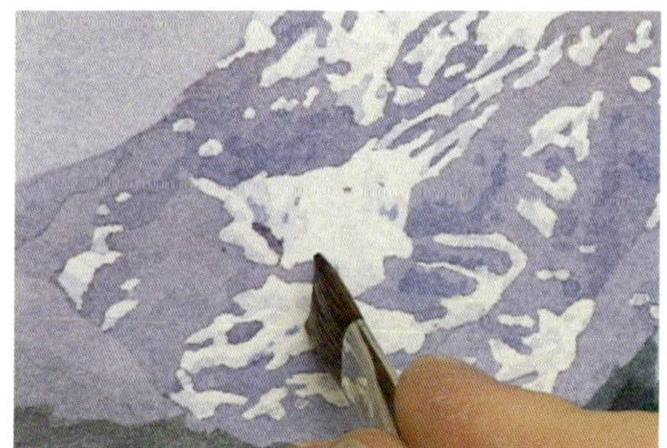

As with the rocks, I progressed to a smaller #4 rigger brush to apply the finer shade details—again tending to shade within a previously shaded area.

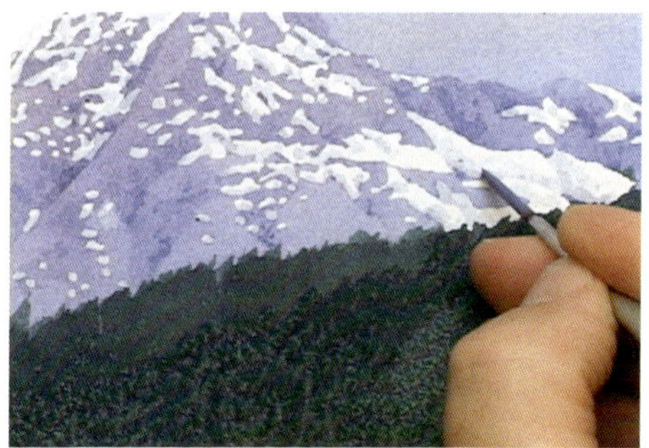

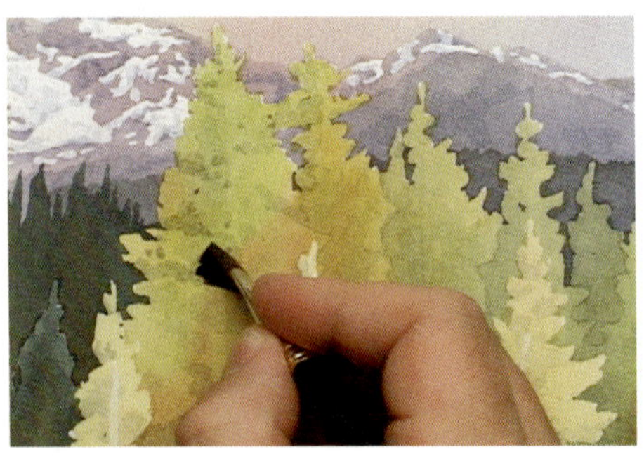

**Step 25:** To shape the trees, I mixed some Ultramarine Blue and Ultramarine Green. With a 1/2" flat brush, I tried to distinguish some branch forms—but only vaguely. I did not want to overwork the trees and lose their base colors. I simply wanted to suggest the various depths of the trees. Here again, I separated shapes with the hard edge of the shade color. The other edges of the shade color were then lost by dabbing or diluting them.

After this first step of shading had dried, I returned with the same colors and shaded more details within the previously shaded areas.

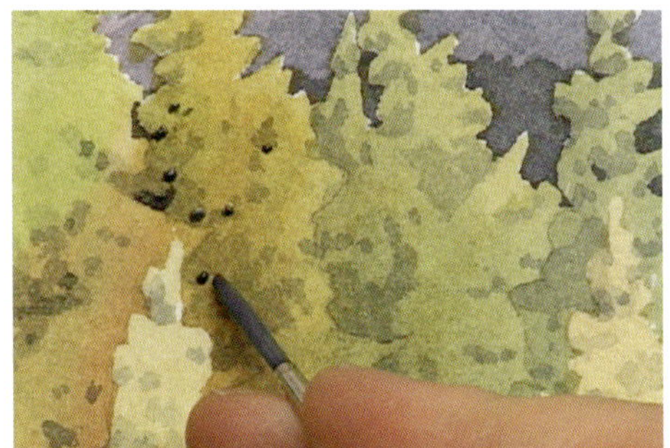

(Step 25 continued)

Then, with #4 rigger brush, I shaded even smaller details—again, tending to stay within the previously shaded areas.

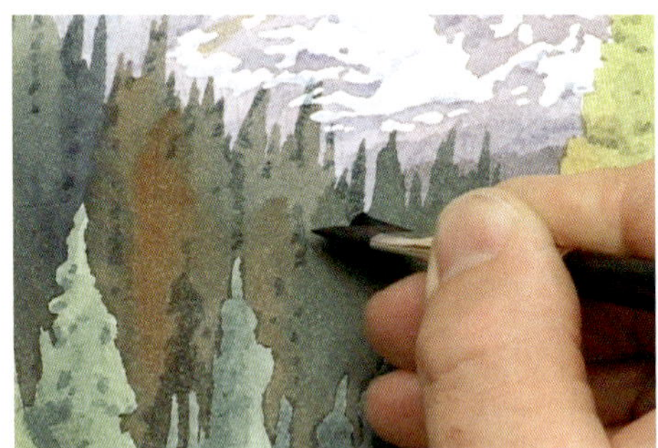

**Step 26:** Switching to their base colors of Phthalo Blue and Phthalo Green, I shaded the midground trees in the same manner. First, I would vaguely define some branch shapes. Then, I would shade details within the previously shaded areas—progressively using a smaller paintbrush.

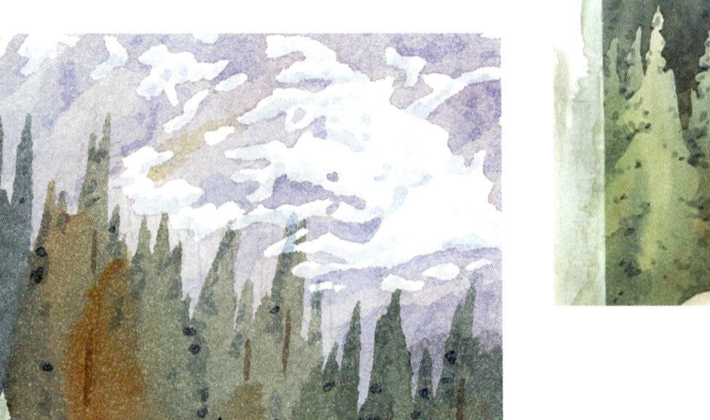

**Step 27:** Using a richer mix of Phthalo Blue and Phthalo Green and a #4 rigger brush, I next painted in some details on the dark, distant, forested hill. Here again, I wanted to do as little as possible—providing the viewer with just enough visual information—without losing the nice texture effects that the salt had created.

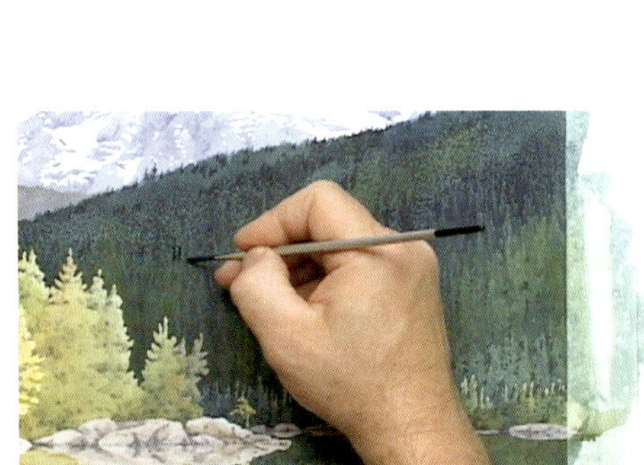

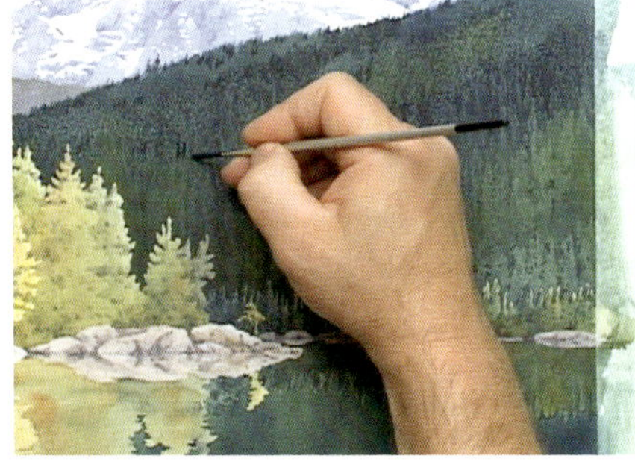

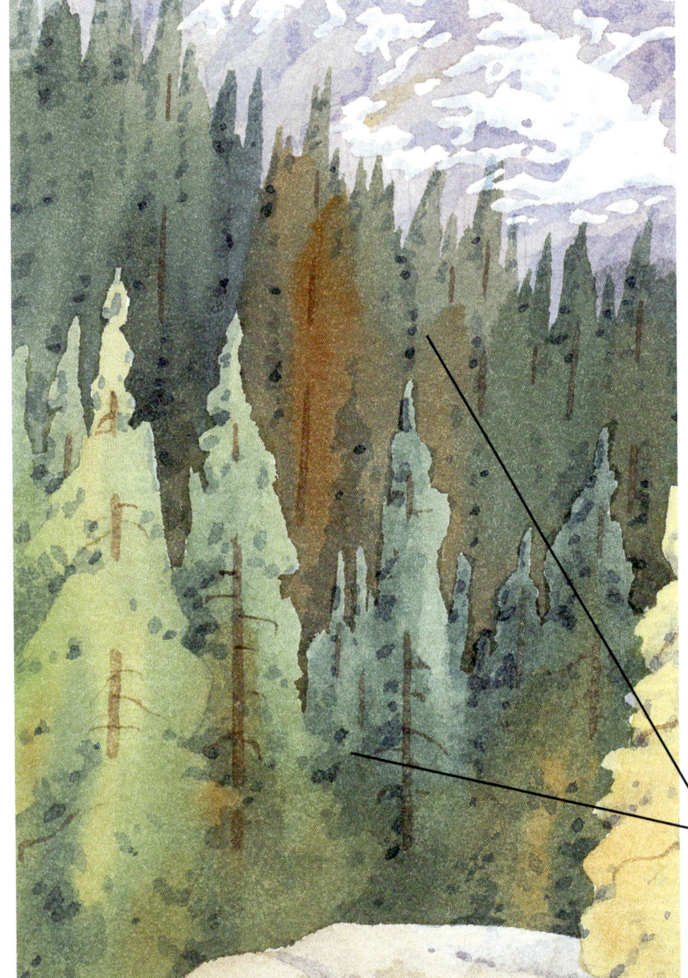

The shading, in this case, only suggests to the viewer that the trees have some depth and shape. I did not want to create photo-realism, nor did I want to cover up the tree base colors. To be sure, much is left to the viewer's imagination.

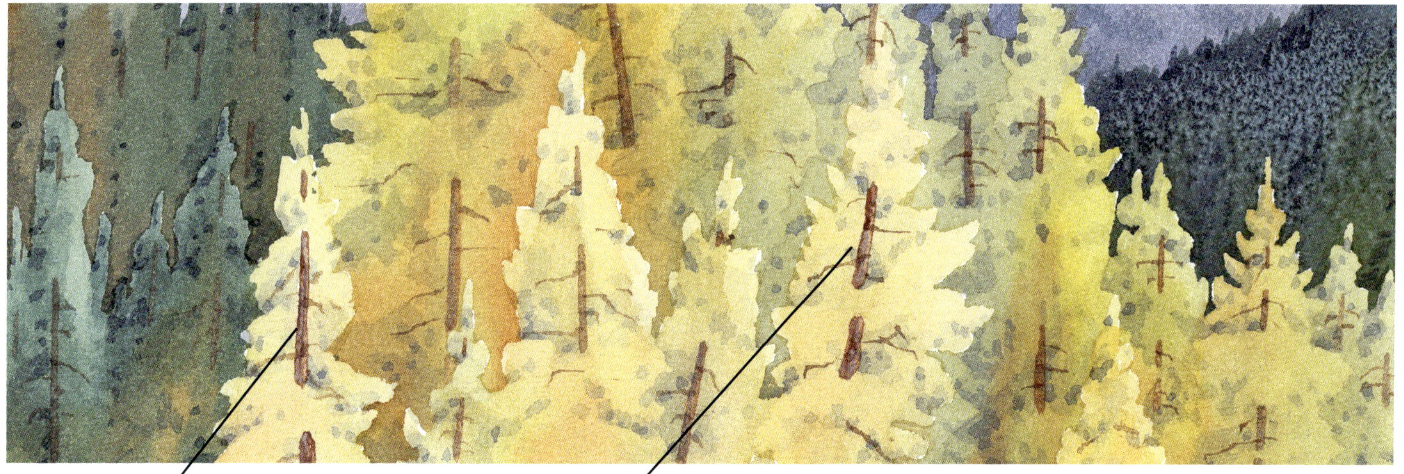

It is important to scrape the bark texture before the paint loses its shine of wetness. If it is scraped too soon, the texture will fill in with paint. If it is scraped too late, the dry paint will not accept the scrape. This is a good procedure to practice first.

I painted in just the visible sections of trunk on the foreground trees. On the more distant midground trees, I did the same—but not on all of the trees.

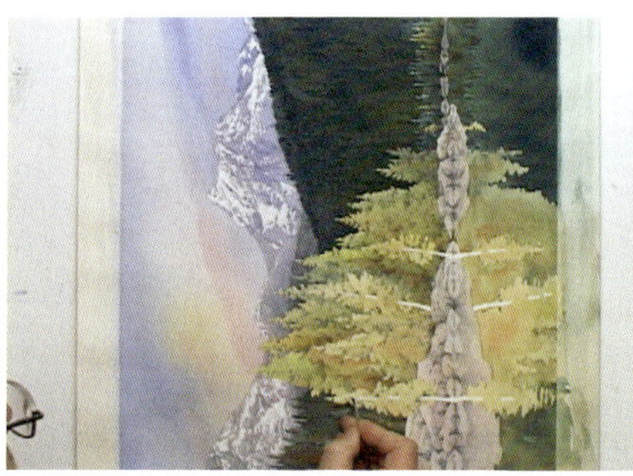

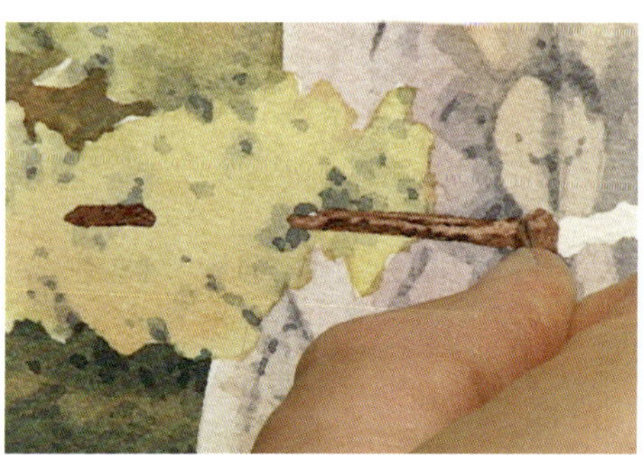

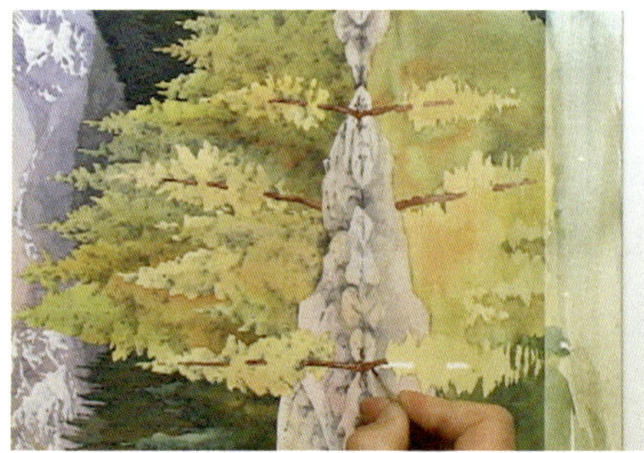

**Step 28:** I peeled off the remaining masking from the tree trunks and their reflections. Then with a mix of Brown Madder and Phthalo Blue and a #2 round brush, I painted these same tree trunks. Before these sections of painted tree trunks dried, I scraped their "up-light" sides with a palette knife. These sections of trunk dried very quickly, so I only painted one or two at a time—depending on their size. If I had painted too many at once, they would have dried before I could have scraped texture into them.

**Step 29:** Without scraping in texture, I also painted in the tree trunk reflections with the same colors.

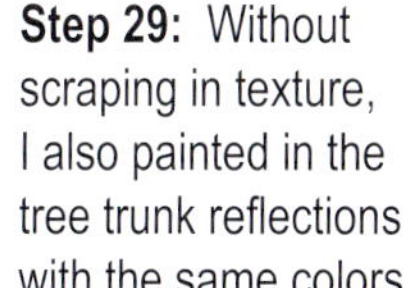

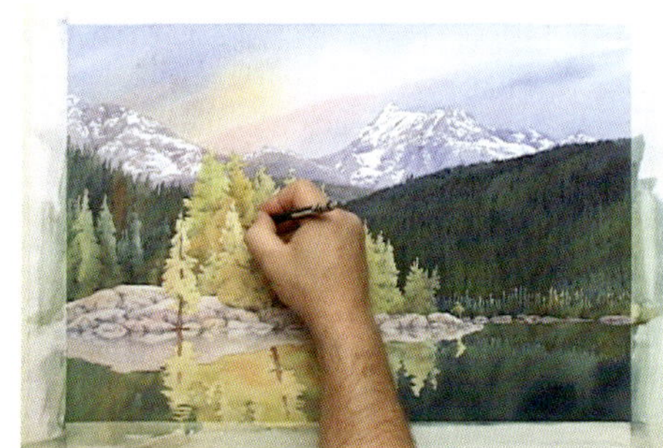

**Step 30:** With an H-lead pencil, I lightly drew in tree trunk guidelines on some of the other foreground trees.

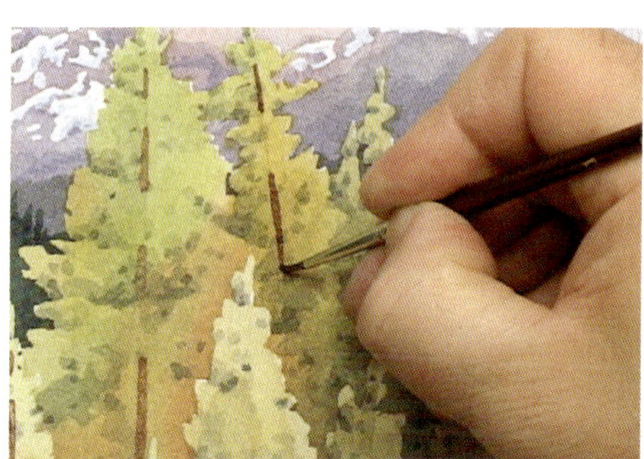

**Step 31:** Then, with the same trunk colors—Brown Madder and Phthalo Blue—and a #1 round brush, I painted in these, slightly, more distant tree trunks. For these, I did not scrape in bark texture.

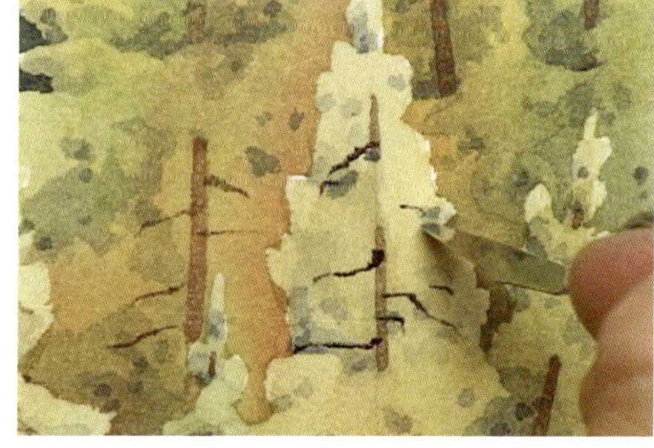

**Step 32:** Dipping my palette knife into the same mix of Brown Madder and Phthalo Blue, I lifted up some of the paint like a quill pen dipped into ink. Then I pulled sporadic branches with the tip of the knife.

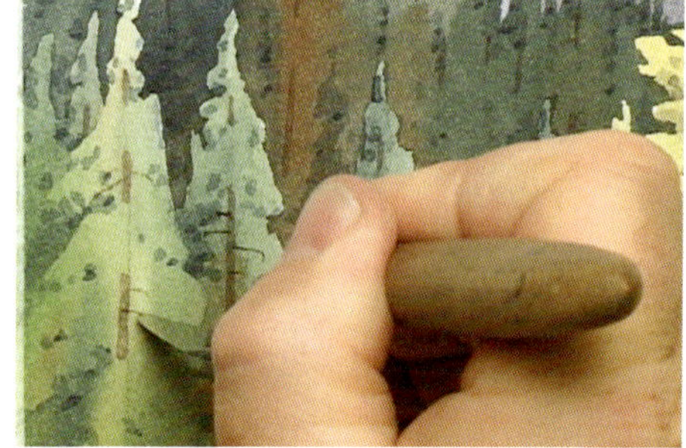

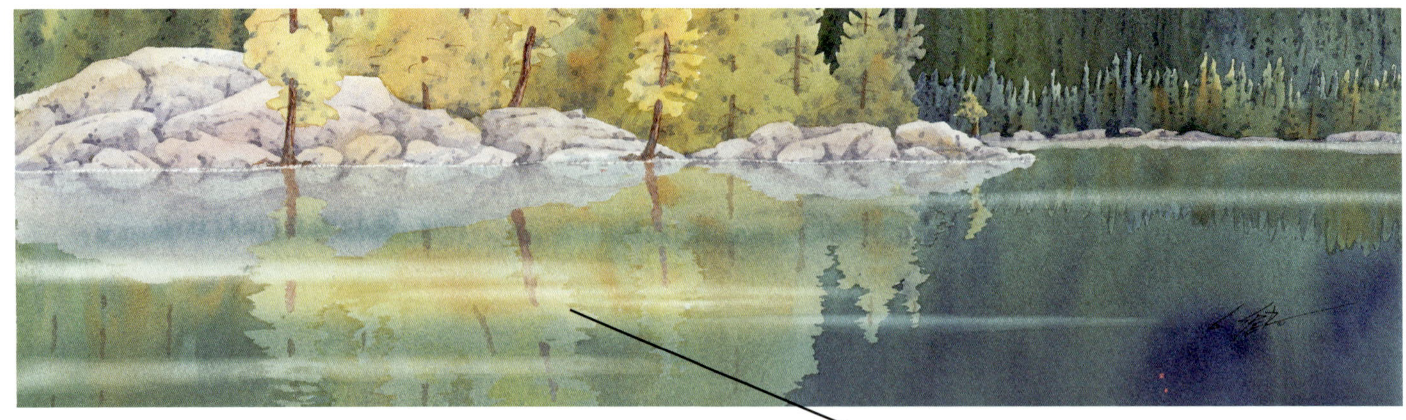

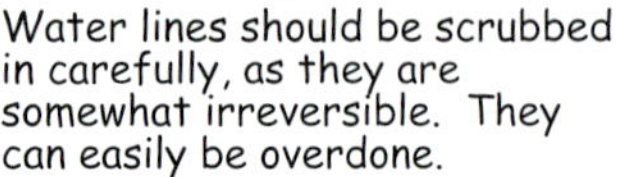

Water lines should be scrubbed in carefully, as they are somewhat irreversible. They can easily be overdone.

I preferred to use a syringe to apply the lake's surface, as it does not make direct contact with the paper. A brush would have likely lifted some of the underlying colors.

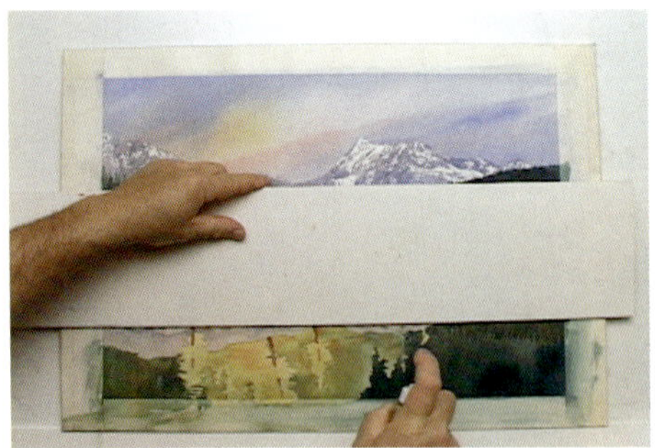

**Step 33:** To prepare for my lake surface colors, I saturated the painting below the shoreline, using a spray bottle filled with water. I held a piece of foamboard above the shoreline to prevent the area above the lake from getting wet.

Before that dried, I followed the lake's edge more precisely with a 2" flat brush loaded with water.

Then quickly, I tipped the painting onto its side and with a syringe loaded with water, I continued to saturate the same lake surface area. Now that the lake's shoreline edge had been defined with the water-loaded brush, this new supply of water did not cross into the painting above the shoreline. Water tends to follow water.

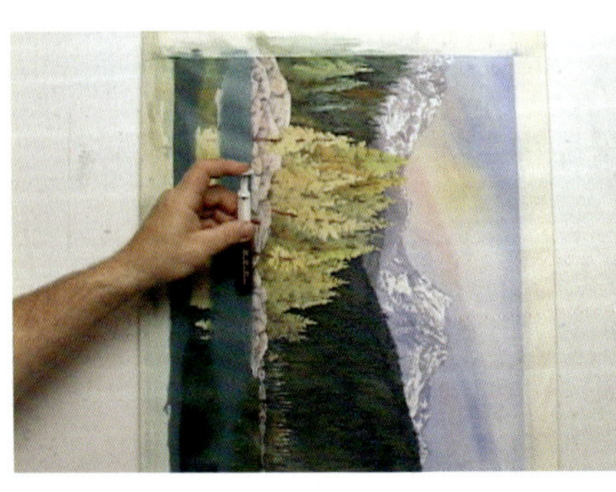

Continuing to work quickly, I loaded the same syringe with a watery mix of Cobalt Turquoise. Then I squeezed the paint onto the lake's surface from its uphill edge. If I applied too much paint, I simply squeezed on some more water. I tried to vary the intensity of the Cobalt Turquoise, purposely not applying it in a uniform fashion.

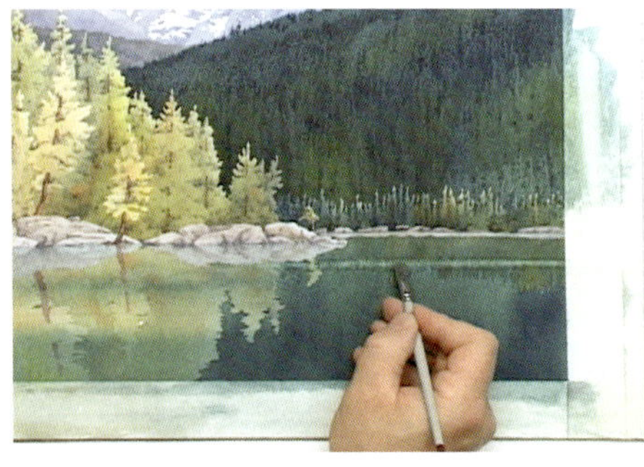

**Step 34:** Once I had thoroughly dried the lake's surface, I added some water reflection lines with a variety of scrubbing brushes. I would simply dip the scrubbing brush into clean water, then scrub horizontally to lift some of the pigment. With a tissue, I would wipe the excess water and paint off of the paper and from the brush. These lines provided more cues to help the viewer distinguish between the landscape and its reflection.

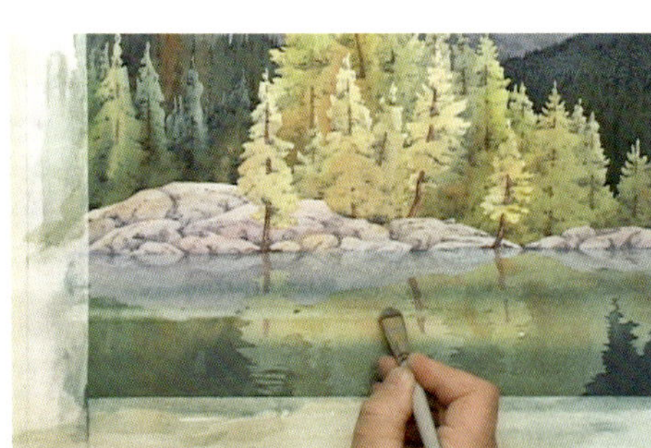

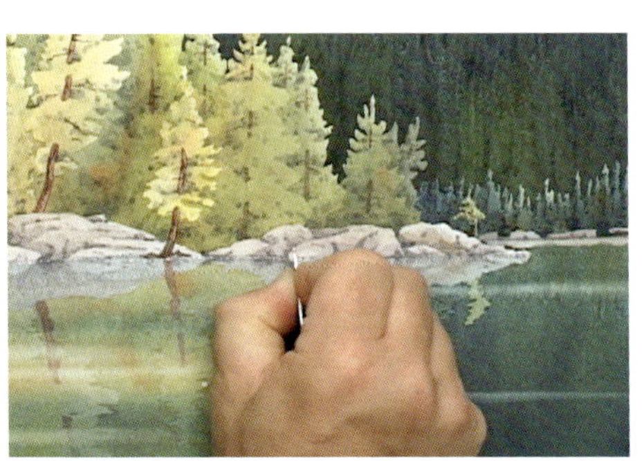

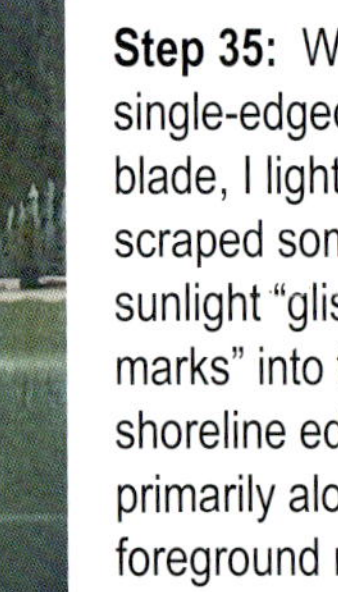

**Step 35:** With a single-edged razor blade, I lightly scraped some sunlight "glisten marks" into the lake's shoreline edge—primarily along the foreground rocks.

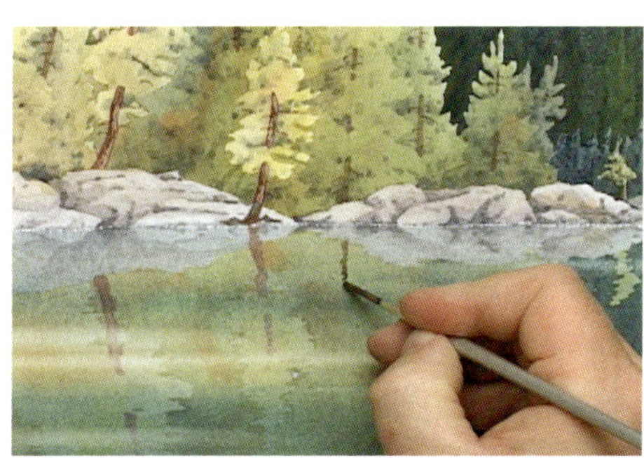

**Step 36:** Then, with a #4 rigger brush and the tree trunk colors—Brown Madder and Phthalo Blue—I painted in the prominent tree trunk reflections that I had missed earlier.

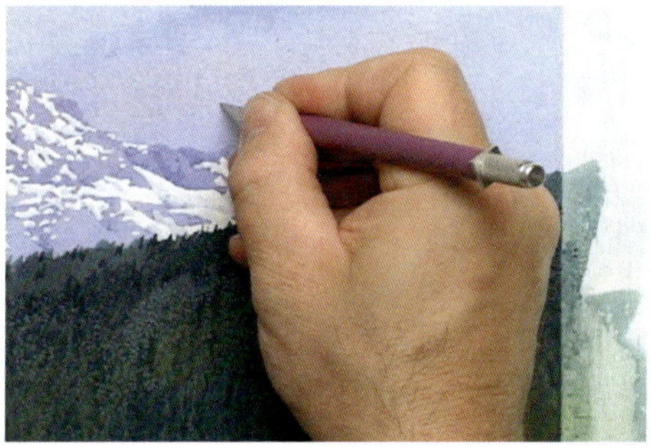

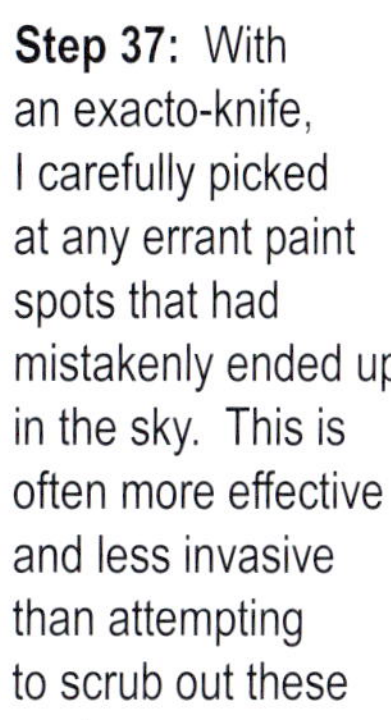

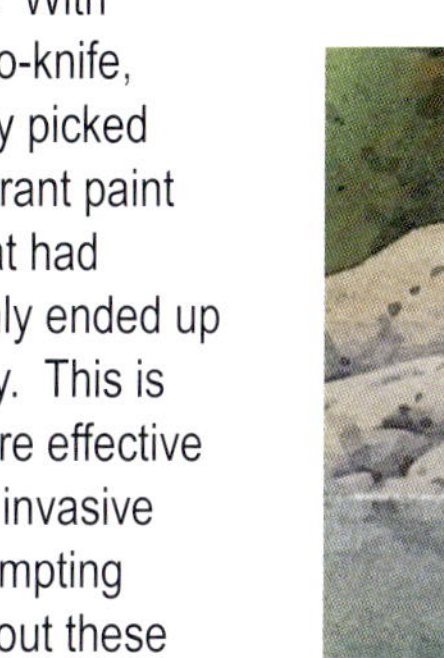

**Step 37:** With an exacto-knife, I carefully picked at any errant paint spots that had mistakenly ended up in the sky. This is often more effective and less invasive than attempting to scrub out these spots.

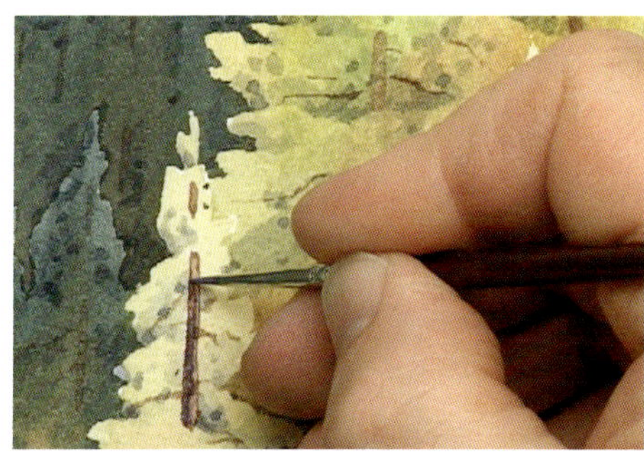

**Step 38:** With a lean mix of Cobalt Blue and a #1 round brush, I painted the downlight side of the visible tree trunks—suggesting dimension.

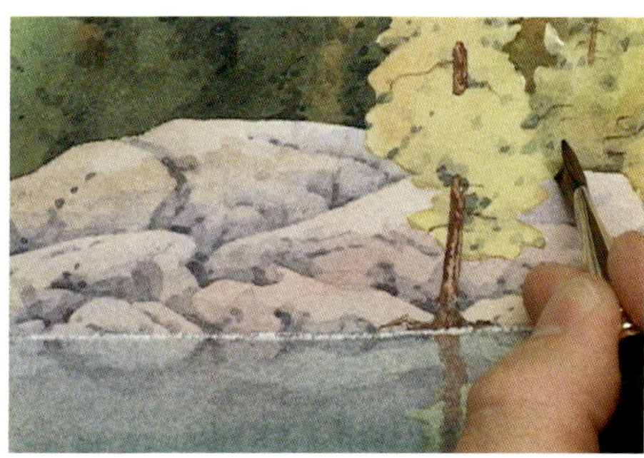

**Step 39:** To help distinguish the rocks from the foreground trees, I added more shade details to the rocks using Cobalt Blue and a 1/2" flat brush.

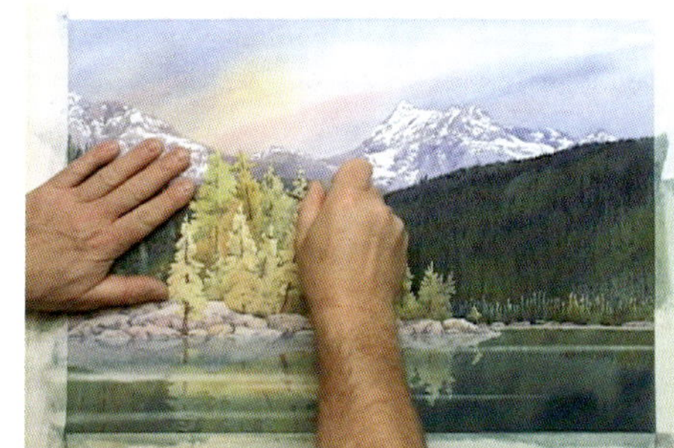

**Step 40:** To conclude the painting, I erased any visible pencil lines with a kneaded eraser.

Both the range of colors, and their values, played a crucial role in creating the illusion of depth in this painting.

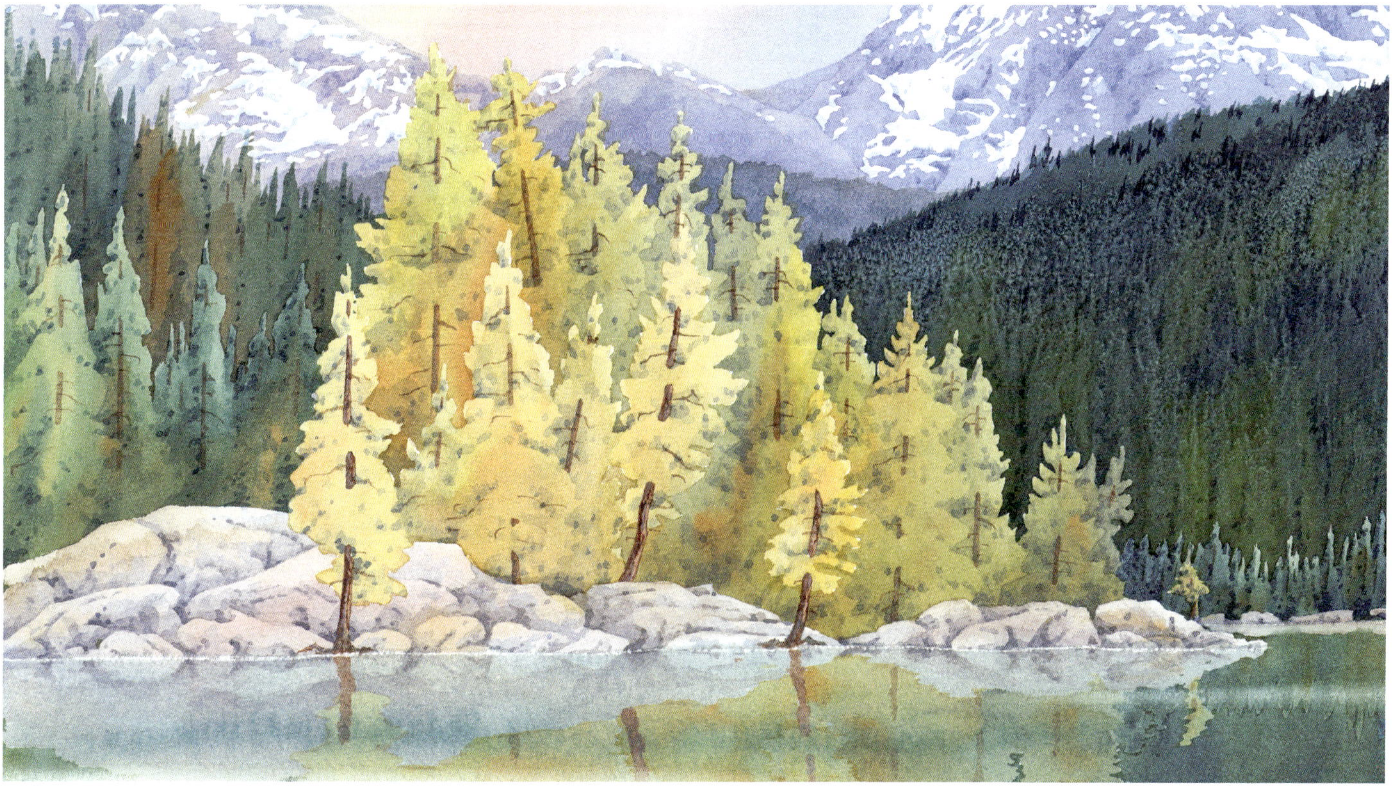

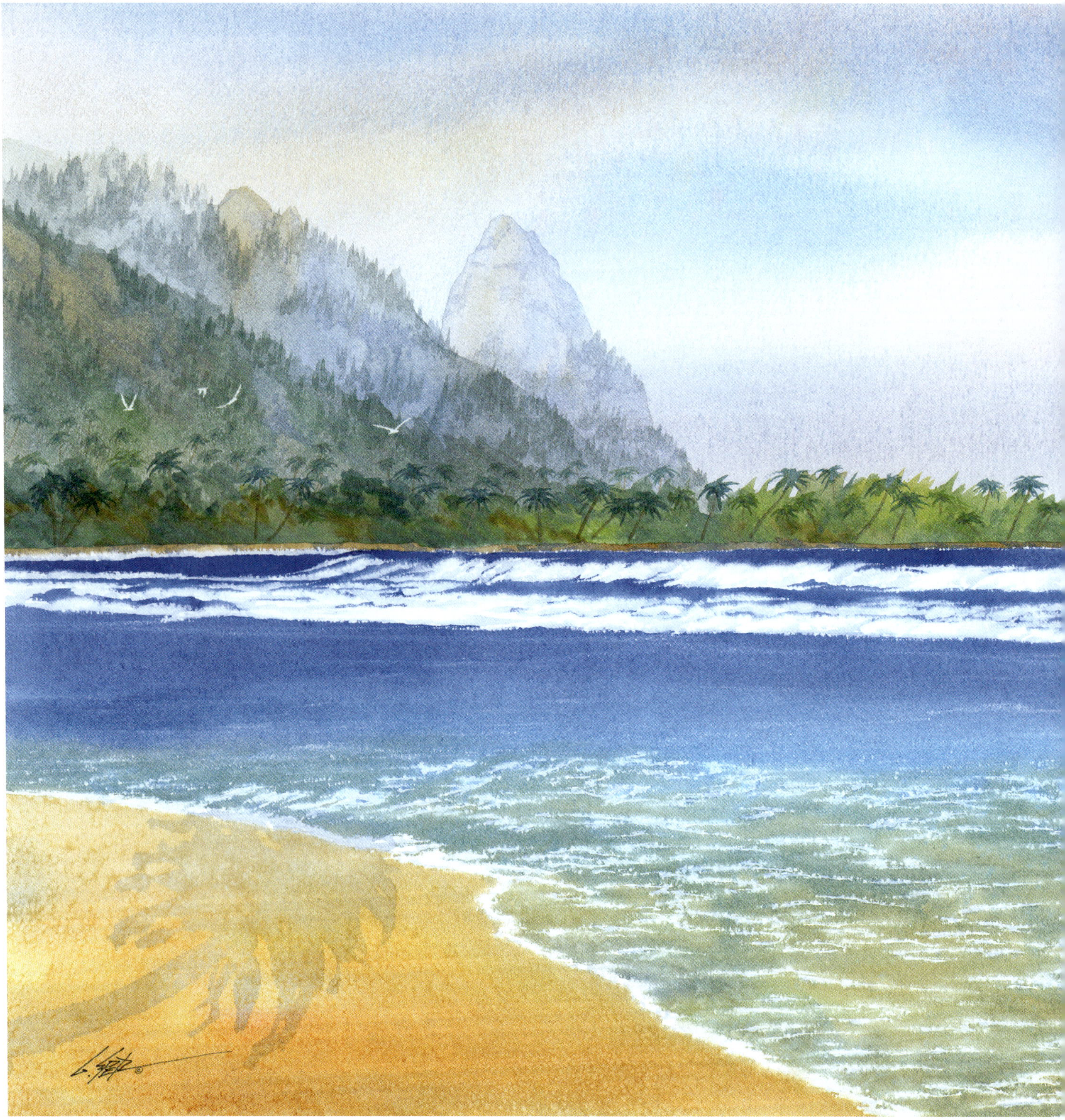

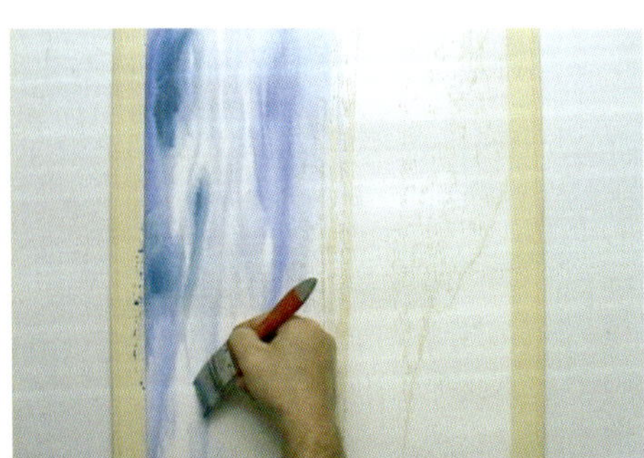

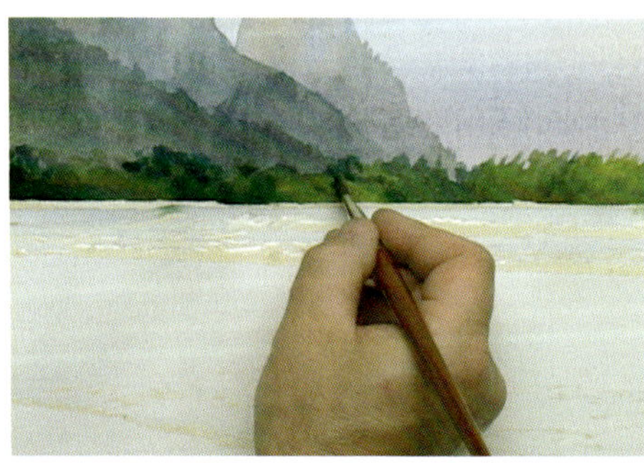

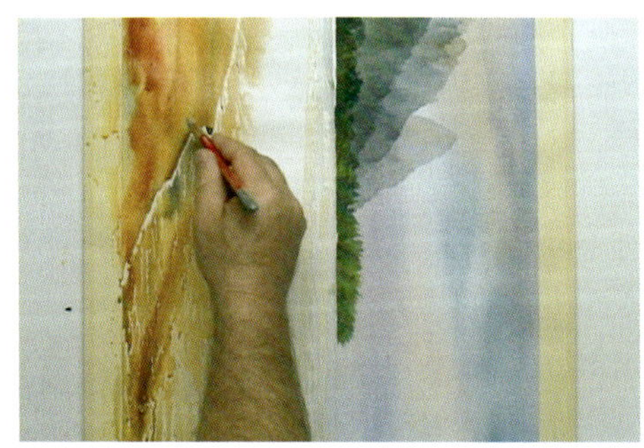

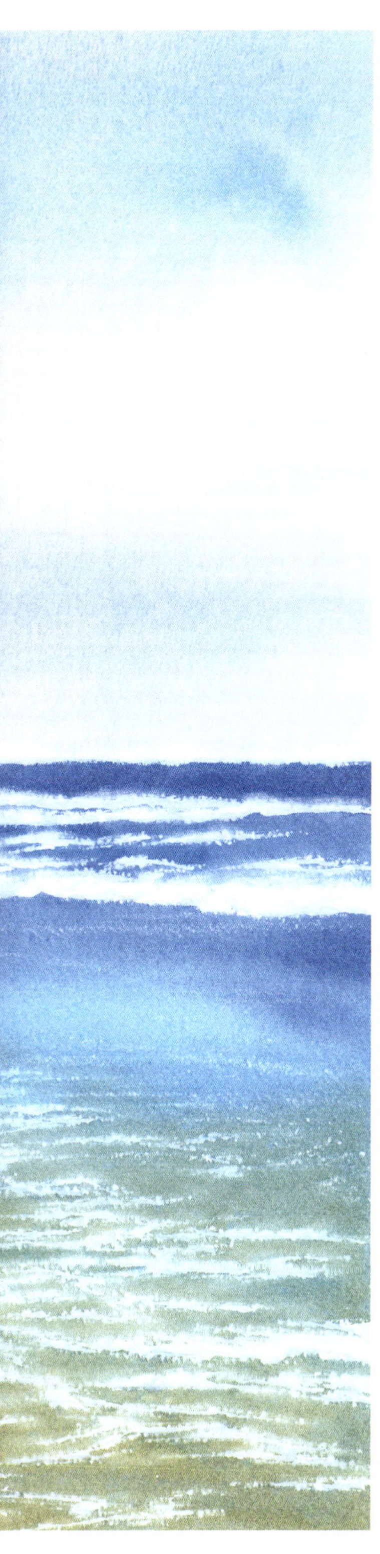

# *BALI HAI*

Few scenes depict the ideal of paradise better than Kauai's Makana Ridge. This Hawaiian Island landmark is recognized by many as Bali Hai from the motion picture, *South Pacific*. Like most wild places, its enchanting power is best felt early in the morning, when the light is low and the people are few.

Aside from this place's vivid array of colors, I was particularly interested in its interaction of shapes: a vast horizontal ocean intersecting, at a sharp angle, a broad flat beach—all backed by a wall of imposing jagged peaks.

Of course, such a scene begs to be painted!

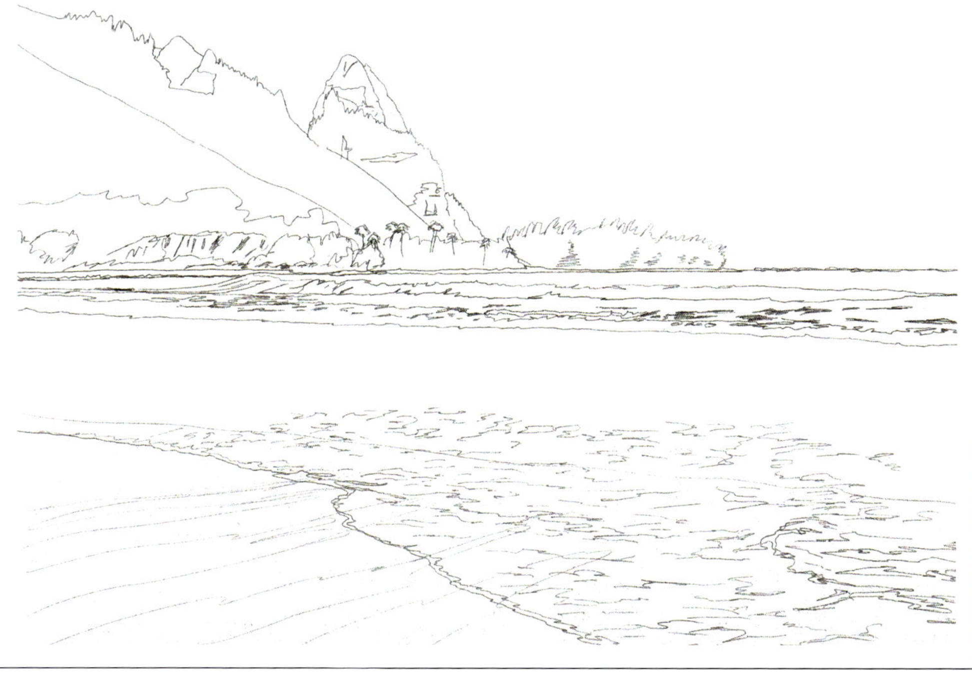

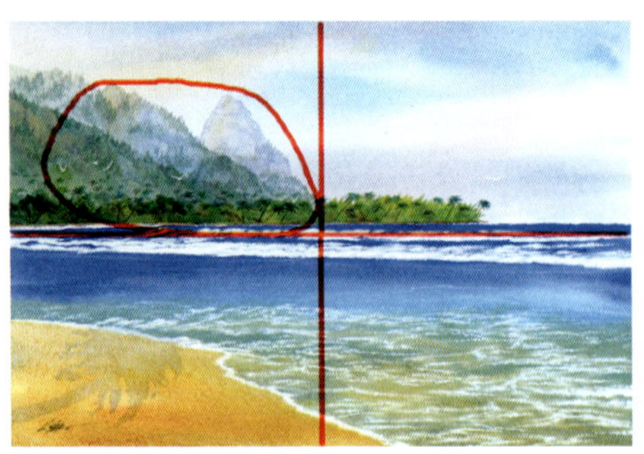

**Step 1:** I drew out my composition while being careful to not center prominent objects or primary focal points. In this case I kept the distant mountain range above and to the left of center.

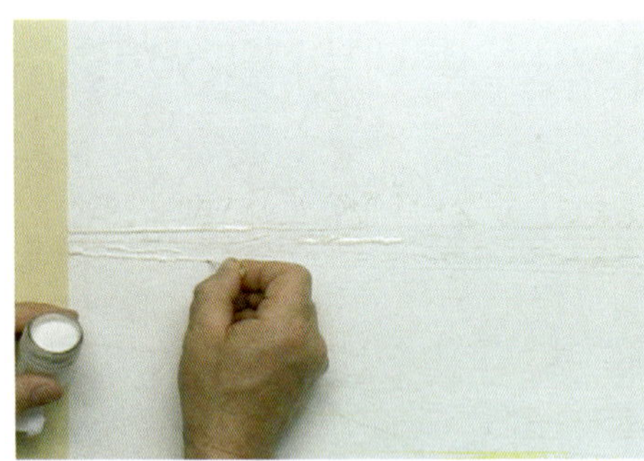

**Step 2:** Next, with liquid masking fluid and a plastic toothpick, I masked out the narrow distant beach.

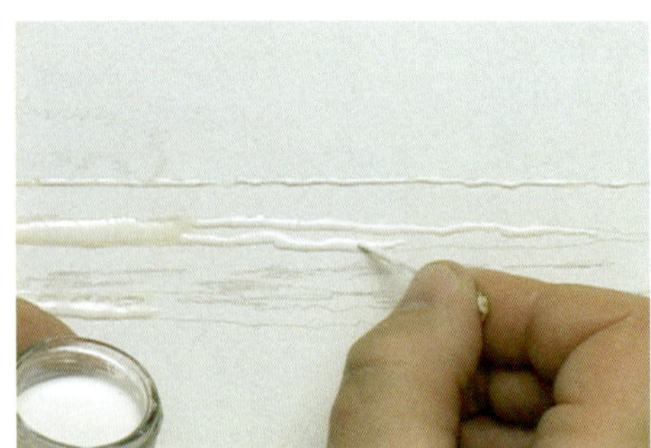

(Step 2 continued)

I also masked the horizontal whitecaps of the many breaking waves.

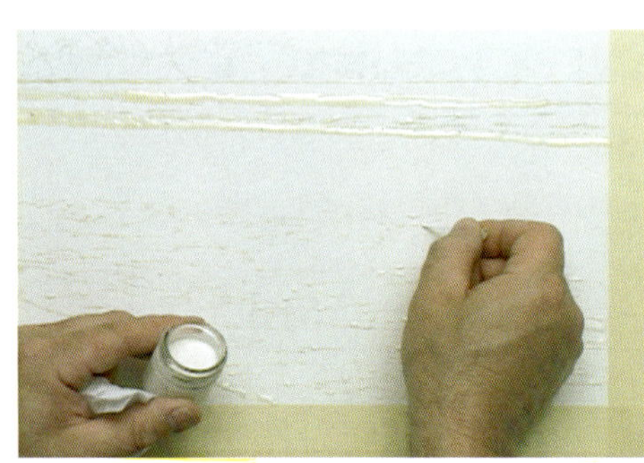

And I masked the intricate shoreline foam patterns.

Investing the time into masking the painting's whites will pay off later by allowing more freedom when painting in the beach and ocean colors.

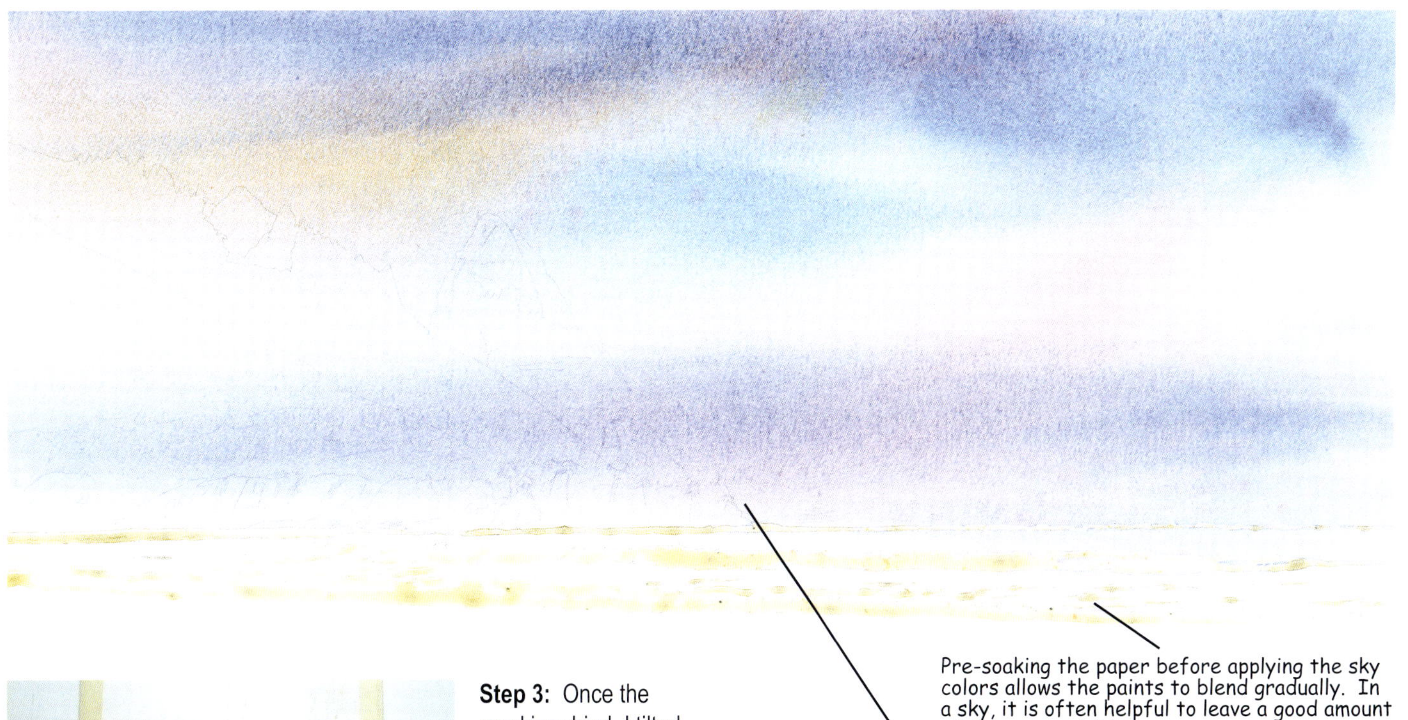

Pre-soaking the paper before applying the sky colors allows the paints to blend gradually. In a sky, it is often helpful to leave a good amount of the paper visible.

If your sky area is still wet and you have applied too much paint, you can still spray some off with water. I have, at times, sprayed my entire sky off and have started over. But, this can only be done if the sky is still quite wet. Some colors, like Cerulean Blue, will not completely wash off, but you should be able to still work it into your next sky wash attempt.

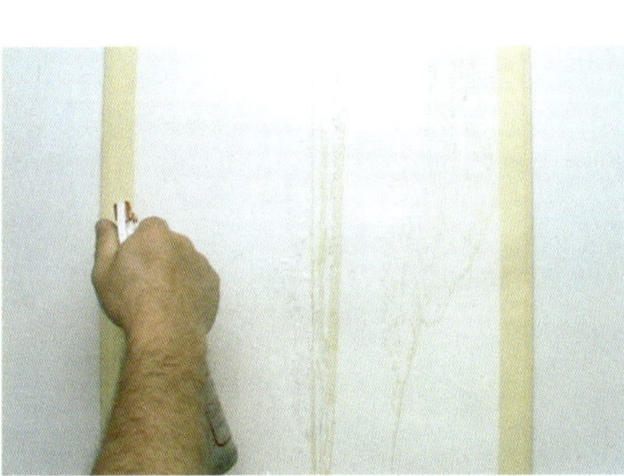

**Step 3:** Once the masking dried, I tilted the painting onto its side (remember, it is already tilted forward on my inclined painting table).

With a spray bottle filled with water, I saturated the entire painting.

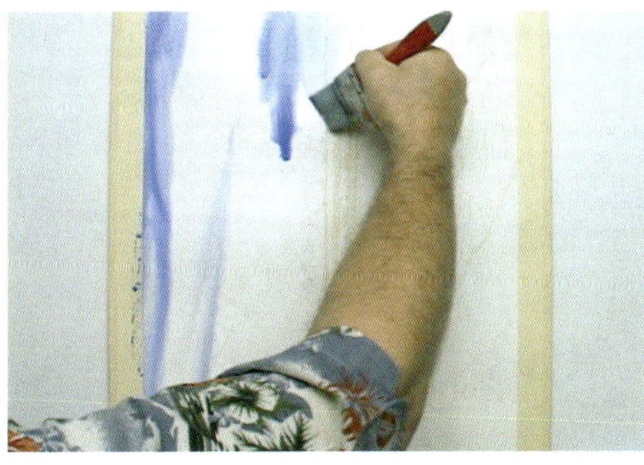

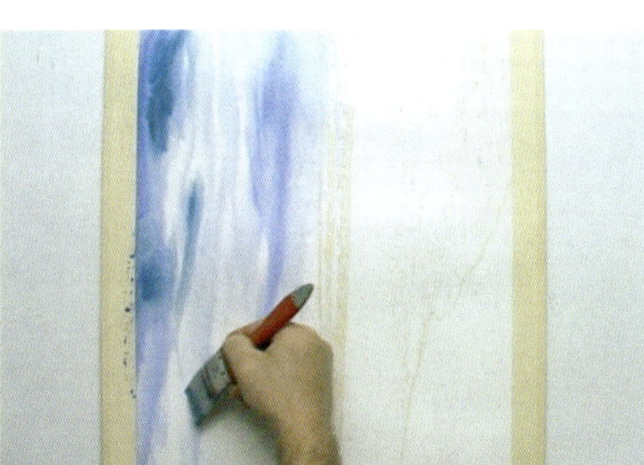

Then, with my 2" flat brush and a rich mix of Cobalt Blue and Cerulean Blue, I worked in erratic stripes of color. I used care to make sure that I did not paint over the entire sky—I wanted much of the paper's white to be remain visible. Since the painting was pre-soaked, these blues blended gradually with the white areas.

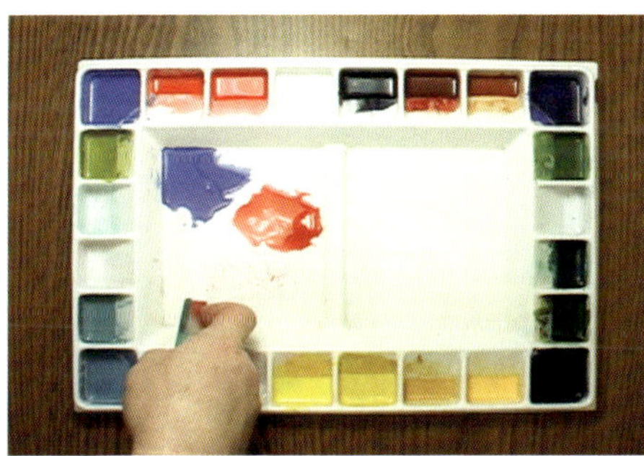

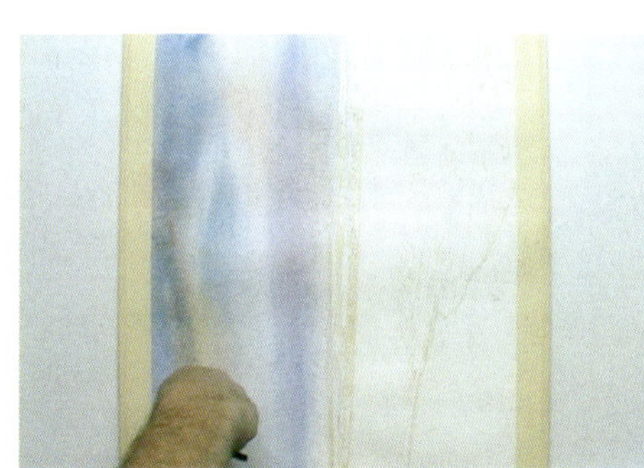

Next, with a stiff-bristled toothbrush, I "flicked" areas of the sky with both Rose and Transparent Yellow—being careful to not center either of these prominent colors. Since the paper was still quite wet, these colors also blended gradually into the sky.

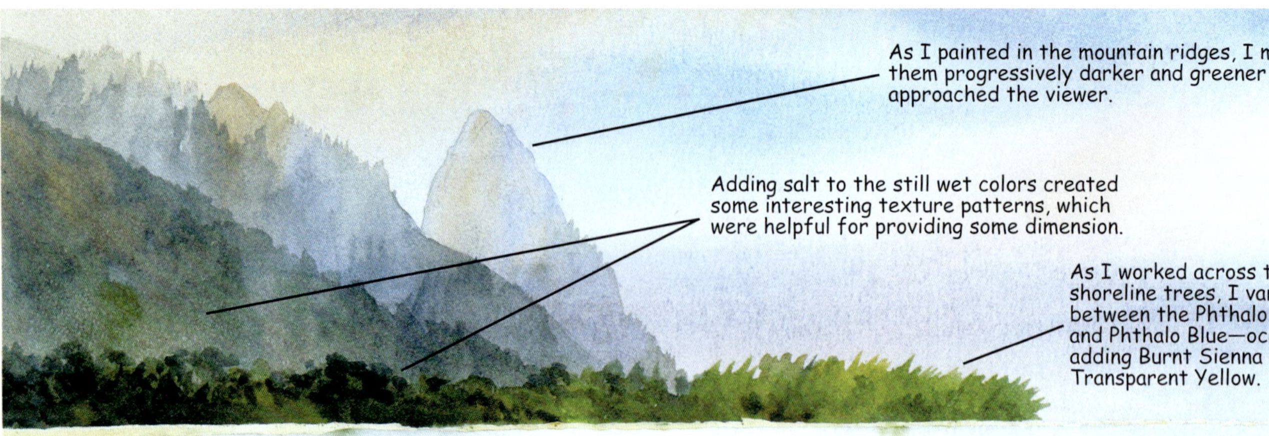


**Step 4:** After drying the sky colors, I saturated everything below the bottom of the mountains. This prevented a hard edge from forming at the base of the mountains while I turned my attention to the mountain's upper edges.

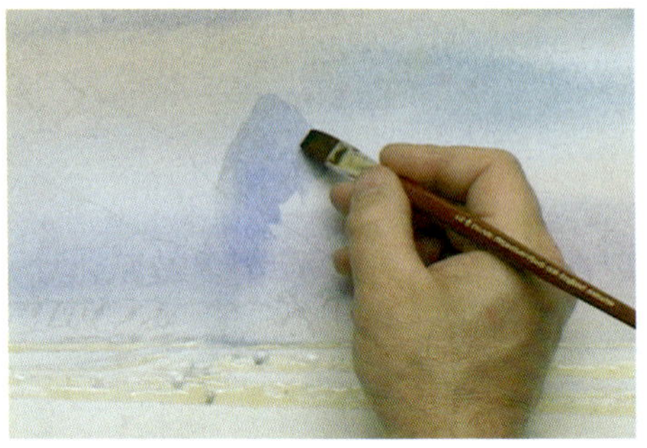

Using a 1/2" flat brush and a lean mix of Cobalt Blue, I painted in the most prominent peak. Quickly, before this paint had dried, I worked in some Burnt Sienna—allowing it to blend with the Cobalt Blue. Then, as I worked towards the bottom of the peak, I began using a mix of Cobalt Green—representing where the rock merged into the vegetation below.

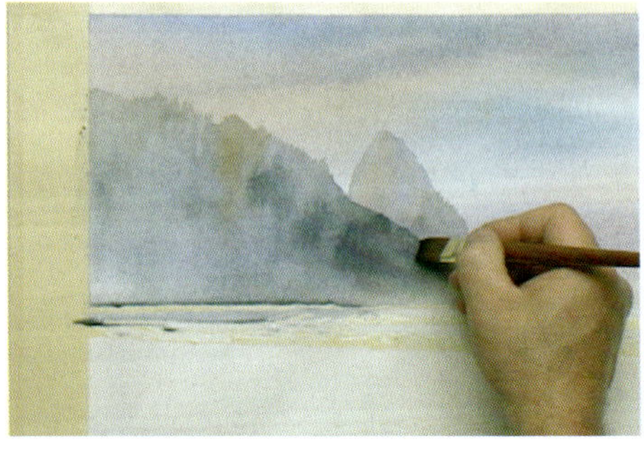

**Step 5:** After I dried the first peak with a blow drier, I again saturated the paper below the mountain base. Then, I began working in the next closest row of mountains—again using the Cobalt Blue and again blending in areas of Burnt Sienna and Cobalt Green. I gave the upper edge of this mountain a bit of a sawtooth shape to suggest distant trees.

**Step 6:** Then, I repeated the process for the next closest mountains: I dried the preceding mountain colors, then saturated everything below them. This time I mixed in some Ultramarine Green and Ultramarine Blue with the Cobalt

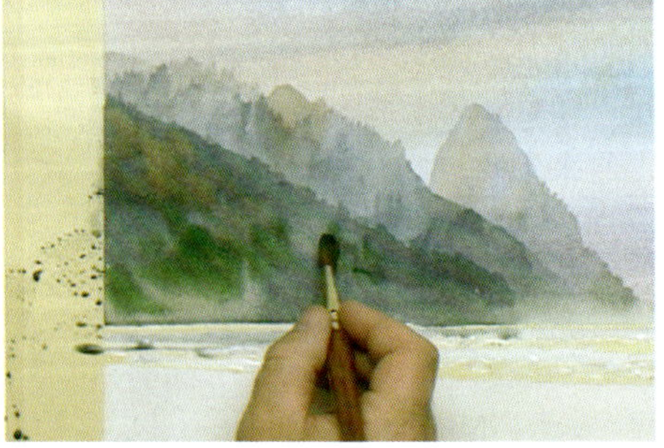

(Step 6 continued)

Green and Cobalt Blue—making this row of mountains stand out a bit more prominently. In areas where I wanted to suggest exposed rock, I worked in some Burnt Sienna while the underlying colors were still wet.

As the colors dried on this row of mountains, I painted in some Ultramarine Green sawtooth patterns to suggest various rows of trees—providing a little more detail as the mountains got closer to the viewer.

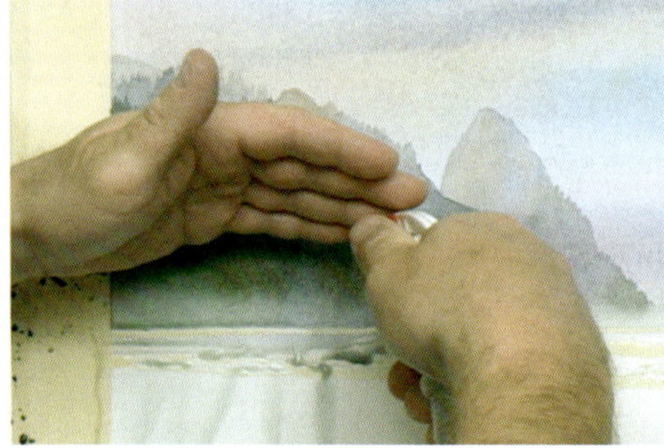

**Step 7:** For the foliage area right above the distant beach, I first sprayed off the lower edge of the previous step. Then I worked in some Phthalo Blue and Phthalo Green with a 1/2" flat brush. These vivid colors stand out against the less prominent Ultramarine Green and Cobalt Green—giving the impression that this foliage is separate and closer to the viewer. Since I applied these colors while the last row of mountains was still wet, I was able to gradually blend the Phthalo Green into the base of the mountain.

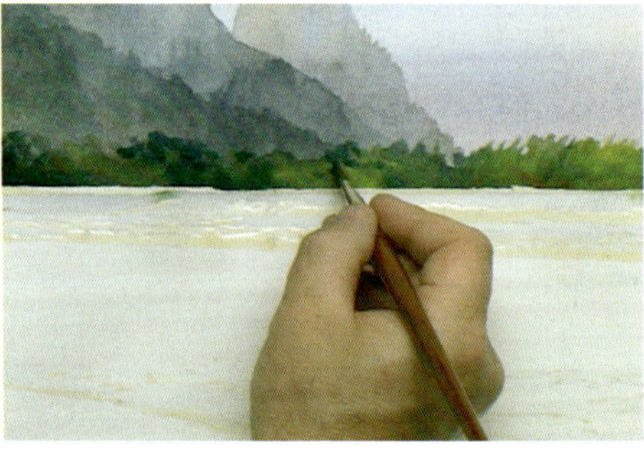

As I worked across the beach foliage, I intermittently added Burnt Sienna and Transparent Yellow to the still-wet underlying foliage colors. And before any of this dried, I added salt to promote a texturing effect.

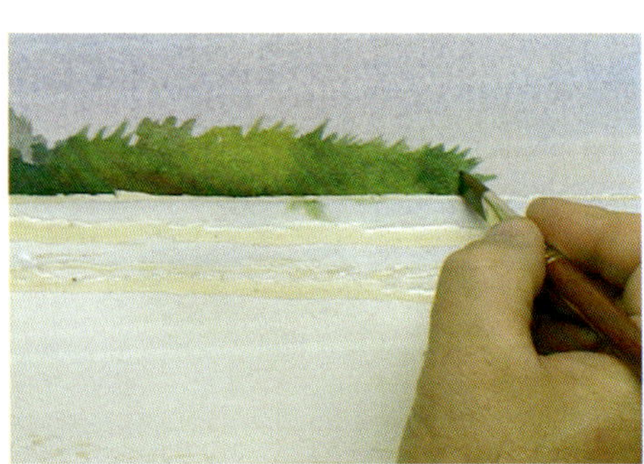

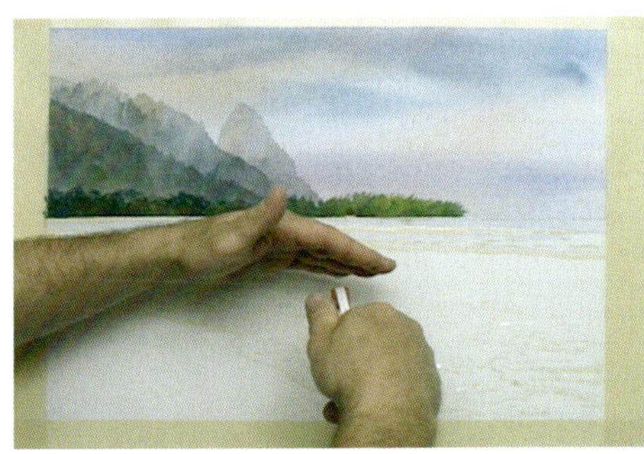

**Step 8:** To achieve the gradual beach-to-ocean effect, I wanted to paint my beach colors in first. So, once again, I saturated the painting below the distant shoreline.

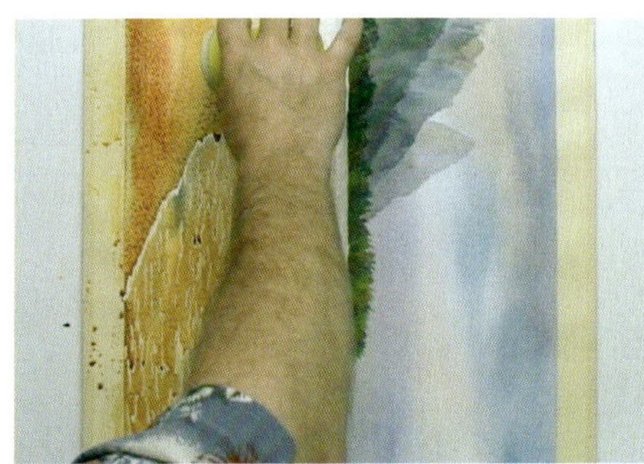

**Step 10:** With the painting still on its side, I loaded my 2" flat brush with water and pre-wetted the entire ocean area. Then I loaded the same brush with a medium mix of Turquoise Green. I carefully painted along the beach foam line, allowing the colors to flow downward on the wet paper. Next, I worked the same color into the remainder of the ocean.

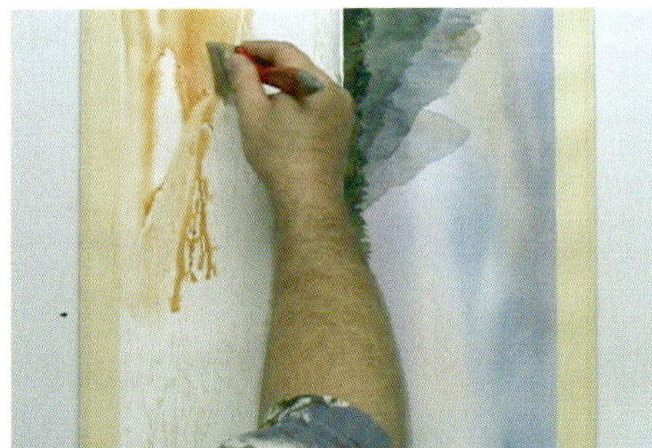

**Step 9:** Again, I tilted the painting onto its side. With a 2" flat brush and a mix of Burnt Sienna, Ultramarine Blue, Transparent Yellow and Rose, I worked in my beach colors—allowing these pure colors to blend right on the wet paper. Since the painting was also tilted forward on my inclined table, these colors ran down into (what would become) the ocean area. Before they dried, I added salt to create a textured effect. Then I thoroughly dried these colors with a blow drier.

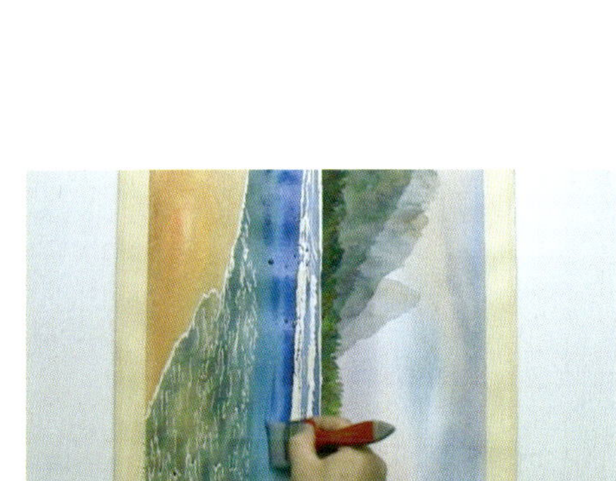

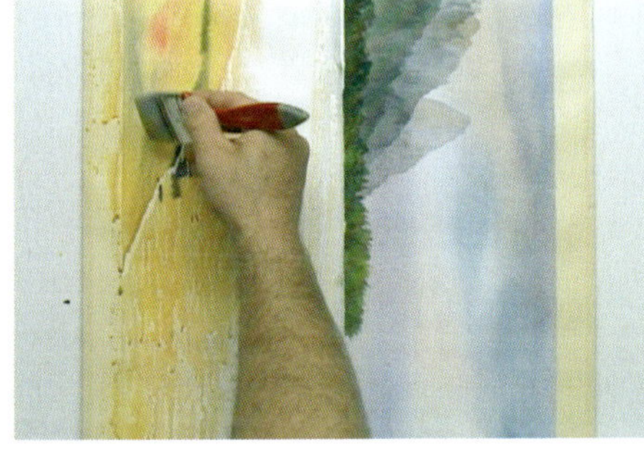

Once the entire ocean was colored, I applied rich streaks of both Turquoise Green and Ultramarine Blue to the more distant areas, allowing them to blend into the still-wet underlying base color.

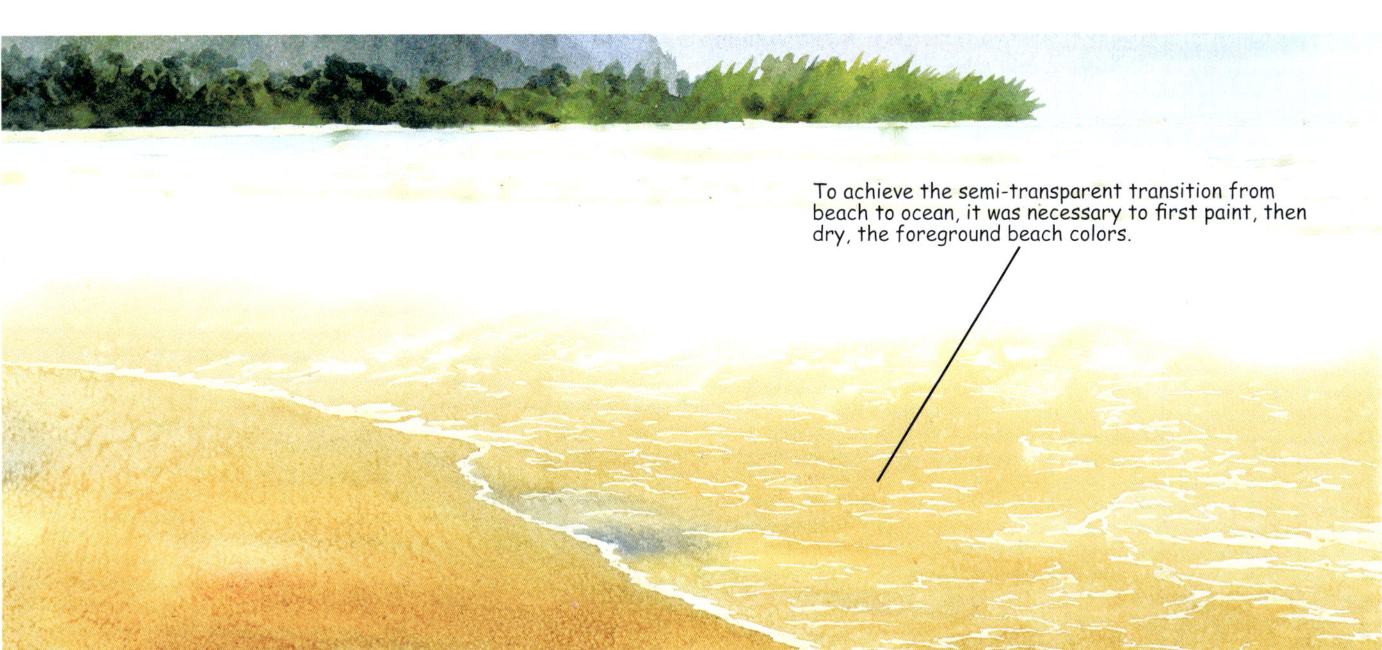

To achieve the semi-transparent transition from beach to ocean, it was necessary to first paint, then dry, the foreground beach colors.

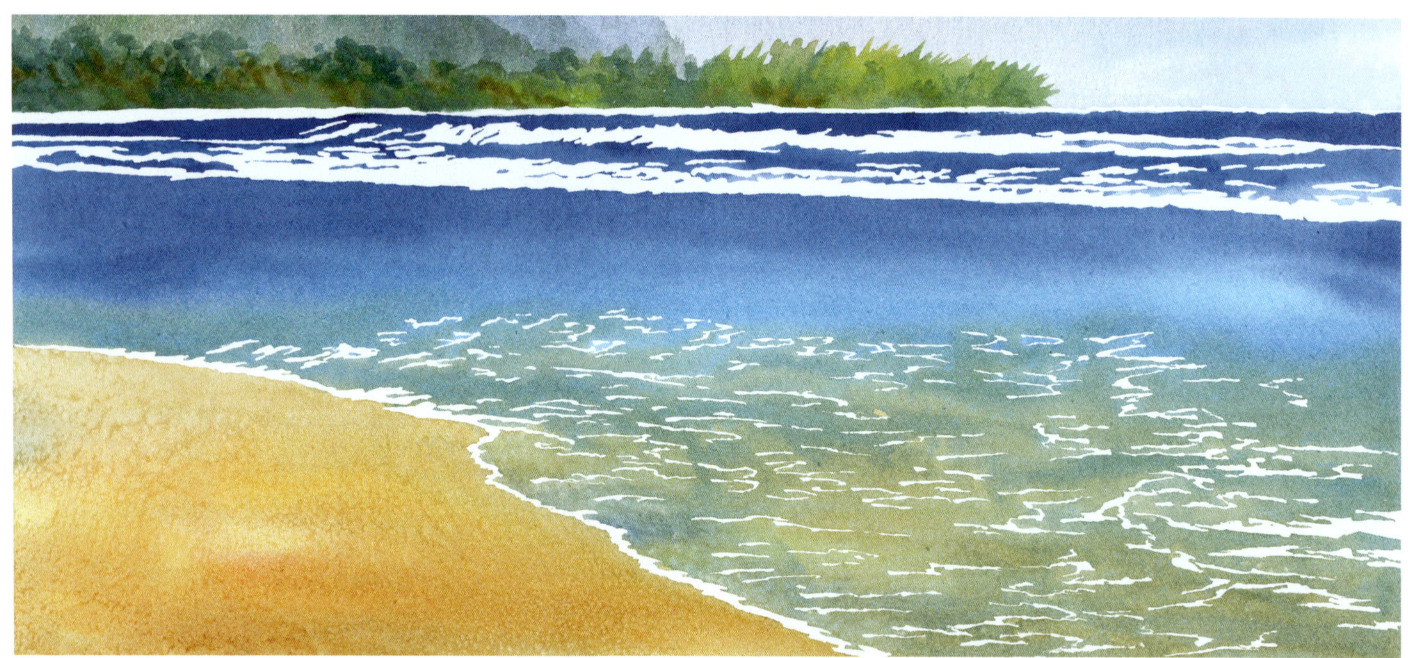

Generally, I tended to scrap the upper edges of the whitecaps, allowing the lower edges to appear defined by the rolling segments of blue water. It is the upper edges of the waves that are falling through the air, creating the confused, white edges.

By using a quality grade of 140 lb. watercolor paper, it is difficult (though not impossible) to scrape through the paper. Practice this technique first to know the paper's limits.

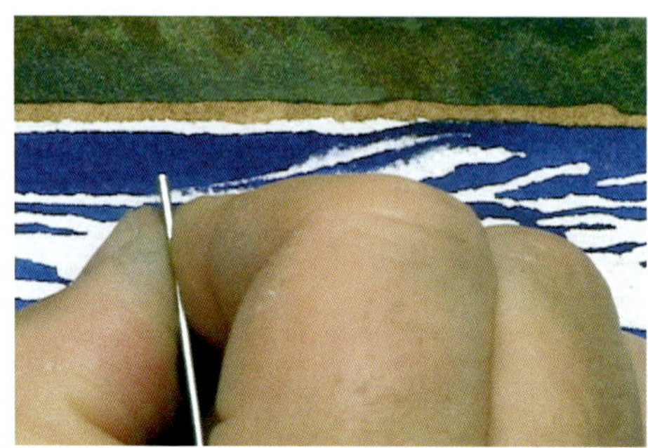

**Step 13:** Peeling off the masking left the ocean whitecap shapes with hard edges. Some of these needed to be softened. So, with a single-edged razor blade, I scraped away at many of them. I worked in a tight circular motion and I tended to gnaw away at the tops of the white shapes—leaving many of their bottom edges hard.

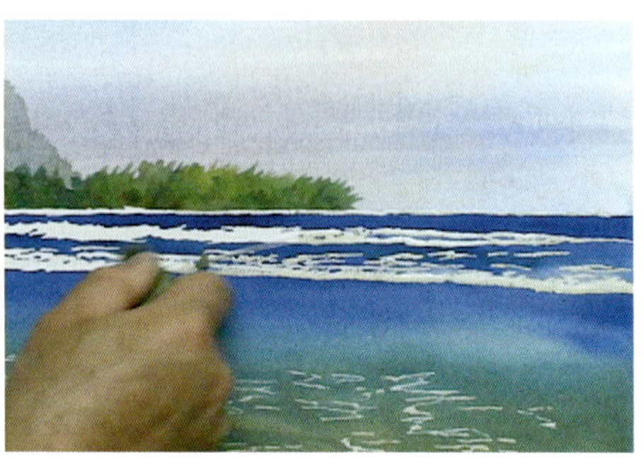

**Step 11:** Next I peeled off all of the masking, exposing once again the white of the paper.

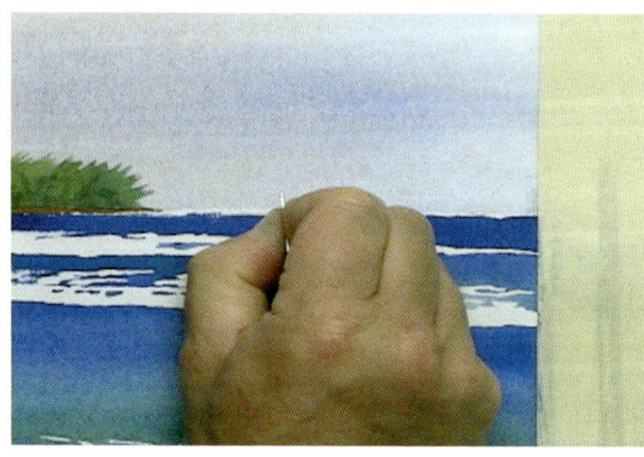

**Step 12:** Then, with a #2 round brush and a mix of Burnt Sienna and Ultramarine Blue, I painted in the distant beach—fluctuating between the two colors as I worked across horizontally. These were painted richer than the foreground beach so that the distant beach would appear darker.

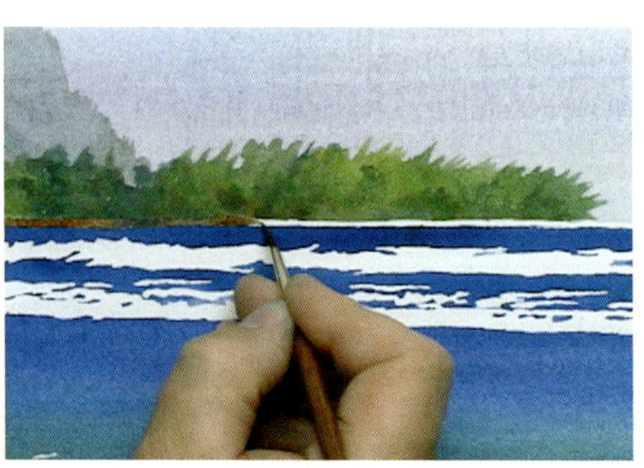

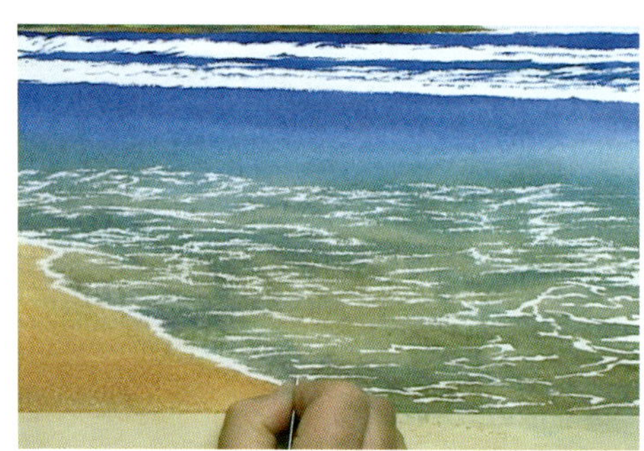

I also scraped away at most of the edges of the foam shapes, too—generally roughening both sides of the shapes.

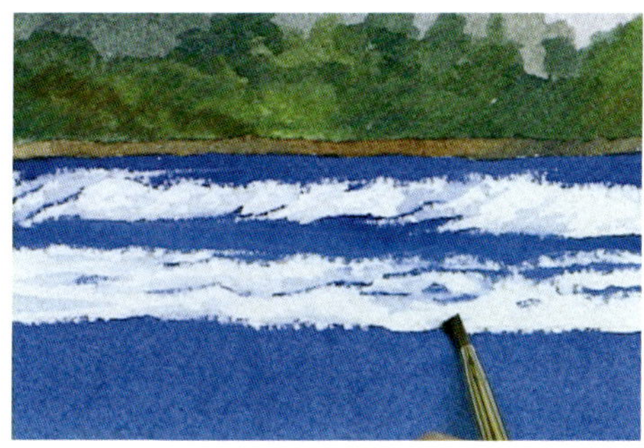

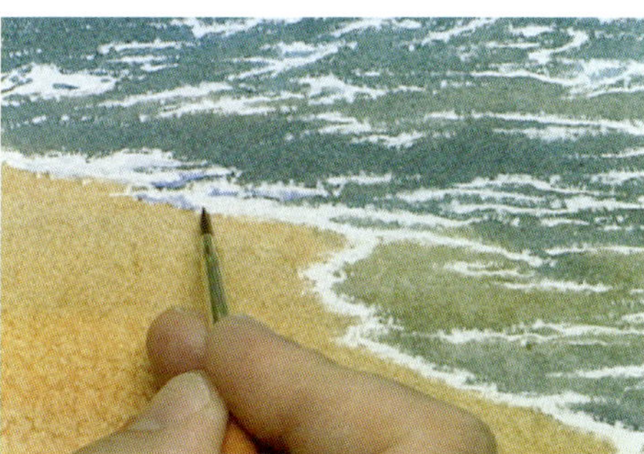

**Step 14:** To provide these white shapes with more dimension, I sorted various sections by shading with a 1/8" flat brush and a lean mix of Cobalt Blue. On the waves, I tended to separate sections with a hard shade edge. The non-separating shade edge was then diffused, using a brush dipped into water. On the foam shapes, I tended to shade their lower downlight sides.

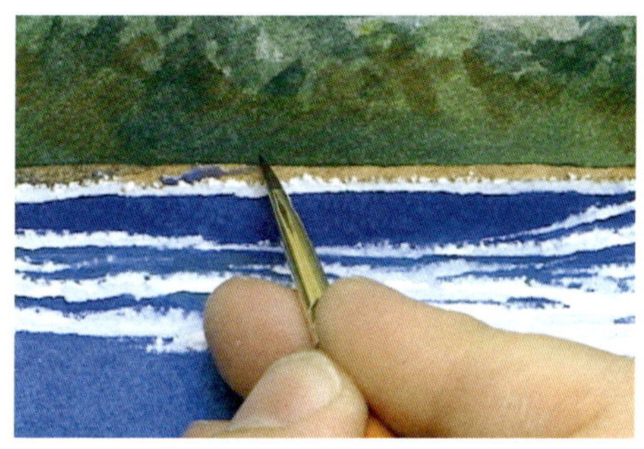

**Step 15:** With Cobalt Blue, I did the same shading to break up the distant shoreline.

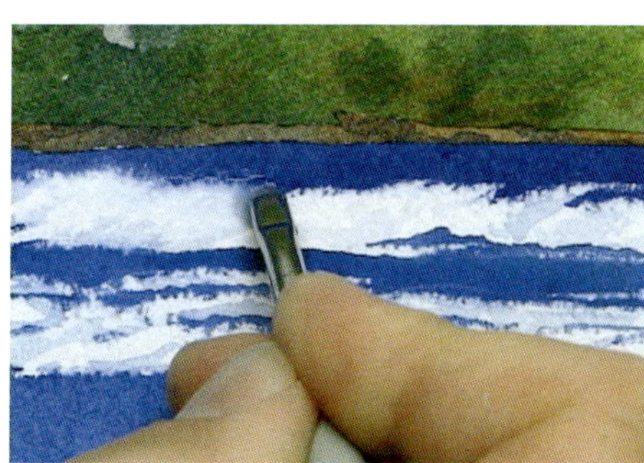

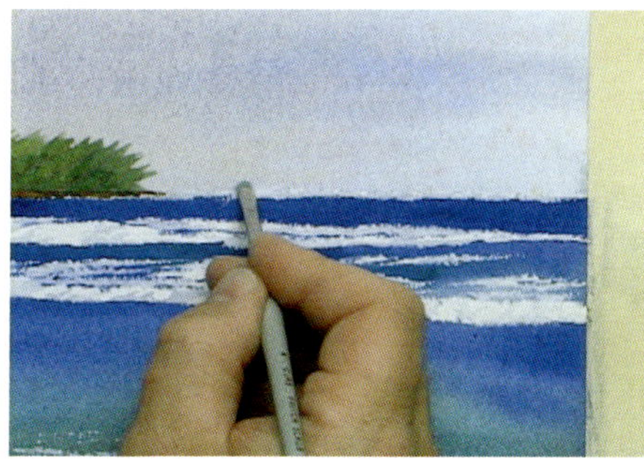

**Step 16:** To give the breaking white water a more natural look, I scrubbed at many of the edges with an assortment of stiff-bristled scrubbing brushes loaded with water. I tended to scrub the previously scraped edges, but I did not scrub all of these edges—preferring to maintain variety.

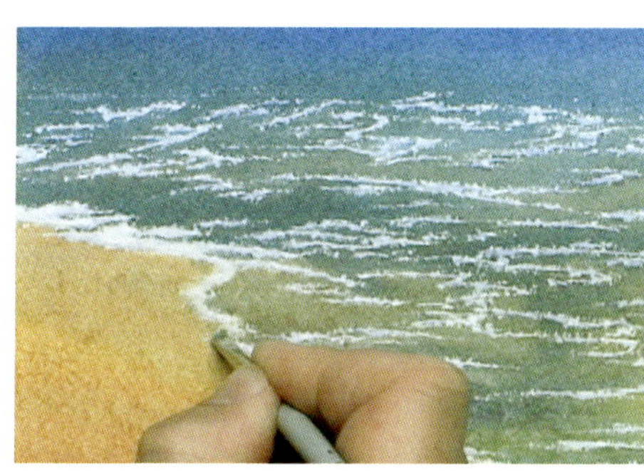

On the foam shapes, I tended to scrub both edges to soften them a bit. I would scrub, then dab and lift the paint with a tissue.

Shading and scrubbing did a lot to soften the harshness of the solid white shapes and make them look more realistic.

It is important to not scrub all of the white water edges. A mix of hard, scraped and scrubbed edges provides a more interesting and natural look.

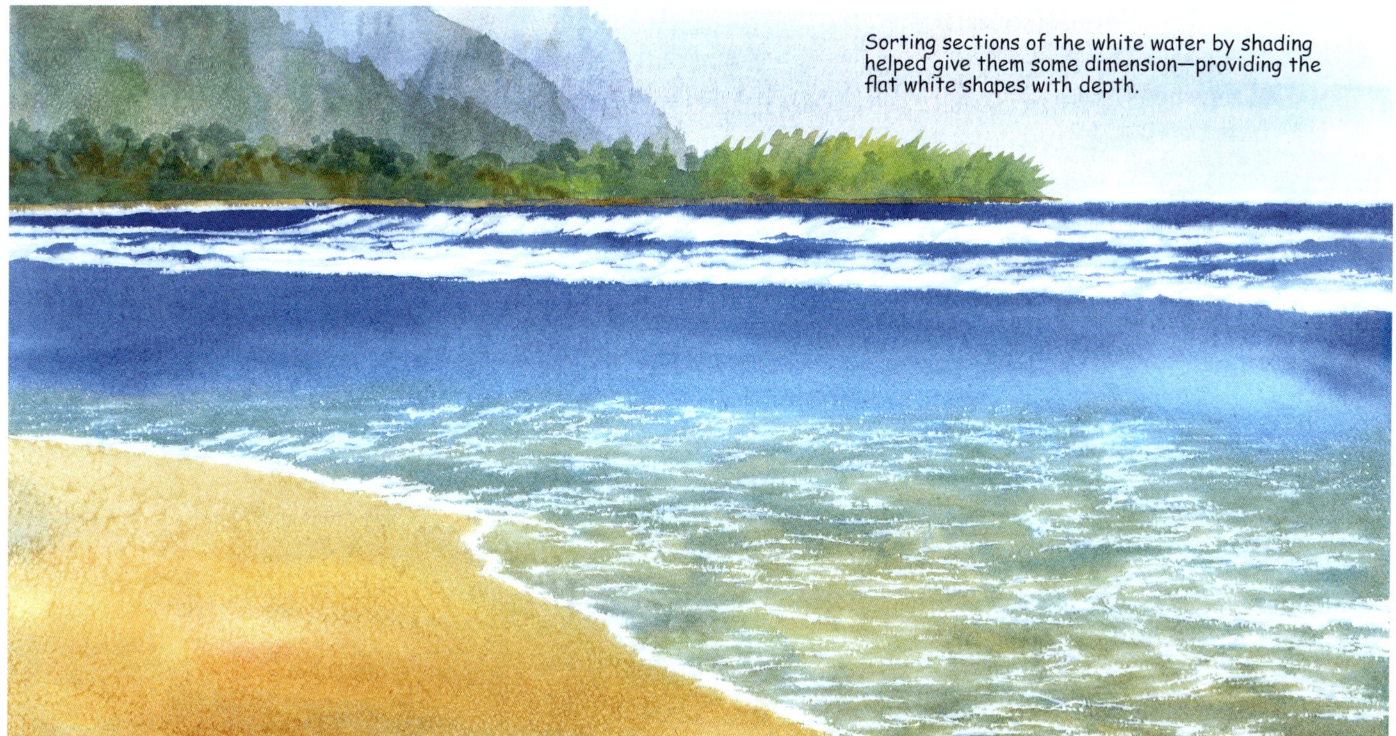

Sorting sections of the white water by shading helped give them some dimension—providing the flat white shapes with depth.

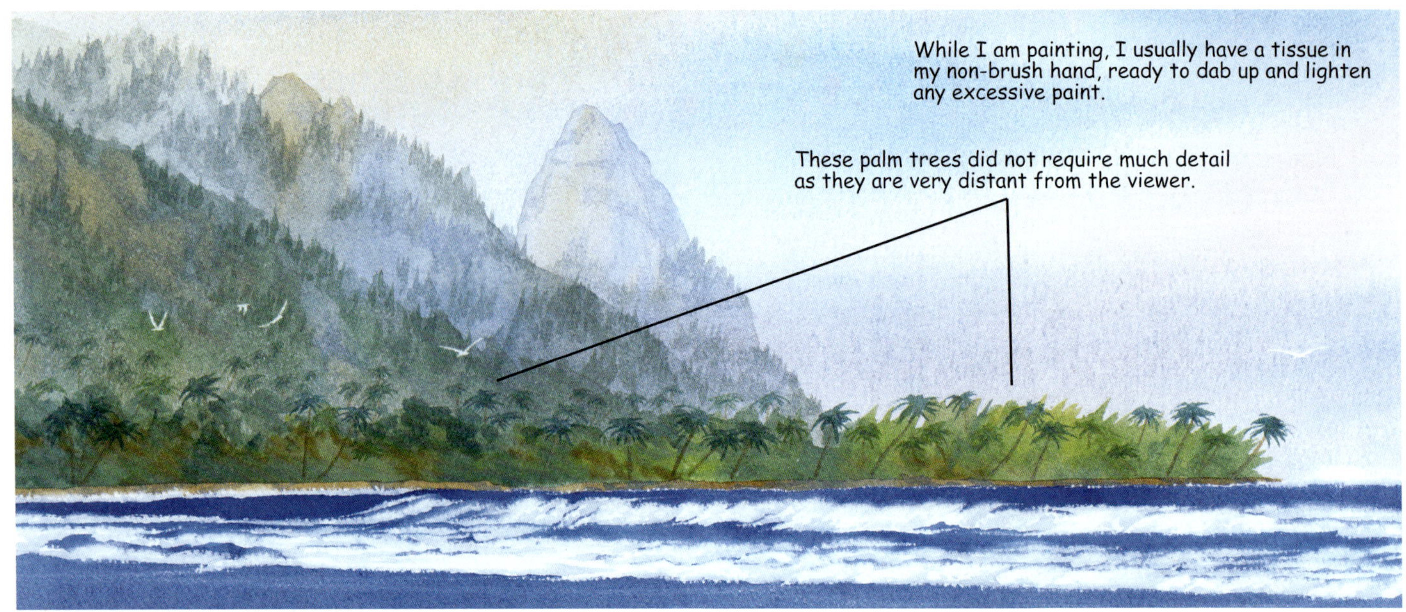


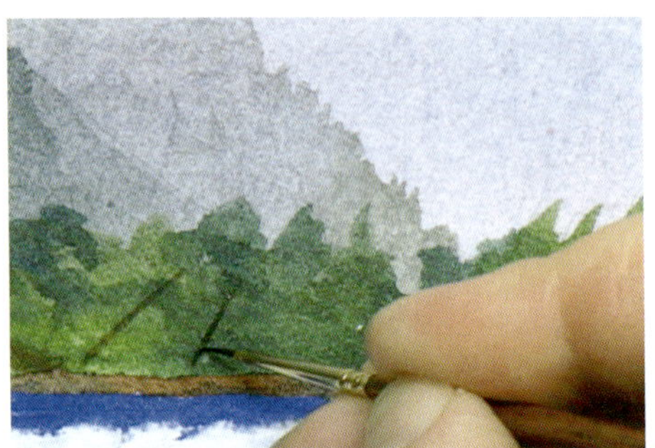

**Step 17:** To provide the distant shoreline foliage with more detail, I painted in some palm trees. First, using a small #2/0 round brush and a mix of Brown Madder and Phthalo Blue, I painted in some simple trunk shapes.

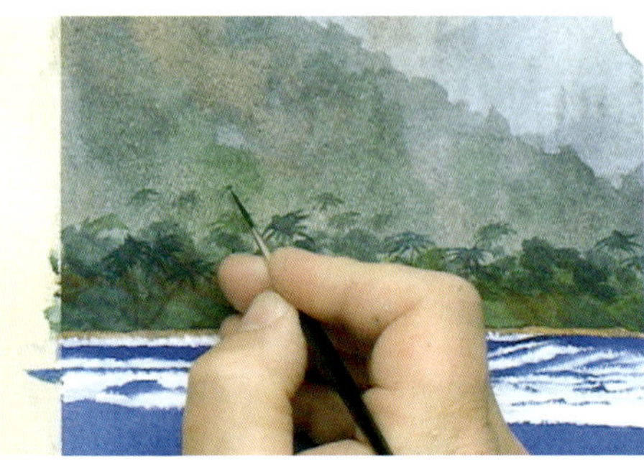

**Step 19:** With the same #2 rigger brush and a mix of Ultramarine Blue and Ultramarine Green, I painted some crude palm tops in the more distant mountain foliage, between the mountains and the shoreline trees—often dabbing at them with a tissue so they would not appear too dark.

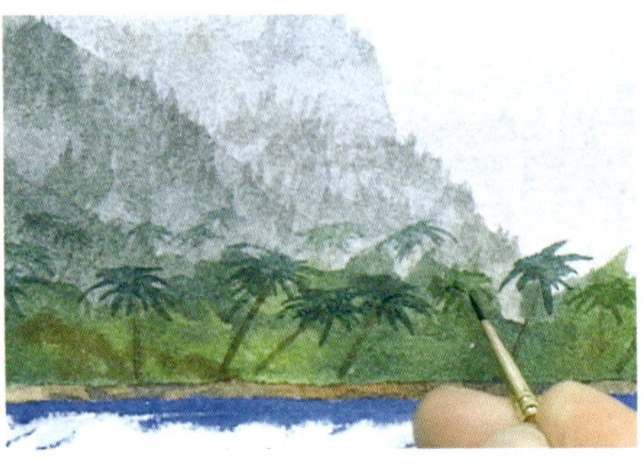

**Step 18:** I followed these by painting in their tops with a larger #0 round brush and a rich mix of Phthalo Blue and Phthalo Green. When I applied them too heavily, I simply dabbed up some of the still-wet paint with a tissue to lighten them.

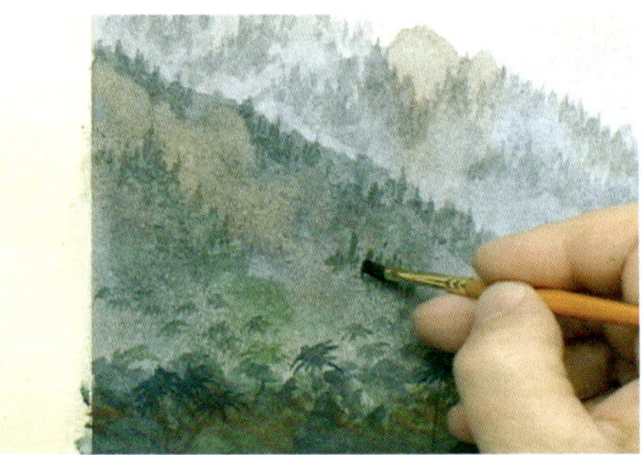

**Step 20:** With a 1/8" flat brush and a mix of Cobalt Blue and Cobalt Green, I painted in more sawtooth tree shapes on the mountainsides—providing them with more dimension. As I worked down the mountainsides, I switched back to the Ultramarine Green.

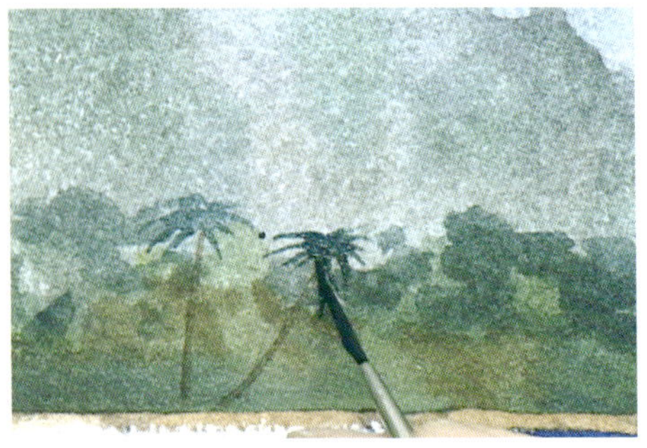

For the more prominent palm tree tops, I used a #2 rigger brush.

**Step 21:** Next, with a 1/4" flat brush and Cobalt Blue, I added some subtle shade details to the exposed rock section of the prominent peak.

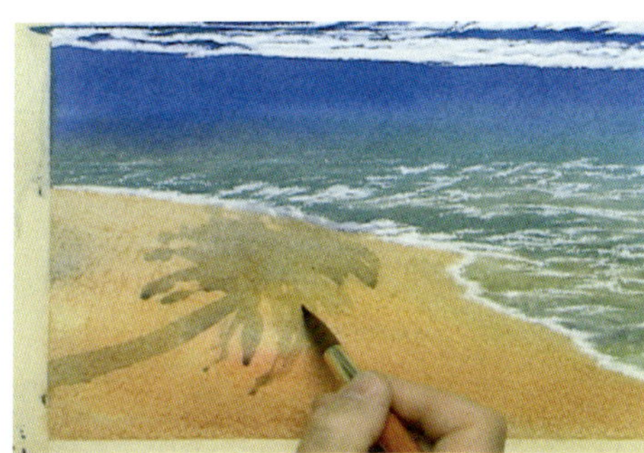

**Step 22:** To break up the large beach shape, I painted in a subtle palm tree shadow. To accomplish this, I used a #10 round brush and a very lean mix of Cobalt Blue. The shadow was painted over the dry sand and partially into the water.

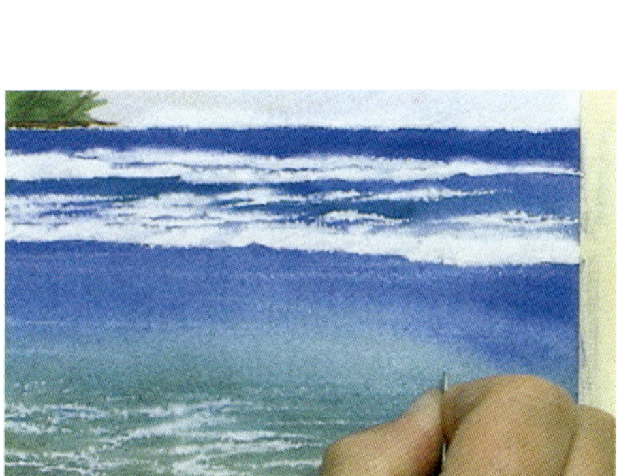

**Step 23:** Using a single-edged razor blade, I added some more ocean details by scraping. First, I scraped white breaking waves along the distant beach. Then, I scraped more white details in the water's midground, making this area graduate into the foreground foam area.

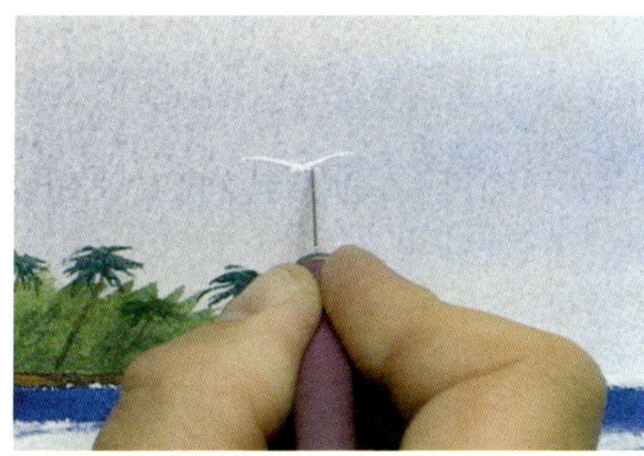

**Step 24:** As a finishing touch, I scraped in some sea gulls with an exacto-knife. I planned their placement and then lightly drew them in beforehand, as they are irreversible. Since they are quite distant from the viewer, they did not require much detail.

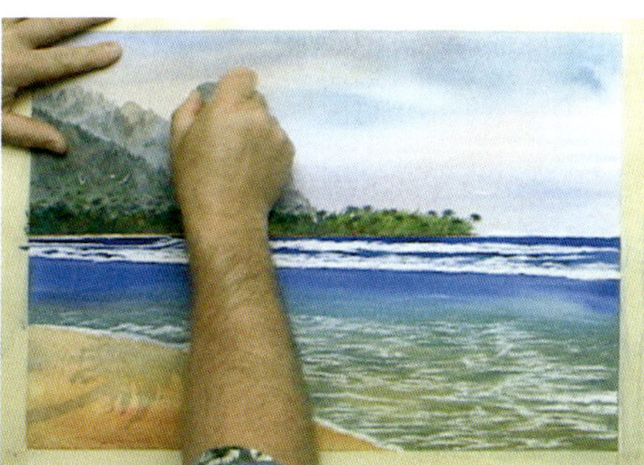

**Step 25:** To complete the painting, I removed any visible pencil lines with a kneaded eraser.

To help the painting's composition, I needed to break up the large beach mass in the foreground. It was simply too large of an uninteresting shape. Adding a subtle palm tree shadow was "just the ticket" for both adding interest to the shape and to the painting as a whole. Are there palm trees behind the viewer?

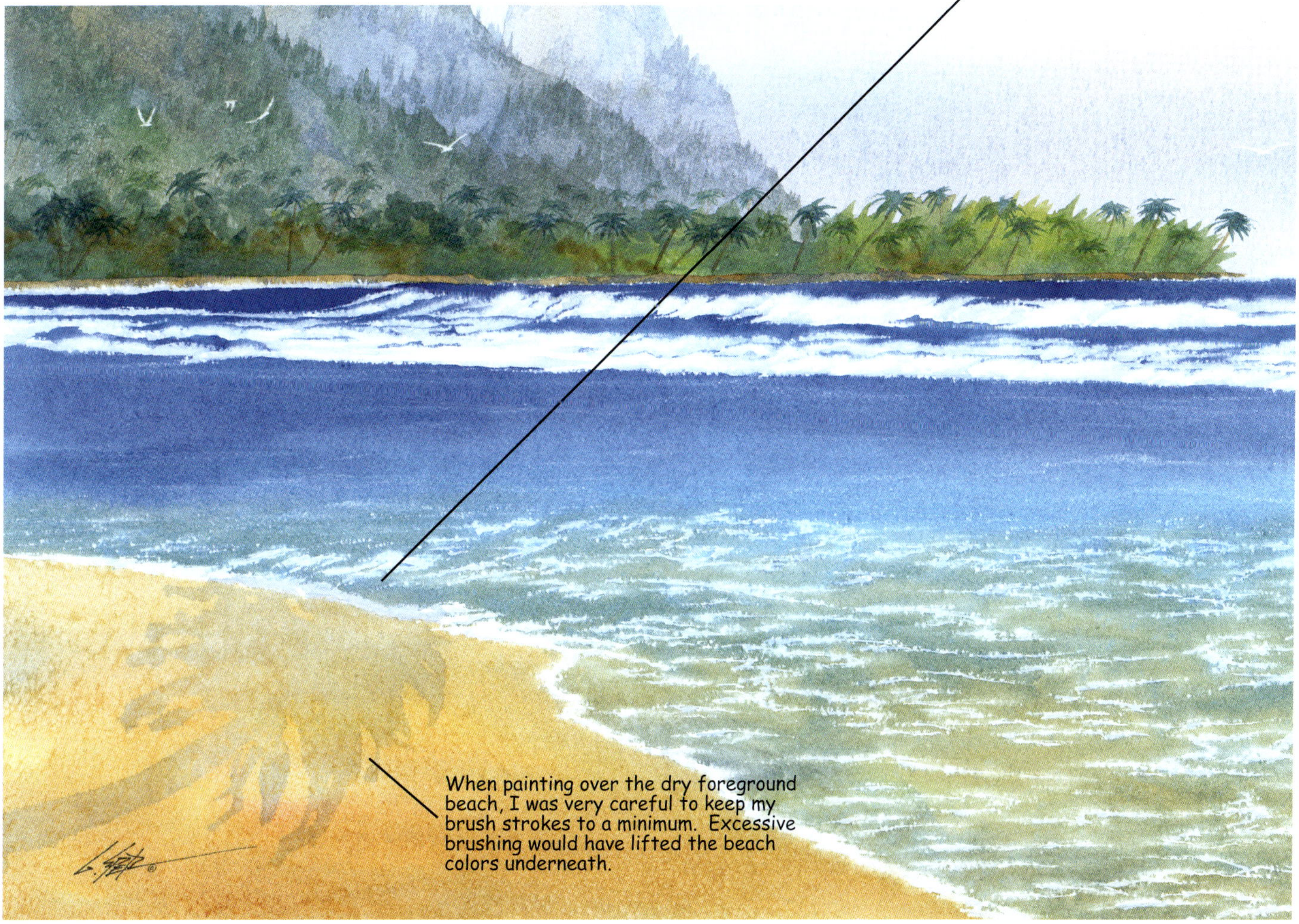

When painting over the dry foreground beach, I was very careful to keep my brush strokes to a minimum. Excessive brushing would have lifted the beach colors underneath.

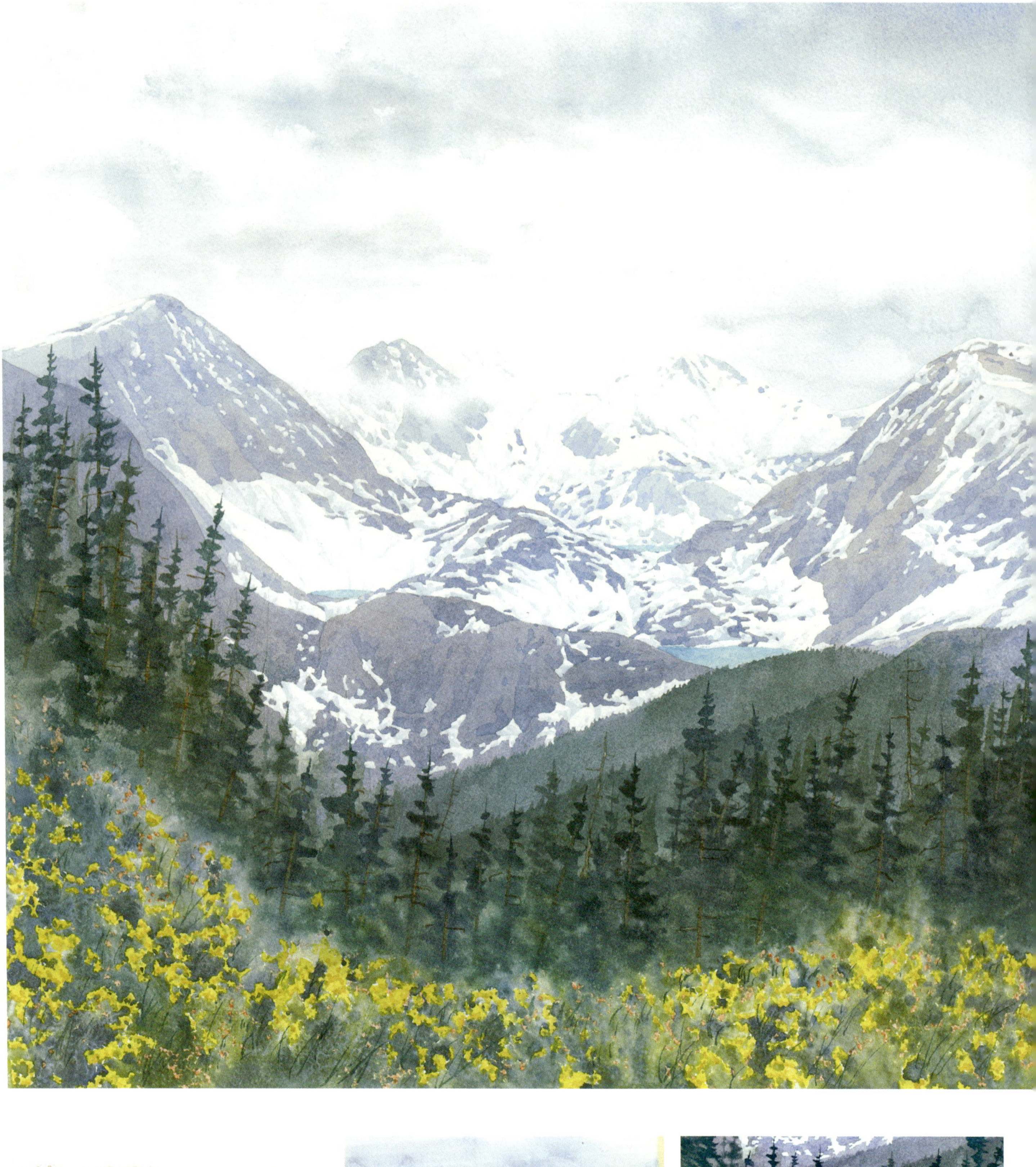

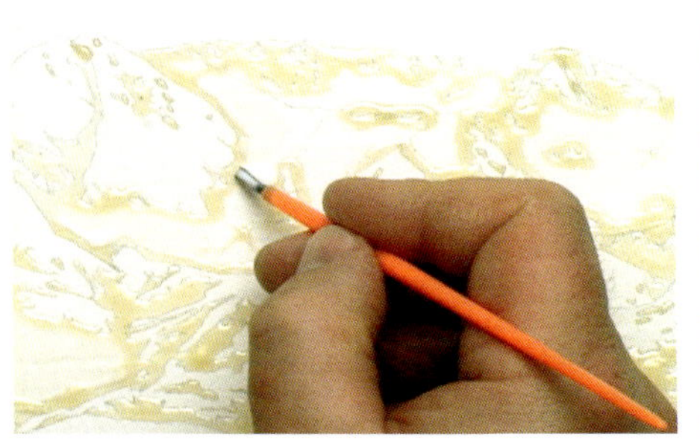

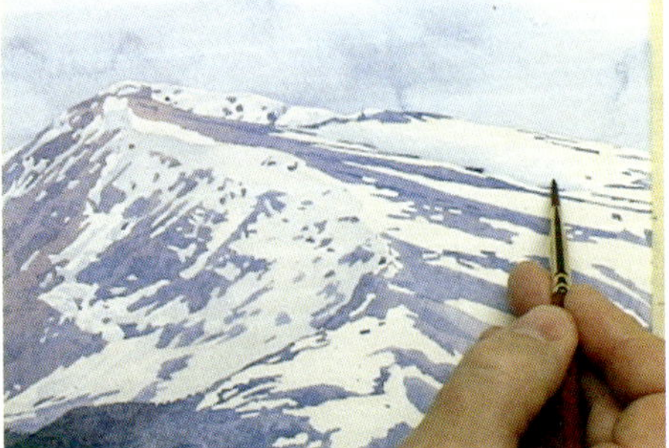

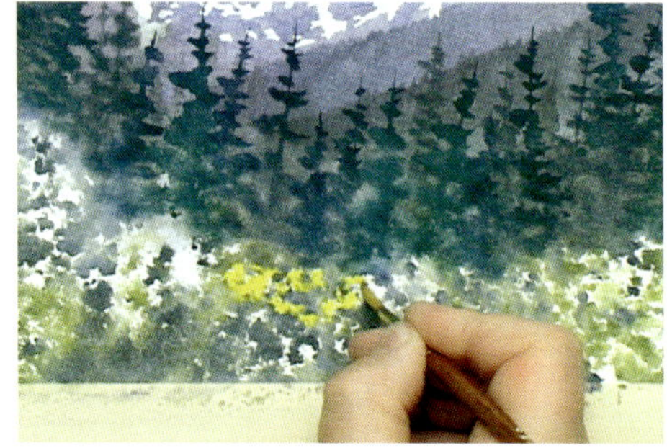

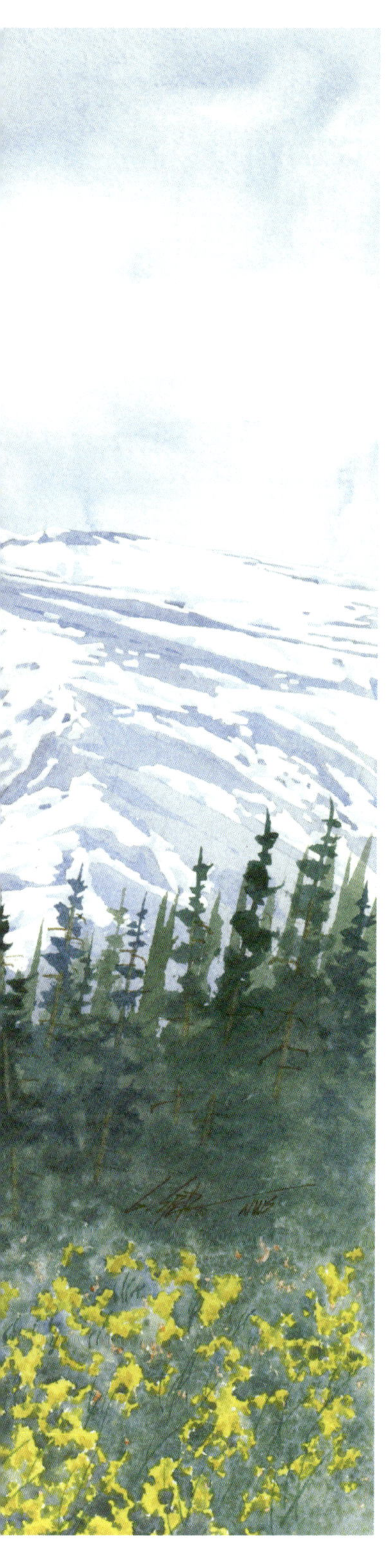

# *TRAIL RIDGE OVERLOOK*

As a landscape painter, few things interest me more than the shapes of mountain snow. I find great beauty in their bold contrast and their intricate, seemingly wild, patterns. When these patterns are combined with a confused, cloudy sky, it is often difficult to determine exactly where the mountain ends and the sky begins. It is a look that I enjoy creating and, lucky for me, it is a job particularly well suited to the medium of watercolor.

With my mountain scenes, I often like to include wildflowers. Unfortunately, the ideal mountain snow conditions rarely coincide with the peak wildflower season. But, while this may present a problem to a photographer, it is not a problem to a painter, who can employ "artistic license." A painter is only limited by his/her imagination. So, in this painting, I am going to *imagine* that there are vivid wildflowers in the foreground.

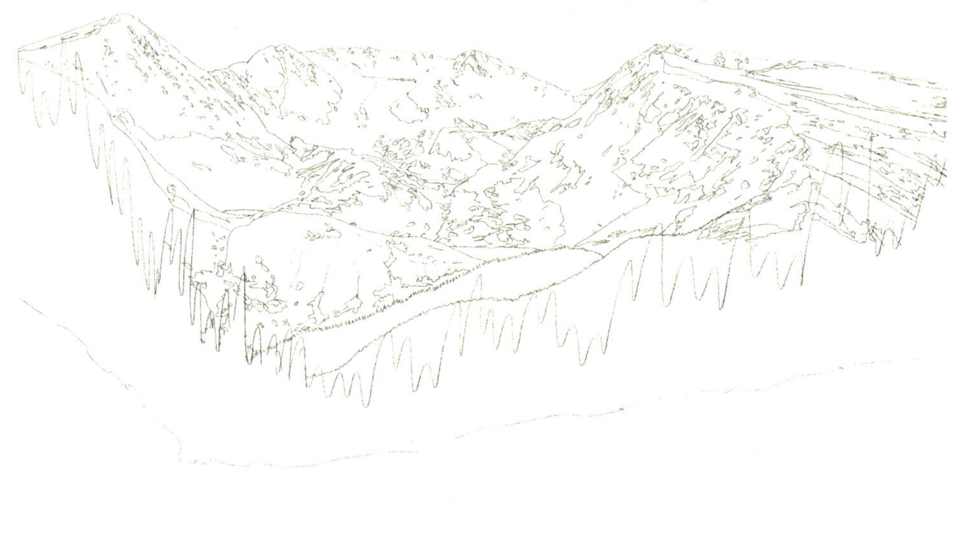

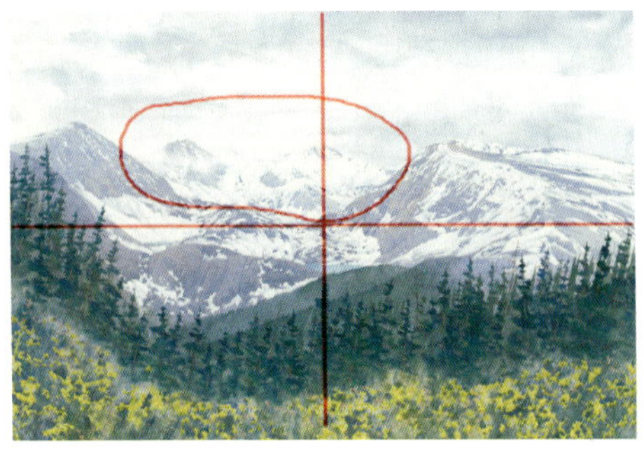

**Step 1:** I first drew out my composition directly on the sheet of watercolor paper. I was careful to not center prominent objects, as in this case the distant mountain peaks. I was also careful to prevent the foreground tree line from forming a symmetrical "V" shape. To help me remember my center points, I marked them both vertically and horizontally on the edges of the painting.

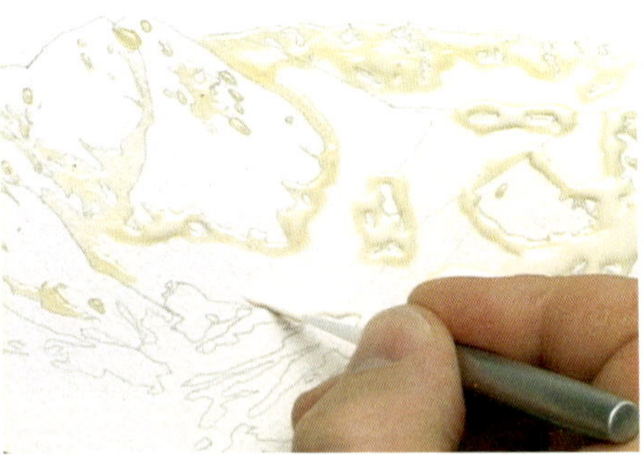

**Step 2:** With liquid masking fluid and a plastic toothpick, I masked out all of the intricate mountain snow shapes. While this may seem like shoveling snow with a spoon, I find that attending to the snow details is a large part of what makes this painting work. It is difficult to achieve the same level of detail with a larger tool, like a brush.

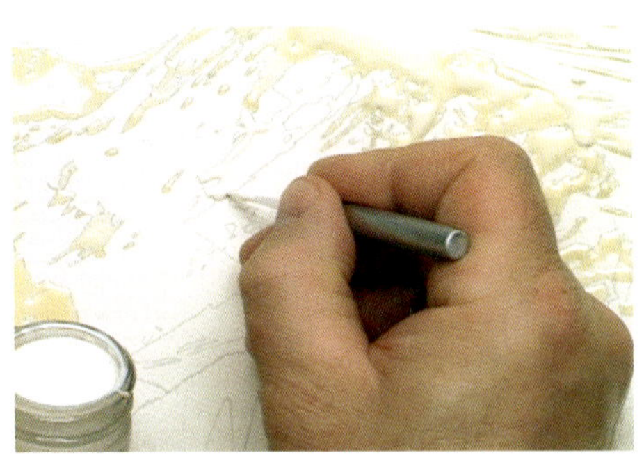

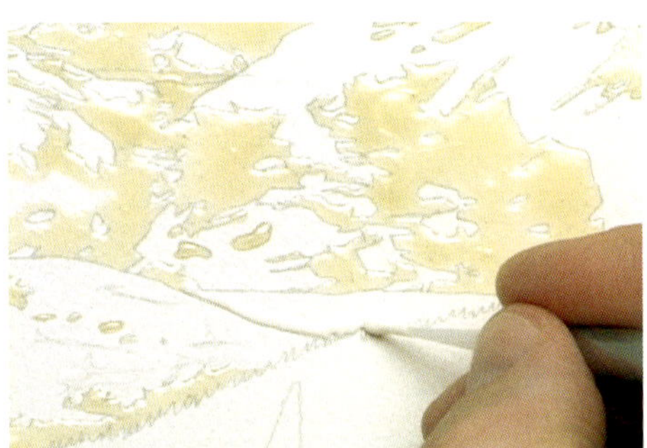

(Step 2 continued)

I also masked out the three distant mountain lakes.

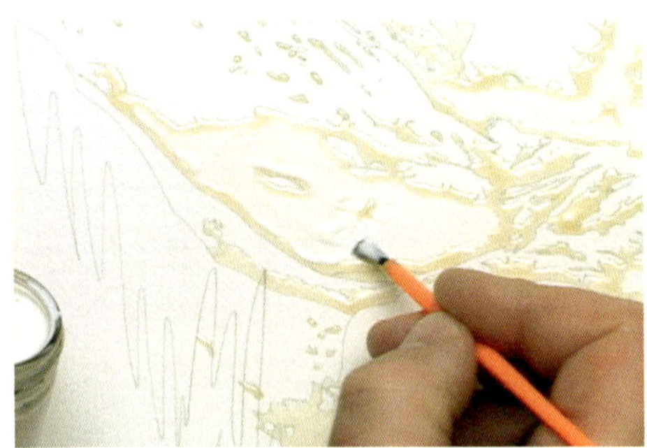

With a disposable paintbrush, I filled in the larger shapes that I had marked with an "X".

Where the treetops intersected the snow shapes, I ignored the tree top drawing—masking right over it.

After the masking had dried, I rubbed my hands over the sky area, trying to detect any drops of masking that may have accidentally ended up there.

Although time consuming, masking all of the intricate mountain snow shapes will pay off big in the end.

I masked right over the intersection with the treeline, ignoring the tree sketch.

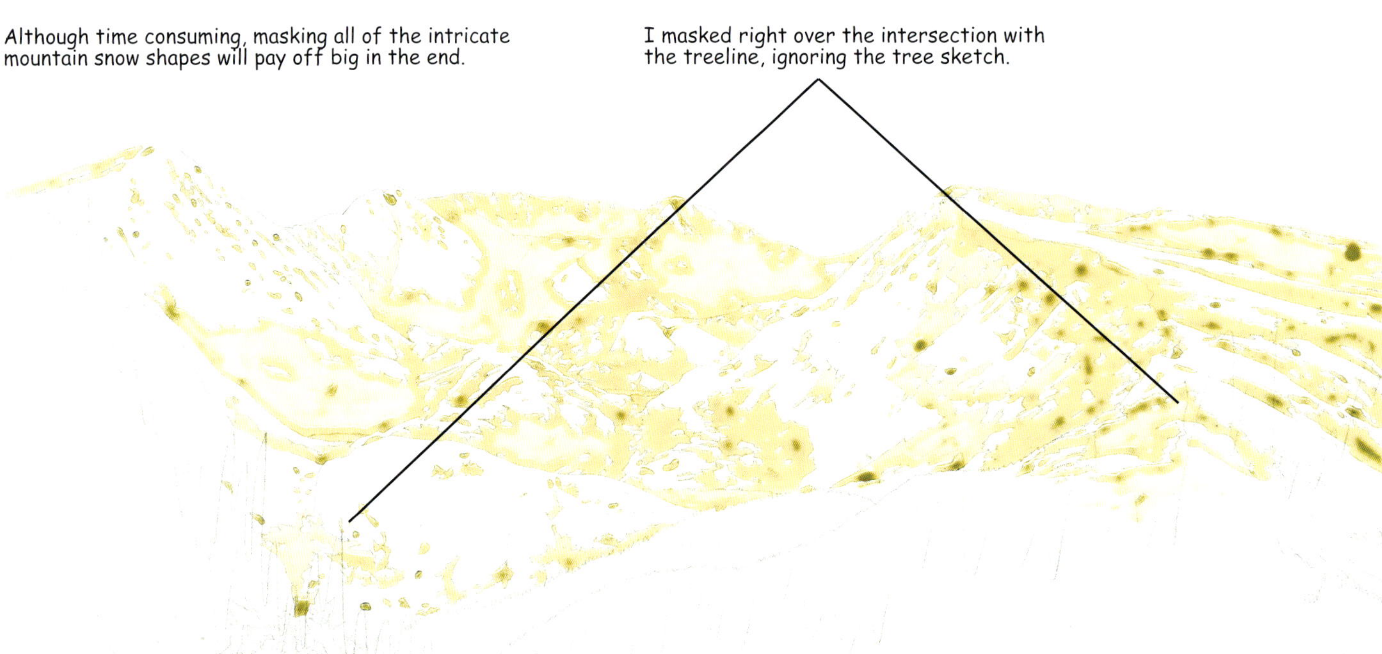

When scrubbing some of the hard edges of the sky, I was careful to not create an obvious pattern of scrubbed and hard edges.

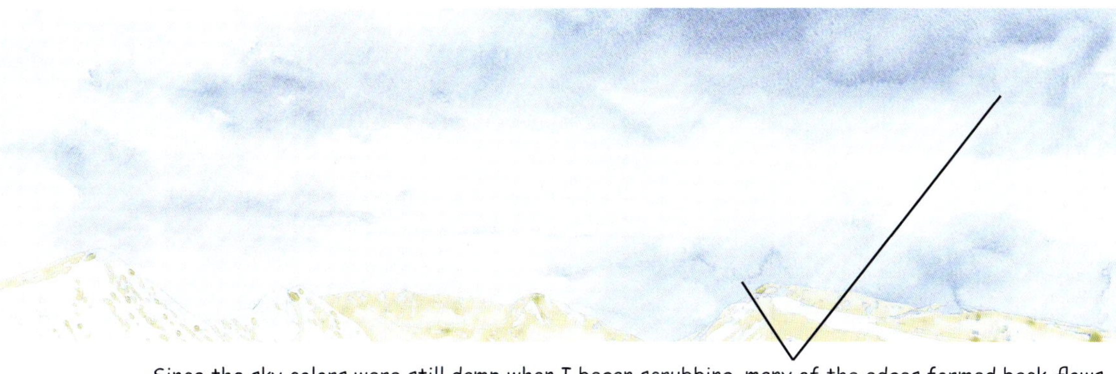

Because the sky paints were still partially wet, I moved back and forth across the sky as I scrubbed. To get consistent results, I did not want to work in one area too long.

Since the sky colors were still damp when I began scrubbing, many of the edges formed back-flows when I touched them with a water-loaded brush. Normally, this type of watercolor distortion would spell trouble, but in this case it was a welcome effect on a turbulent sky.

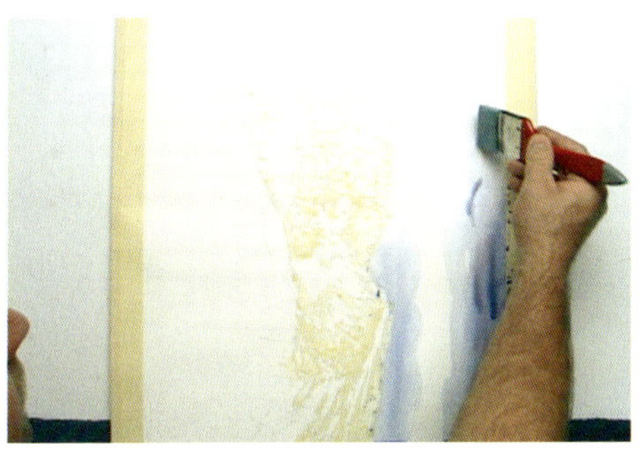

**Step 3:** Employing "artistic license," I wanted to paint the sky more turbulent and dynamic than it actually was on the day of my visit. To accomplish this, I worked in areas of Cobalt Blue and Rose with a 2" flat brush. This time I did not pre-wet the paper, as I wanted some hard edges to be created. I tended to paint horizontal streaks, leaving much of the white of the paper exposed.

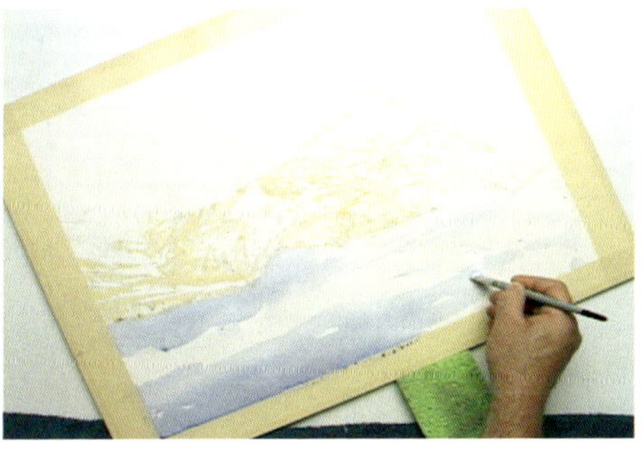

**Step 4:** Once these colors had dried enough so that they would not run, I turned the painting nearly upside down. Using a stiff-bristled scrubbing brush loaded with water, I softened some of the hard edges. I would scrub into the painted edge, then frequently dab at the lifted paint with a tissue. I did not soften all of the hard edges, as I wanted to retain some variety.

As the scrubbing brush collected paint in its bristles, I would occasionally dab it onto a white unpainted area of the sky. This would help give the white shapes some dimension. I would in turn scrub at these paints, too.

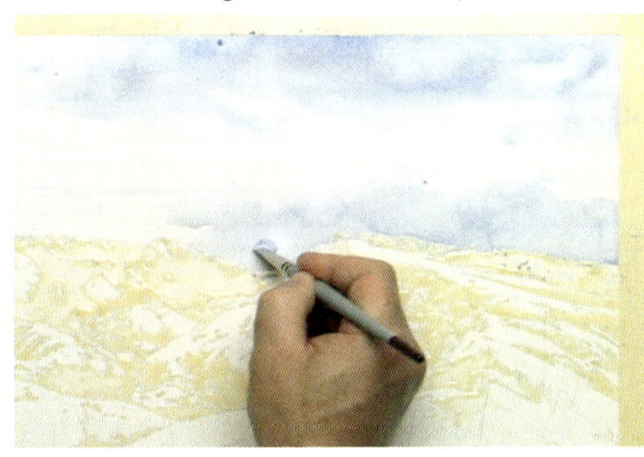

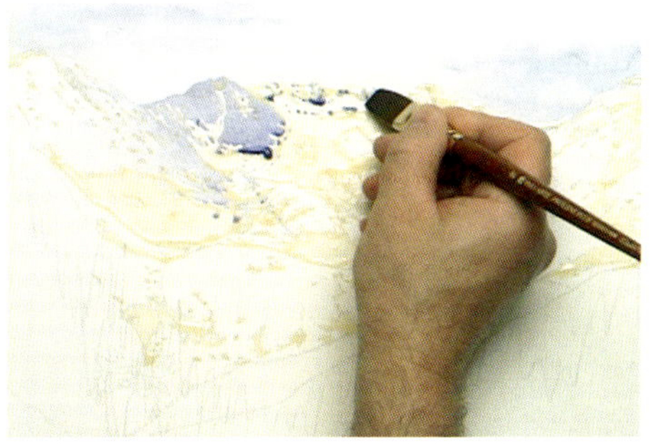

**Step 5:** After the sky was dry, I painted in the most distant mountains with Cobalt Blue, Rose and a 3/4" flat brush. I carefully followed the mountain's upper edges, but frequently diluted the mountains lower edges with a water-loaded brush to prevent hard edges from forming. These colors were applied only slightly darker than the sky. I tried to vary between these two colors without creating an obvious pattern.

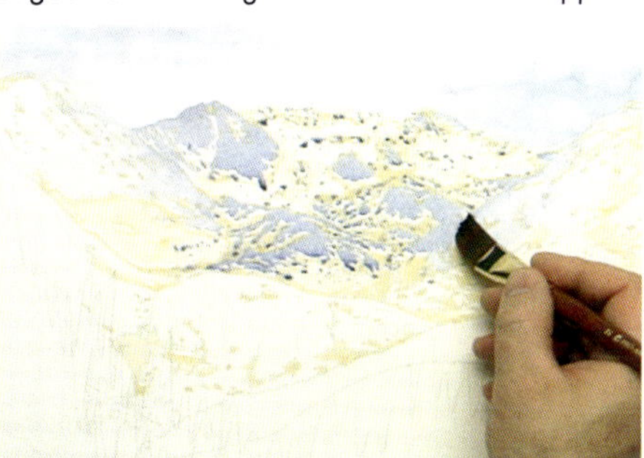

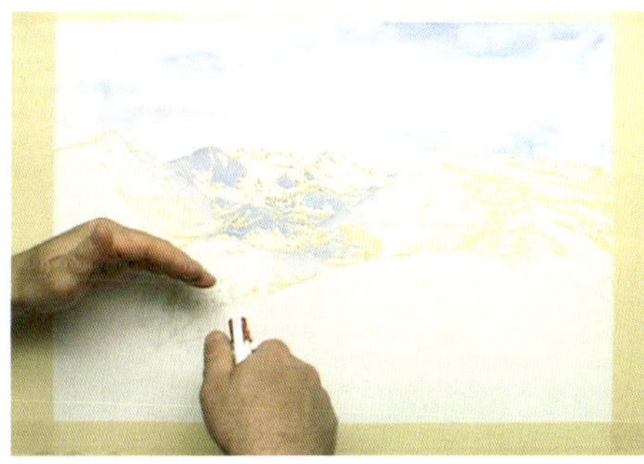

**Step 6:** When the distant mountains were dry, I pre-wet everything below the base of the next closest set of mountains. This time, with a 1-1/4" flat brush, I repeated the previous step on these mountains. Again, I tried to vary the mix of Cobalt Blue and Rose. And, I made sure that I worked the mountain's lower colors into the pre-wet area to prevent hard edges from forming. I applied these colors slightly darker than I had on the previous mountains.

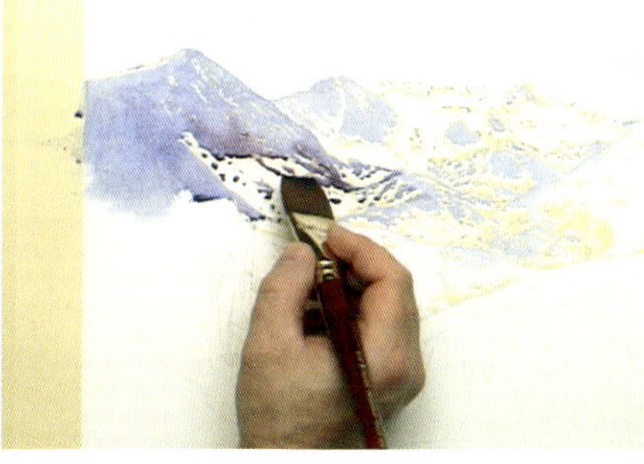

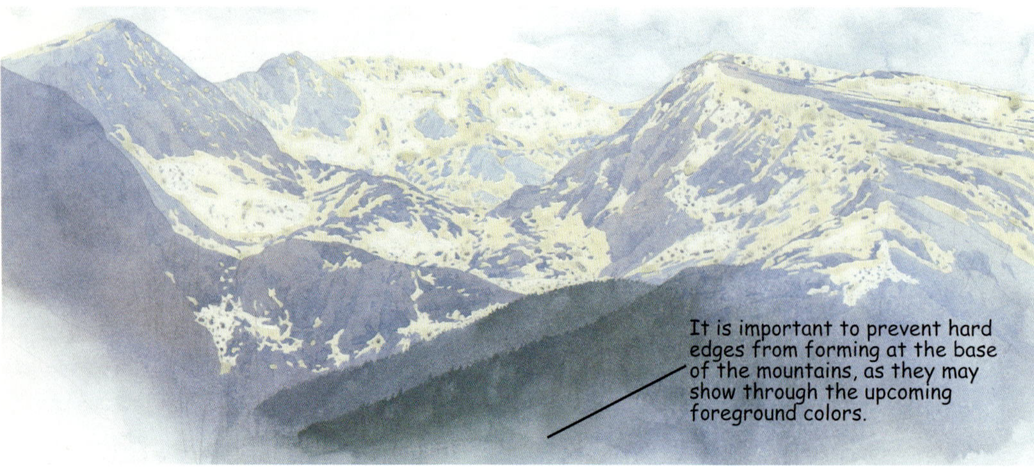


When shading and shaping the mountains, I would look for what appeared to be obvious ridge lines and sections of mountain that needed to be separated or sorted from one another. Often the snow shapes would provide clues to this. But, I did follow my instincts here—not being too concerned if I replicated the exact shapes of the mountains.

Making the mountain color values progressively darker helps create the illusion of depth.

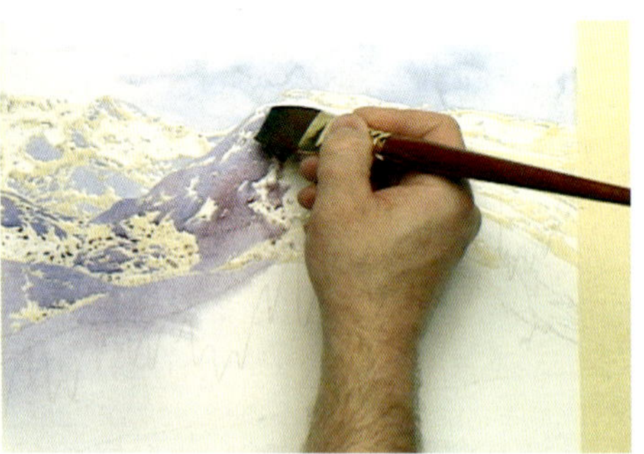

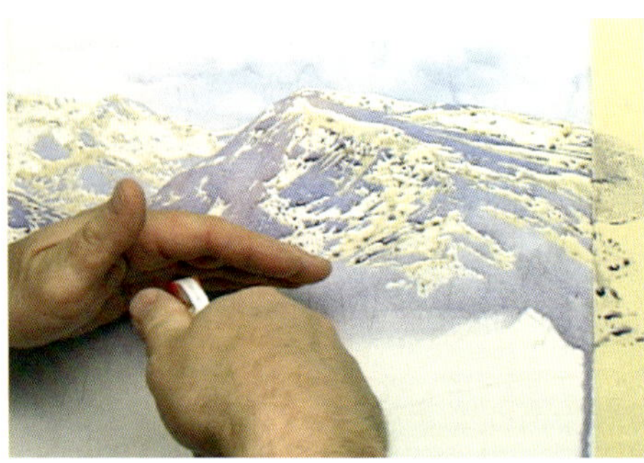

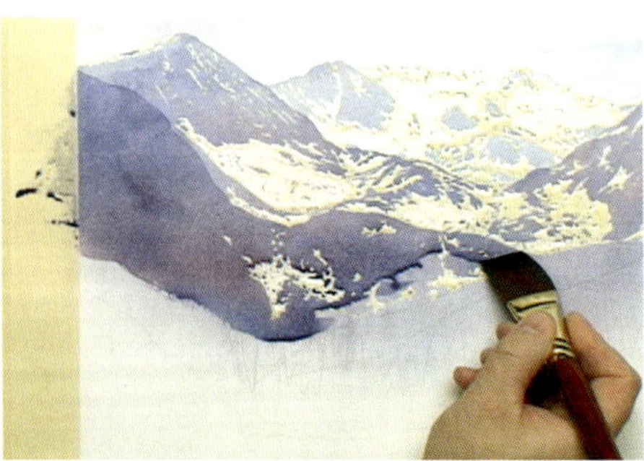

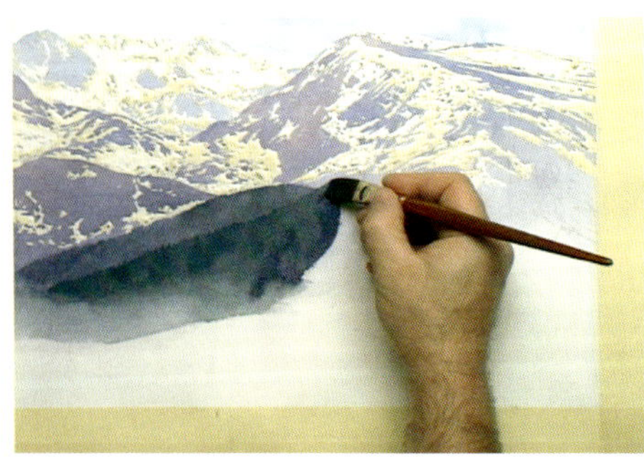

You can see that the darker value makes this set of mountains stand out against the more distant ones.

**Step 7:** Repeating the process, after I had dried the previous set of mountains with a blow drier, I pre-

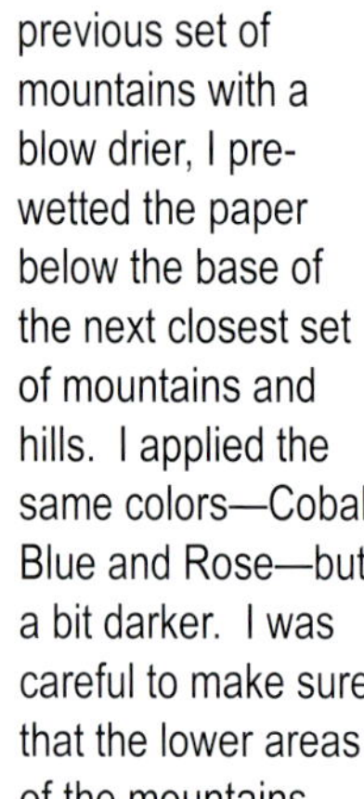

wetted the paper below the base of the next closest set of mountains and hills. I applied the same colors—Cobalt Blue and Rose—but a bit darker. I was careful to make sure that the lower areas of the mountains were diffused into the wet paper below them.

**Step 8:** After drying the previous step, I painted in the next closest set of ridges (which were hills). For these

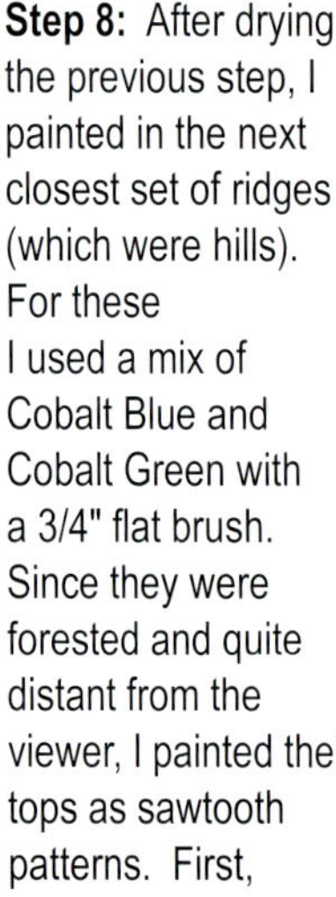

I used a mix of Cobalt Blue and Cobalt Green with a 3/4" flat brush. Since they were forested and quite distant from the viewer, I painted their tops as sawtooth patterns. First,

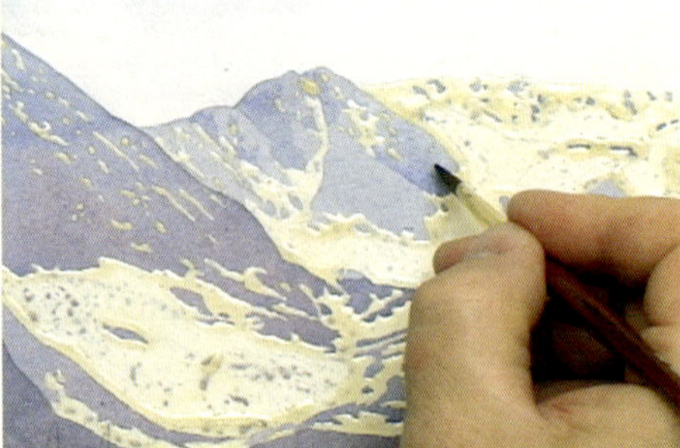

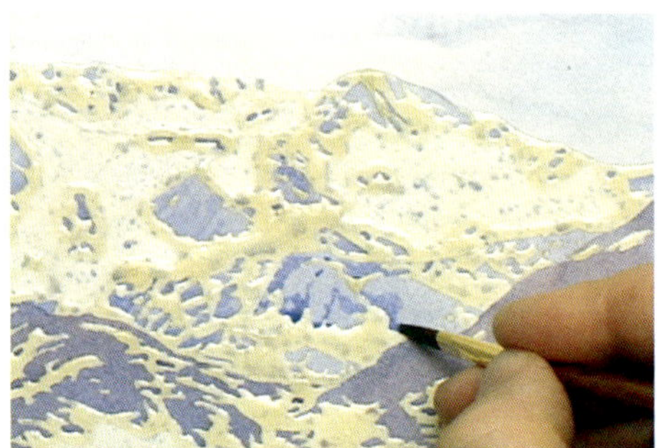

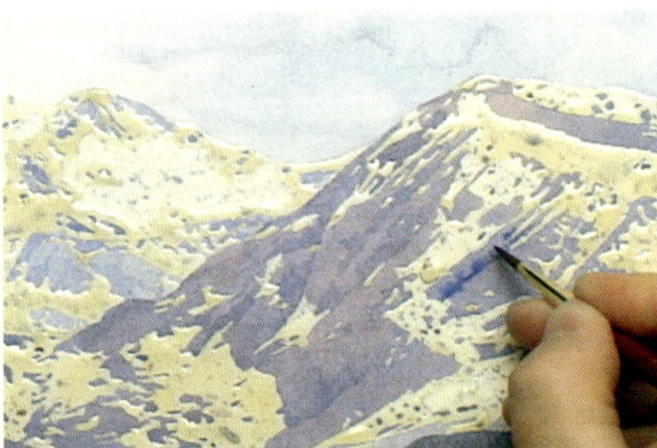

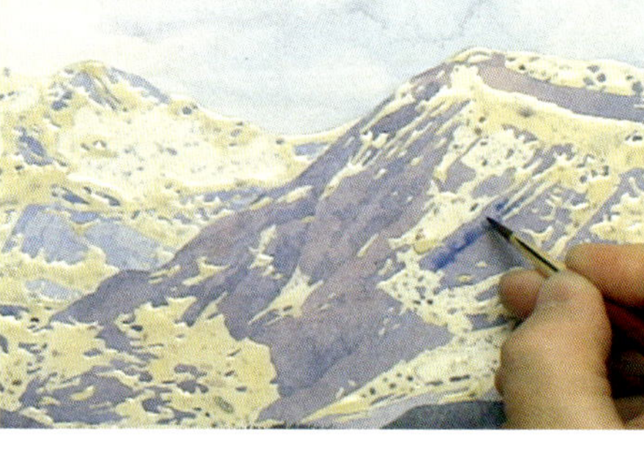

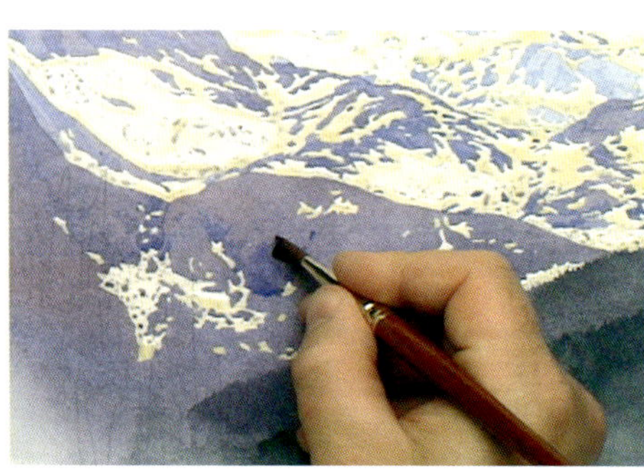

(Step 8 continued)

I painted in one ridge, then as it dried, painted in the next, slightly darker. Before either ridge had dried, I sprinkled on some salt to promote texture.

**Step 9**: Next, I shaped the mountains with some shading. For this I used Cobalt Blue and a 1/4" flat brush. I separated one section of mountain from another with a hard edge. Then, typically, I would lose the other shade edges by lifting with a tissue or diluting with a water-loaded brush.

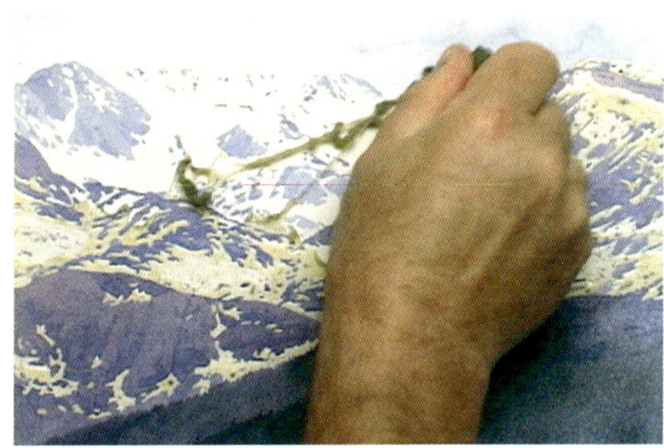

**Step 10:** After the painting had been thoroughly dried again with a blow drier, I peeled off all of the mountain snow masking, revealing the white of the paper.

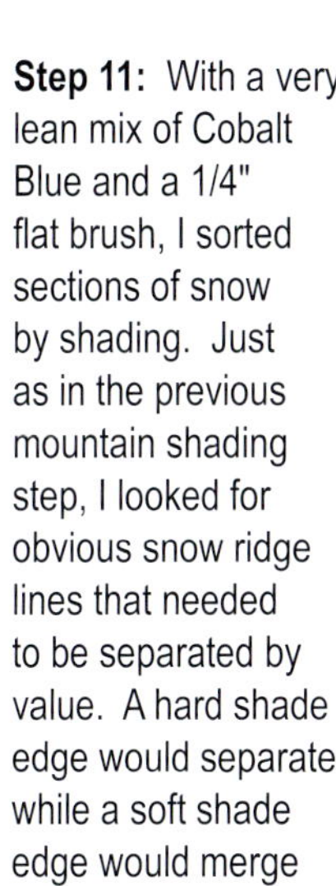

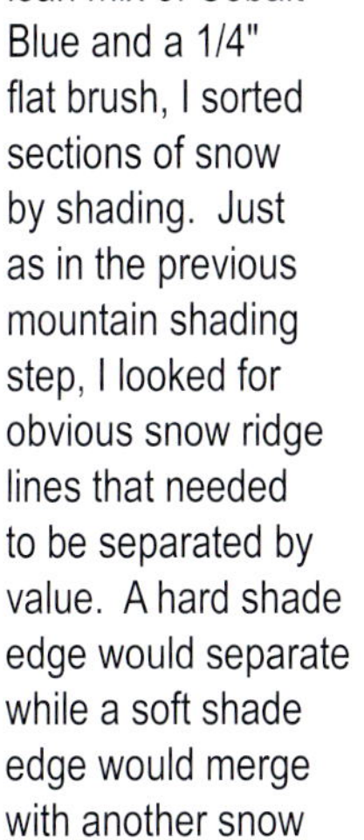

**Step 11:** With a very lean mix of Cobalt Blue and a 1/4" flat brush, I sorted sections of snow by shading. Just as in the previous mountain shading step, I looked for obvious snow ridge lines that needed to be separated by value. A hard shade edge would separate while a soft shade edge would merge with another snow section. On this step, I would avoid detail by limiting my shading to general snow section sorting.

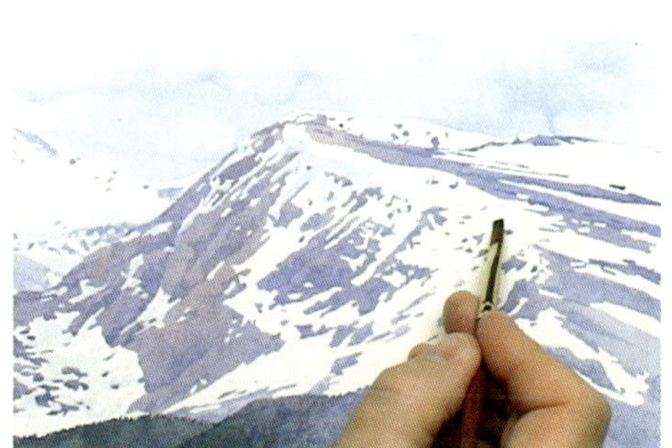

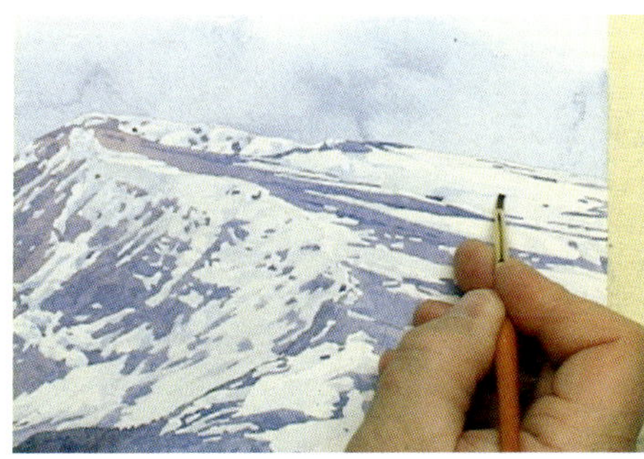

**Step 12:** Then on the next step, I would use the same lean mix of Cobalt Blue to shade within the previously shaded areas of snow. This was intended to create some detail within the snow shapes—helping to provide them with some depth.

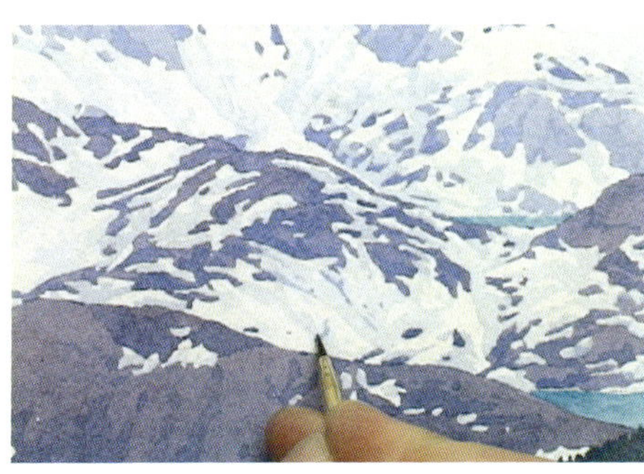

**Step 13:** After that step dried, I returned with Cobalt Blue, but this time with a smaller 1/8" flat brush. Again I tended to paint within the previously shaded areas—the smaller brush providing greater details.

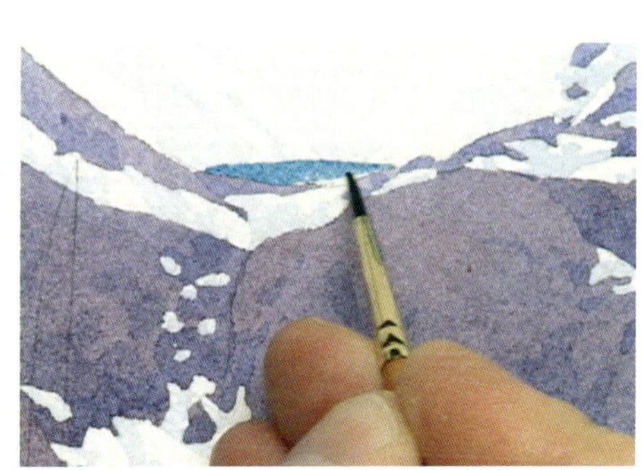

**Step 14:** Since I was already working in the same area, I also painted in the small mountain lakes with Turquoise Green and a #1 round brush.

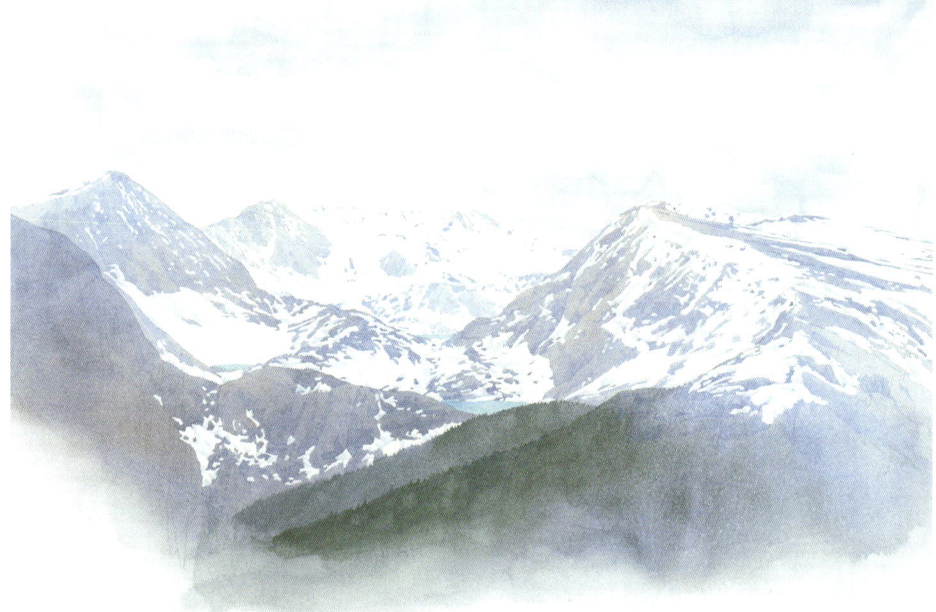

Show shading is easily overdone. I used a very watery mix of Cobalt Blue. And, I was careful to not apply shading to all areas of the white snow. I left much to the viewer's imagination.

Without the shading, the snow shapes would appear flat. The shading helps create the illusion that they have depth.

Individually, the snow shades are not greatly detailed. However, viewed as a whole, these shades make the snow and the mountains far more believable to the viewer.

**Step 14:** With the mountains completed, I began work on the painting's foreground area. To prepare for this, I tilted my steeply inclined painting table down to a near-level position. Then I covered the sky area with rags to protect it from errant drops of paint. The following steps can be messy!

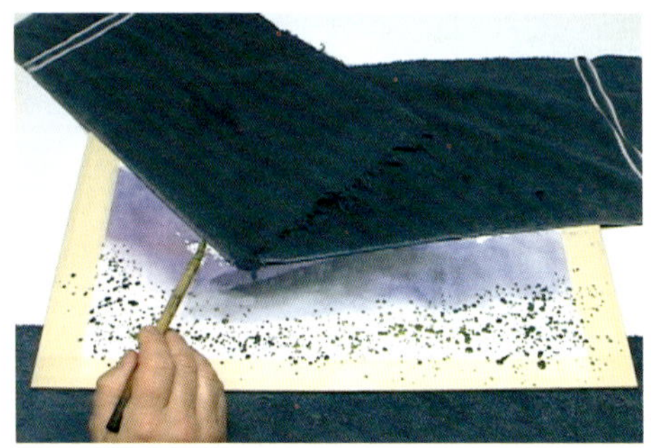

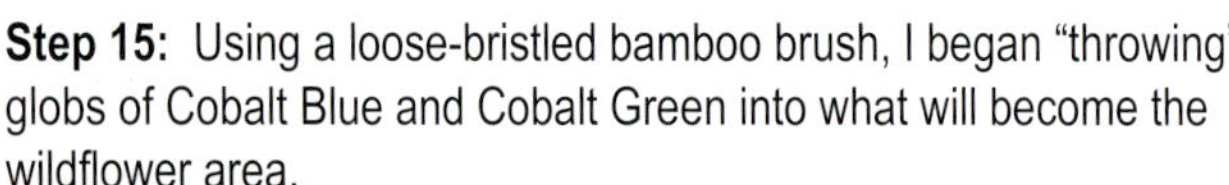

**Step 15:** Using a loose-bristled bamboo brush, I began "throwing" globs of Cobalt Blue and Cobalt Green into what will become the wildflower area.

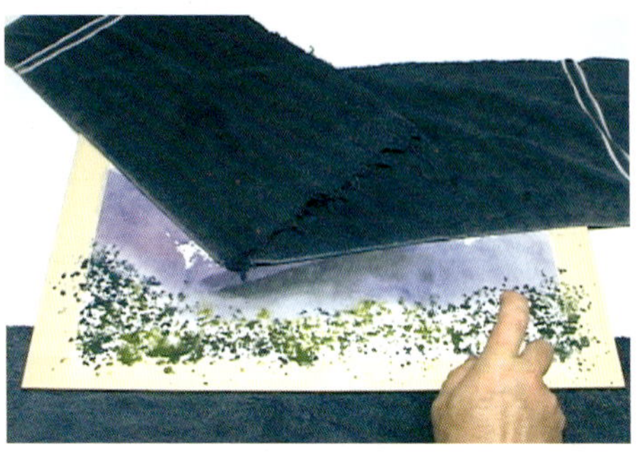

**Step 16:** Then quickly, using a spray bottle filled with water, I "spurted" water droplets onto the paint globs. I was very careful to not saturate the entire area. Rather, I spurted just enough water droplets to fuse the paint globs to one another. I wanted to retain white spaces between the paint globs. These were the areas of paper that did not get wet.

Before this area dried, I sprinkled it with salt to create a textured effect.

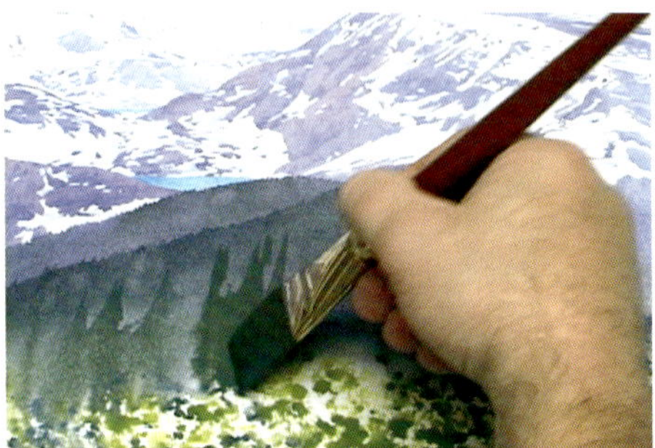

**Step 17:** While these colors were still wet, I used a 1-1/4" flat brush to pull some of the paint puddles upward to form sawtooth tree shapes. I did this all of the way across the painting to create a background row of trees.

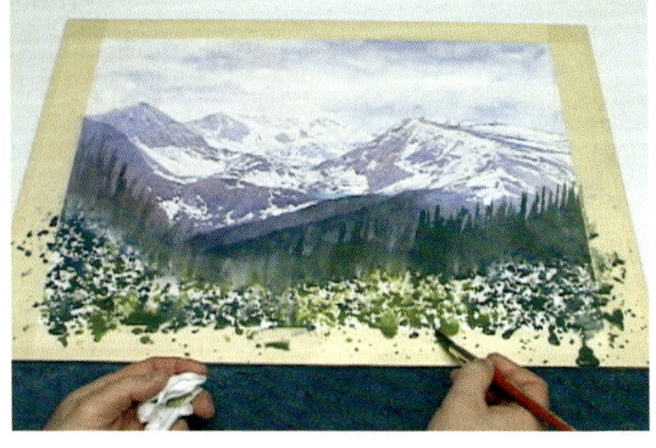

With a thirsty brush and a tissue, I then picked up any other paint puddles that remained.

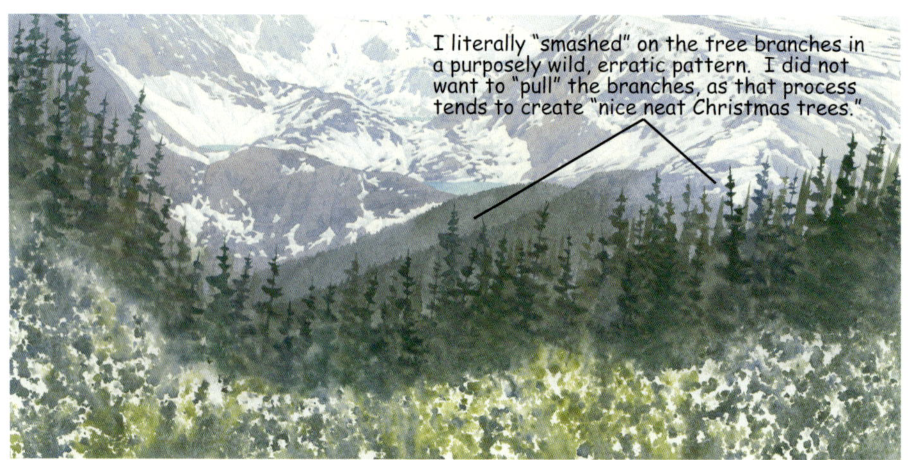


For "spurting" water droplets, the more erratic the spray pattern, the better. Plunger-type pump spray bottles tend to have coarser spray patterns than trigger-type pump spray bottles, making them the preferable choice for this task.

It is very easy to over-spray (with water) the wildflower area. It is important to retain the white spaces between the paint globs. These white spaces provide the shapes for the flowers.

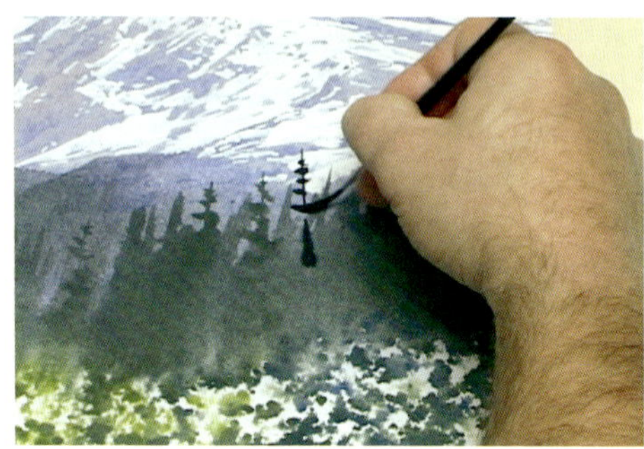

**Step 18:** As the background row of trees slowly dried, I began pulling more detailed tree shapes into them with a #4 rigger brush and a rich mix of Ultramarine Blue and Ultramarine Green. I simply pulled the trunk up from the bottom, then literally "smashed" on branches in an erratic pattern. As with the sky, I worked back and forth across the entire painting—not wanting to work in one area too long. The underlying paints were continually drying, so this necessitated "jumping around" with the paintbrush. Of course, I also varied between the blue and the green.

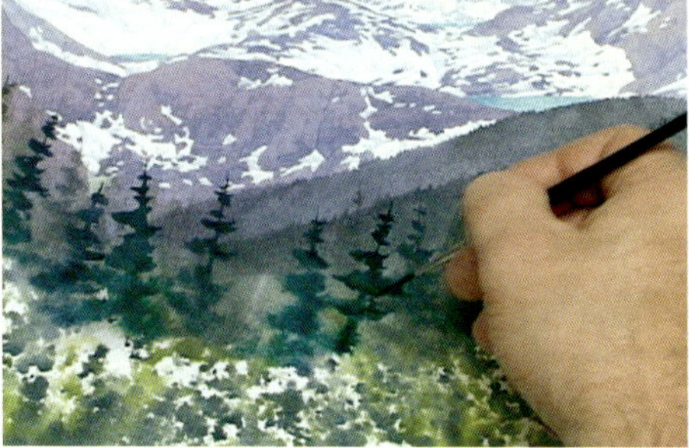

While these paints were still wet, I switched to the more vivid Phthalo Blue and Phthalo Green. As the underlying paints dried, the overlying trees became more and more defined (since they were blending less and less with the drying background trees). This helped create the impression that the latter trees were closer to the viewer—which, of course, helped create the illusion of depth.

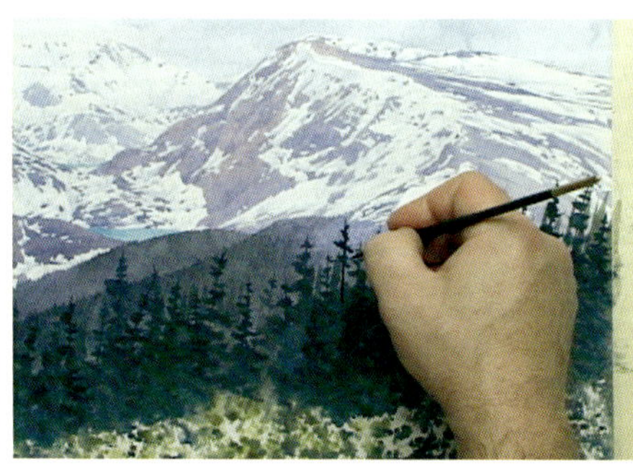

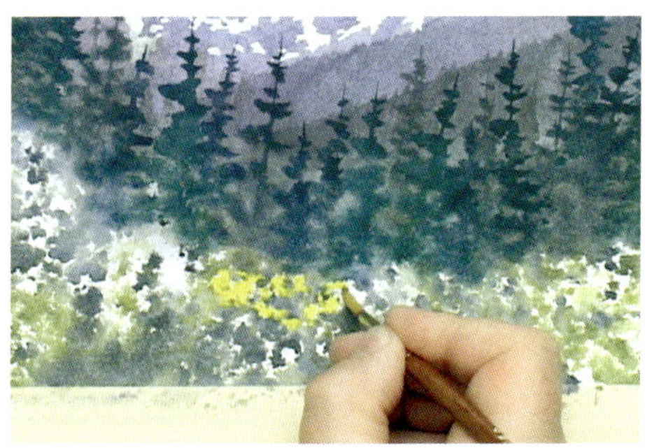

**Step 19:** Once the foreground foliage area had been thoroughly dried with a blow drier, I began painting in the base wildflower colors. Using a #6 round brush and a rich mix of Transparent Yellow, I painted most of the white spaces that resulted in the previous step. These white areas were spaced and shaped irregularly, making an interesting template to fill in with flowers. In this case, I filled nearly every large white space with yellow. And, I filled in most of the remaining small spaces with Rose, using a #2 round brush.

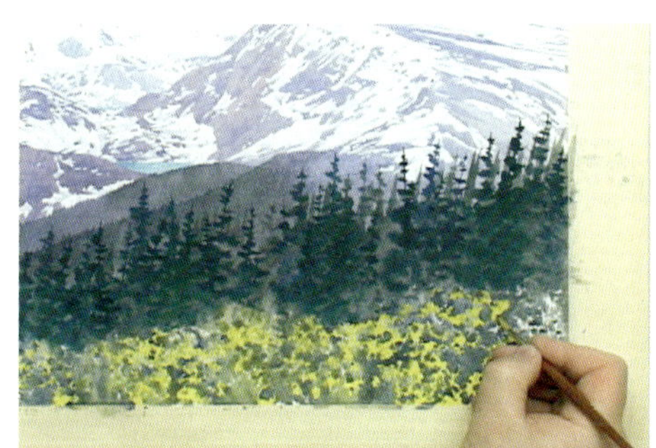

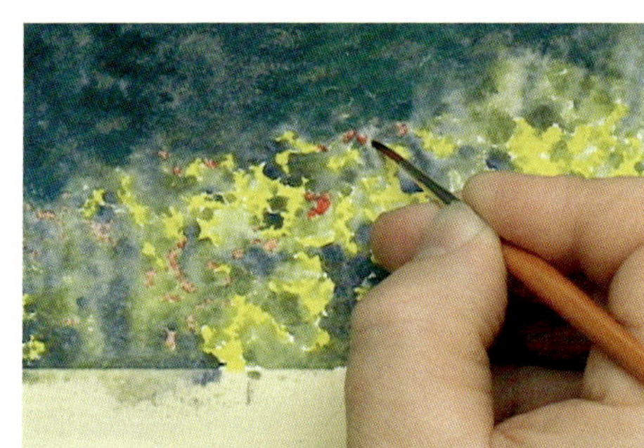

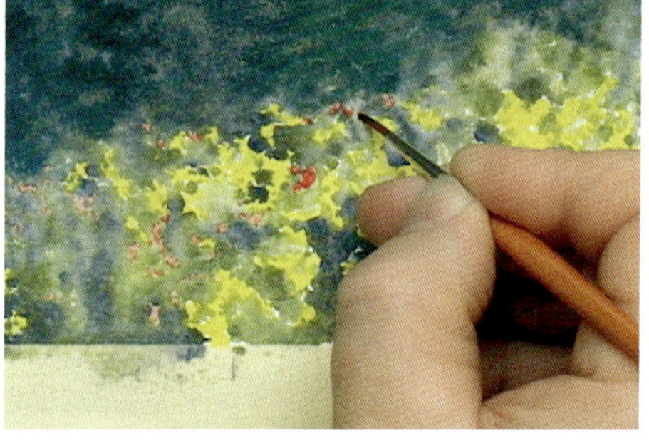

(Step 19 continued)

I tried to not create any unnatural pattern of colors.

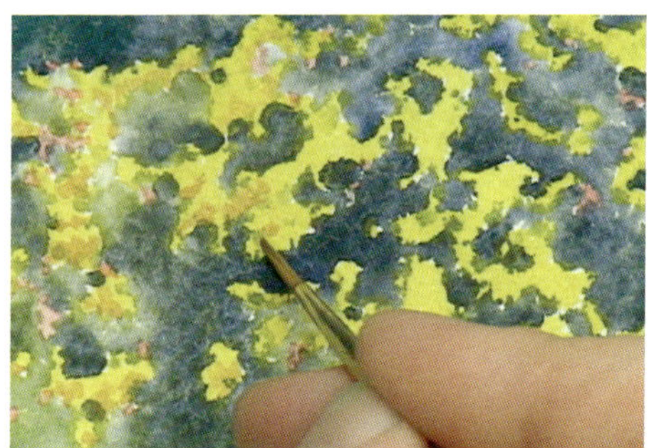

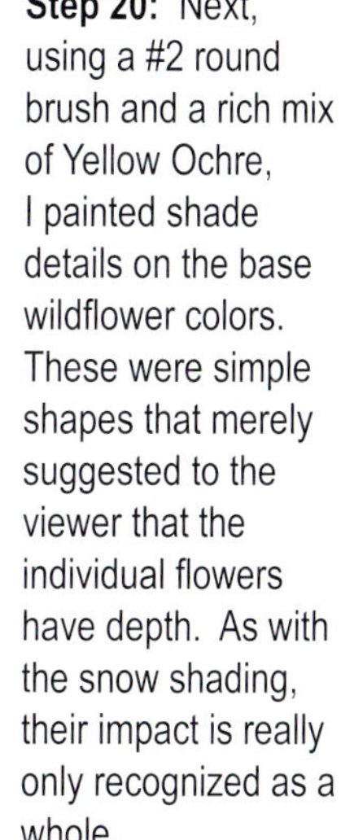

**Step 20:** Next, using a #2 round brush and a rich mix of Yellow Ochre, I painted shade details on the base wildflower colors. These were simple shapes that merely suggested to the viewer that the individual flowers have depth. As with the snow shading, their impact is really only recognized as a whole.

I did the same on the Rose base wildflower colors, simply shading with Rose over Rose.

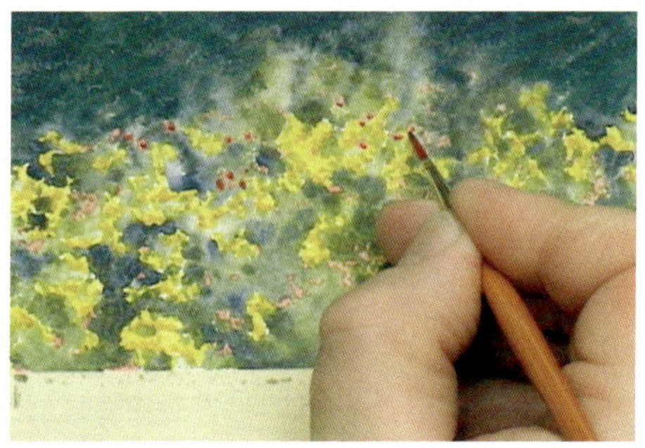

I was not particularly careful about applying the wildflower base colors. It was actually preferable to allow some of these colors to spill over into their surrounding green foliage—casting yet more color variance around the flowers.

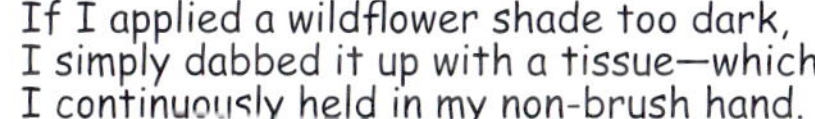

If I applied a wildflower shade too dark, I simply dabbed it up with a tissue—which I continuously held in my non-brush hand.

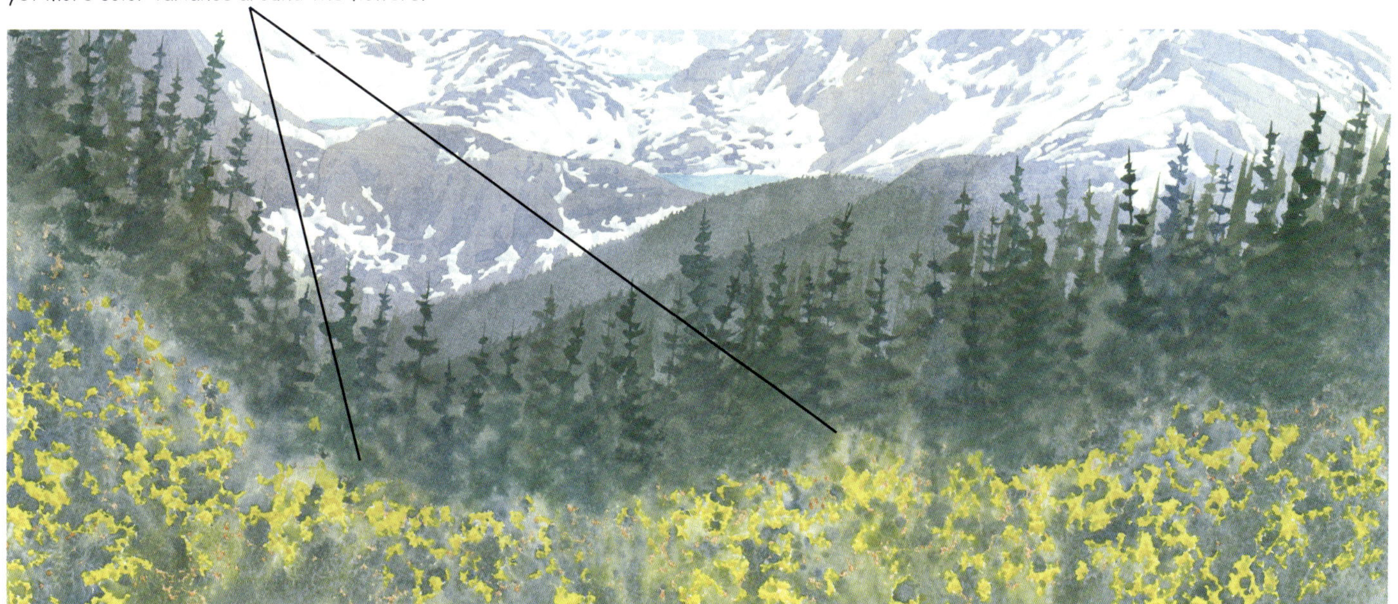

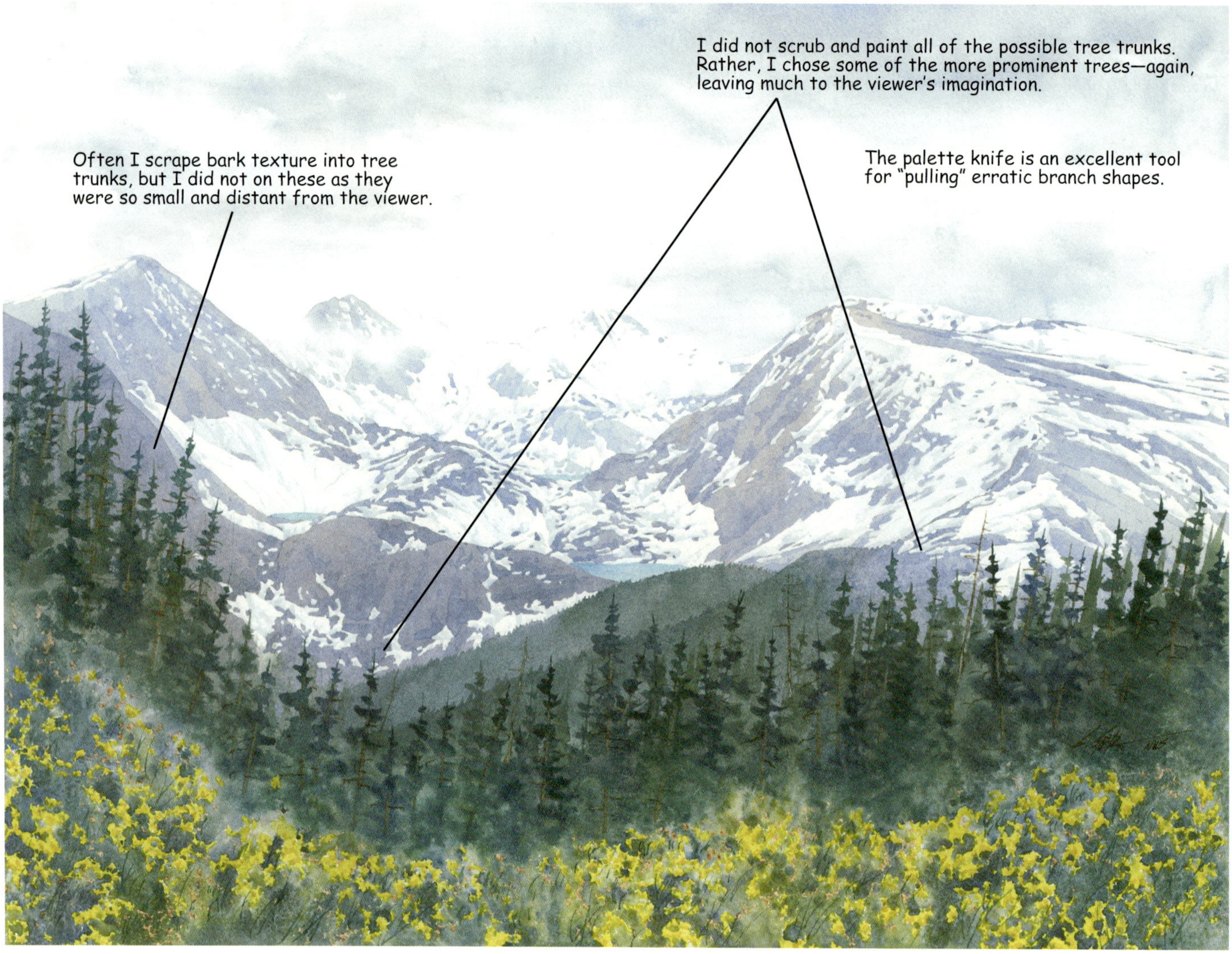

I did not scrub and paint all of the possible tree trunks. Rather, I chose some of the more prominent trees—again, leaving much to the viewer's imagination.

Often I scrape bark texture into tree trunks, but I did not on these as they were so small and distant from the viewer.

The palette knife is an excellent tool for "pulling" erratic branch shapes.

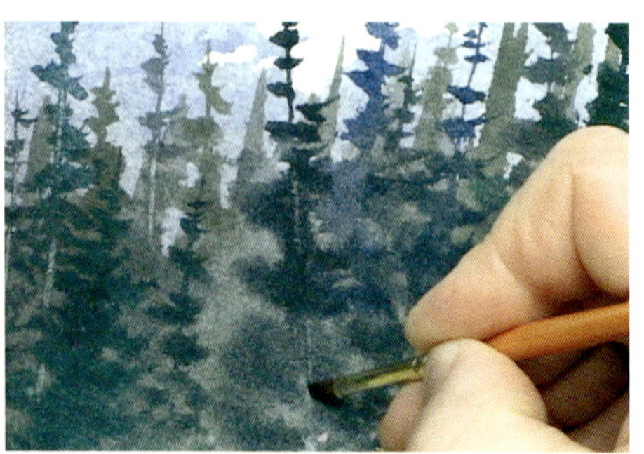

**Step 21:** With a 1/8" flat brush loaded with water, I scrubbed visible trunk shapes into the tree forms that I had created previously. This was done carefully, as it is very easy to scrub these shapes out too wide.

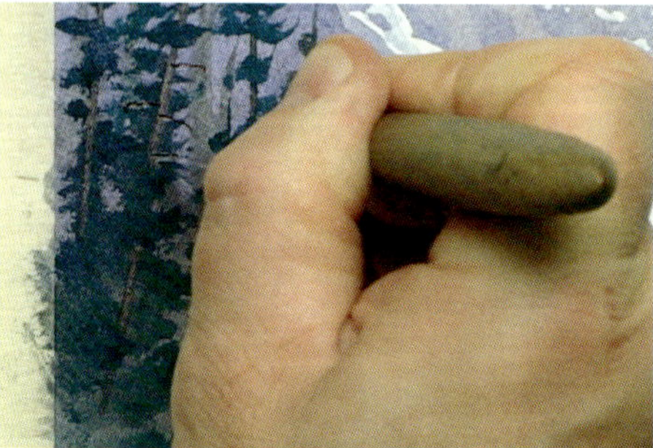

**Step 23:** By dipping a palette knife into the same two colors, I was able to use it much like a quill pen dipped into ink. I loaded it with paint and "pulled" branches off of my newly painted tree trunks.

I also pulled some dead trees—first pulling the trunk upward, then pulling branches outward.

Again, I held a tissue in my non-palette hand so that I could immediately dab up any excess paint.

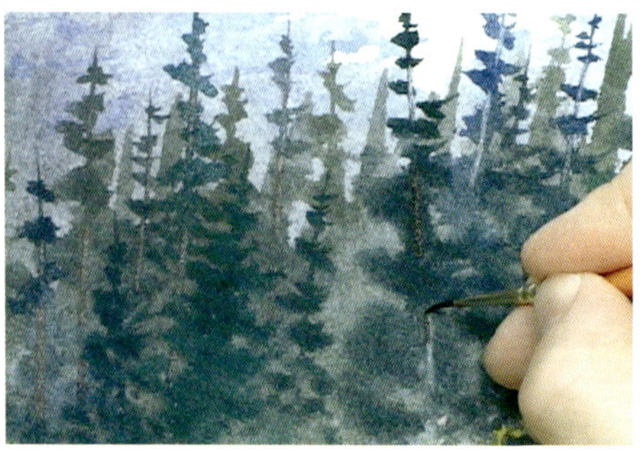

**Step 22:** Then, with a #1 round brush and a mix of Brown Madder and Phthalo Blue, I painted in these shapes. When I painted them in too darkly, I quickly dabbed at them with a tissue to lighten them.

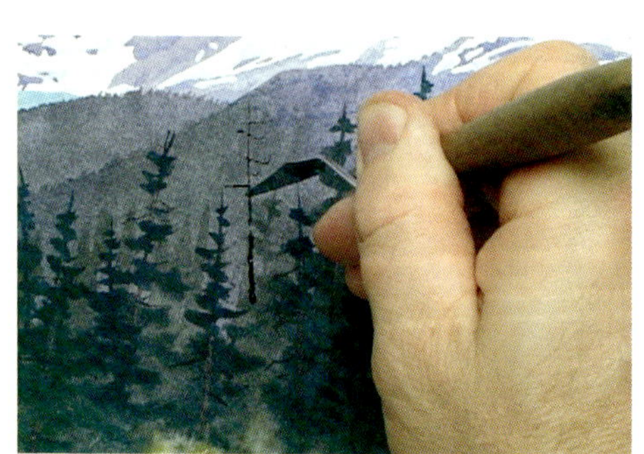

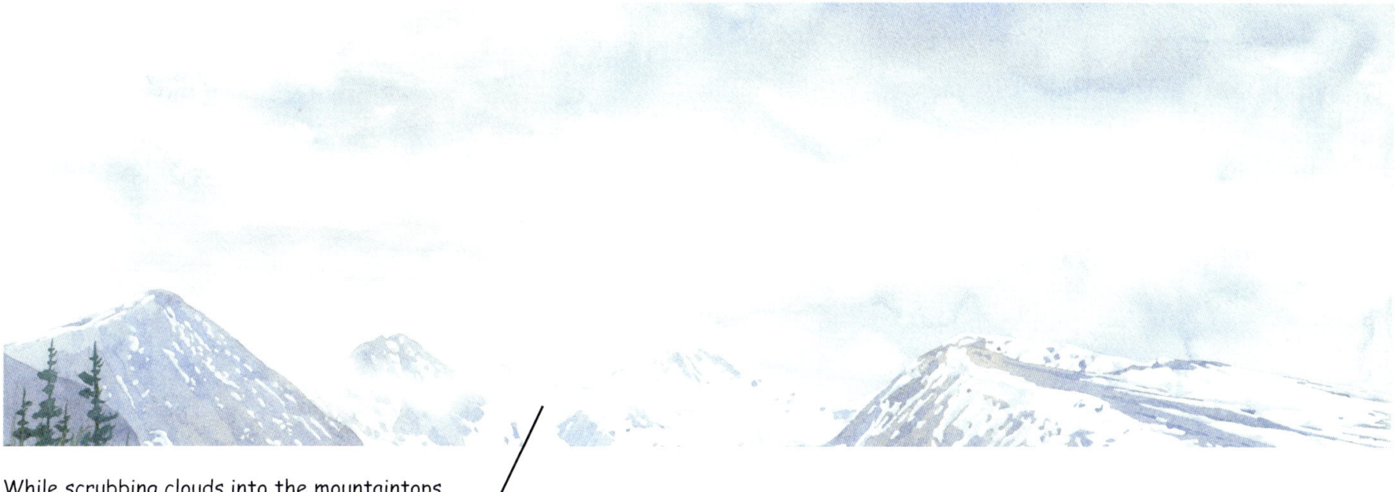

While scrubbing clouds into the mountaintops, I frequently dipped the brush into clean water.

Like most scrubbing techniques, scrubbing the clouds into the mountaintops is easily overdone. It is best to scrub a little, then sit back and assess what scrubbing might still be needed.

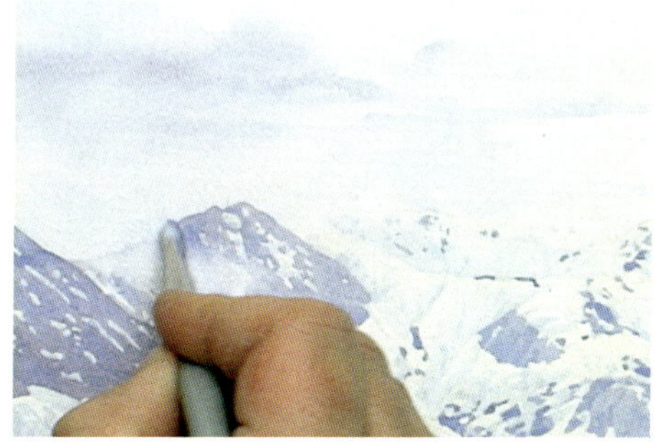

**Step 25:** Nearing the end, I returned to the mountaintops with a stiff-bristled scrubbing brush that was loaded with water. Carefully, I scrubbed some of the cloud shapes right into the mountains—subtly blending some of the mountain into the sky. As I scrubbed, I lifted the paint with a tissue.

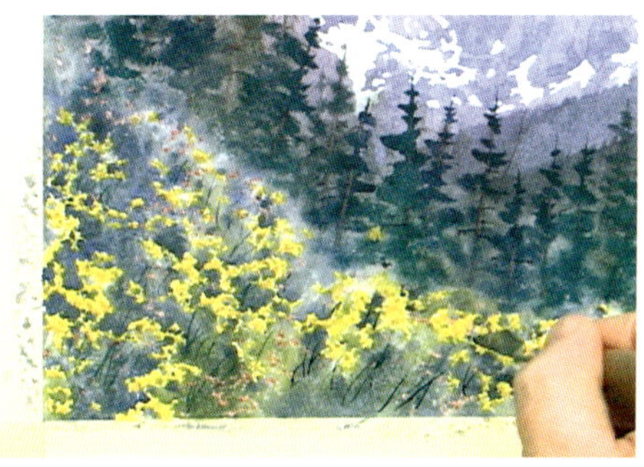

**Step 24:** Continuing with the palette knife, I loaded it with a rich mix of Phthalo Blue and Phthalo Green. Then I pulled sporadic flower stems and grass blades in a similar fashion to what I had done previously with the branches. Again, I dabbed at any excess paint with a tissue.

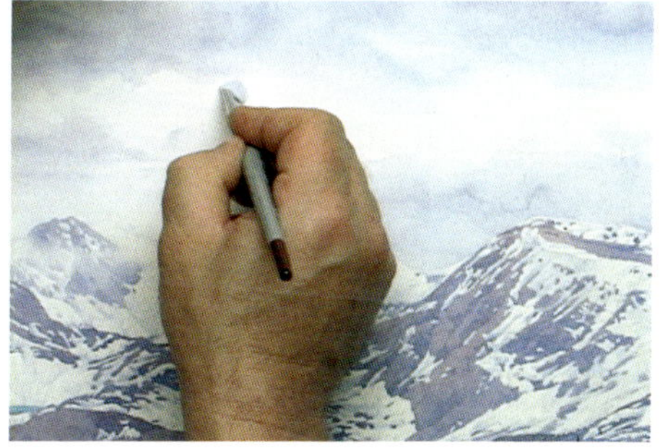

Since this is a turbulent sky, I also had the freedom to scrub out any errant drops of paint that may have landed, accidentally, in the sky area. Since the sky was so dynamic, it was usually easy to blend any such repair into its background without compromising the sky's overall impact.

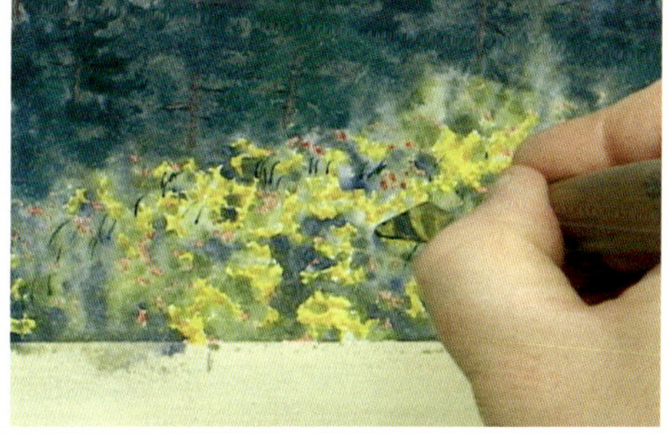

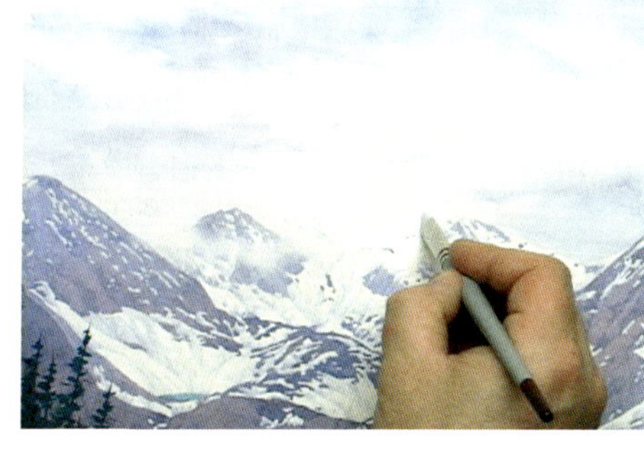

**Step 26:** Finally, after I was certain that the entire painting was dry, I used a kneaded eraser to rub out any remaining visible pencil lines.

The stems and grass blades added much needed detail to help inform the viewer that these rather abstract shapes were actually flowers.

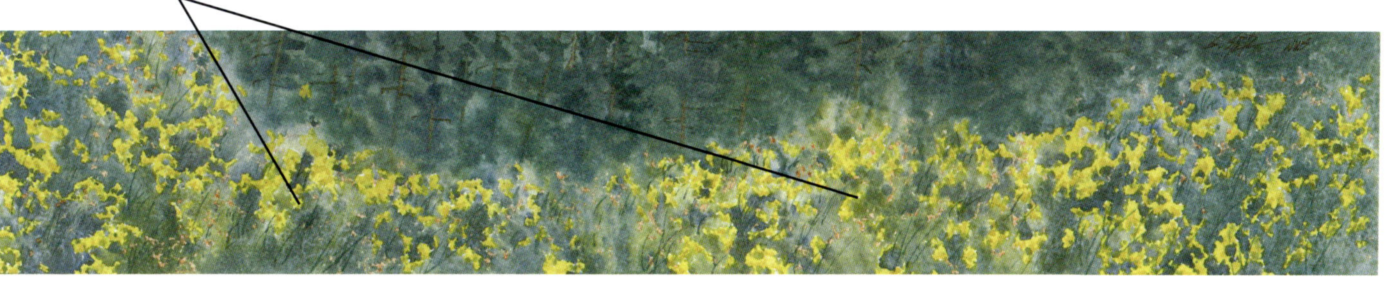

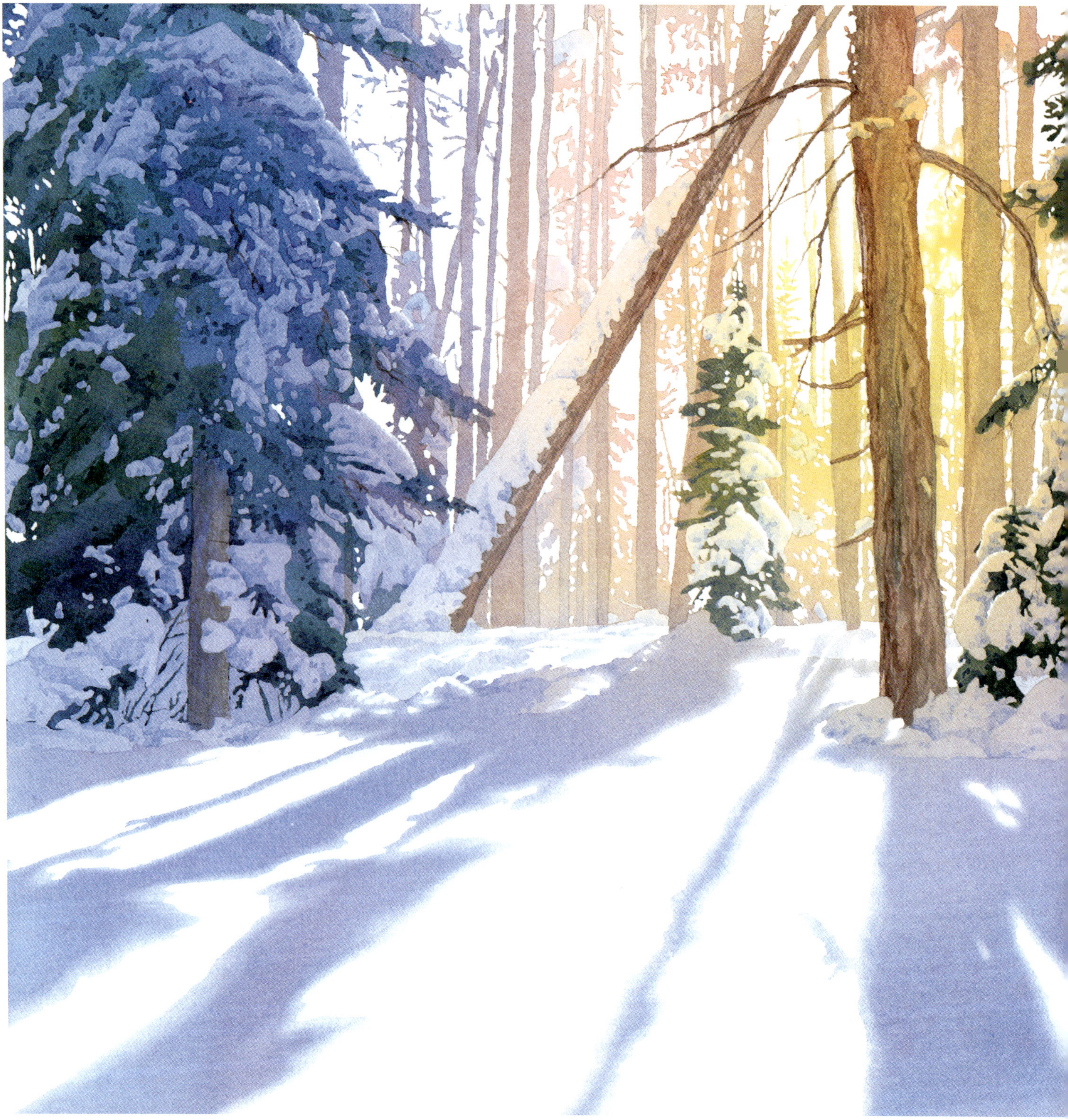

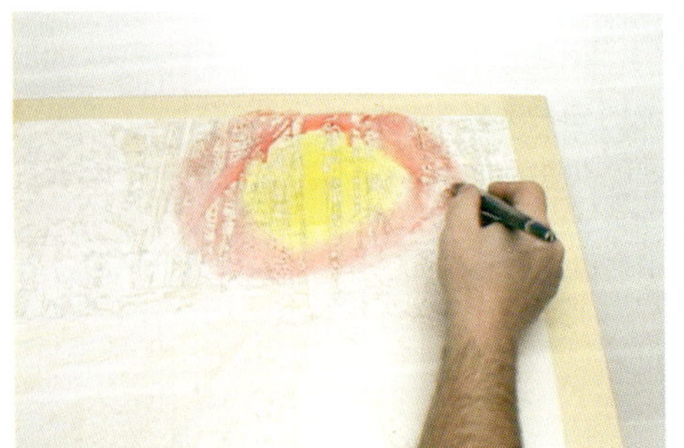

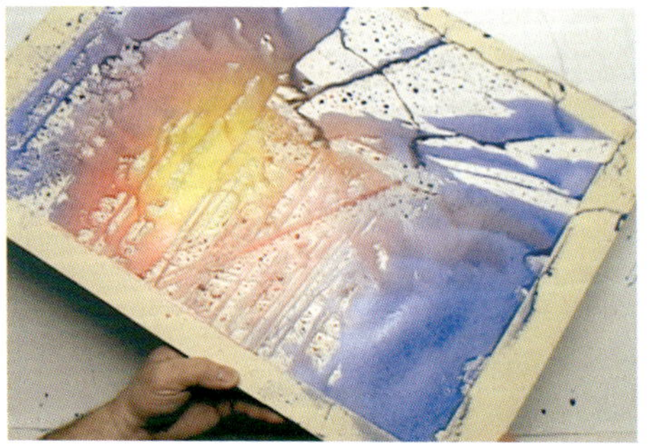

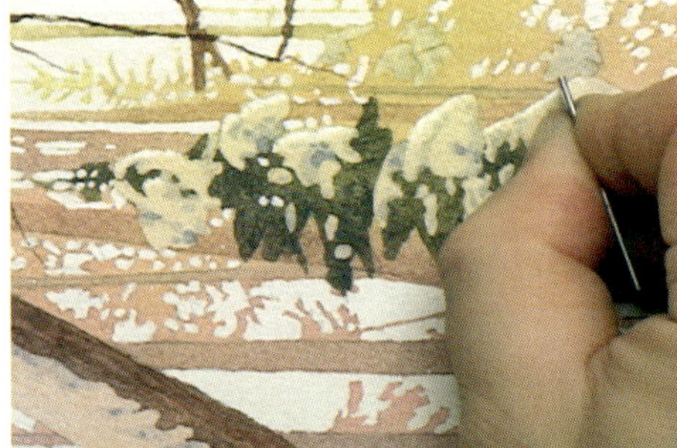

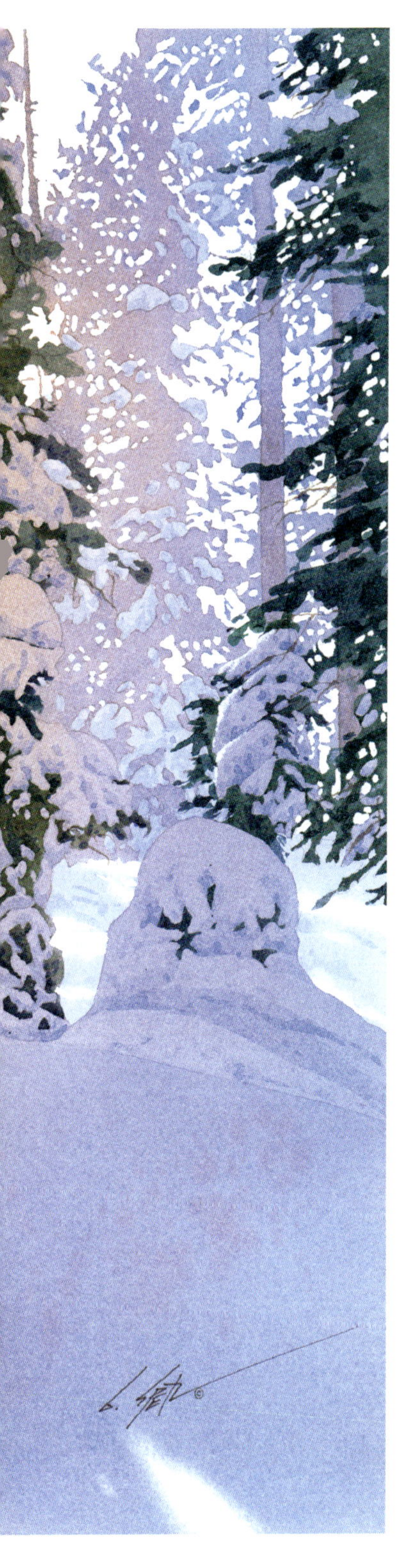

# WINTER'S LIGHT

Although seemingly contradictory, there is such a thing as a "warm winter snow scene"—or at least there can be in art! Low sunlight and long shadows—on the stark white of fresh snow—offer endless opportunities to the landscape watercolor painter. No other painting medium can command the use of white in the way that transparent watercolors can! This is no small feat, considering that watercolor painters, such as myself, very rarely use white paint! Why apply white paint to cover up perfectly good white paper, we ask?

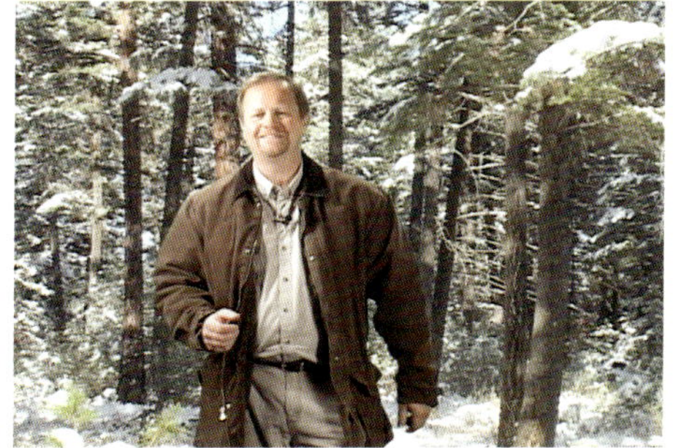

Saving the white of the paper—and seeing through paints to the white of the paper—is what transparent watercolors are all about. On this painting I will do both. If you have enjoyed the (arguably tedious) masking tasks on my other lessons, then you are going to love this one! Winter's Light takes masking to a whole other level. But, the "toils with the toothpick" will be worth well worth the effort!

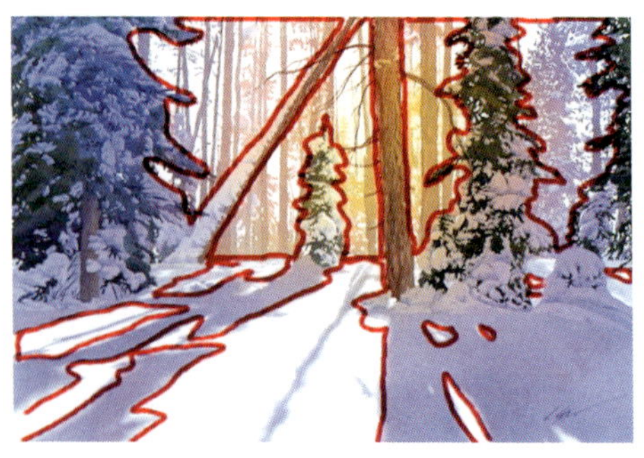

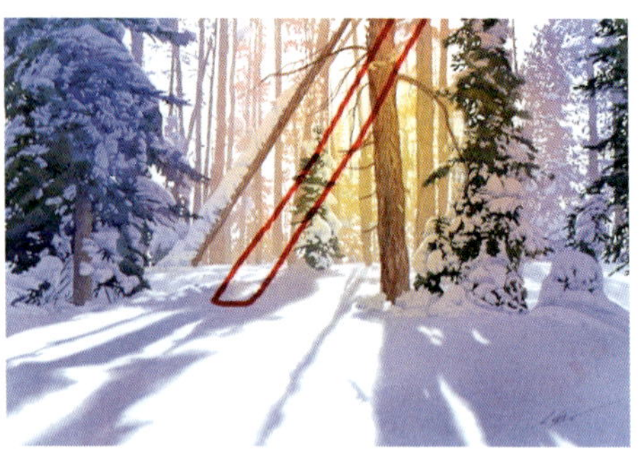

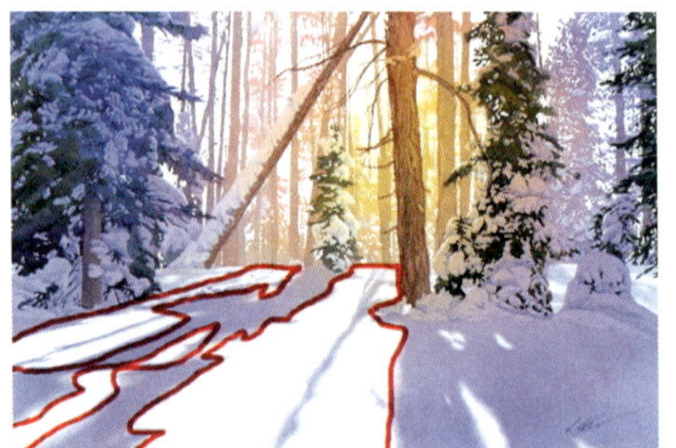

**Step 1:** I began by drawing out my composition on the watercolor paper. Marking my horizontal and vertical center points on the sides of the painting helped remind me to not center prominent objects or prominent colors. In this case, I made sure that the bold yellow of the sunlight source was above and to the right of the painting's center. I also was careful to not center any of the prominent tree trunks. And, the same is true of the large area of sunlit snow.

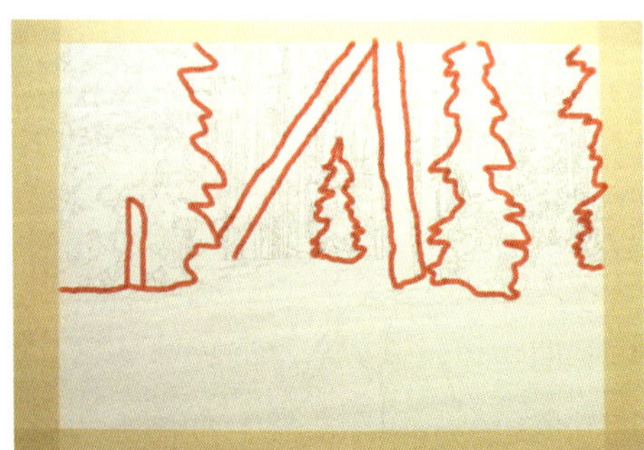

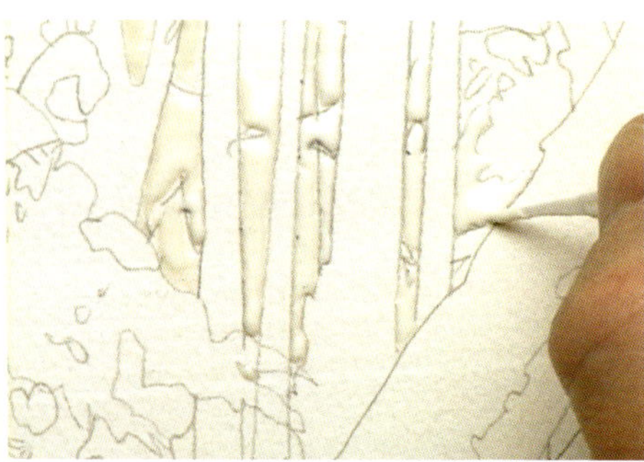

**Step 2:** Using liquid masking fluid and a plastic toothpick, I began the lengthy job of masking out the background areas of intense sunlight. Although the drawing may make all of these intricate shapes look complicated, they really are not. In my mind, I tried to isolate the foreground trees and trunks from the remainder of the painting. On this step, I did not want to mask out any of the snow on

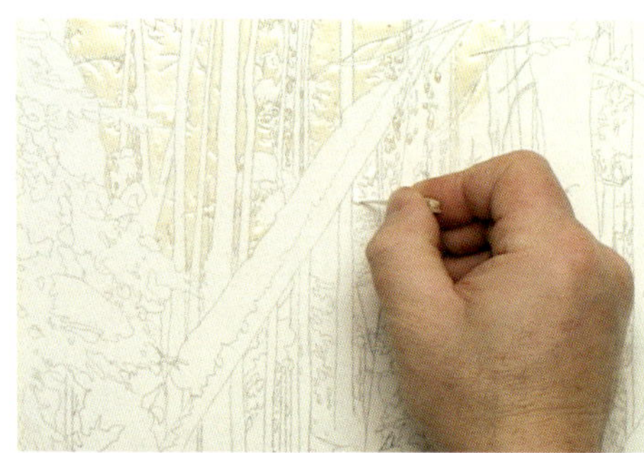

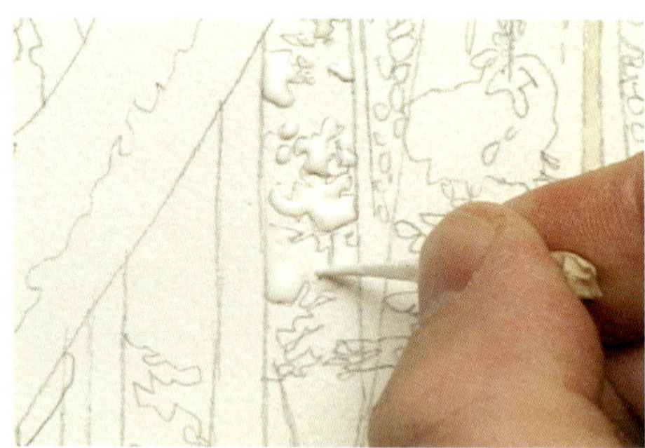

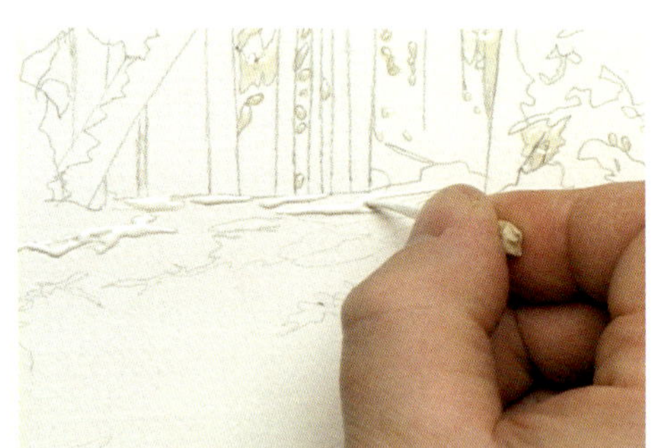

(Step 2 continued)

these trees. I only wanted to mask out the background silhouettes—the shapes of backlight.

While it is true that there were a confusingly large number of these shapes, once I started masking them, they became easier to read. Indeed, once the backlight shapes had been masked, the foreground tree snow shapes became much easier to identify.

Of course, when I accidentally masked the wrong shape, I simply allowed it to dry before peeling it off.

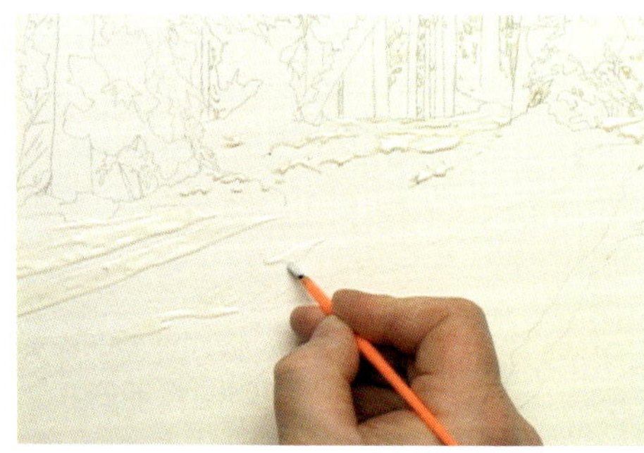

I also masked out the areas of sunlit snow. Since these were simpler and often larger shapes, I used a disposable paintbrush to apply the liquid masking.

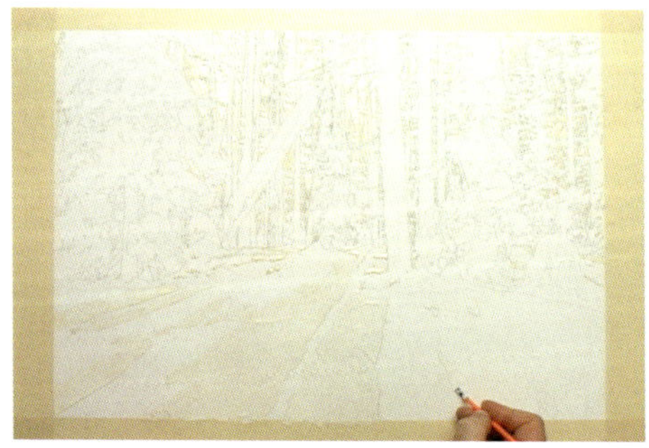

When this was completed, I hurried along the drying process with a blow drier.

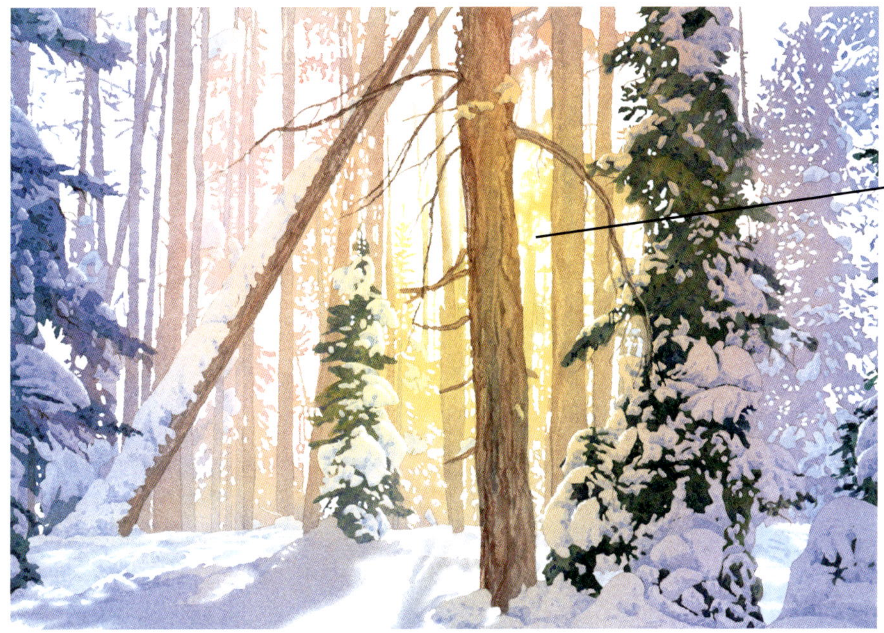

Controlling shapes with masking—in this case, shapes of backlighting—enabled greater freedom to blend the painting's base colors.

The "color bull's eye" creates drama in this composition—which will tend to draw the viewer's attention to this area of the painting.

It was crucial to thoroughly dry the painting between the color bull's eye steps. If masking fluid is applied to damp paint, it will likely lift some of it when it is peeled off. And, even worse, it could tear the paper. Once I believe that I have got the painting dry, I dry it some more!

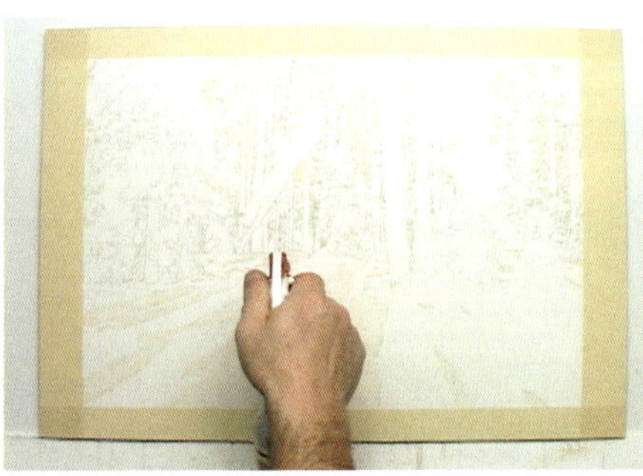

**Step 3:** Once the masking had dried, I tilted my inclined painting table down to a near level position. Then, with a spray bottle filled with water, I saturated the entire painting.

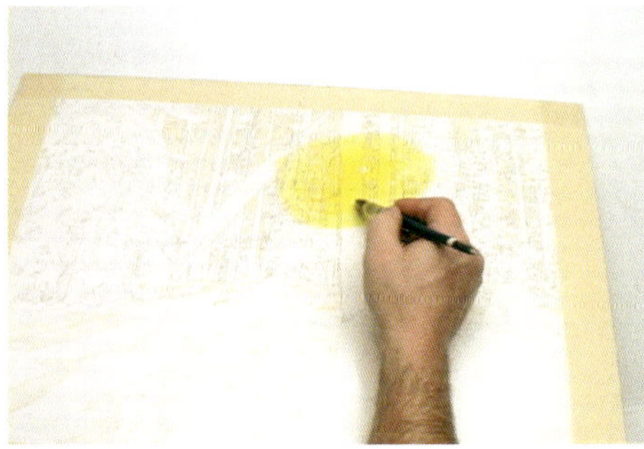

**Step 4:** Using a #20 round brush loaded with a rich mix of Transparent Yellow, I painted a large dot over the center of the composition's light source—which happens to be behind the largest tree trunk, above center.

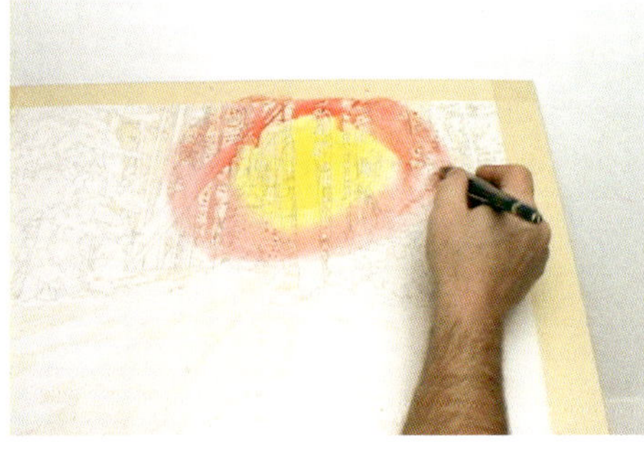

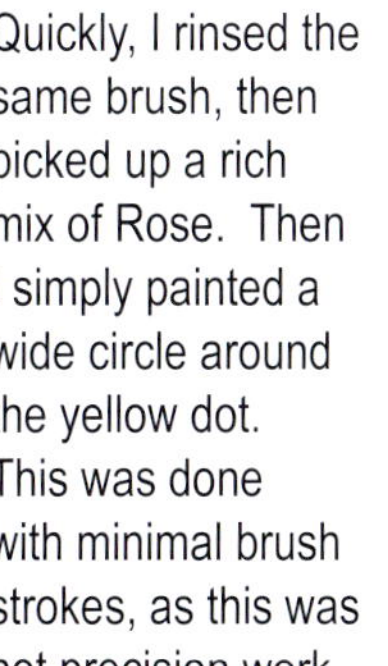

Quickly, I rinsed the same brush, then picked up a rich mix of Rose. Then I simply painted a wide circle around the yellow dot. This was done with minimal brush strokes, as this was not precision work.

(Step 4 continued)

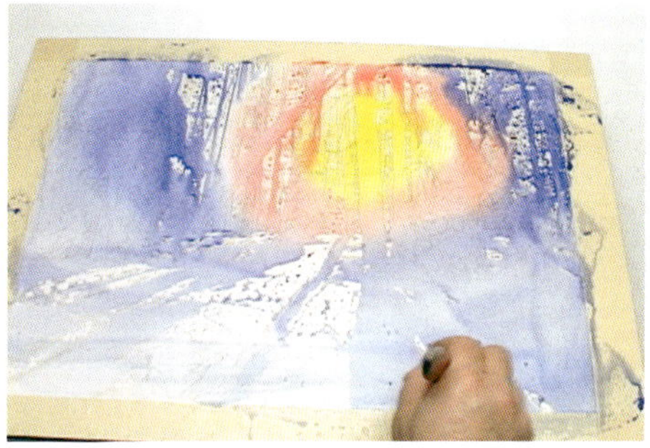

While the painting was still very wet, I surrounded both colors with a rich mix of Cobalt Blue. Since this entailed covering the remainder of the painting, I switched to a 2" flat brush.

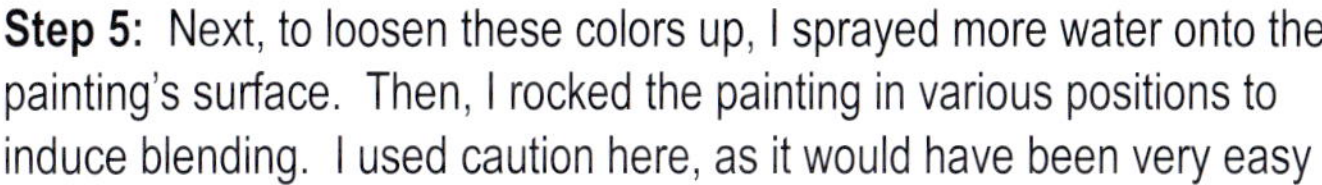

**Step 5:** Next, to loosen these colors up, I sprayed more water onto the painting's surface. Then, I rocked the painting in various positions to induce blending. I used caution here, as it would have been very easy to over blend and loose the "color bull's eye's" impact.

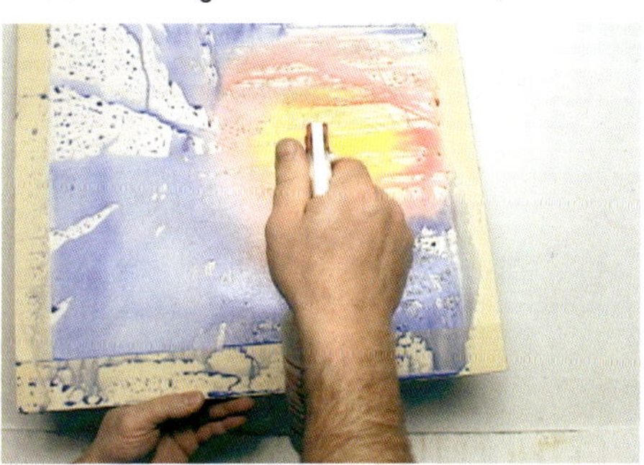

As I rotated the painting, I continuously used a tissue to lift the puddles of paint that formed along the edges. Sometimes I used a "thirsty brush" to wick up puddles that formed inside of the painting's edges.

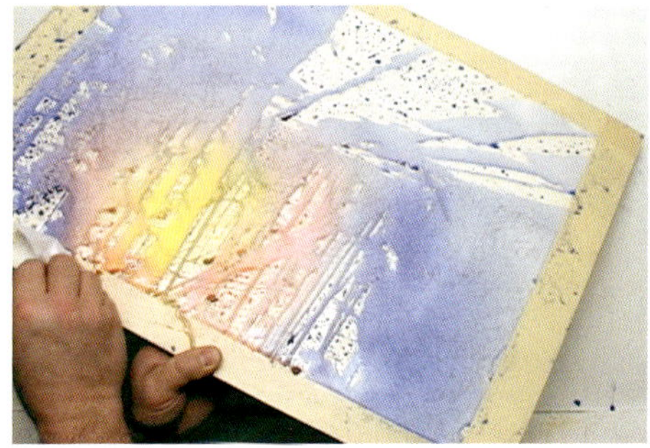

After I achieved the gradual blending effect that I wanted, I locked these colors by drying them with a blow dryer. Indeed, I very thoroughly dried the painting, as this was essential for the following step.

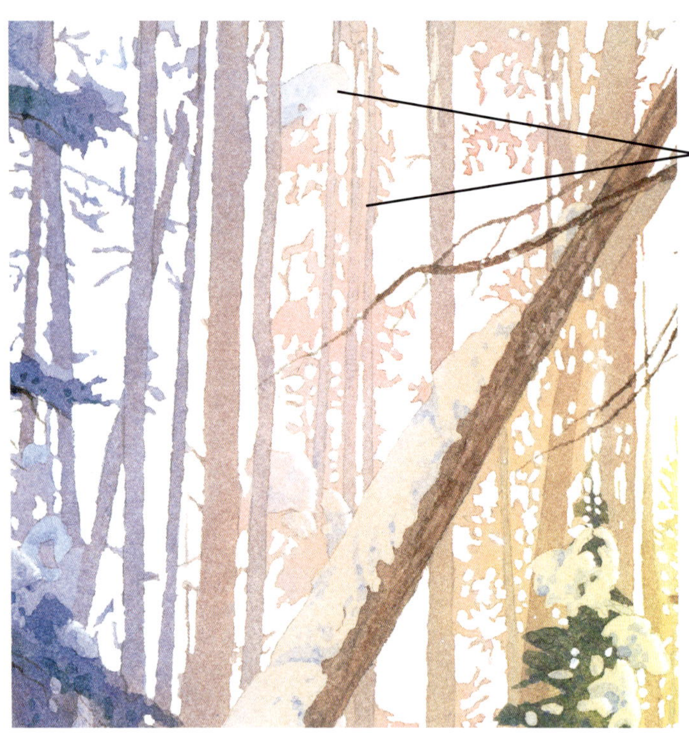

The second phase of masking included the snow clumps of the tilted tree, the pine tree below it and all of the background trees. It did not include the snow clumps of the foreground row of trees.

Masking in stages, between color washes, creates an interesting display of values.

It was easier to identify the snow of the background trees after the shapes of the backlighting had been masked. What had been a somewhat confusing drawing to read, became much more understandable.

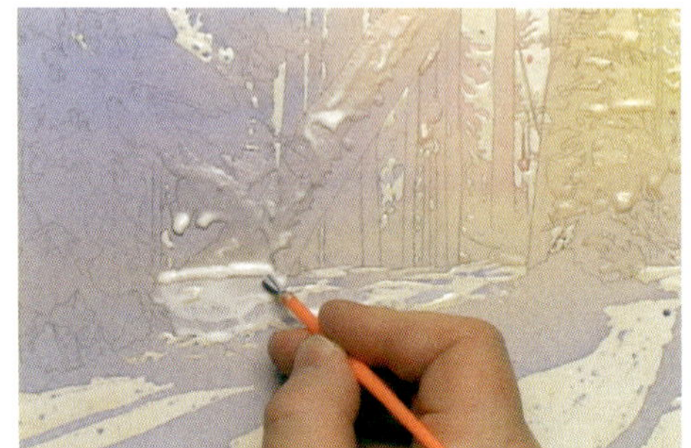

(Step 6 continued)

For the larger, simpler shapes, I used a disposable paintbrush.

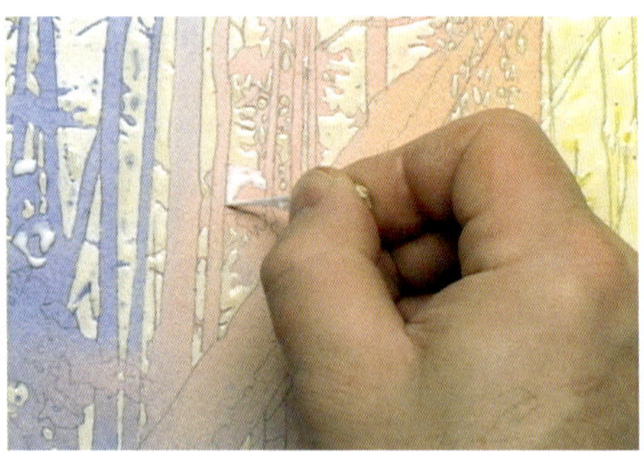

**Step 6**: Again, using liquid masking and a plastic toothpick, I masked out the clumps of snow that were on the background trees. This did not include what I will call the foreground trees, but did include the tilted tree trunk and the small pine tree below it.

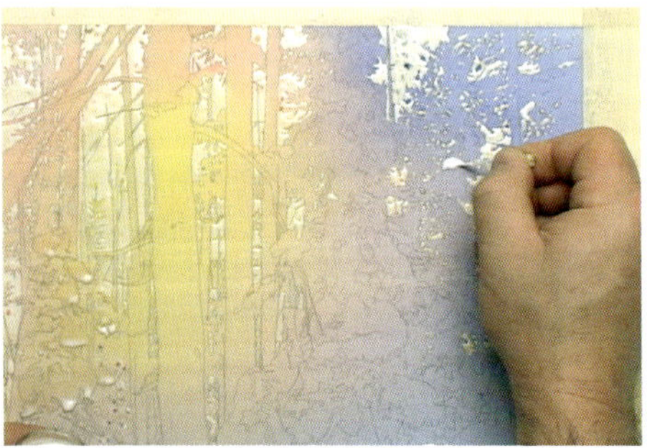

With the shapes of backlighting already masked out, the drawing was much easier to read while applying this step of masking.

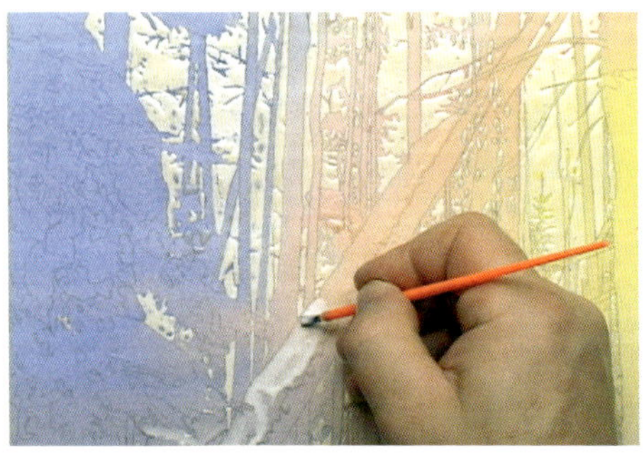

I also masked out the snow on the tilted tree, as it was one of the more distant background trees.

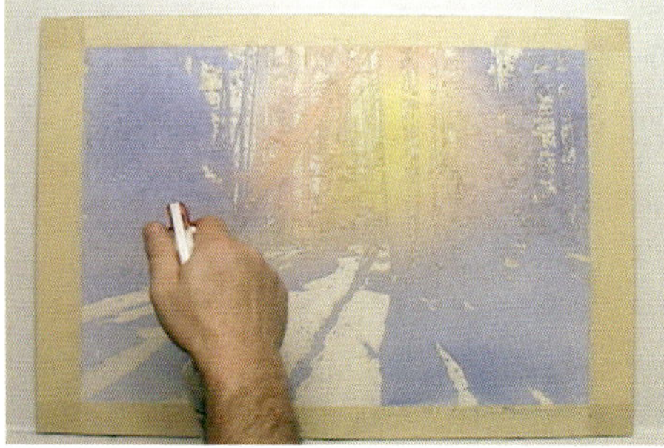

**Step 7:** Once the masking was dry, I made sure that my working table was at a near level position (as opposed to steeply inclined). Then, with a spray bottle of water, I again saturated the entire painting.

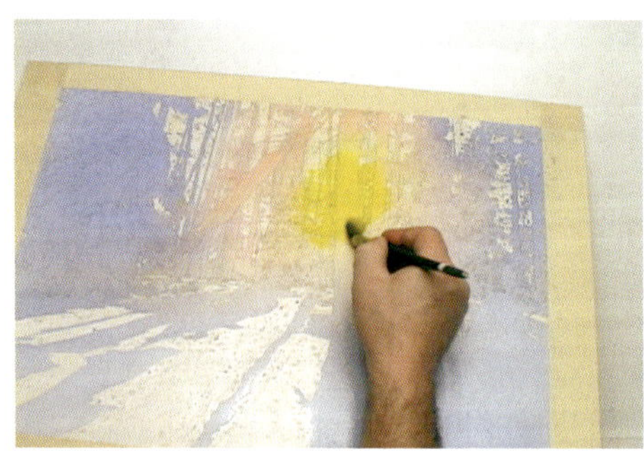

**Step 8:** Following the same sequence as before, with a #20 round brush, I painted another large Transparent Yellow dot right over the previous one.

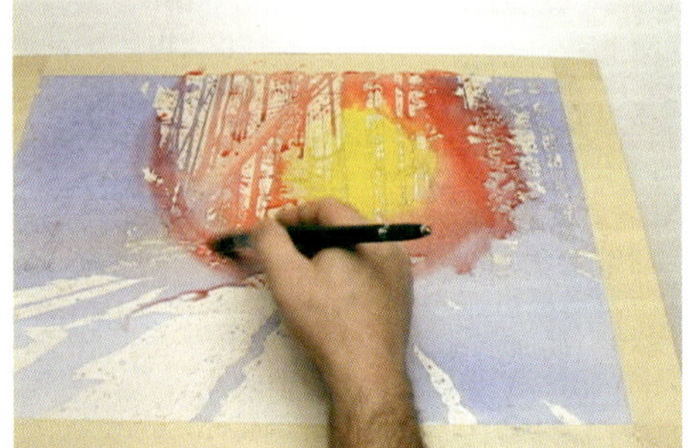

Next, I encircled this dot with a wide ring of Rose.

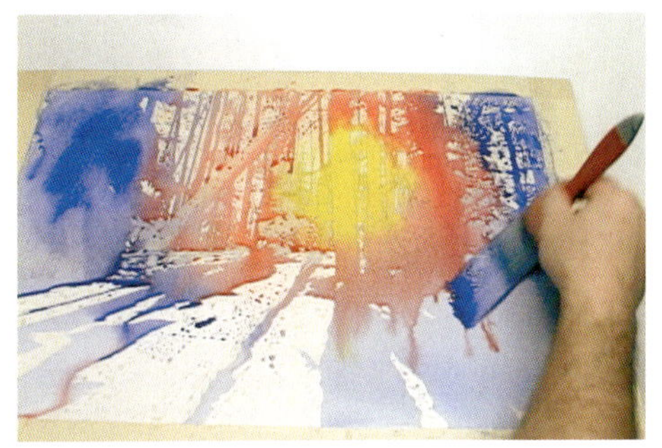

(Step 8 continued)

And switching to a 2" flat brush, I covered the remainder of the painting with another layer of Cobalt Blue.

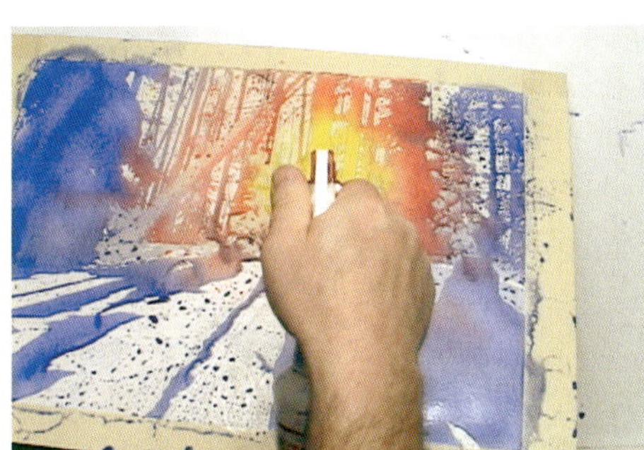

**Step 9:** To loosen these colors up for blending, I sprayed more water onto the painting.

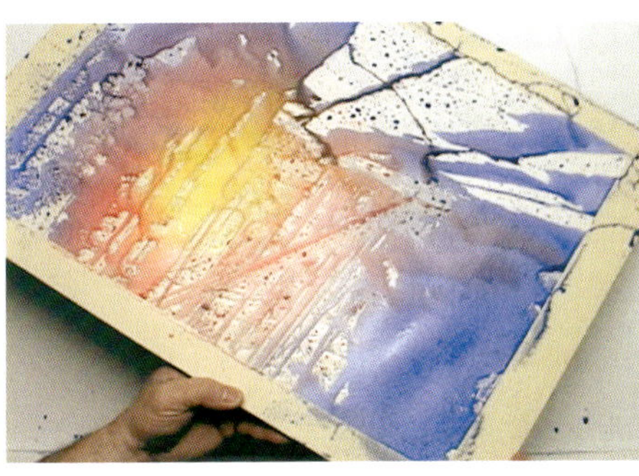

Then, I again rotated and rocked the painting to induce blending—using care to not blend too much.

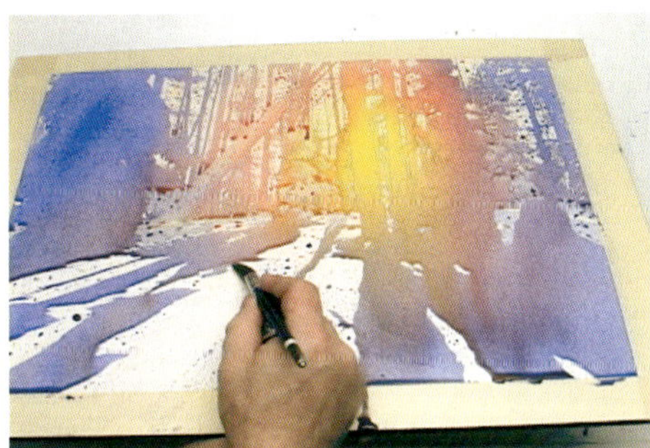

With a thirsty brush and a tissue, I wicked up any excess puddles of paint. When I had the look that I wanted, I thoroughly dried the painting to lock in the colors. Again, before I went on to the next masking step, I made sure that the painting was "bone dry."

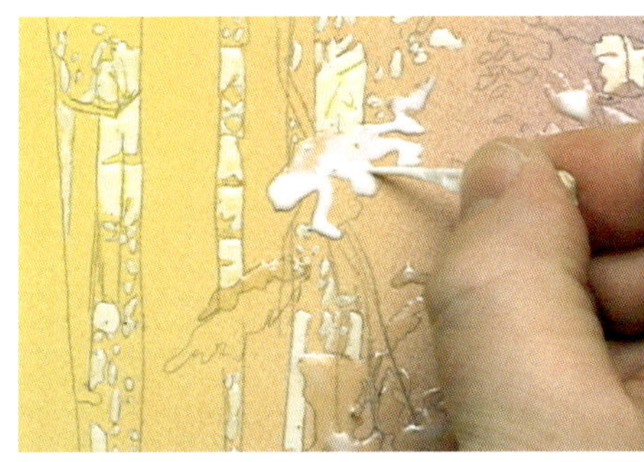

**Step 10:** This time—using a plastic toothpick for the small, intricate shapes and a disposable paintbrush for the larger and simpler shapes—I masked out the snow clumps on the foreground trees.

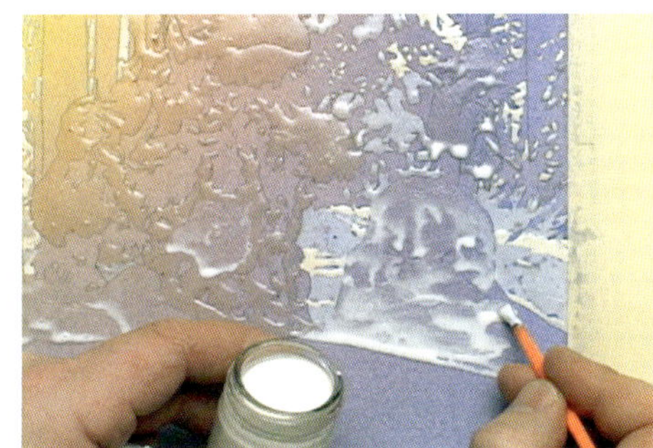

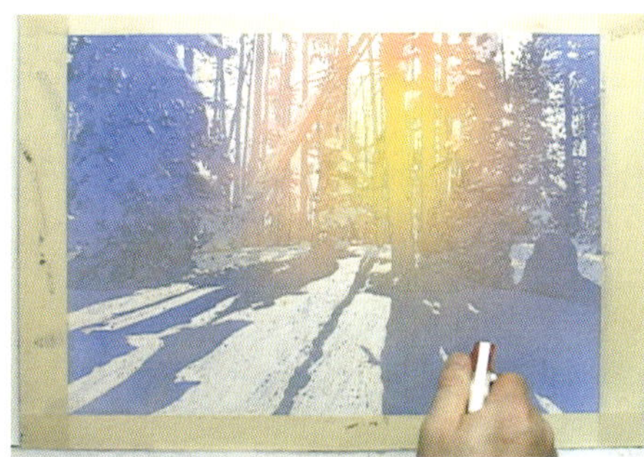

**Step 11:** After the masking had dried, I saturated the foreground snow area with water.

**Step 12:** Using a 2" flat brush with Cobalt Blue, I gave the snow shadows one more layer of color to differentiate this snow from the other snow areas. While the underlying blue paint was still wet, I "flicked" on some Rose with a toothbrush.

As Yogi Berra once quipped, "This is like déjà vu all over again." Following the same sequence as before, I painted and blended another color bull's eye right over the previous one.

This time I masked the snow clumps on the foreground trees. However, I did not mask the shadowed snow in the foreground.

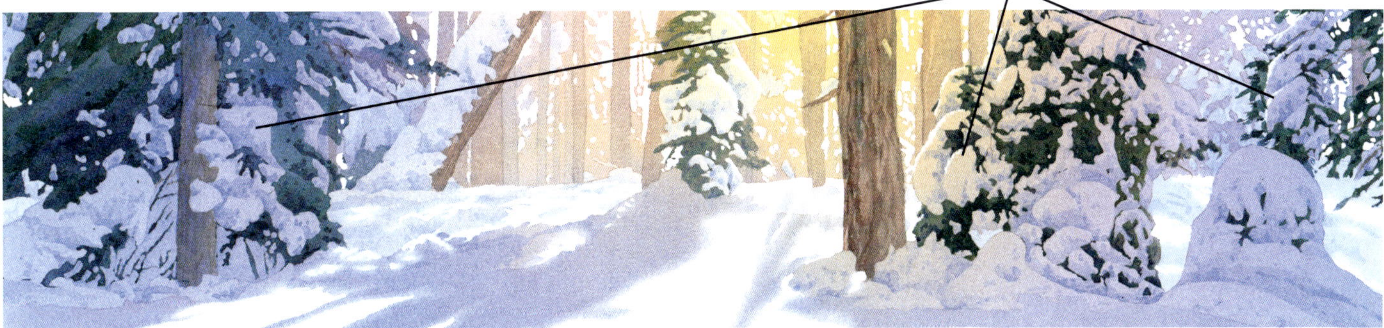

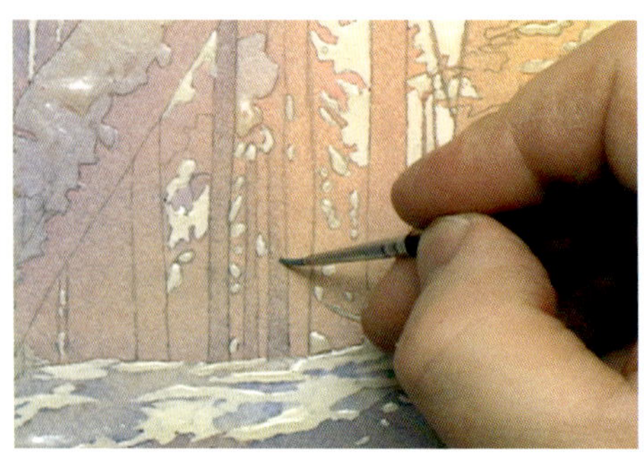

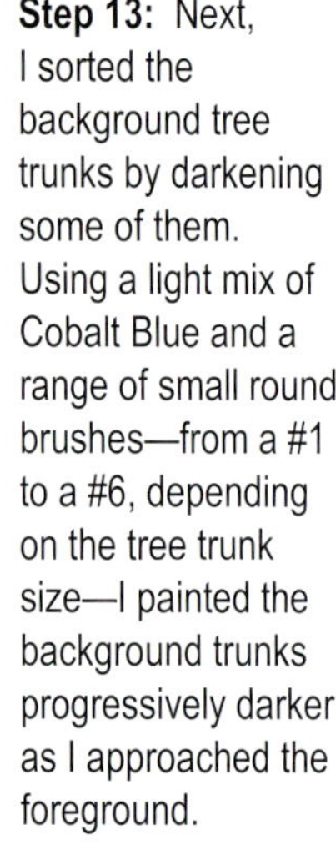

**Step 13:** Next, I sorted the background tree trunks by darkening some of them. Using a light mix of Cobalt Blue and a range of small round brushes—from a #1 to a #6, depending on the tree trunk size—I painted the background trunks progressively darker as I approached the foreground.

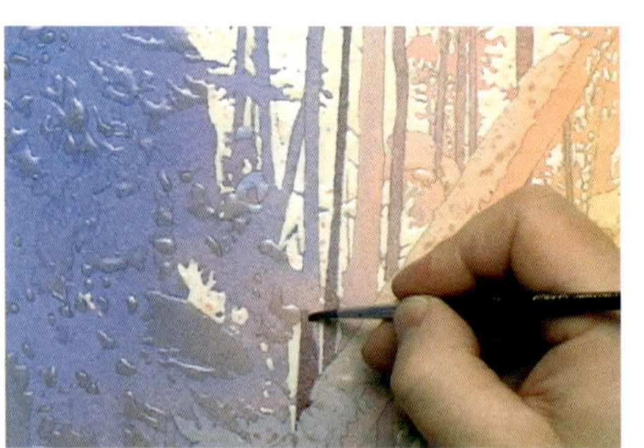

Gradually, I worked in some Brown Madder with the Cobalt Blue on the closer trees.

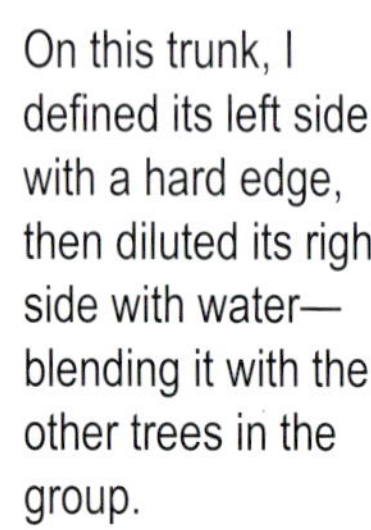

On this trunk, I defined its left side with a hard edge, then diluted its right side with water—blending it with the other trees in the group.

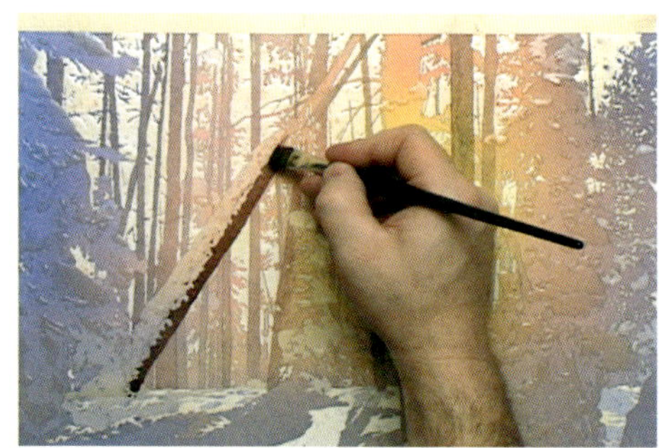

**Step 14:** For the largest tree trunks, I switched to a 1/2" flat brush and a mix of Brown Madder and Phthalo Blue. Again, I gradually darkened the value as the trees approached the viewer.

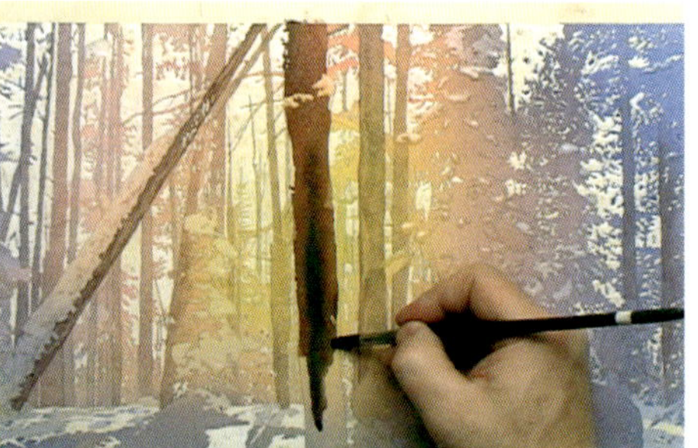

I varied the mix between the two colors—avoiding one solid brown color.

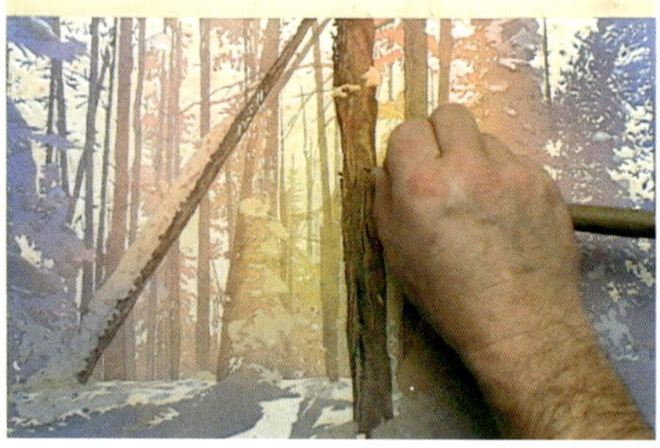

For these larger tree trunks, I scraped in bark texture with the tip of a palette knife. This was done before the paint had lost its sheen of wetness, so I painted and scraped these larger trunks one at a time.

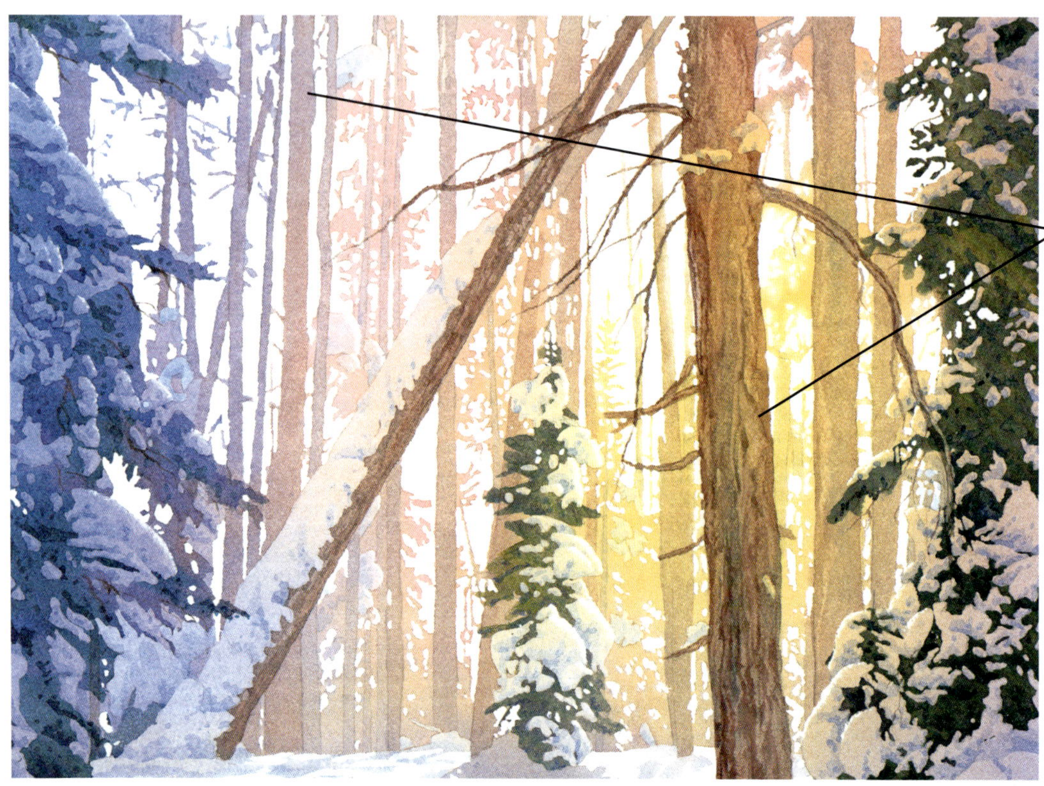

The tree trunks were painted progressively darker and progressively "browner" as they approached the viewer. This range of color and value helps cue the viewer into realizing that this scene has depth.

Since the snow clumps had been protected with masking, the tree colors could be applied quickly and freely.

I used different colors of green on the trees to emphasize their varying distances from the viewer. These subtle differences all added up in the end to convey the depth of field to the viewer.

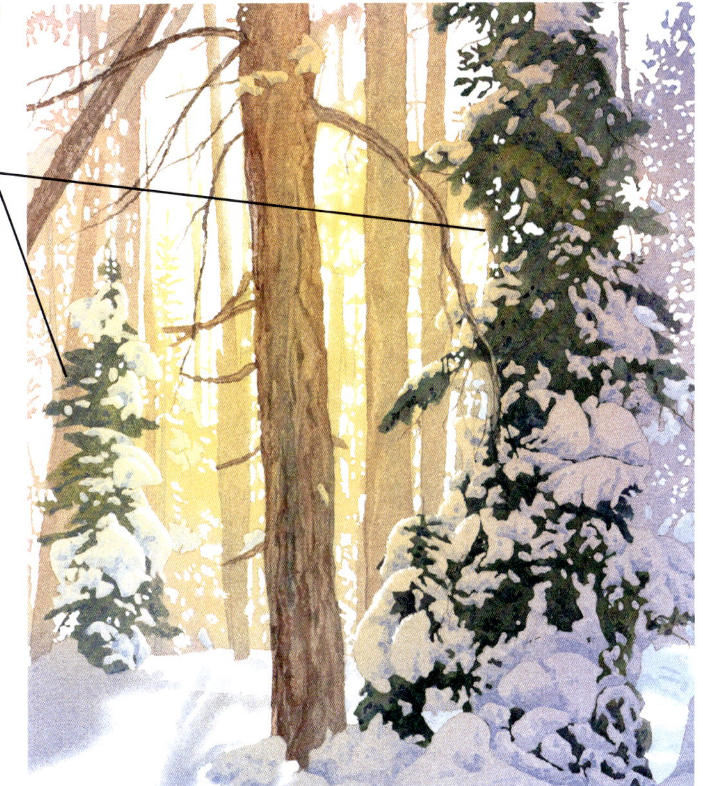

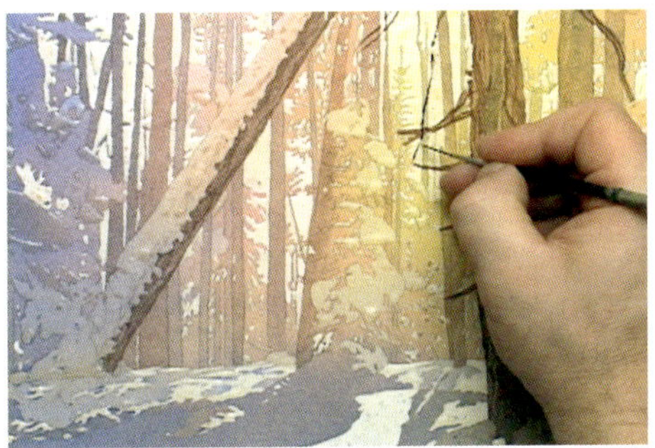

**Step 15:** Using various sized rigger brushes and the same trunk colors—Brown Madder and Phthalo Blue—I painted branches onto the most prominent tree trunk. I would paint two or three at a time, then immediately scrape bark texture into them with a palette knife before they dried.

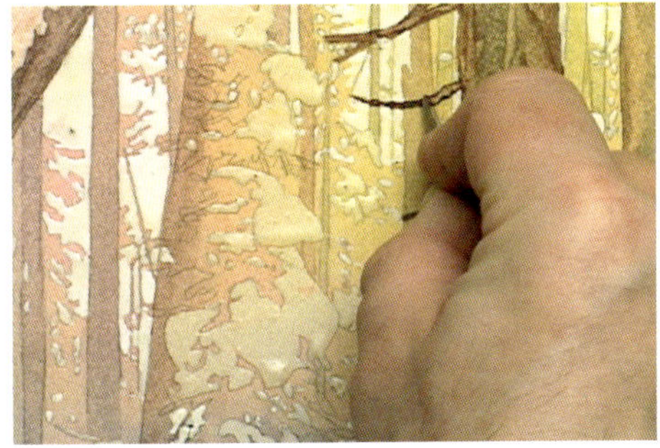

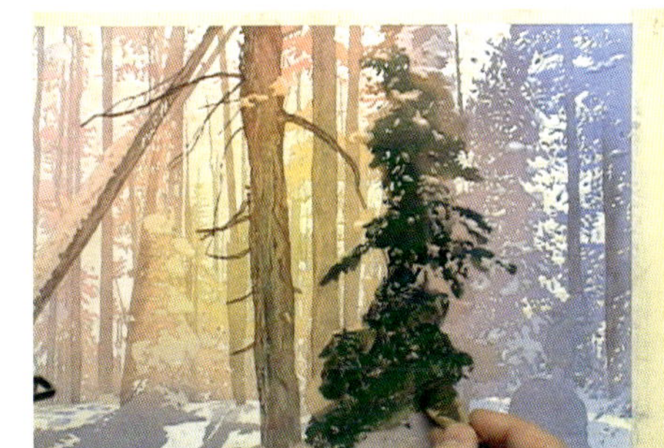

(Step 16 continued)

Here I switched to Ultramarine Blue and Ultramarine Green...

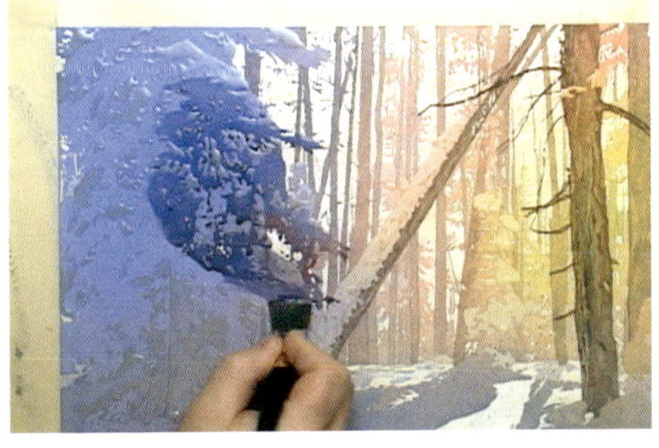

**Step 16:** Next, I painted in the tree foliage colors. Beginning with the left side, I started with a mix of Cobalt Blue and Rose, using a 3/4" flat brush.

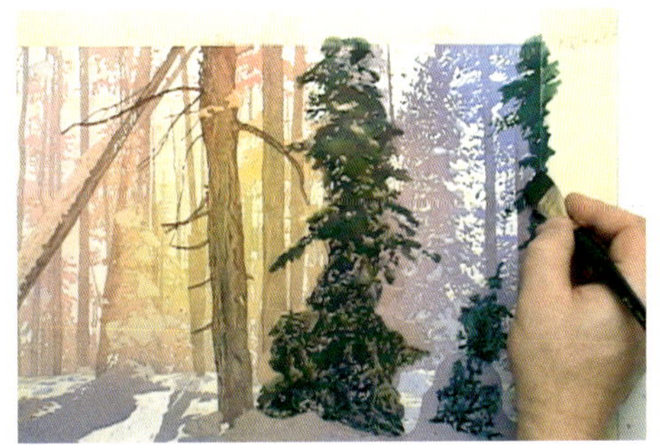

then back to Phthalo Blue and Phthalo Green.

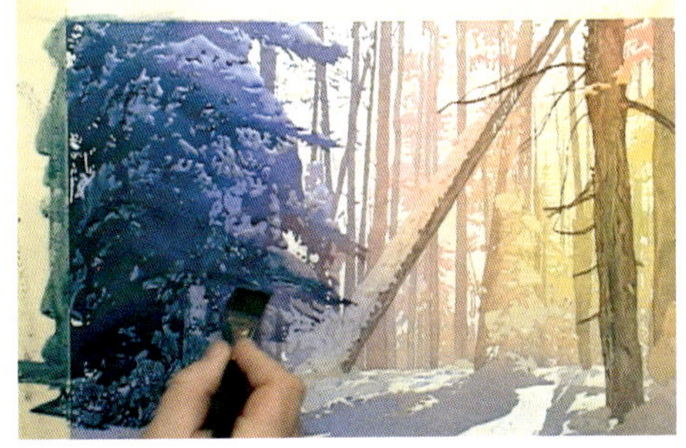

As I worked towards the left, I merged these colors with Phthalo Blue and Phthalo Green.

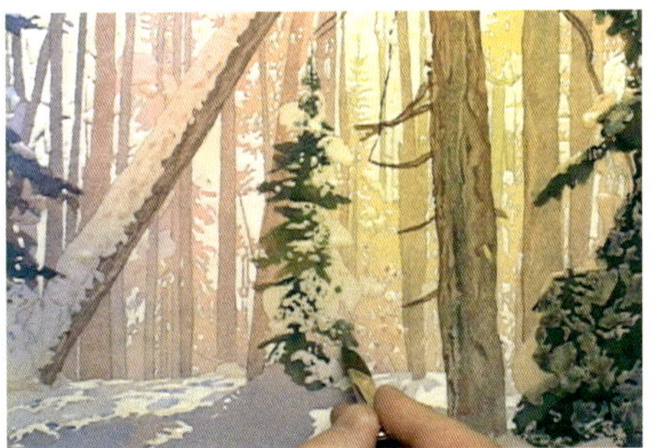

For the more distant foliage, I used a mix of Cobalt Blue and Cobalt Green, applied with a 1/2" flat brush.

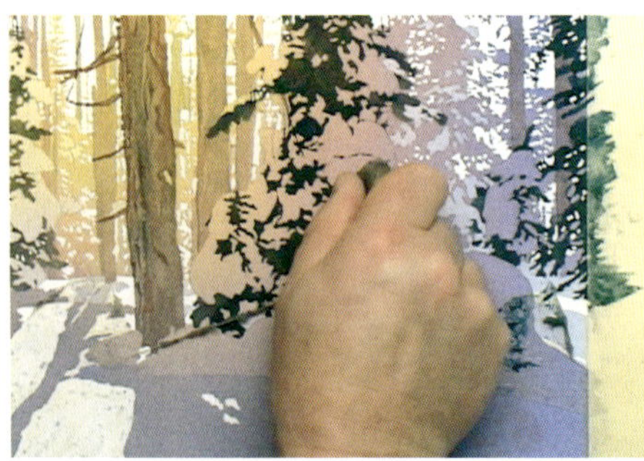

**Step 17:** With all of the painting's base colors applied, I next peeled off the masking. This exposed snow shapes that required some subtle shaping.

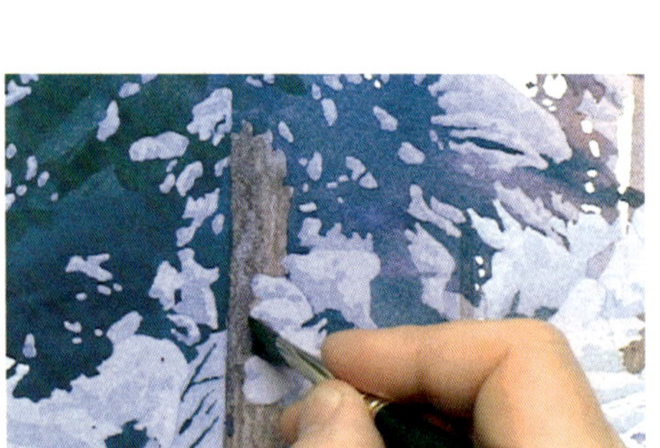

**Step 18:** Using a lean mix of Cobalt Blue and a 1/2" flat brush, I sorted various sections of snow from one another. Typically, I would separate two areas with a

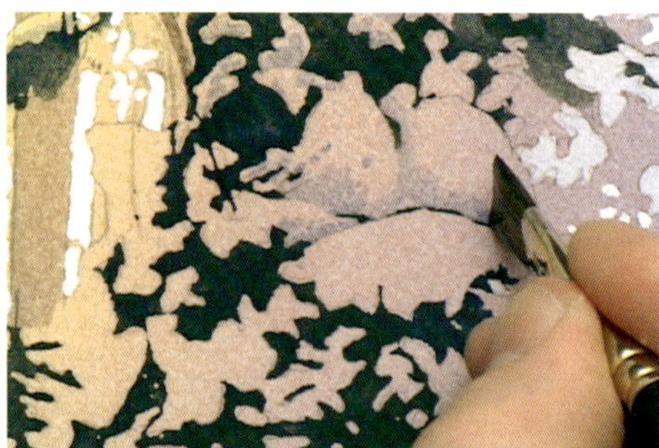

(Step 18 continued)

hard edge, then lose the shade's other edges by dabbing them with a tissue or diluting them with a water-loaded brush.

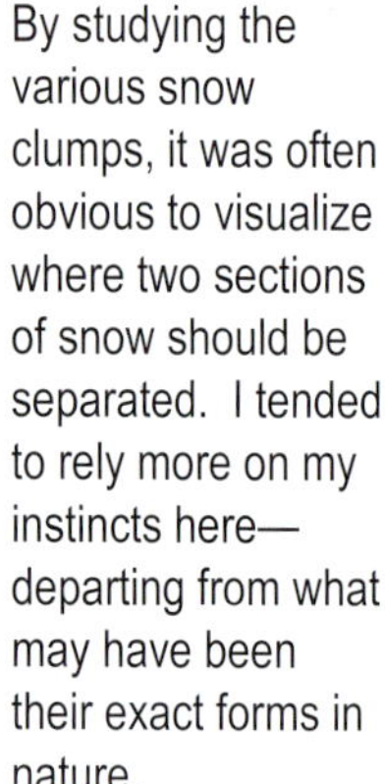

By studying the various snow clumps, it was often obvious to visualize where two sections of snow should be separated. I tended to rely more on my instincts here—departing from what may have been their exact forms in nature.

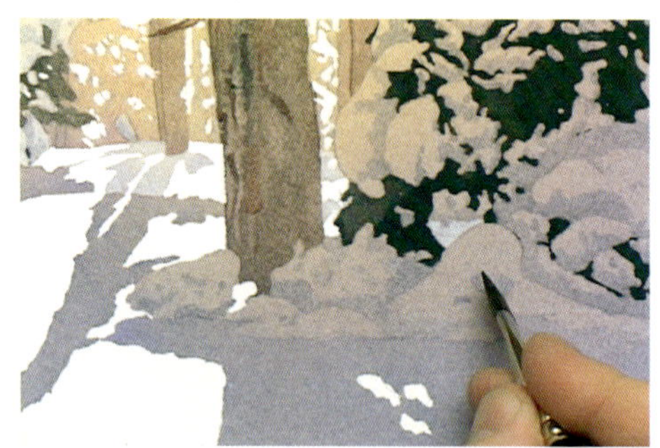

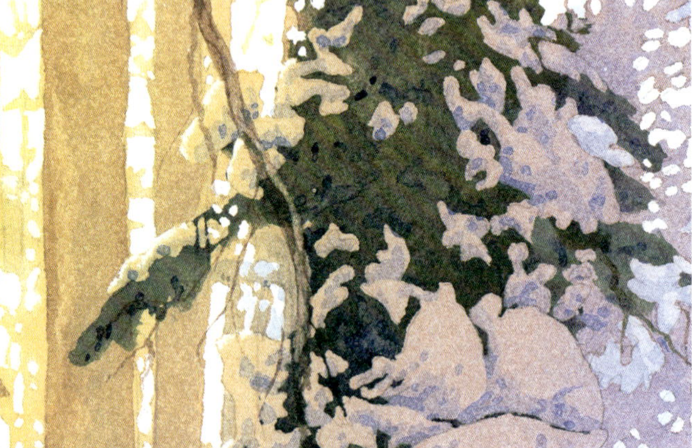

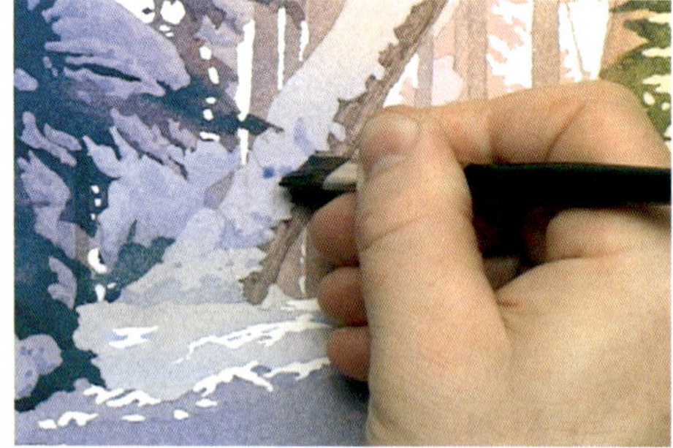

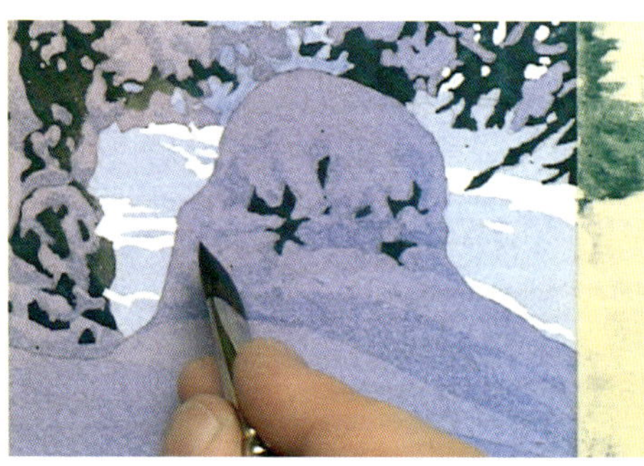

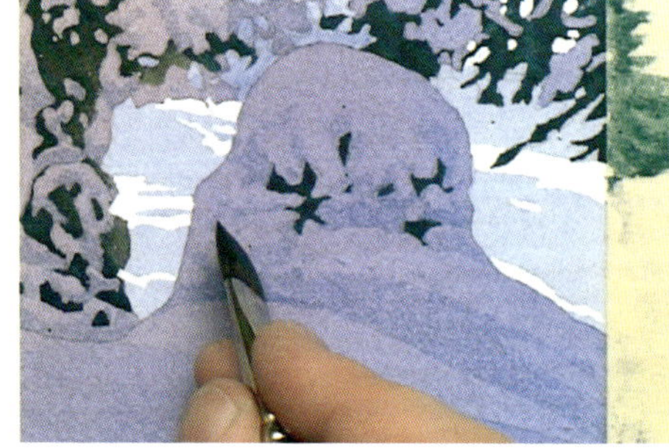

After the first round of sorting was completed, I went back through the snow clumps and added more shade details. These tended to be shades within the previously shaded areas. I was careful to not cover the entire snow clump shape with Cobalt Blue, which—used in excess— would undermine the impact of initial bull's eye washes.

Without the subtle shade details, the snow clumps would have appeared flat—thus lessening the effectiveness of the painting's overall depth of field.

Removal of the masking revealed all of the painting's color values together for the first time. The effectiveness of its depth of field was now apparent. What remained was, essentially, detailed finish-work.

To soften the shadow's edges, I used a variety of stiff-bristled scrubbing brush sizes. If the shape size permitted, I may have also used a toothbrush. But, I always continuously study the shapes as I progress with the scrubbing, as it is easy to scrub too much. Similar to the carpenter's adage of "measure twice, cut once!", I would argue to "look twice, scrub once!" A little scrubbing can go a long way!

While scrubbing, if I smeared paint onto the white snow areas, I simply scrubbed the spot and lifted the paint with a tissue—preferably while it was still wet. Of course, it is important to always use clean water when scrubbing around whites.

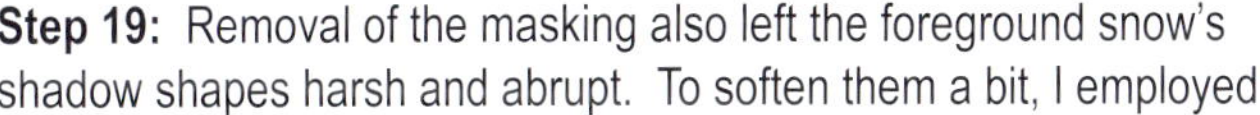

**Step 19:** Removal of the masking also left the foreground snow's shadow shapes harsh and abrupt. To soften them a bit, I employed various sized stiff-bristled scrubbing brushes. I dipped them in clean water, then scrubbed away at the shadow's edges. As I scrubbed, I frequently dabbed up the lifted paint with a tissue.

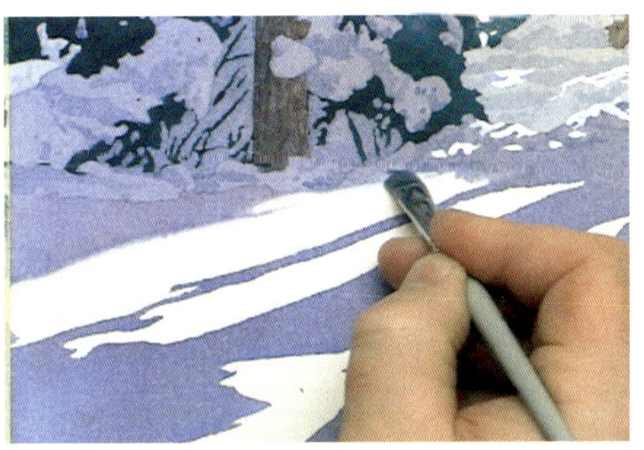

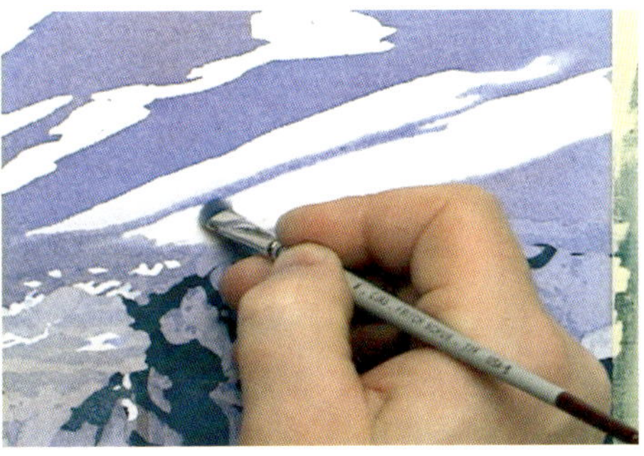

Often, I found it useful to tip the painting upside down so that I could scrub at the upper edges of the shadows more effortlessly.

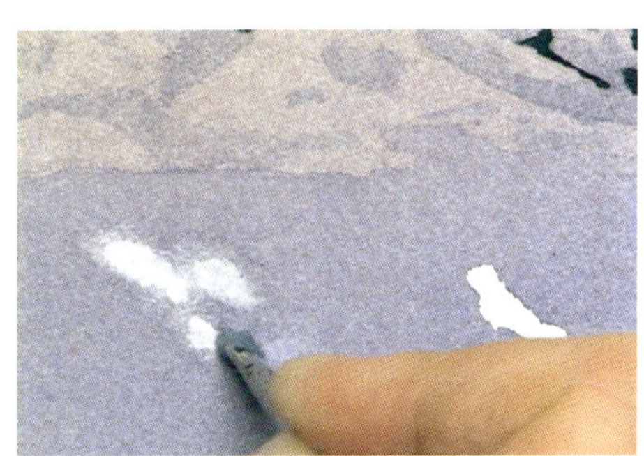

(Step 19 continued)

For smaller sunlit spots, I softened the edges with a smaller scrubbing brush.

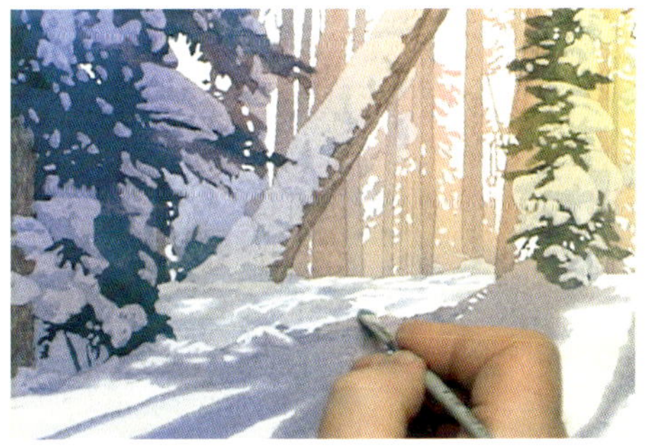

I tended to soften all of the shadow edges in the foreground of both large and small shapes.

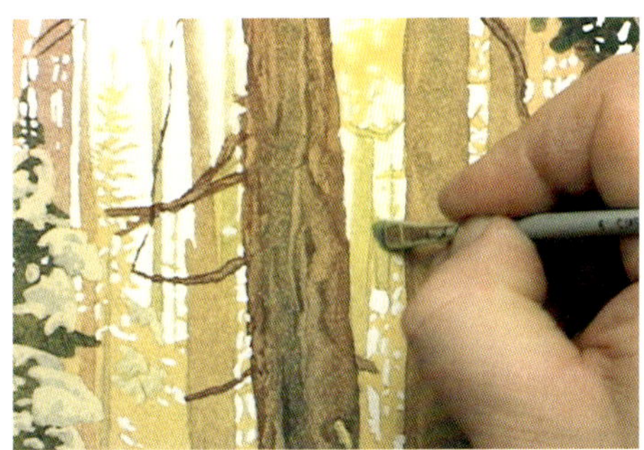

**Step 20:** Then, with a small scrubbing brush, I also softened the backlight shapes that represented where the sun was shining through the trees. The further I worked from the sun's center, the less I scrubbed.

I really did not provide much shade detail; rather I only implied areas of depth within the trees. Again, these simple details help the viewer recognize depth, while leaving much to imagination.

It was important to not make the snow clump shade details too numerous or too dark. I wanted them to be subtle—to only imply dimension. Excessively dark snow shade details would have introduced a distracting element to the overall painting.

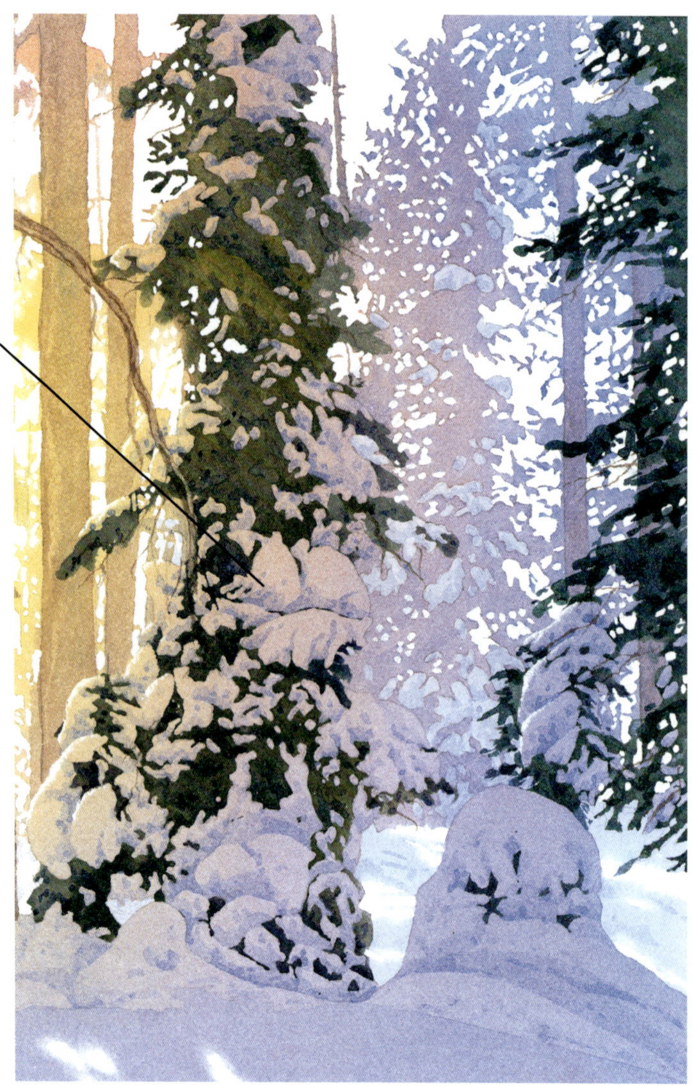

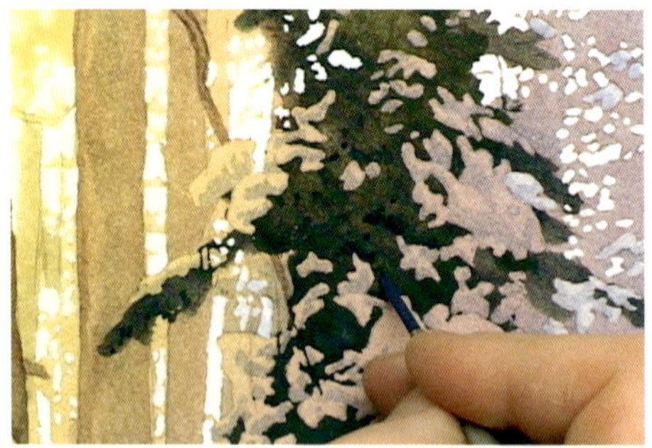

**Step 21:** As I did with the snow clump shapes, I added some darker values to the tree greens to imply depth and dimension. Here, using a mix of Ultramarine Blue and Ultramarine Green with a #2 rigger brush, I highlighted areas that tended to be on the underside of vaguely defined branch shapes.

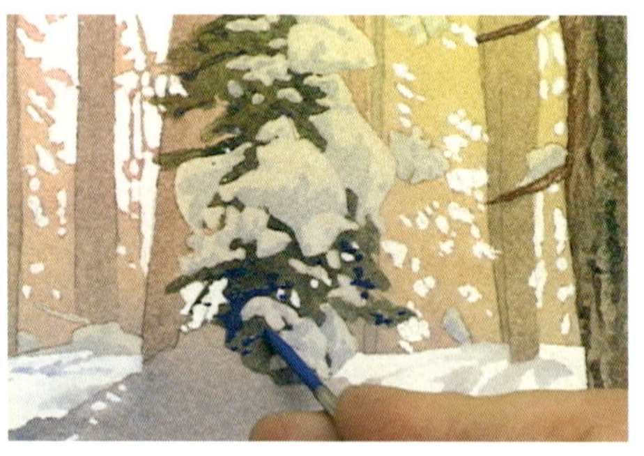

I shaded with the same colors as the tree's base colors: Cobalt Blue and Cobalt Green here…

and Phthalo Blue and Phthalo Green here.

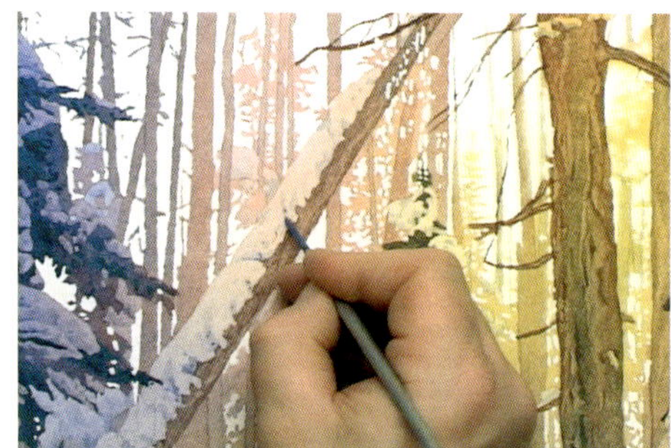

**Step 22:** Continuing with a #2 rigger brush—this time loaded with Cobalt Blue—I painted in more snow clump shade details. These, again, tended to be painted within the previously shaded areas. I consciously tried to limit these additional details as they can easily be overdone. I did not want the snow shapes to look too busy.

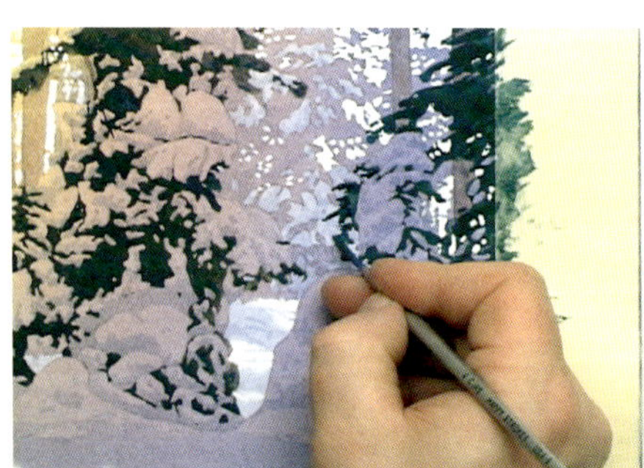

With the masking removed, I also took the opportunity to extend some of the branches to better shape the tree.

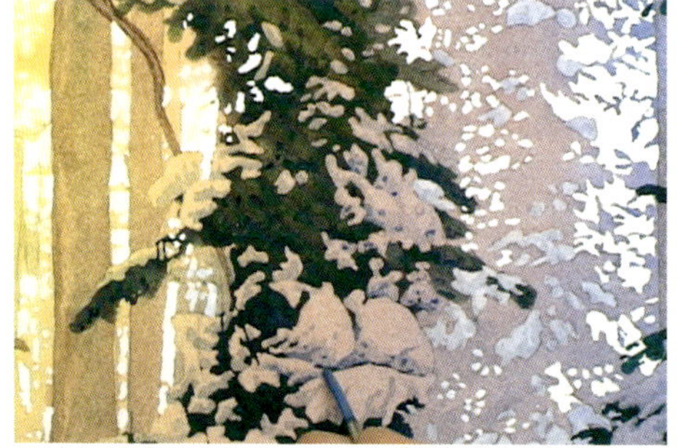

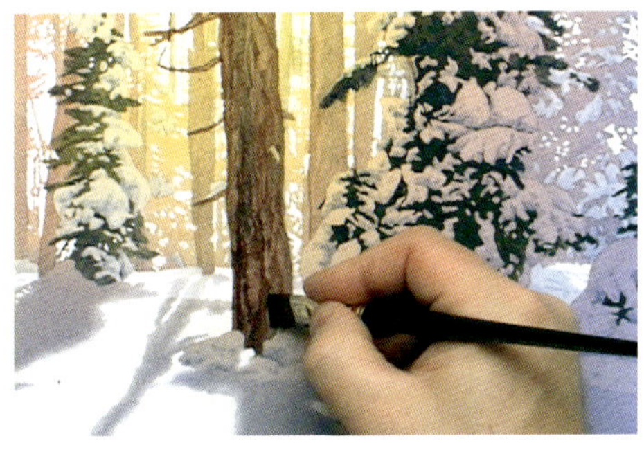

**Step 23:** Beginning the final "touch-up" phase of the painting, I noticed that the most prominent tree trunk needed some shape modification. I believe that I had initially read the drawing wrong, making the trunk a bit too narrow in one area. But this shape anomaly was easily resolved. To alter its existing shape, I employed the tree trunk colors—Brown Madder and Phthalo Blue—and a 1/2" flat brush. I simply filled in the omitted area of trunk, then blended the colors into the previous trunk colors. Quickly, I scraped additional bark texture lines into the new paint. This also helped the repair job blend more naturally into the previously painted area.

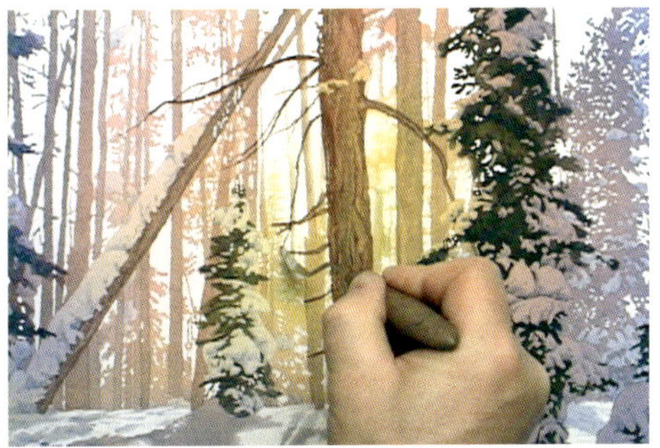

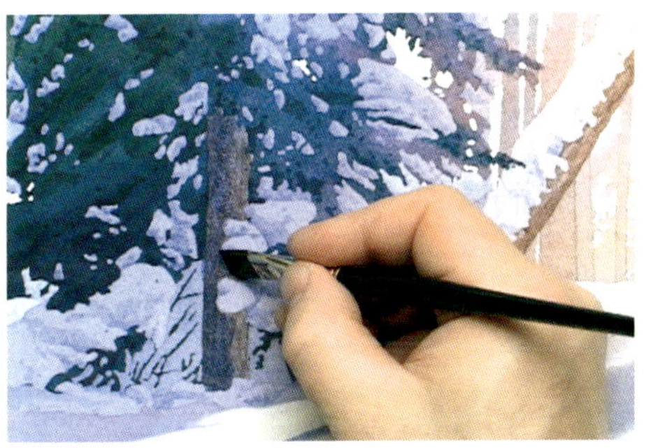

**Step 24:** Next, I shaded with Cobalt Blue any obvious downlight sides of objects, such as this tree trunk.

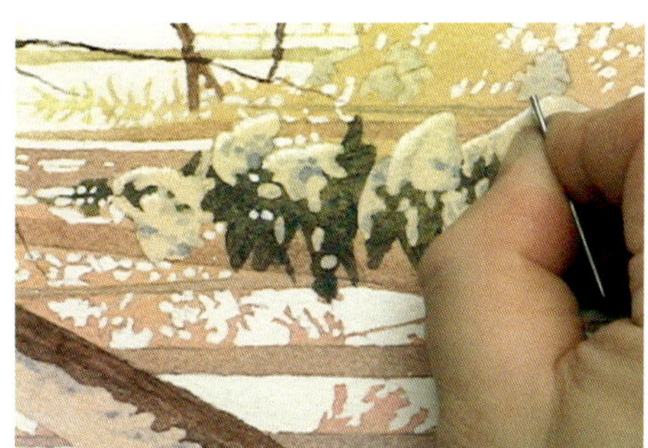

**Step 25:** To emphasize the direct sunlight that came through the trees, I highlighted the edges of some of the snow clumps by scraping them with a single-edged razor blade. I would carefully and lightly scrape, but still I purposely cut down into the white of the paper. Depending on the position of the shape, often this was easier to accomplish by tipping the painting.

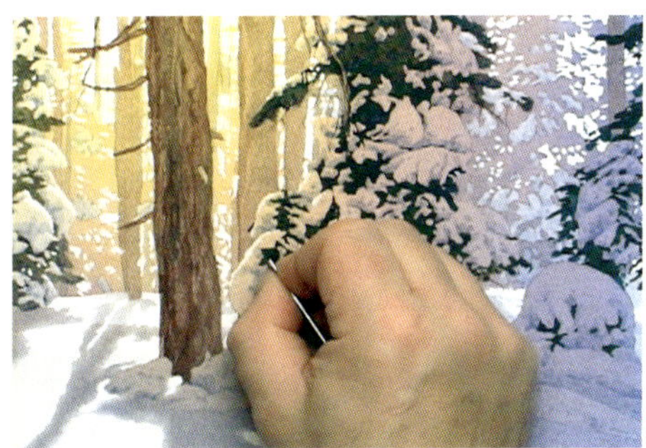

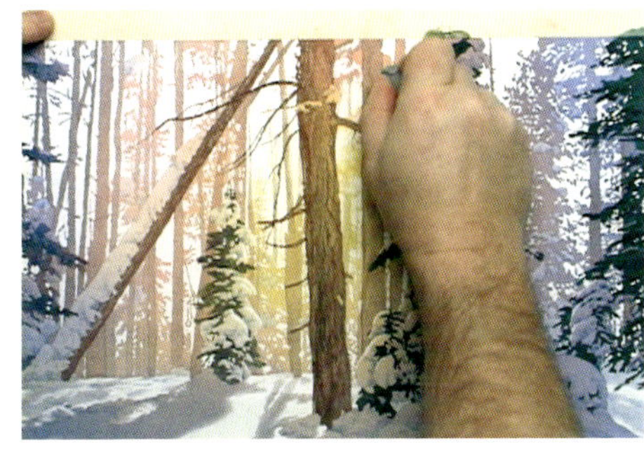

**Step 26:** Finally, I completed the painting by using a kneaded eraser to remove any pencil lines that were still visible.

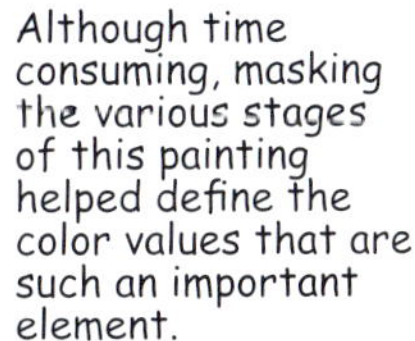

Although time consuming, masking the various stages of this painting helped define the color values that are such an important element.

Each of the subtle differences in value helps establish the painting's depth of field. Often with watercolor paintings, success is narrowly defined by these subtleties.

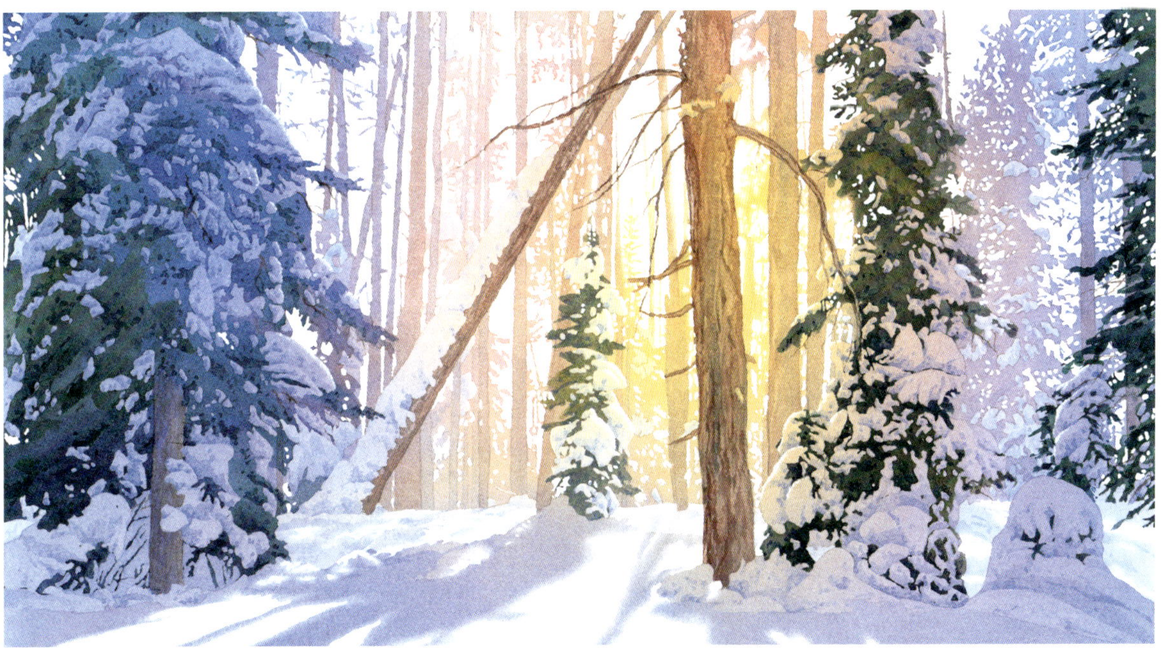

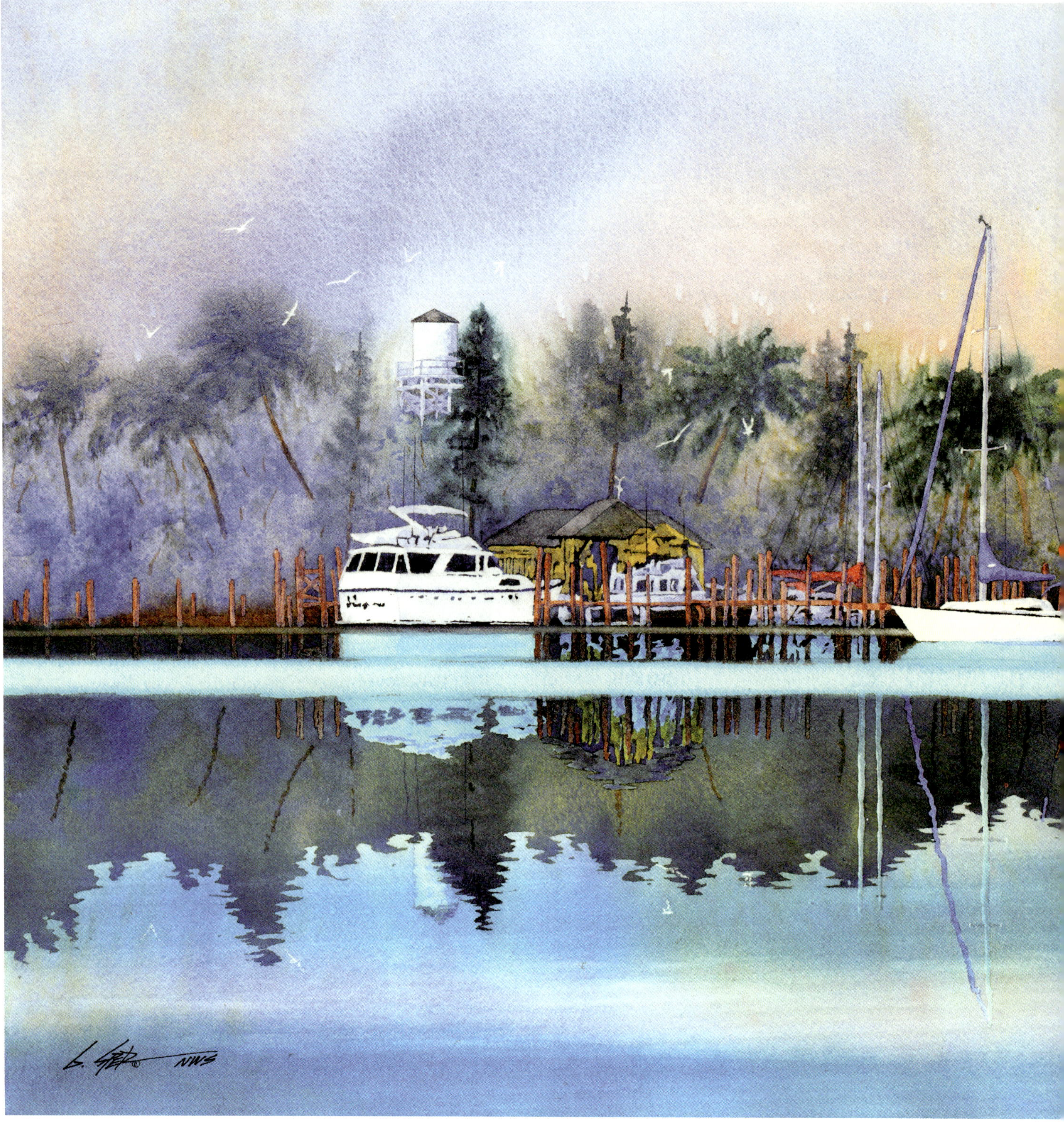

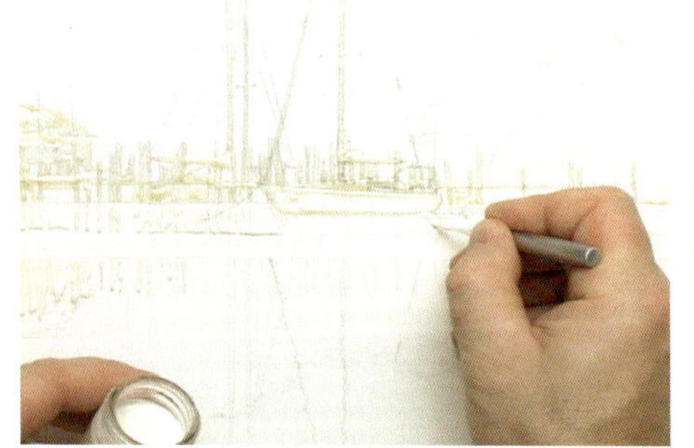

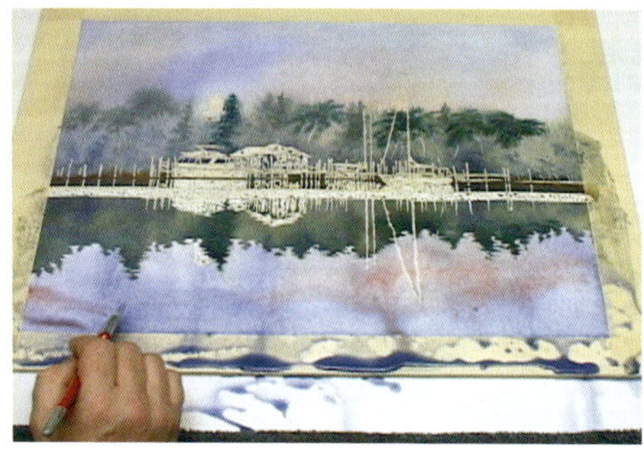

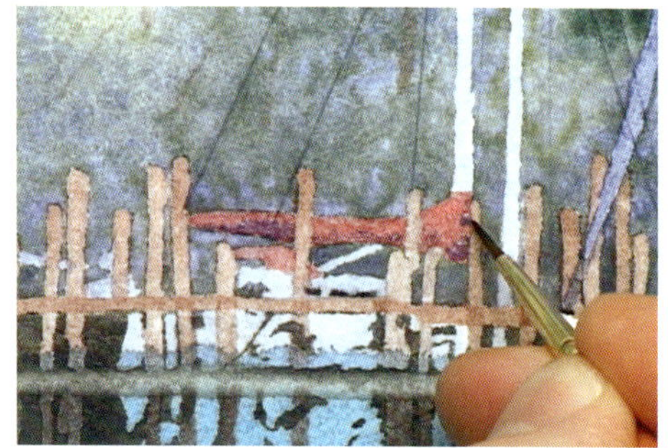

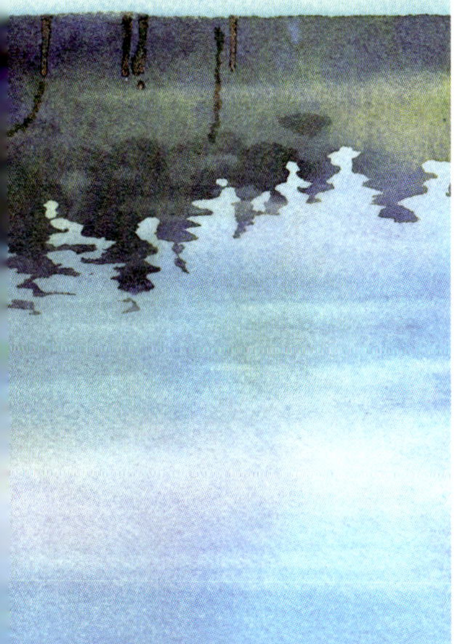

# CABBAGE KEY

One of the great advantages of using masking fluid with watercolors is that it enables me to control recognizable shapes, such as a boat, a dock, a water tower or a building. Once these shapes are protected, I can freely paint in things like the trees and the sky, without concern of painting over crucial shapes.

Without masking, the sky and trees in this painting of Cabbage Key might be hard to "read." There would not be enough recognizable shapes. But when the protective masking was peeled off, the painting came together to make sense to the viewer. This lesson demonstrates how one can create a fairly detailed painting, while still leaving most of the space quite loose.

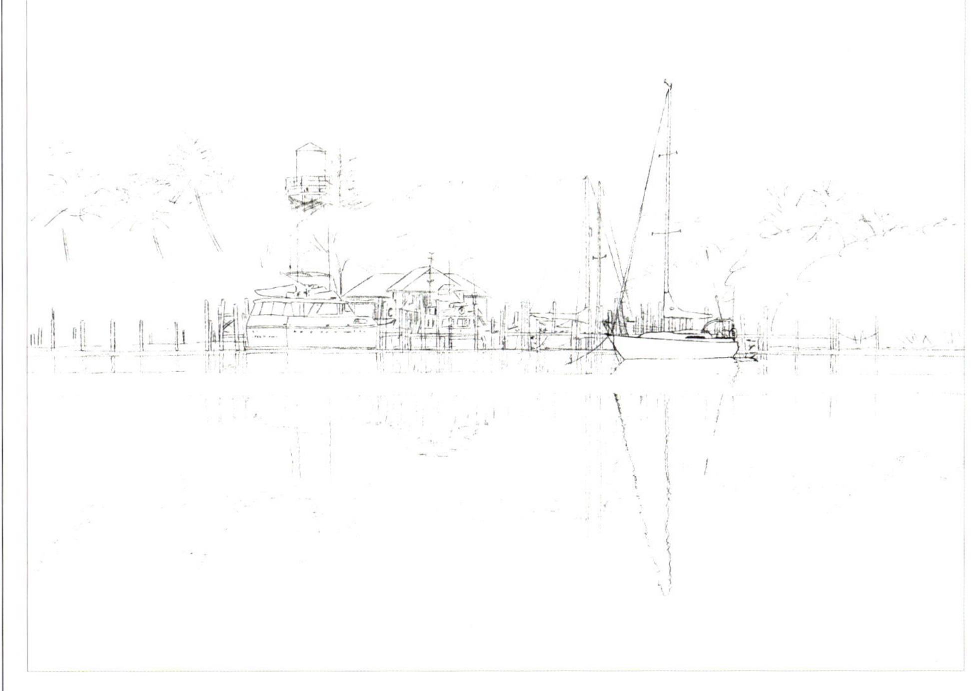

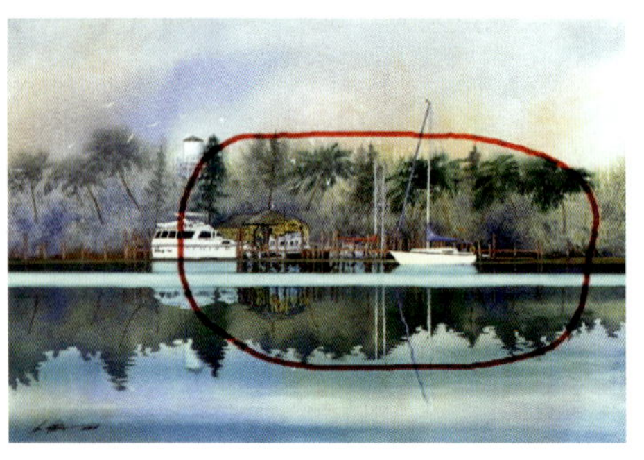

**Step 1:** I drew my composition out on the watercolor paper after marking the horizontal and vertical center points on the sides of the painting. The shoreline was kept below center and the sailboat focal point was kept below and to the right of center. The foliage was painted darker on the right two-thirds of the composition to help shift the focal point in this direction.

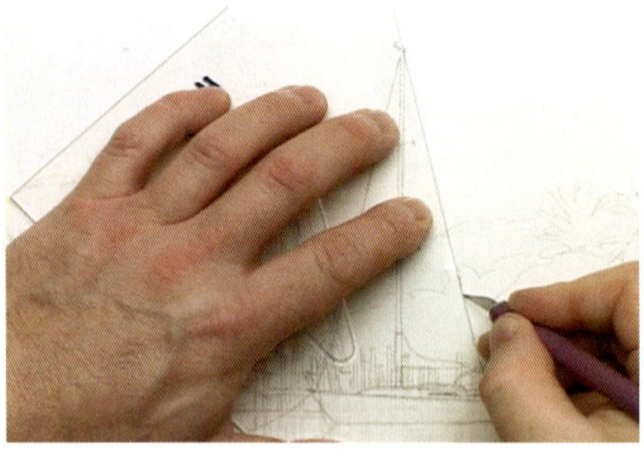

**Step 2:** Using a straightedge and an exacto-knife, I carefully scraped the many sailboat riggings. Although nearly invisible when I created them, they filled and disproportionately darkened with paint after I applied the sky wash. "Close does not count" here, so I planned these carefully before scraping.

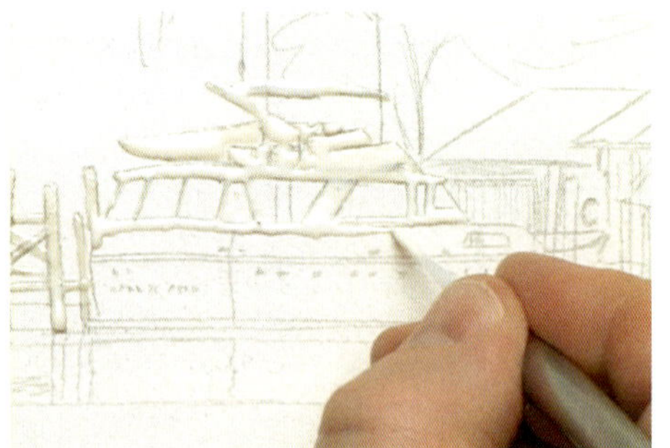

**Step 3:** With liquid masking fluid and a plastic toothpick, I meticulously masked out each of the man-made objects in this painting.

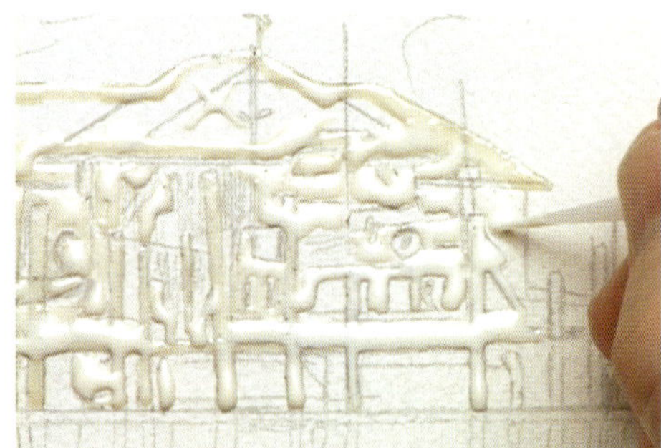

(Step 3 continued)

On the marina building, I masked out the various shapes that were apparently of a lighter value. I was not always certain as to what these varied shapes were, but since the building was so distant from the viewer, it did not require much detail. So, I simply focused on depicting the values of these (unknown) details.

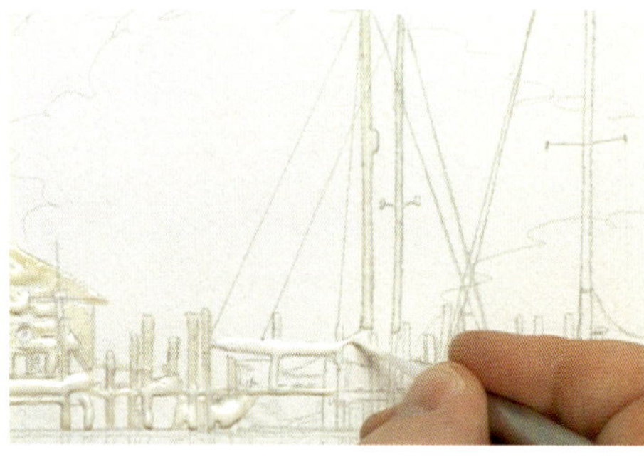

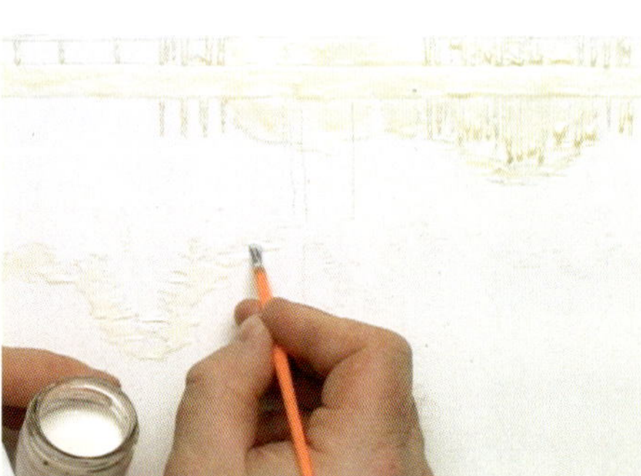

Then with a disposable paintbrush, I masked out the sky's reflection in the water. I first followed and masked the tree's jagged edges and then I quickly filled in the remainder of the paper below the tree line's reflection.

It is a good idea to first practice the scraping of rigging lines. Since they are virtually invisible until paint is applied to them, it is essential that you know that you are scraping them correctly the first time. A misplaced rigging against a painting's sky could be irreversible. But, done correctly, this can be a very convincing way to depict rigging and other subjects.

After the masking had dried, I rubbed my hand through the sky area to detect any errant drops of masking fluid that may have accidentally landed there.

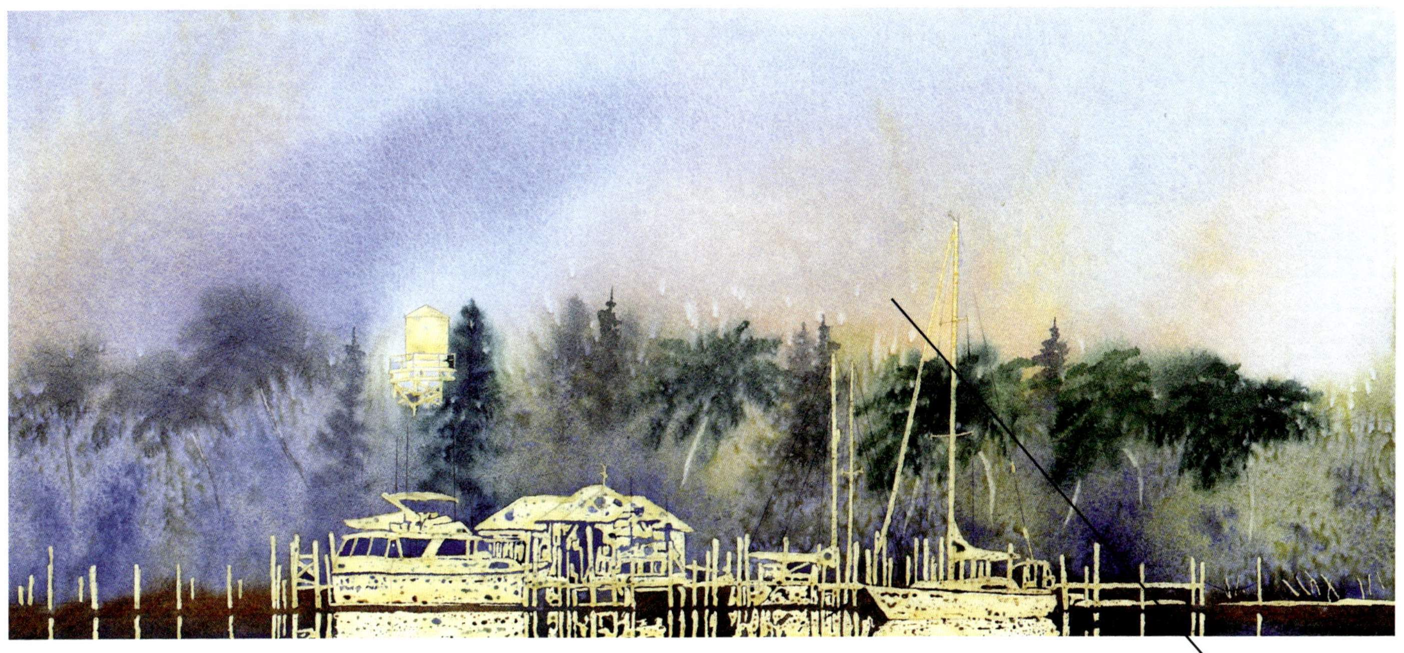

Skies offer a great opportunity to introduce broad colors into a painting, shifting its overall color emphasis. I am usually guilty of taking great liberties in my depictions of skies, paying little attention to the way they had actually had appeared.

I was careful to not center prominent colors like the Rose or Yellow Ochre.

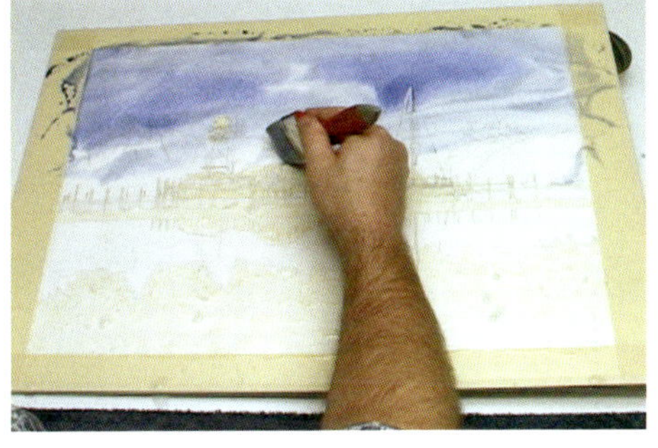

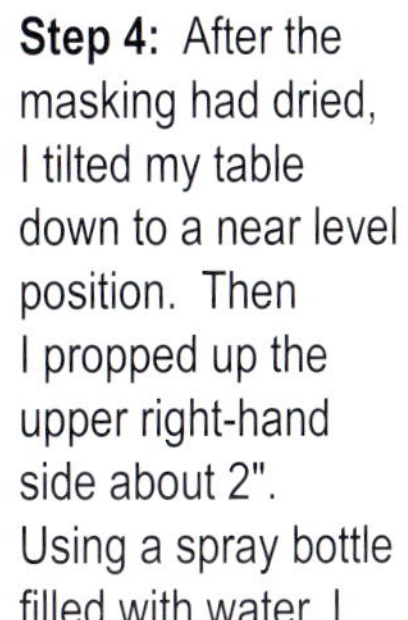

**Step 4:** After the masking had dried, I tilted my table down to a near level position. Then I propped up the upper right-hand side about 2". Using a spray bottle filled with water, I saturated the entire painting's surface.

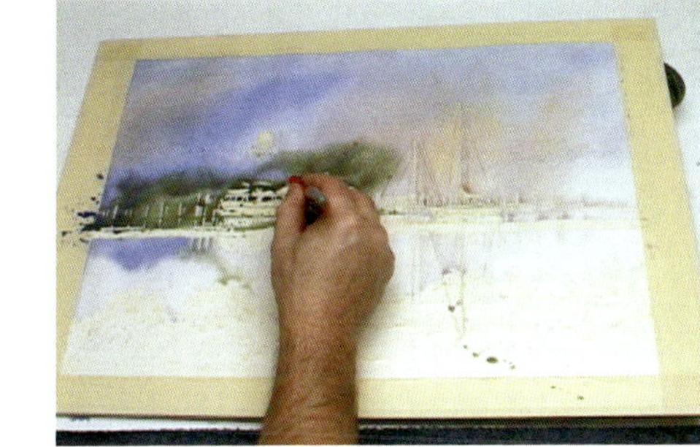

**Step 6:** Moving quickly before the sky dried, I began working in my base foliage colors, beginning with a rich mix of Cobalt Blue and Cobalt Green. These colors blended slightly with the sky color above.

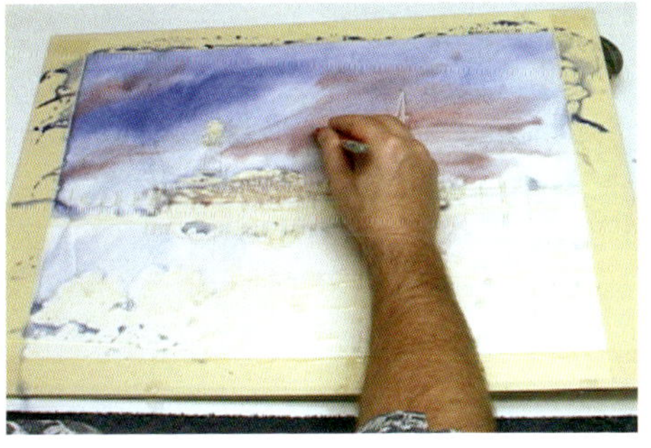

**Step 5:** Quickly, while the paper was still very wet, I began working streaks of Cobalt Blue onto the sky area with my 2" flat brush. I did not cover the entire sky, as I wanted to leave much of the paper's white surface visible. On the still-wet paper, I added some Rose, allowing it to blend slightly with the blue.

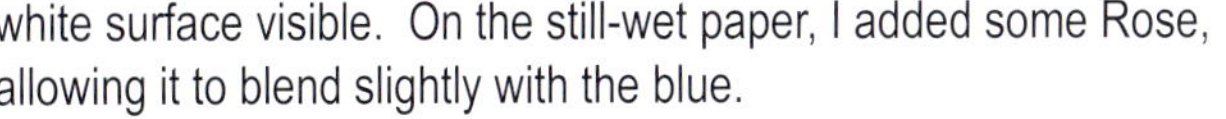

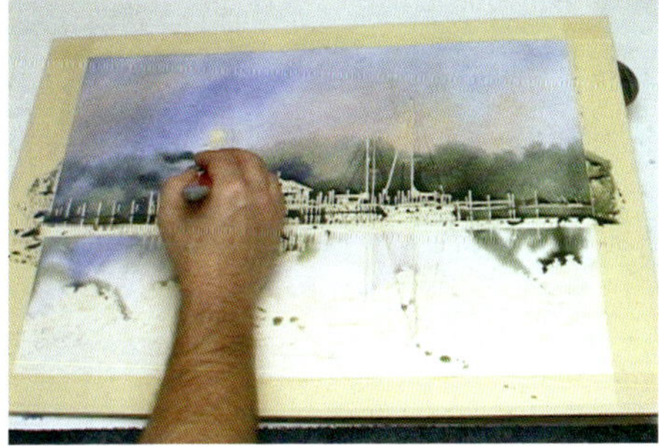

As I worked towards the right, I switched to a rich mix of Ultramarine Blue and Ultramarine Green, then finally Phthalo Blue and Phthalo Green.

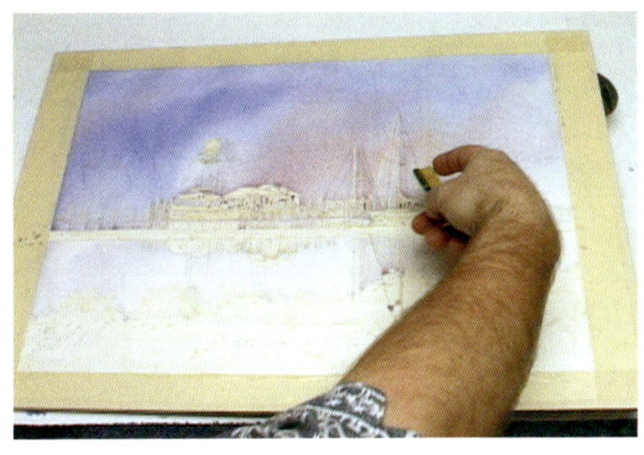

Then, with a toothbrush, I "flicked" Yellow Ochre onto the lower right-hand side of the sky.

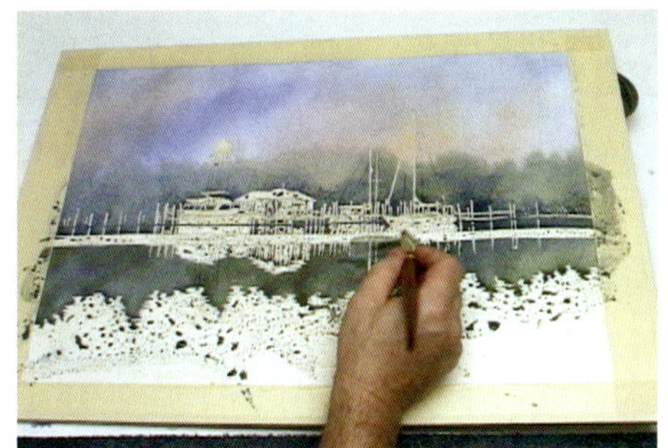

With a 1-1/4" flat brush, I mimicked the same colors in their reflection below.

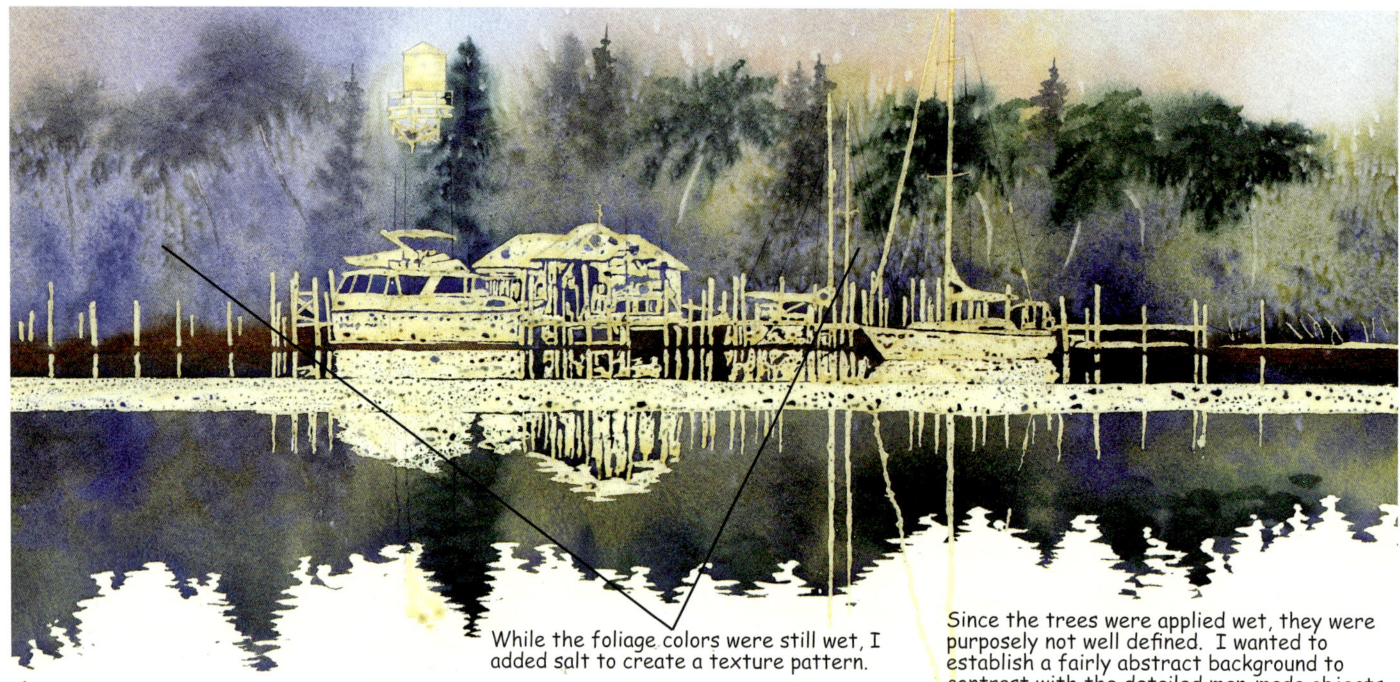

While the foliage colors were still wet, I added salt to create a texture pattern.

Since the trees were applied wet, they were purposely not well defined. I wanted to establish a fairly abstract background to contrast with the detailed man-made objects.

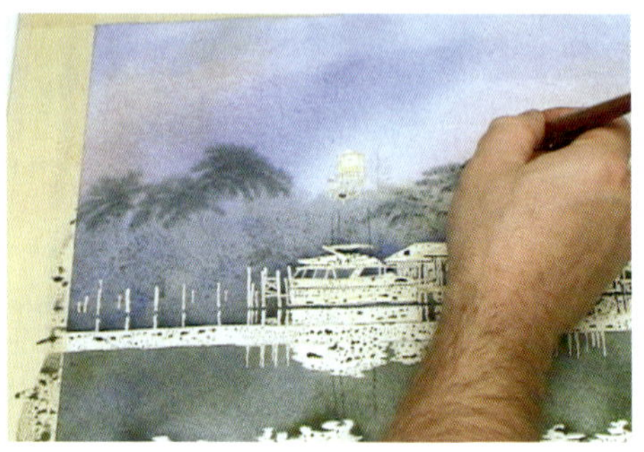

**Step 7:** While the foliage colors were still damp, I began painting in palm treetops with a #2 rigger brush. These shapes softened as they blended with the underlying colors. I used a mix of Cobalt Blue and Cobalt Green on the left side, then switched over to Ultramarine Blue and Ultramarine Green as I worked towards the right. Eventually on the right side, I worked in some palm tops with the vivid Phthalo Blue and Phthalo Green.

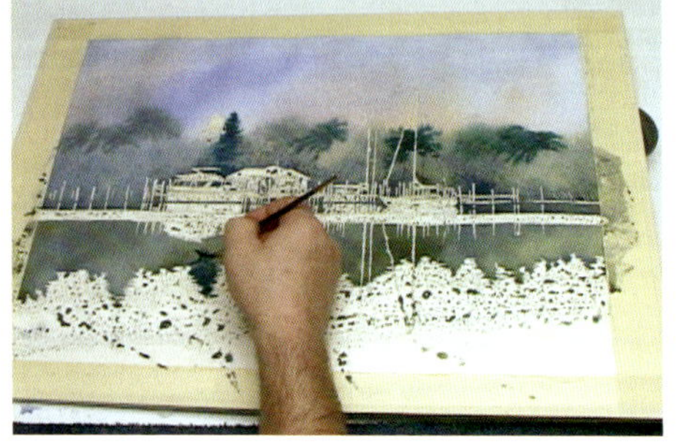

I also pulled some pine trees with the rigger brush. First I would pull the trunk upward, then I would literally smash in the branches as I worked downward on the tree. The smashed branches gave the trees a more realistic appearance than would have occurred if I had pulled the branches outward, as well.

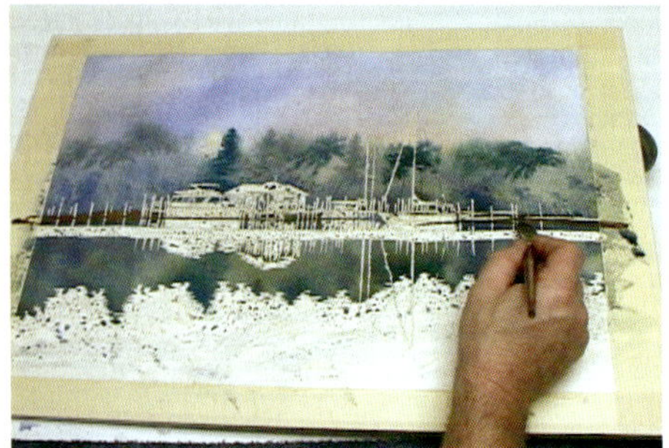

In the midst of working on the trees, I quickly laid in a rich mix of Burnt Sienna and Ultramarine Blue with a 3/4" flat brush to represent the shoreline.

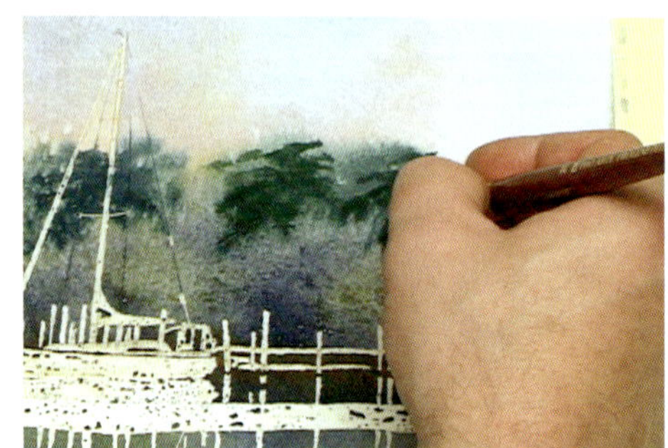

(Step 7 continued)

Since the paper was slowly drying, I did not work the trees in one area too long. Rather, I jumped around the full width of the foliage. But, I did weight the tree's values towards the right side.

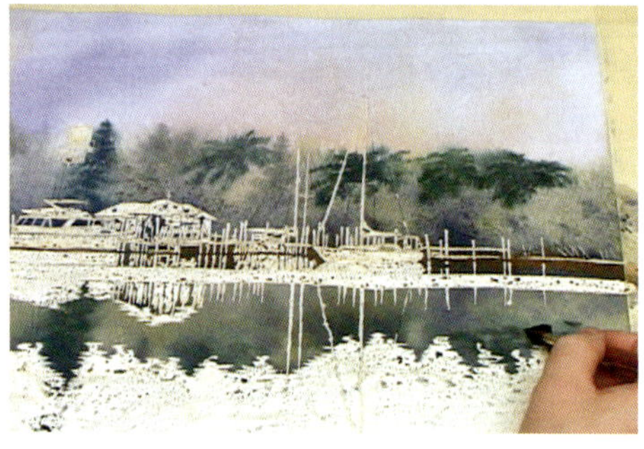

As I worked across, I also mimicked the same colors in their reflection below.

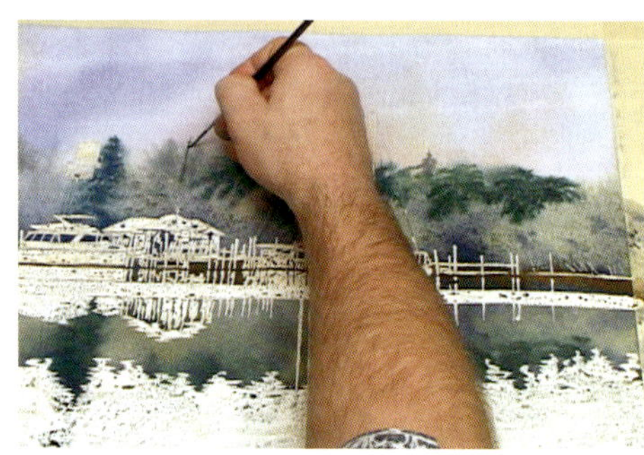

As the underlying foliage colors dried, the added trees blended less and became more defined.

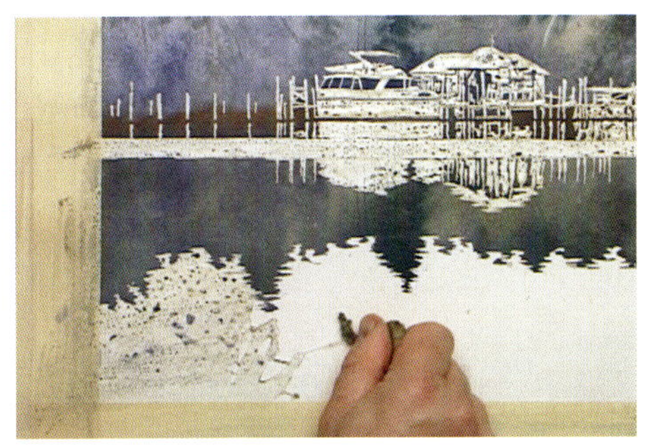

**Step 8:** After drying these colors, I peeled off the masking that covered the sky reflection area. While doing this, I held down the sailboat mast reflections with my thumb—in the tree reflection area—to prevent them from being peeled off, too.

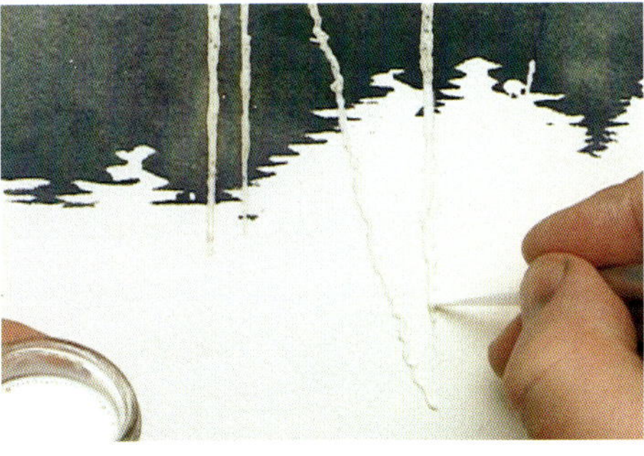

**Step 9:** Then, I re-masked the sailboat masts where needed. Since I was able to hold down most of their protective masking from the previous step, only the reflections of their tops needed to be masked again.

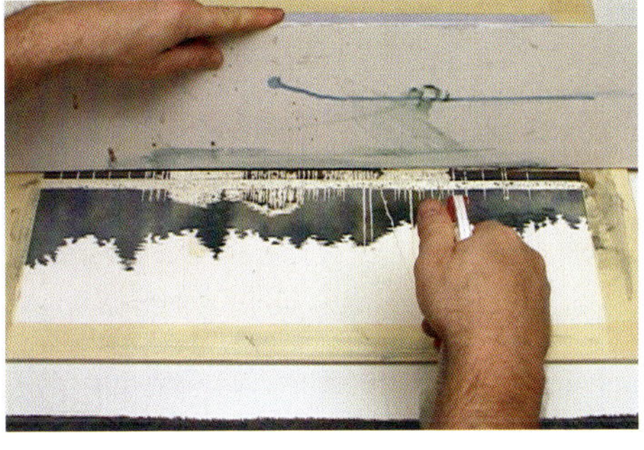

**Step 10:** Once this masking had dried, I saturated everything below the shoreline using a spray bottle filled with water. I held a piece of foamboard along the shoreline to prevent water from getting above.

While painting the sky's reflection, I kept my table in a level position, but I did prop up the top of the painting about 2".

It was better to pre-wet the reflection area and allow the sky reflection colors to flow through this wet surface, rather than brush them over the tree reflections. The brush strokes would have lifted some of the tree reflection colors.

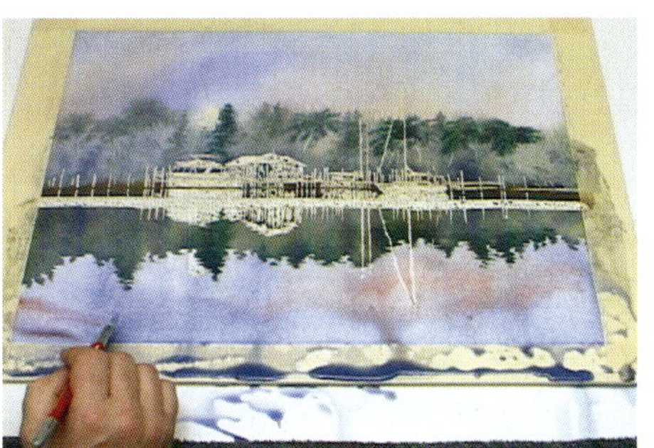

**Step 11:** Quickly, while the paper was still very wet, I began working in streaks of Cobalt Blue and Rose with a 2" flat brush. I tended to work only in the white area, keeping brush contact with the treetop reflections to a minimum. Of course, I tried to mimic the colors in the sky above.

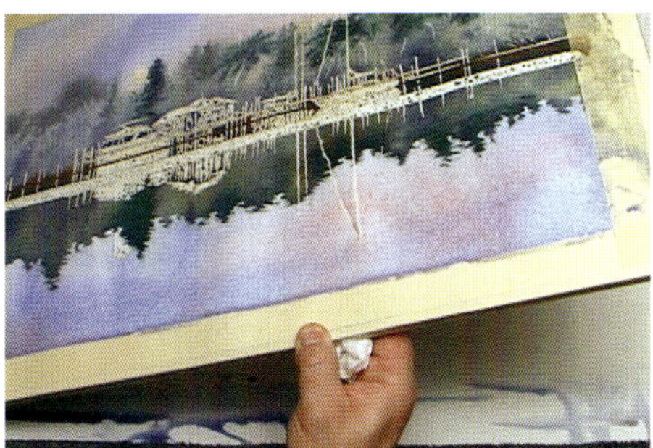

**Step 12:** While the paper was still very wet, I tilted and rocked the painting to promote blending. This action allowed some of the sky reflection colors to blend into and over the tree reflection colors without distorting them.

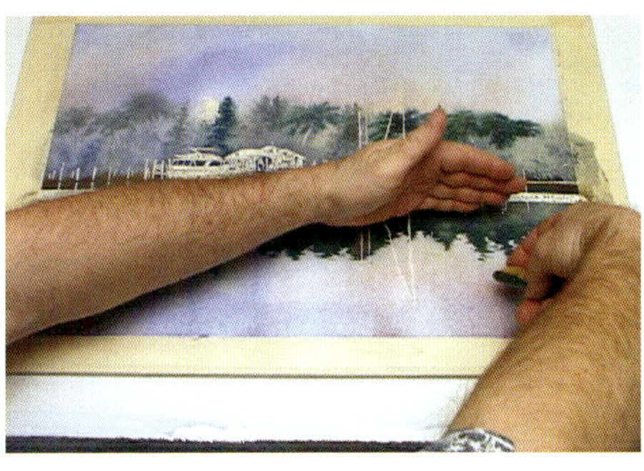

**Step 13:** With the paper still wet, I "flicked" some Yellow Ochre onto the sky's reflection with a toothbrush. Again, I tried to replicate the placement of the Yellow Ochre in the sky above. Once I had the look that I wanted, I locked the colors in by drying them with a blow drier.

On this step, I only peeled off the masking that covered the sky reflection area. I did not want to remove the masking from the dock, boats or buildings, yet.

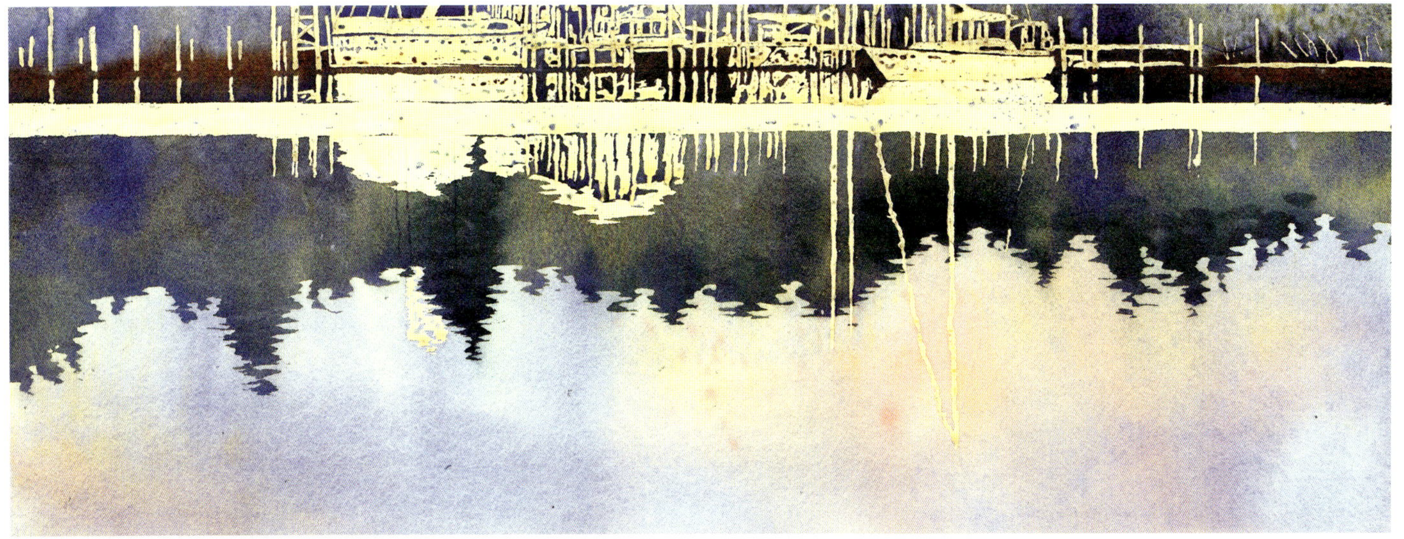

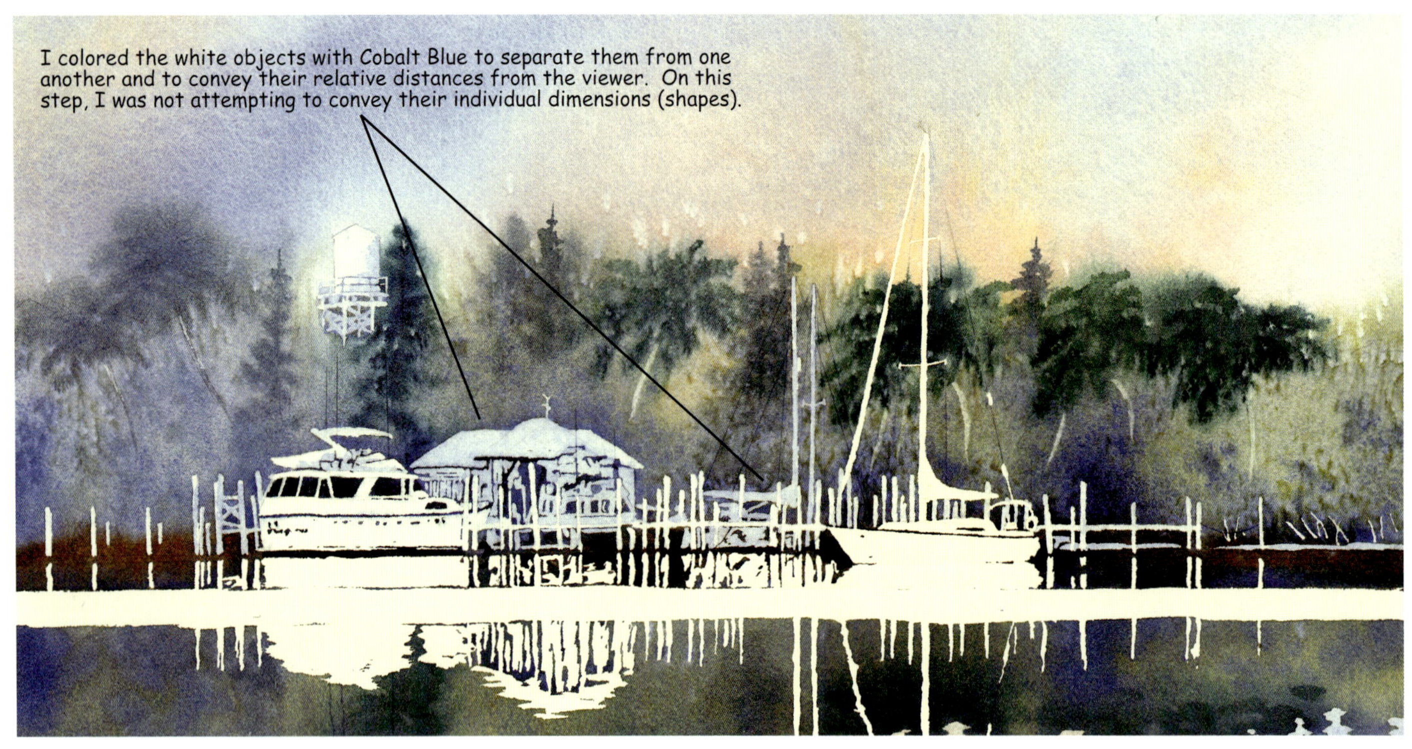


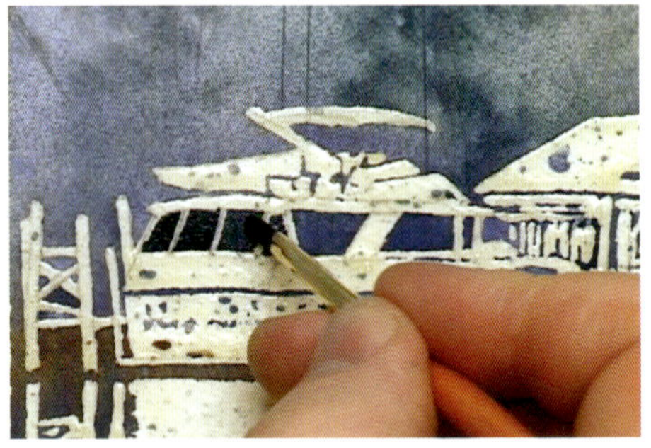

**Step 14:** Next, I painted in some dark areas under the docks and on the boats and buildings. This was easy to do since the masking was still protecting these shapes. With Payne's Gray and a 1/4" flat brush, I darkened the boat windows…

and I darkened some of the areas underneath the docks.

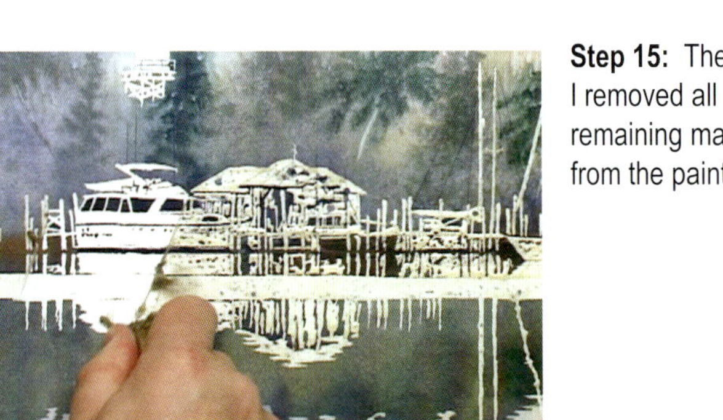

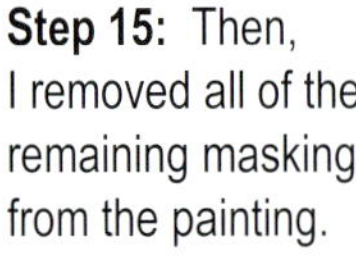

**Step 15:** Then, I removed all of the remaining masking from the painting.

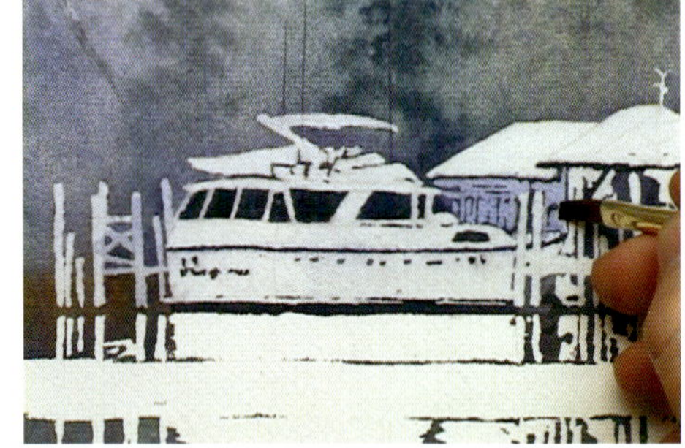

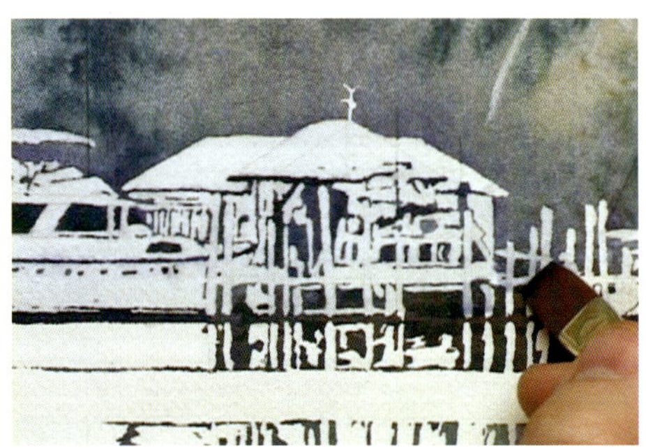

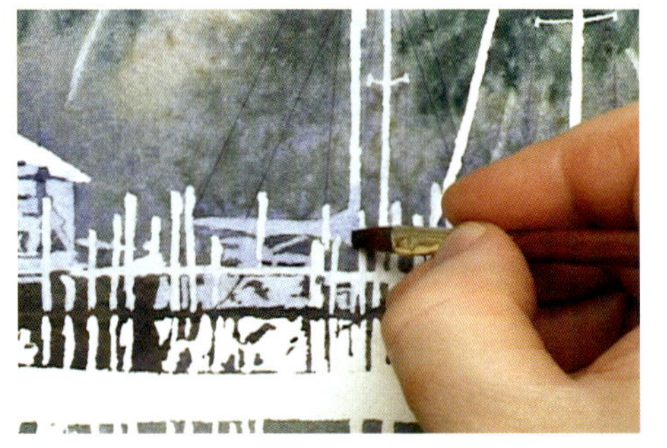

**Step 16:** Once the masking was removed, I had a large mass of recognizable shapes, but they were all the same value—thus making them flat. With a lean mix of Cobalt Blue and a 1/4" flat brush, I worked in subtle layers of color to distinguish the varying distances from the viewer. Since the lone sailboat (on the right side) was the closest subject to the viewer, I did not color it. But, I did give all of the other white objects a slight tint of blue. Then, I gave the next furthest set of items an additional layer of blue. As the subjects got further from the viewer, I made them progressively darker (bluer).

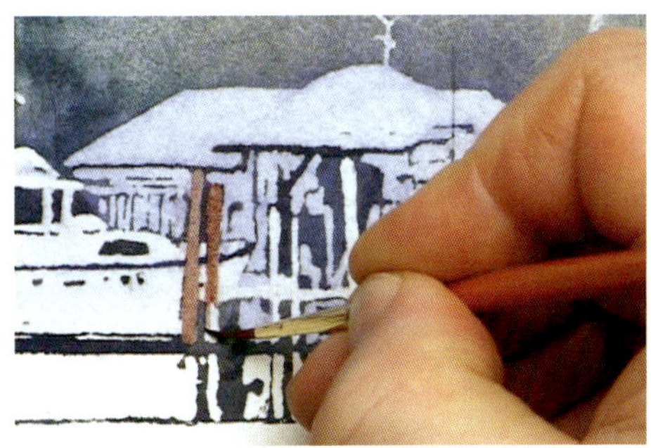

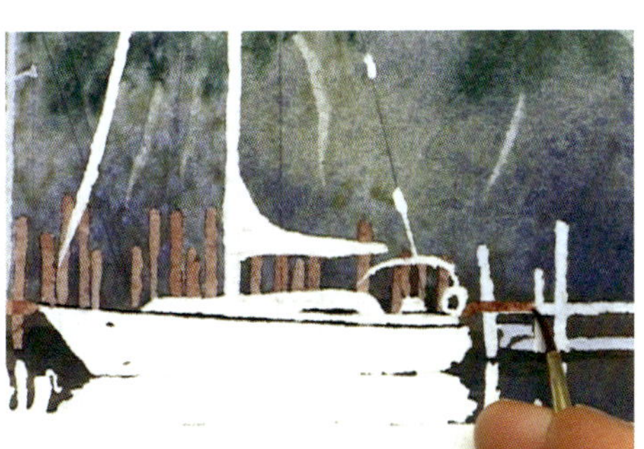

**Step 17:** Next, I sorted the various objects by coloring them. Using a 1/4" flat brush with a mix of Brown Madder and Phthalo Blue, I painted the dock and pilings. As I worked across them, I would vary the mix between the two colors only slightly. With these objects separated by color, the remaining objects became easier to identify.

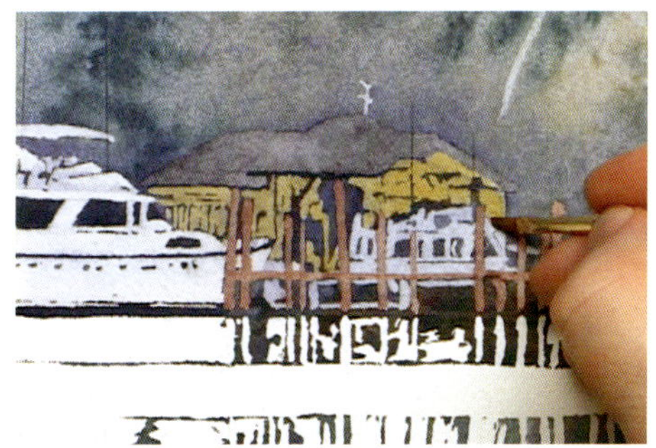

(Step 17 continued)

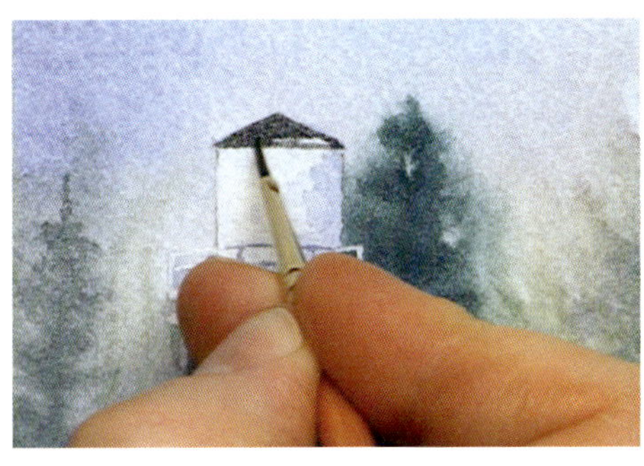

Switching to a #2 round brush, I painted in the base colors of the other objects. The roof of the water tower received Payne's Gray…

as did the roof of the marina building. I used Yellow Ochre on the building's walls.

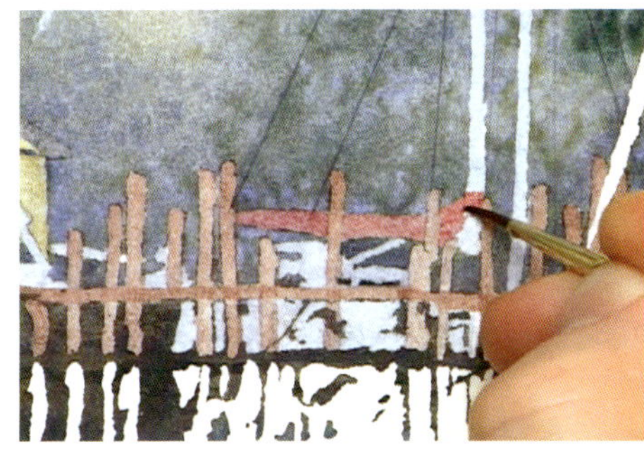

I also painted in this sail cover, using Rose…

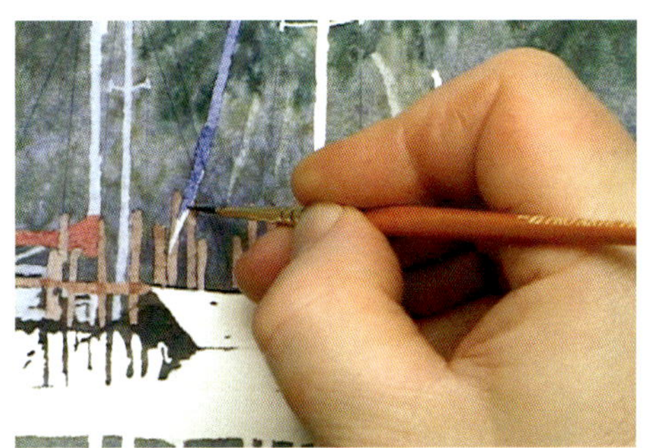

and this sail cover using Ultramarine Blue.

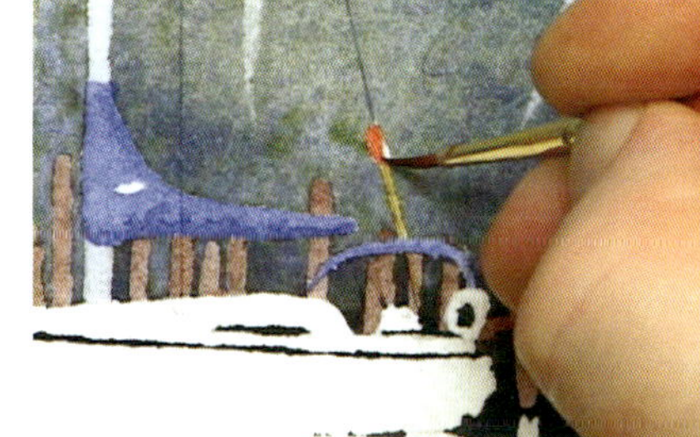

With a mix of Yellow Ochre and Rose, I painted in such details as this emergency overboard buoy.

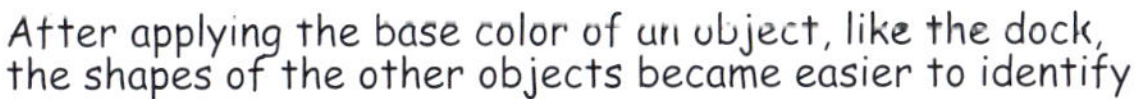

After applying the base color of an object, like the dock, the shapes of the other objects became easier to identify.

These objects could have been painted virtually any color. I often stray from a setting's actual colors—particularly when painting man-made objects. I chose to use colors that would stand out against the green foliage background.

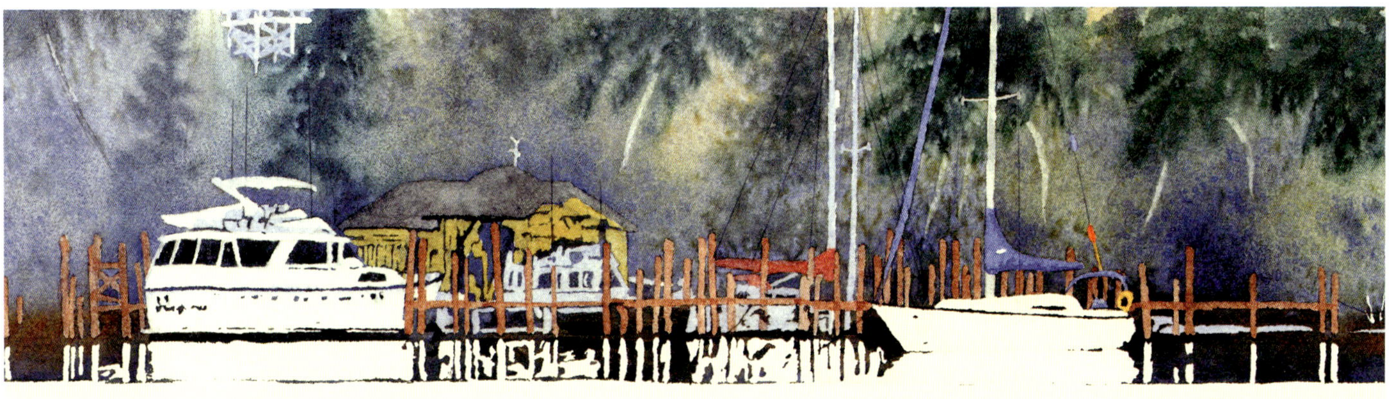

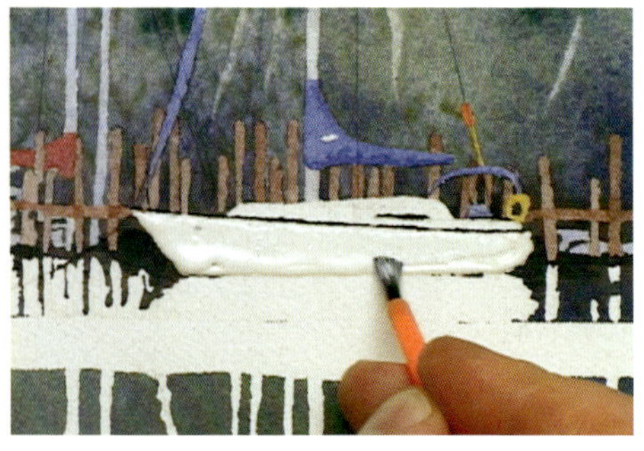

**Step 18:** Before proceeding to the next step of applying the water's surface colors, I masked out the hull of the prominent sailboat. Since it was anchored in front of the dock, rather than tied to it, the shoreline is actually above the bottom of its hull.

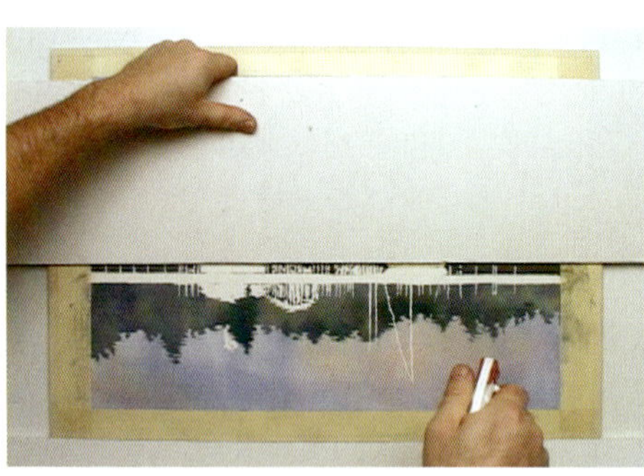

**Step 19:** After the hull masking had dried, I saturated everything below the shoreline with a spray bottle filled with water. Once again I protected the painting above the shoreline with a foamboard.

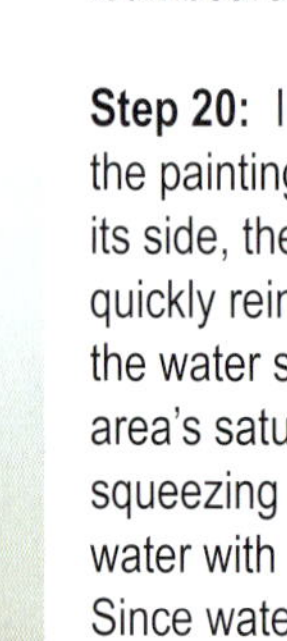

**Step 20:** I tilted the painting onto its side, then quickly reinforced the water surface area's saturation by squeezing on more water with a syringe. Since water tends to follow water, there was little chance that this downward flowing water would cross into the land area above the shoreline.

Quickly, I loaded about 25 percent of the large syringe with a rich mix of Turquoise Green. Then I drew in water to fill the remaining 75 percent. This was then squeezed onto the top edge of the painting's pre-wet area. Since the painting was steeply inclined, the Turquoise Green mix

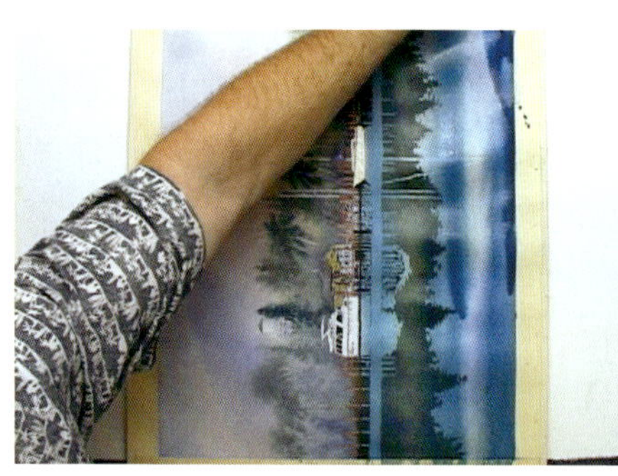

(Step 20 continued)

flowed downward and blended onto the water's surface. Once I achieved the look that I wanted, I locked the colors in by thoroughly drying them with the blow drier.

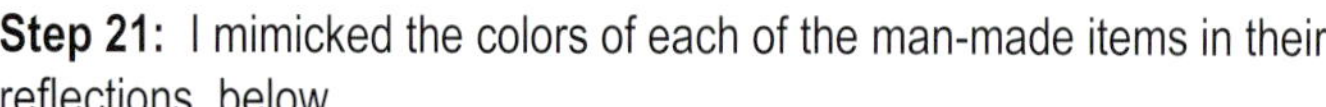

**Step 21:** I mimicked the colors of each of the man-made items in their reflections, below.

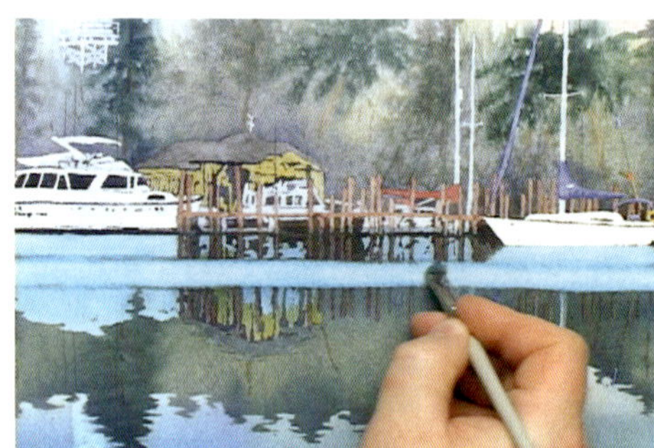

**Step 22:** Next, with a variety of sizes of stiff-bristled scrubbing brushes, I scrubbed and softened the edges of the prominent water "light reflection line." This had been masked, but removal of the masking had left it with hard edges. I loaded the brush with clean water, then scrubbed and lifted along the water line's edge. With a tissue, I dabbed up or rubbed off any lifted paint.

Then, with a smaller scrubbing brush, I lightly lifted a water line along the shoreline. I protected the edges of the prominent sailboat with the edge of a palette knife.

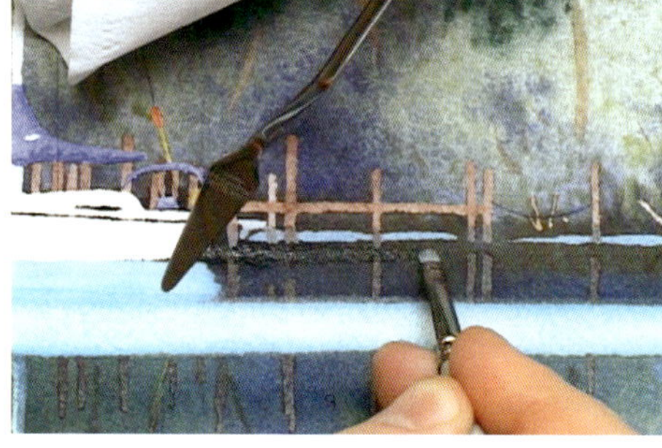

With various sized soft-bristled brushes, I also lifted some "light reflection lines" in the lower area of the painting, too.

To apply the water's surface color, I tilted my painting table to a steep incline—about 45 degrees. This put gravity on my side when I squeezed paint onto the wet paper.

It was preferable to squeeze water and paint over the tree reflection colors, as brushing them would have likely lifted some of their colors.

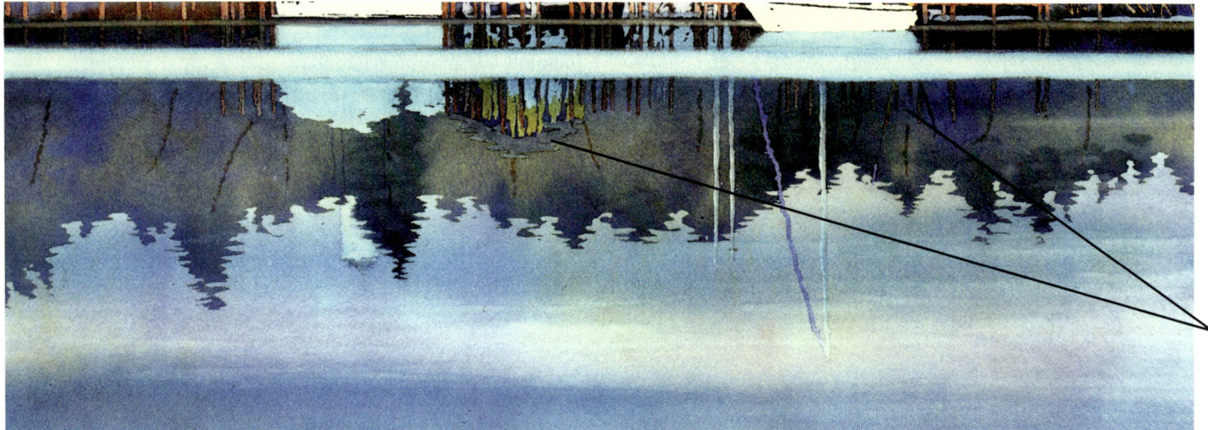

If necessary, a blemish in the sky reflection colors can often be removed with a strategically positioned "light reflection line."

The reflected colors of the dock, boats and marina building were painted in prior to scrubbing the "light reflection lines."

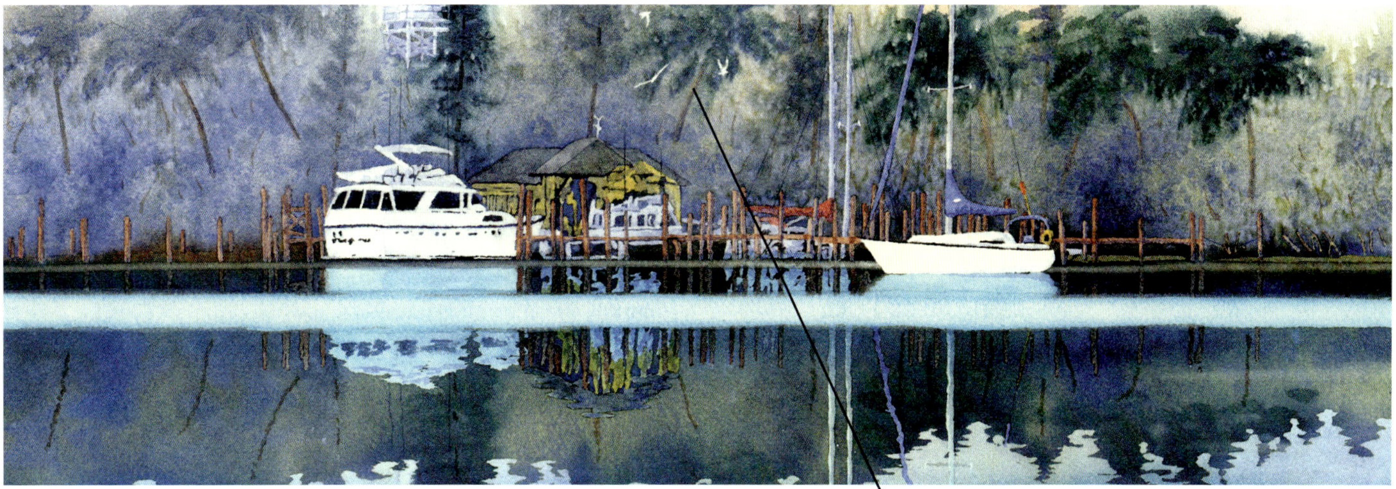

With an exacto-knife, I scraped in some distant sea gull shapes.

Final shade details helped provide the illusion of depth.

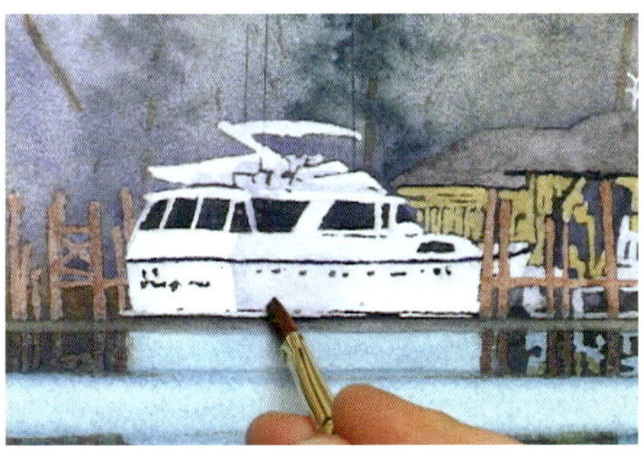

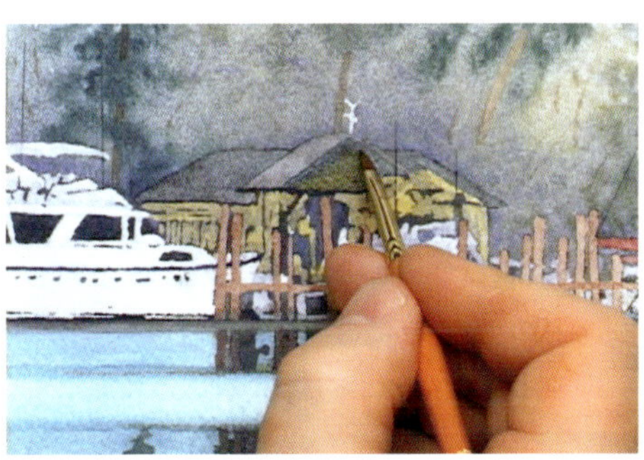

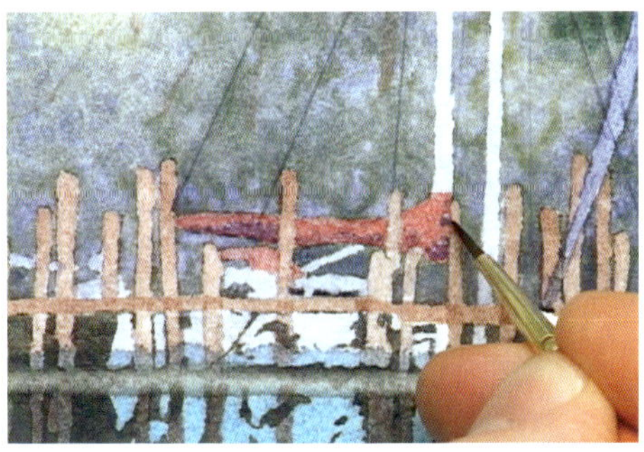

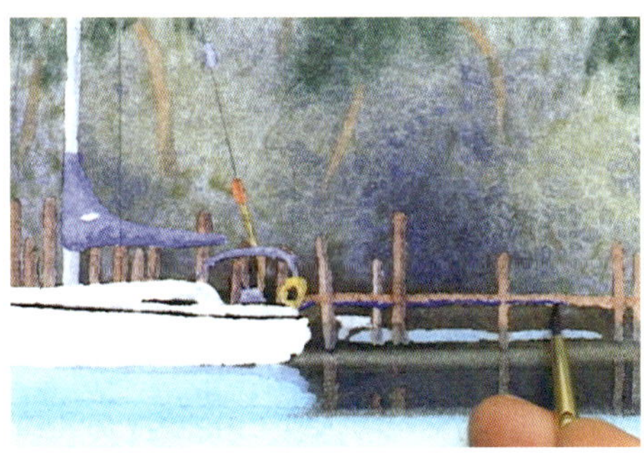

**Step 23:** The low morning sunlight created very distinct shading, so by alternating between a 1/4" and 1/8" flat brush and a lean mixture of Cobalt Blue, I shaded the downlight side of the most prominent objects. The transom of the boat received full sunshine, while the visible side of the hull did not, so I separated the two with a distinct hard edge.
I diluted the shade's opposing edge as I worked forward on the side of the boat.

I was also able to sort sections of the building's roof, by painting their shaded sections.

For both the sail covers and the dock sections, I shaded their lower and right-hand sides.

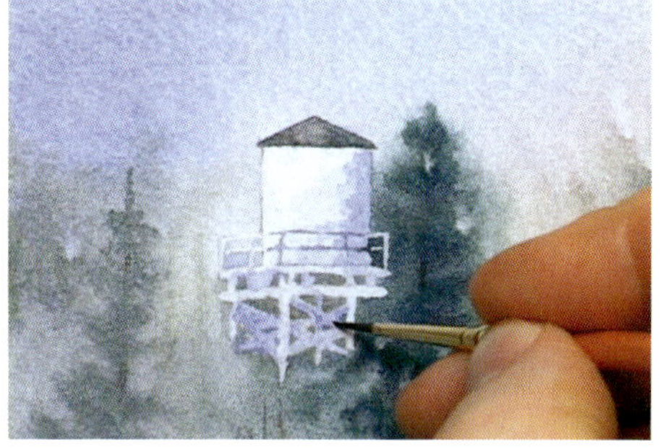

(Step 23 continued)

The water tower required a graduating shade that was darkest on its right side and then became progressively lighter towards its left side. This helped imply roundness. Its legs also needed to be sorted with a variety of subtle Cobalt Blue values—as was done with the marina building and boats—then shaded to emphasize its sunlit left side.

**Step 24:** Without any great detail, I painted in the tree trunk shapes (scraped in previously) with a mix of Burnt Sienna and Ultramarine Blue and a #2 round brush.

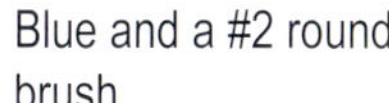

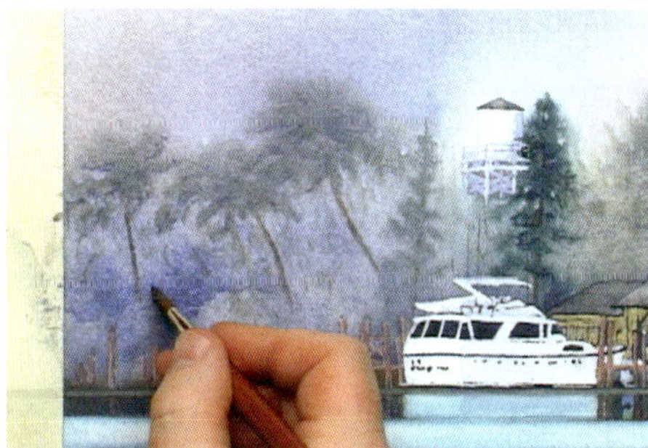

**Step 25:**
I also sorted the background foliage by distinguishing the tree trunk areas from the foreground brush. With a lean mix of Cobalt Blue, I created a hard edge to separate the areas, depending on their distance. Then I softened the shade's upper edge.

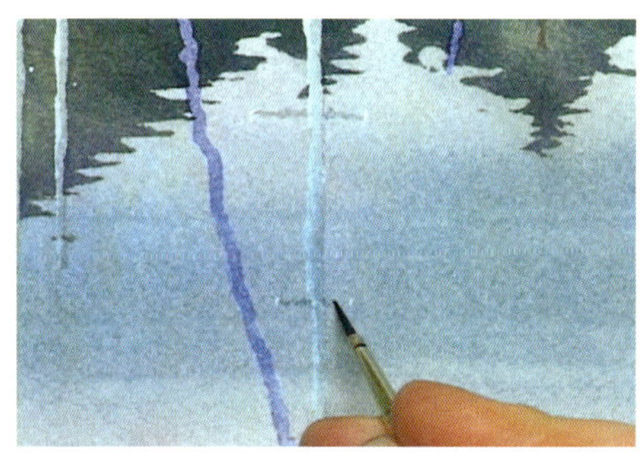

**Step 26**: I finished the painting by working in details, such as the mast spreader reflections. I also scraped in some distant sea gulls with an exacto-knife.

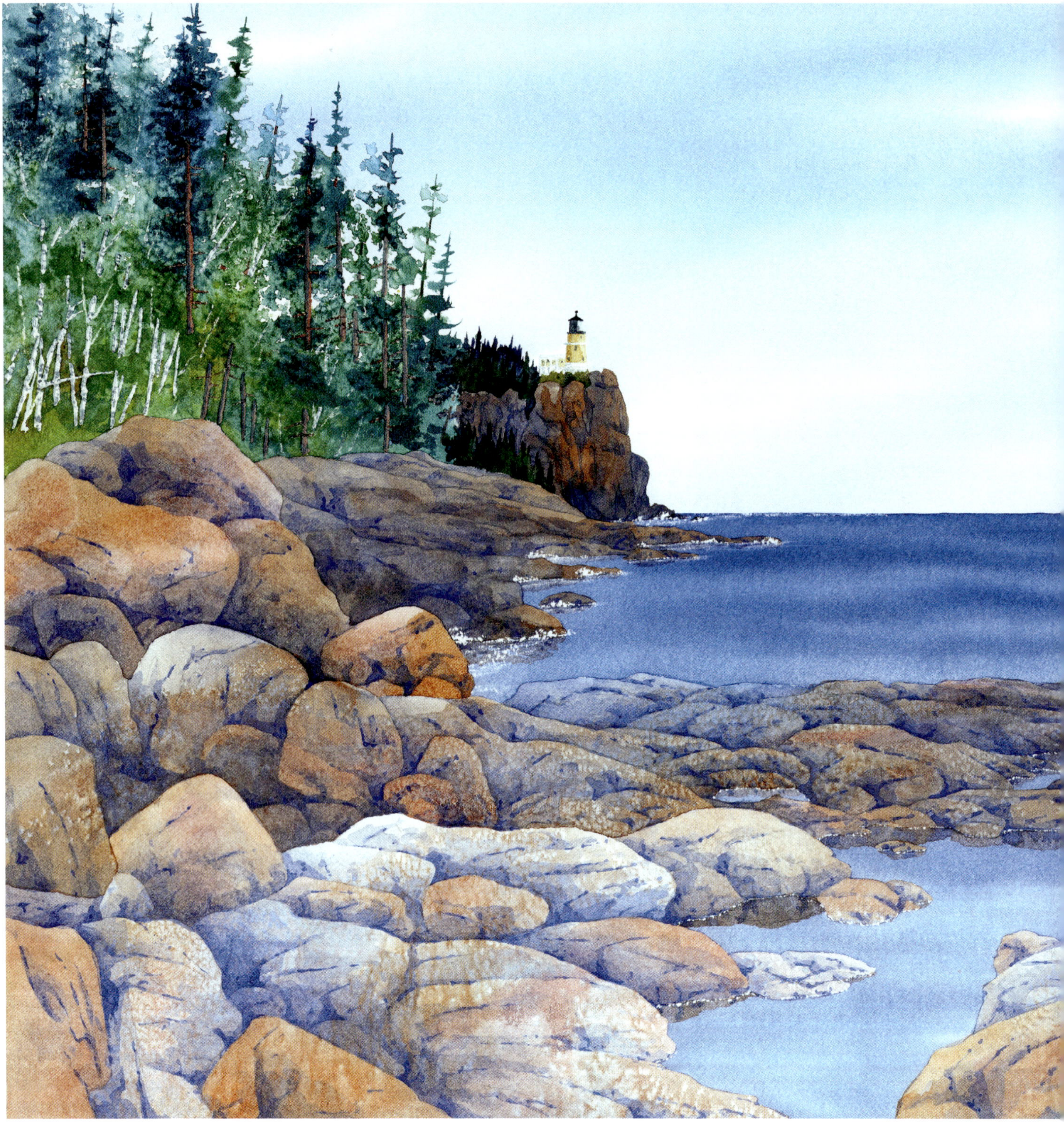

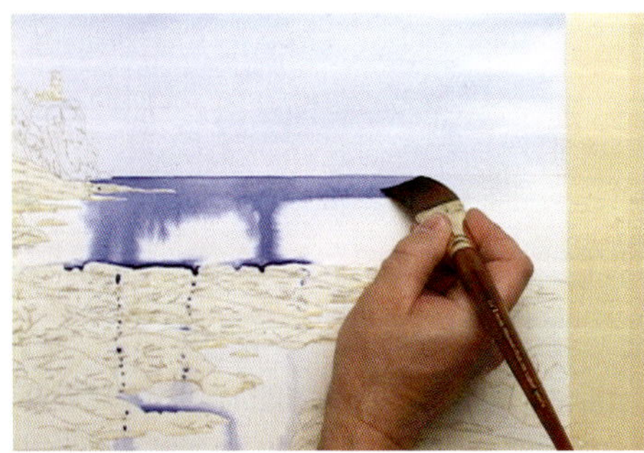

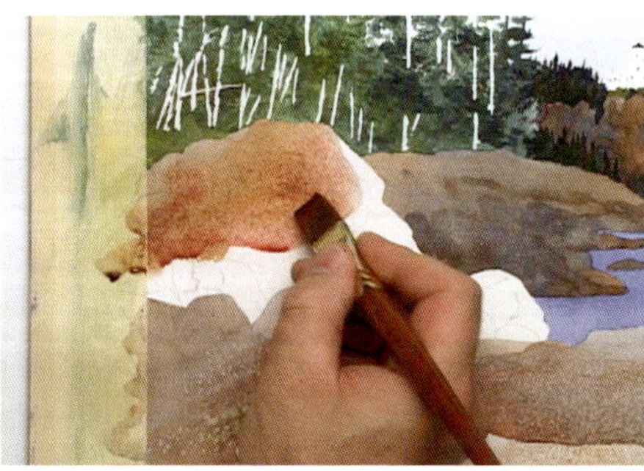

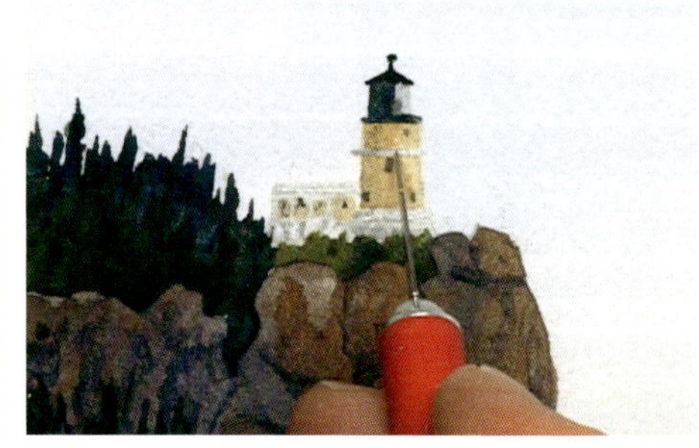

# *SPLIT ROCK LIGHTHOUSE*

I have trekked the rocky shores of Lake Superior on countless occasions and in every season. For years this inland ocean with its wild rocky shores was only a couple of hours from my home—at least, one small portion of it was. Its power, beauty and solitude made it always a big lure.

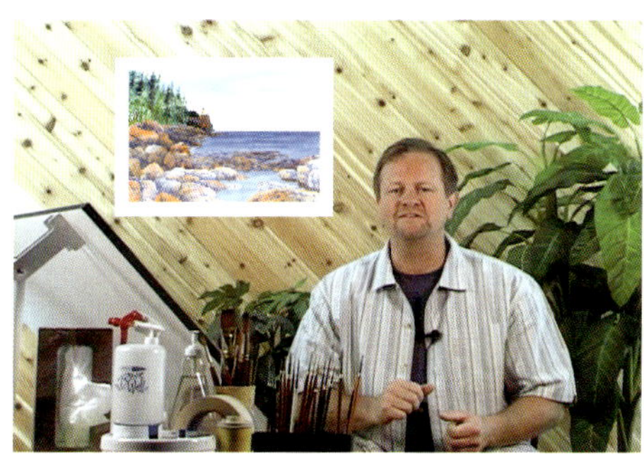

Despite its name, this vast body of water is more ocean than not. Looking out from the shoreline, there is no opposing side—only an endless horizon of water. When the wind blows, its seas can rise to frightful levels. Indeed, it has a cold deep bottom that is littered with decades of shipwrecks. When Superior is calm, its large gentle swells make you keenly aware that this is a giant merely napping. It is an imposing place of endless beauty; surrounded by rugged rocky shores, vast woodlands and a long, colorful history.

I stand in a long line of artists who have attempted to capture her grandeur on canvas and paper.

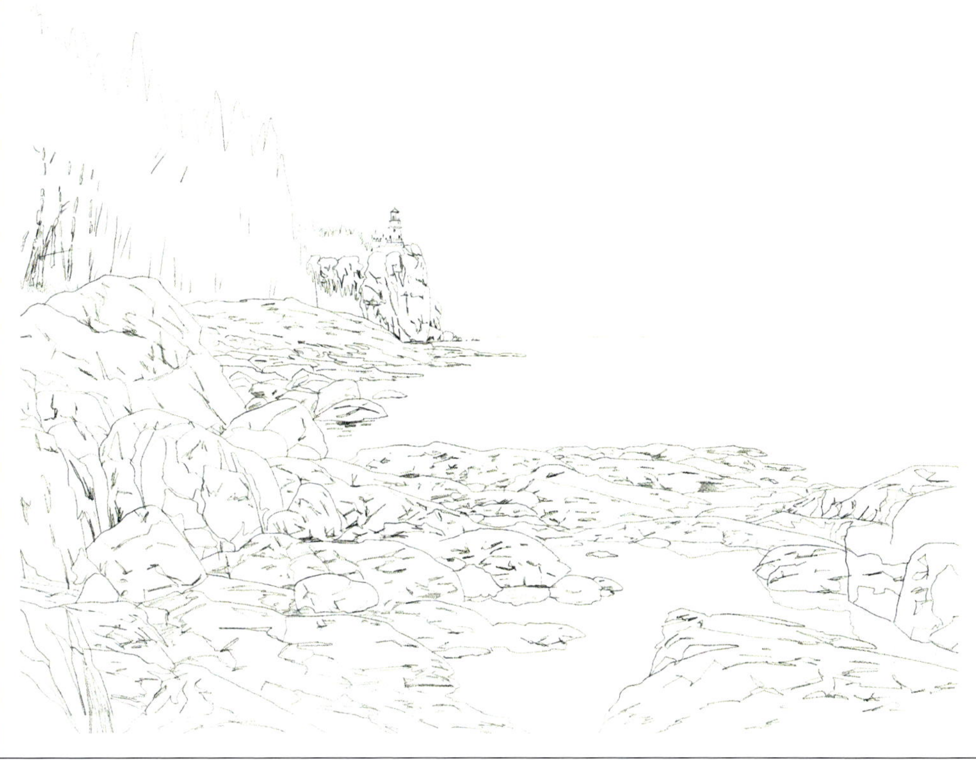

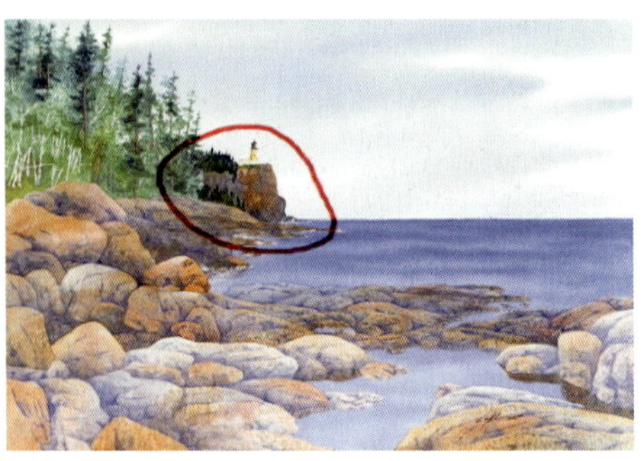

**Step 1:** I drew out my composition on the watercolor paper. As usual, I had marked my horizontal and vertical center points on the sides of the painting to help remind me to not center the prominent objects. You can see that this painting's focal point—the distant cliff-top lighthouse—is above and to the left of center. I was also careful to not center the lake's horizon line. Also, the foreground rocks are depicted in an asymmetrical pattern.

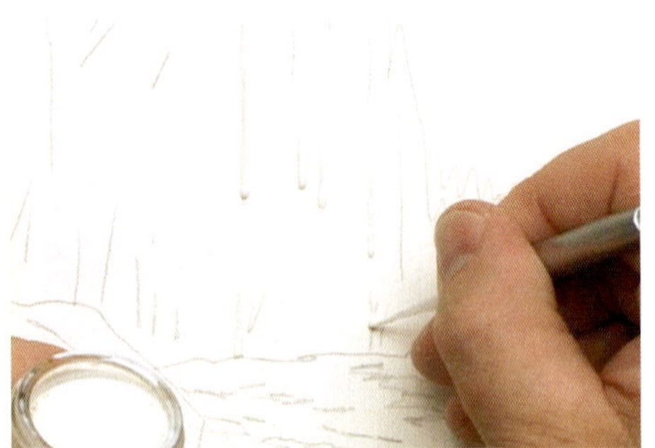

**Step 2:** With liquid masking fluid and a plastic toothpick, I masked out the visible tree trunks.

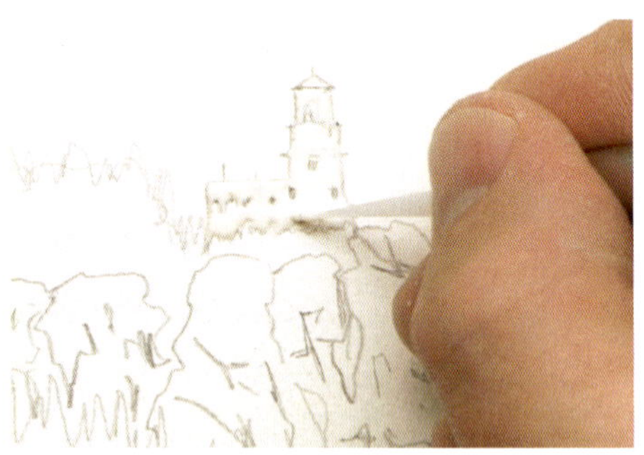

I also carefully masked all but the top portion of the lighthouse, leaving the windows and doorways unmasked.

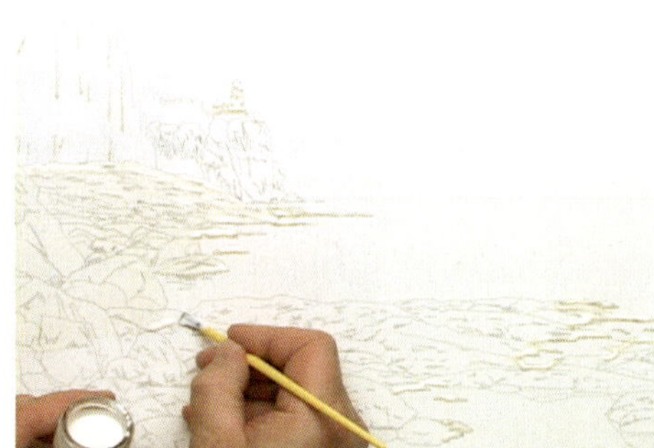

(Step 2 continued)

Then, with a disposable paintbrush, I masked out all of the foreground rocks.

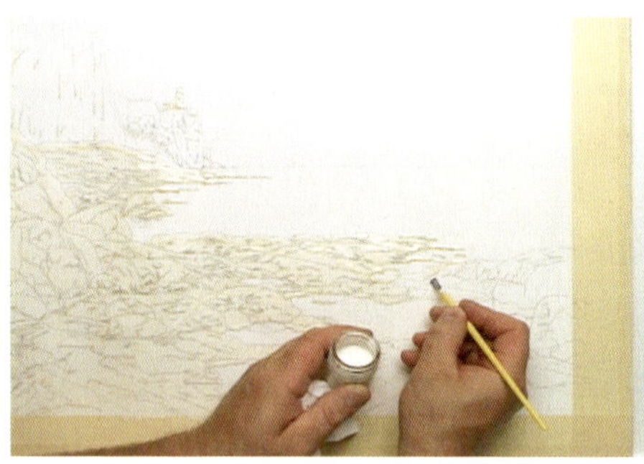

I was careful to not mask over the large pool of water.

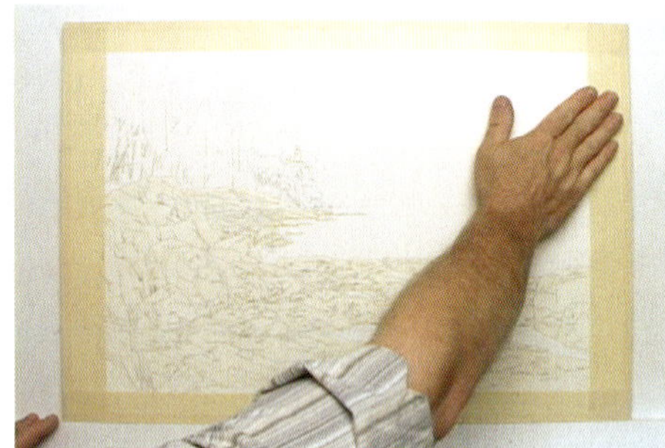

After the masking had dried, I rubbed my hand across the sky to feel for any errant drops of masking that may have accidentally landed there.

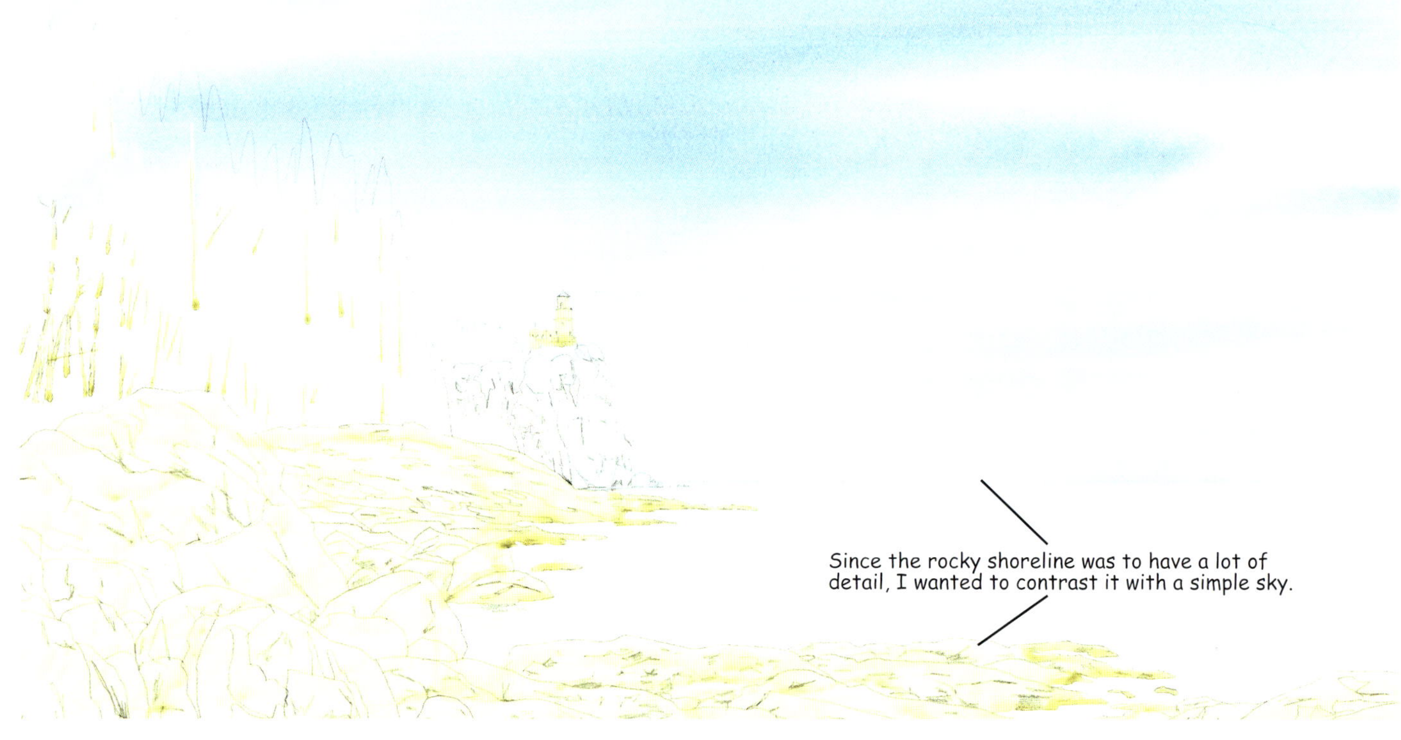

Since the rocky shoreline was to have a lot of detail, I wanted to contrast it with a simple sky.

I purposely graduated the color value of the water—making it progressively darker as it approached the horizon.

I also created variance within this graduation so as not to create an unrealistic uniform blend.

This scene depicts an unusually calm day on Lake Superior. But, this tranquil state of the water actually helped emphasize the complexity of the shoreline rocks. Neither the sky nor the lake competes for the viewer's attention.

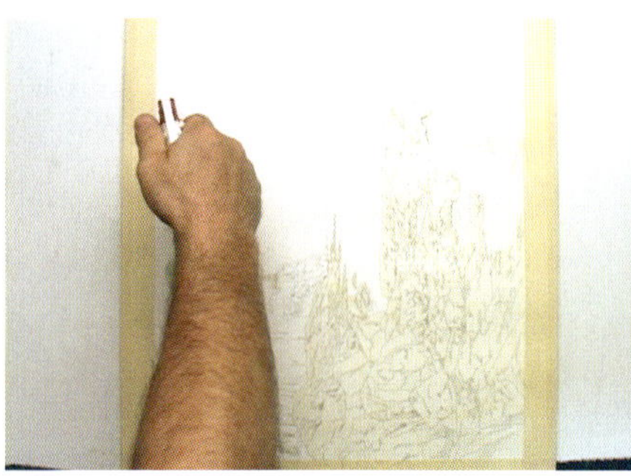

**Step 3:** I tipped the painting onto its side, then saturated it with a spray bottle filled with water.

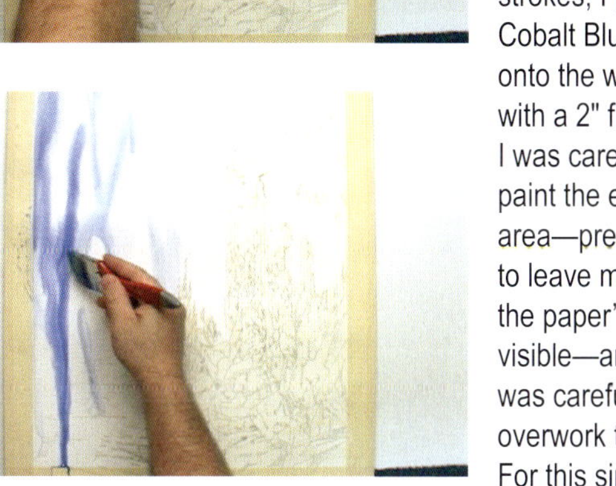

**Step 4:** With just a few brief brush strokes, I painted Cobalt Blue streaks onto the wet paper with a 2" flat brush. I was careful to not paint the entire sky area—preferring to leave much of the paper's white visible—and I was careful to not overwork the sky. For this simple sky, "less was more!"

With a tissue, I wicked up the excess paint and water that puddled up on the painting's lower edges. After allowing the Cobalt Blue to blend a bit into the wet paper, I locked in the sky pattern by thoroughly drying it with a blow drier.

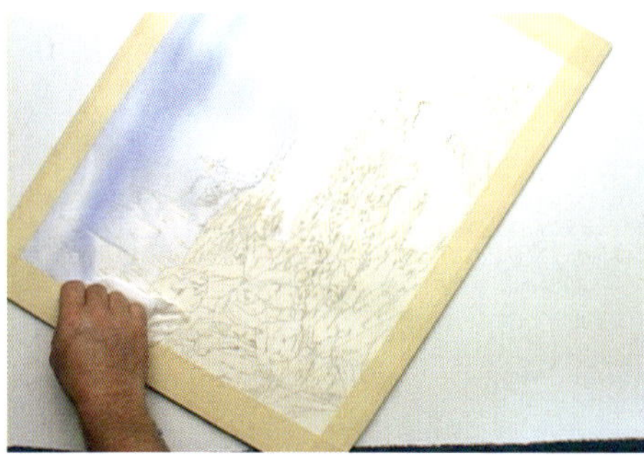

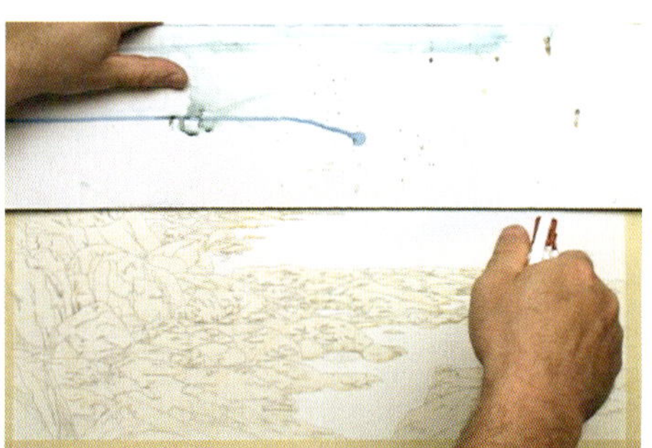

**Step 5:** Tilting the painting back into its normal position, I saturated everything below the lake's horizon line with water. I held a piece of foamboard just slightly below the lake's horizon line to prevent this line, and everything above it, from getting wet.

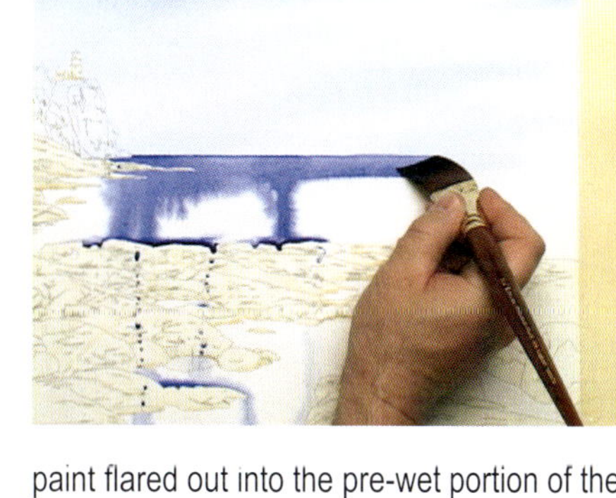

**Step 6:** Then, with a rich mix of Ultramarine Blue and a 1-1/4" flat brush, I carefully painted along the horizon line. As I worked across, trying to maintain a straight upper edge, the lower edge of the paint flared out into the pre-wet portion of the paper. This prevented a hard line from forming below the horizon. After defining the horizon line with paint, I quickly carried these colors downward into the remainder of the lake.

While still wet, I tilted the painting back onto its side, then resumed painting Ultramarine Blue streaks onto the lake and foreground pool.

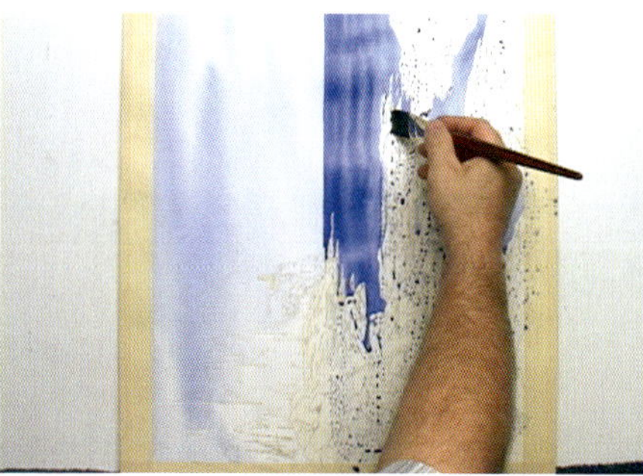

I graduated this color, by regulating its water mix, so that it was darker as it approached the distant horizon. When I had the look that I wanted, I again locked the colors in with a blow dryer.

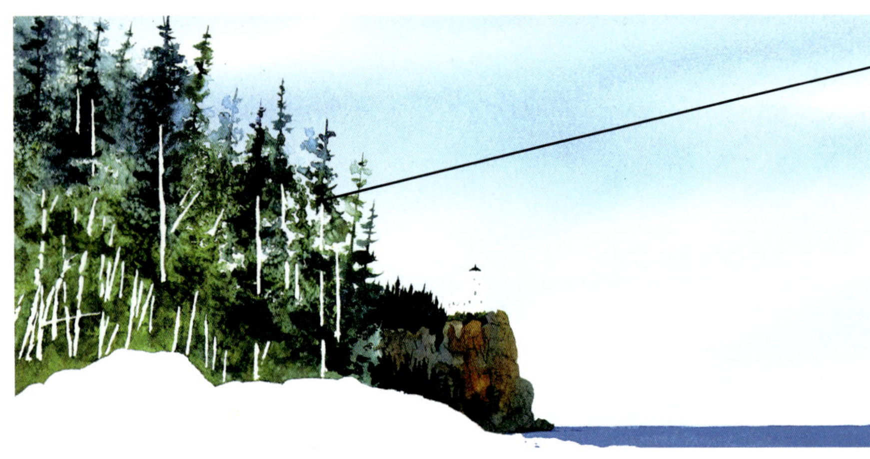

While "spurting" the paint globs, I was careful to not saturate the paper. I wanted to maintain white areas—where the paper never got wet—to represent where the viewer could see through the foliage.

As I painted in the treetops, they would typically appear sharp on the dry paper above. Then, as I worked downward—applying branches—they would blend into the underlying wet colors.

When I added branches to the "pulled" treetops, I literally smashed the rigger brush bristles onto the trunk. This gave the branches a wild natural look.

**Step 7:** For this next step I lowered my inclined painting table into a near level position. Then I covered the sky and lake areas with rags to protect them from an accidental paint splatter—the following step can get messy! With a spray bottle filled with water, I saturated everything below the tree area.

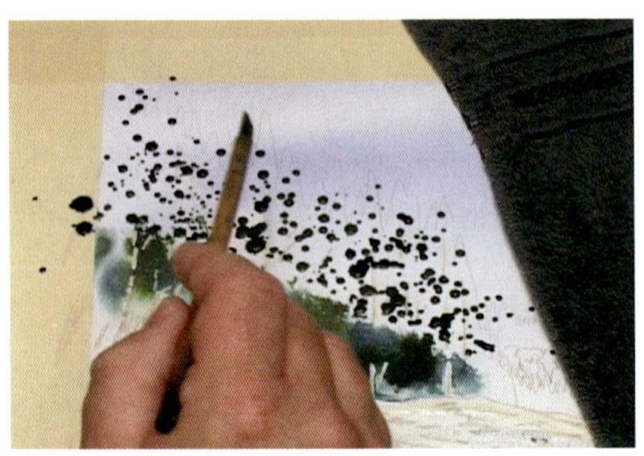

**Step 8:** With a rich mix of Phthalo Blue and Phthalo Green, I literally threw globs of paint onto the tree area with a long loose-bristled bamboo brush. I tried to vary between these two colors so as not to create a pattern of only one color.

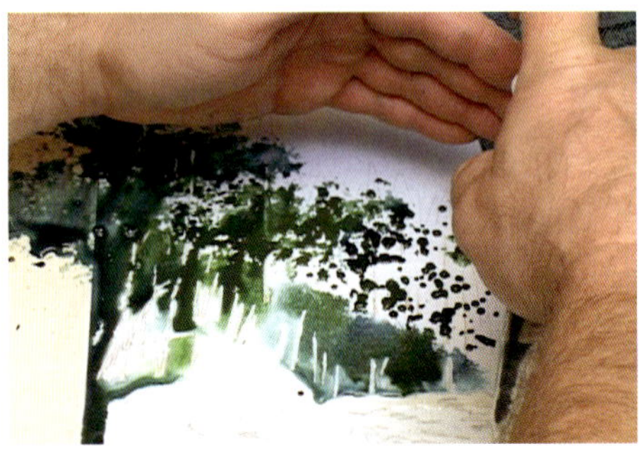

**Step 9:** Then, with a plunger-type pump spray bottle, I "spurted" these paint globs to partially fuse them together with water. I did not want to saturate this area. Rather, I wanted to spurt on just enough water droplets to connect the paint globs while still retaining white (paper) spaces in-between. As I spurted these paint globs, I allowed the excess paint and water to run down into the pre-wet area, below.

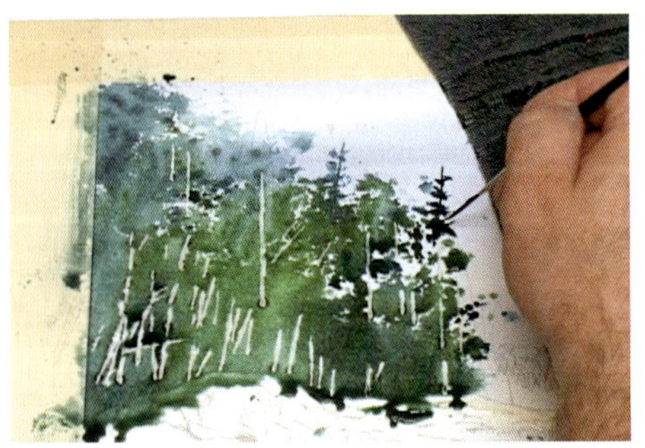

**Step 10:** Before these colors dried, I sprinkled on salt to promote texture.

**Step 11:** And as these colors dried, I "pulled and smashed" pine treetops with a #0 rigger brush. Sometimes I pulled a tree trunk upward from the existing wet paint. But, usually, I added these tree tops with a rich mix of Phthalo Blue and Phthalo Green.

(Step 11 continued)

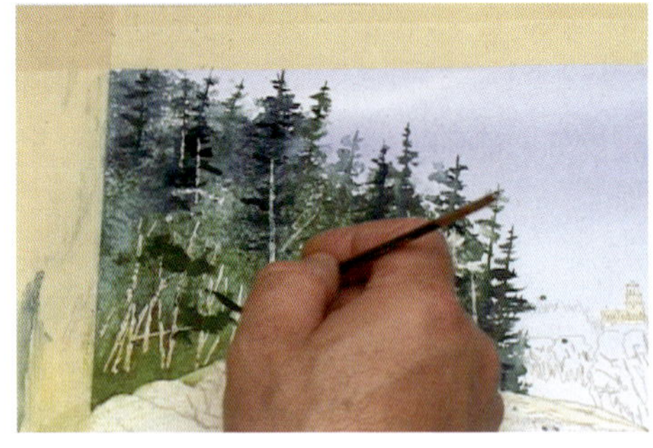

Occasionally, while pulling tree tops, I would introduce some darker values into the lower areas of the still-wet foliage to create variance of color values—suggesting depth.

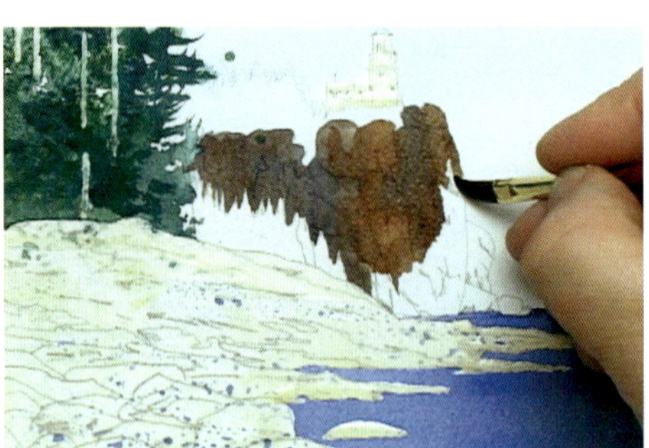

**Step 12:** After I had dried the trees, I painted in the distant cliff with a mix of Burnt Sienna and Ultramarine Blue and a 1/4" flat brush. I varied between these two colors and applied them as a relatively dark value.

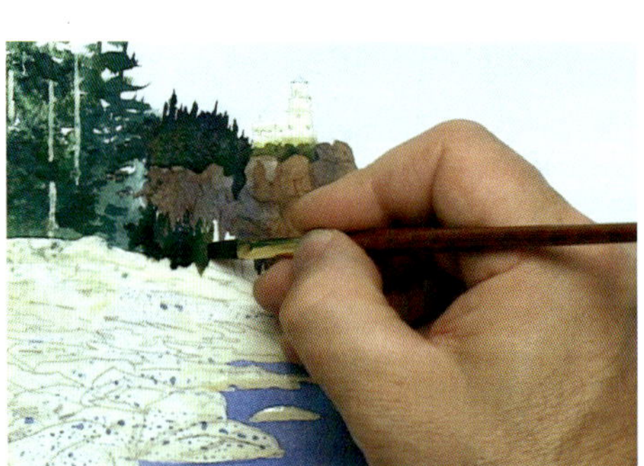

**Step 13:** Then, with the same brush and a mix of Ultramarine Blue and Ultramarine Green, I painted in the cliff trees. These were also painted in dark. Since they were so distant from the viewer, I painted them as simple sawtooth patterns.

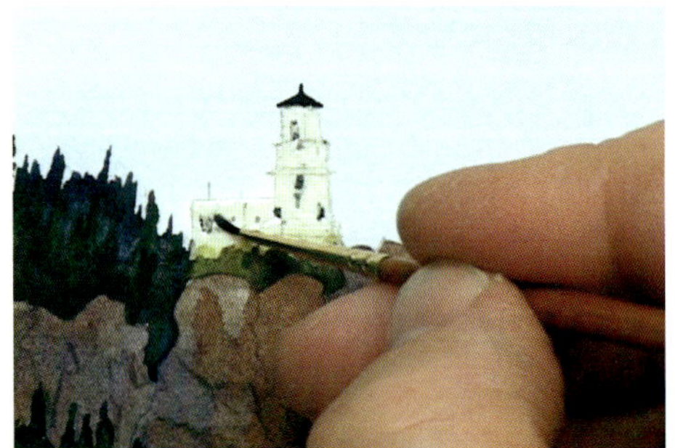

**Step 14:** Next, I used a #3/0 round brush and a rich mix of Payne's Gray to paint the lighthouse roof and to darken its unmasked windows and doorways.

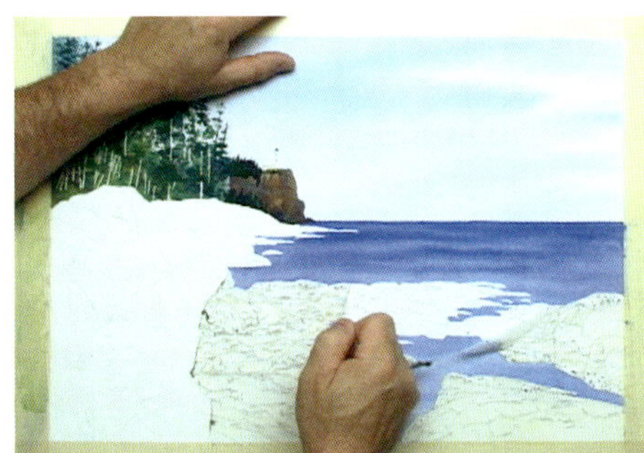

**Step 15:** After thoroughly drying the painting, I peeled off all of the masking.

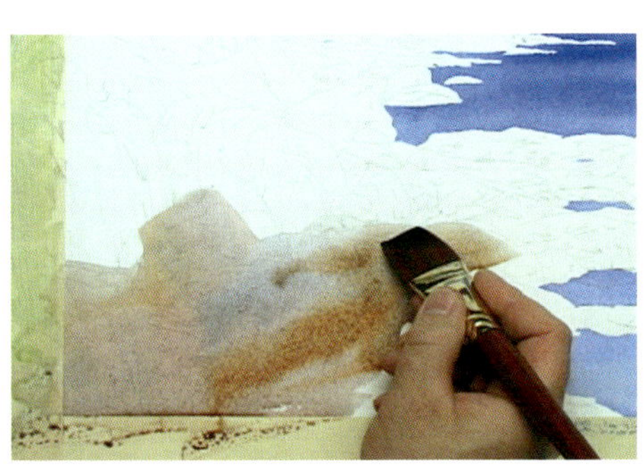

**Step 16:** Then, section by section, I painted in the rock base colors with a mix of Burnt Sienna, Ultramarine Blue and Rose. Depending on the area that I worked on, I varied the flat brush sizes between 1-1/4" and 1/2". It was my intent to vary between these colors to make the rocks interesting. I did not want boring solid brown rocks! It was also my intent to gradually darken the rock color values—section by section—as I worked back towards the horizon. In my mind, I divided these shorelines rocks into subsections—dependent on their relative distance from the viewer.

Before the paint had dried, I added salt to each section to create a textured effect.

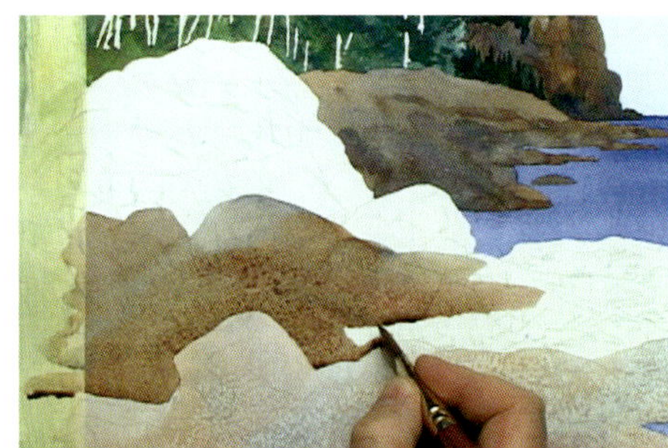

(Step 16 continued)

This rock section was painted in darker than the one below it, but used the same three colors: Burnt Sienna, Ultramarine Blue, and Rose.

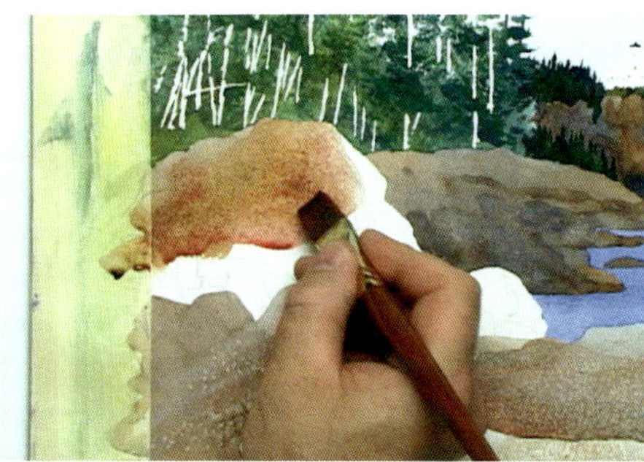

I continuously varied between the colors and avoided a predictable color pattern.

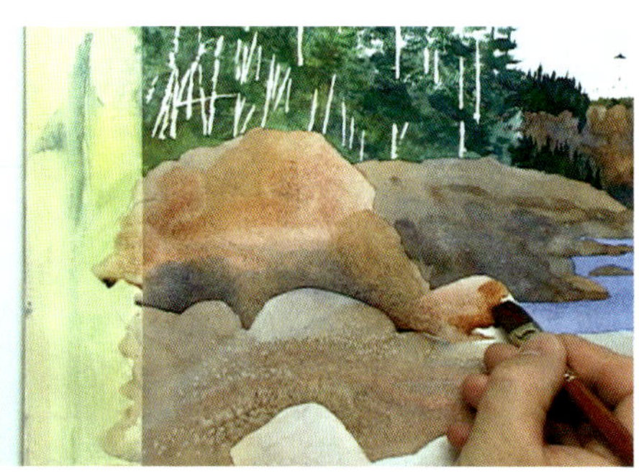

It was helpful to first paint in the closest and the furthest shoreline rocks. This established the value limits in which the intermediary shoreline rocks would fall between.

I avoided the creation of "boring solid brown rocks" by varying the colors and adding salt for texture.

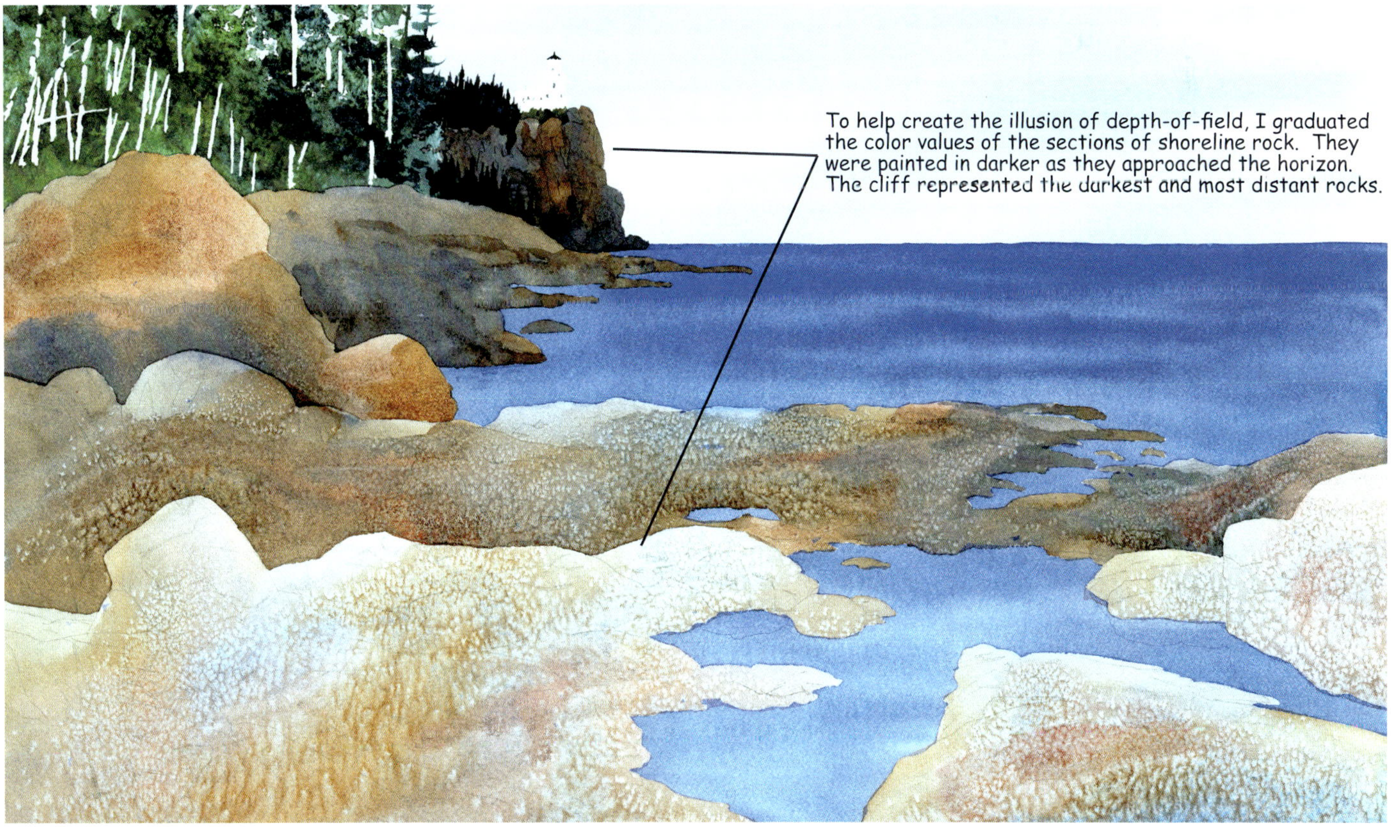

To help create the illusion of depth-of-field, I graduated the color values of the sections of shoreline rock. They were painted in darker as they approached the horizon. The cliff represented the darkest and most distant rocks.

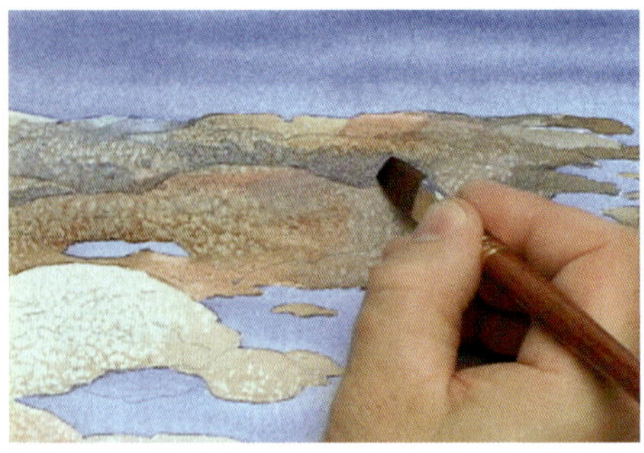

**Step 17:** After I had dried the rock base colors, I began "sorting" within each rock section to distinguish individual rocks. I accomplished this by shading and intermixing hard and soft shade edges.

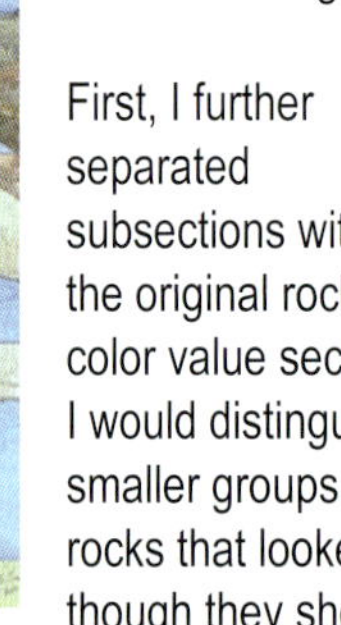

First, I further separated subsections within the original rock color value sections. I would distinguish smaller groups of rocks that looked as though they should grouped together, distance-wise. Using a lean mix of Ultramarine Blue and a 1/2" flat brush, I would create a hard shade edge to distinguish between two groups of rocks. The other (non-dividing) edges would be either dabbed up with a tissue or diluted with water. Essentially, I wanted to lose the non-dividing edges, in most cases.

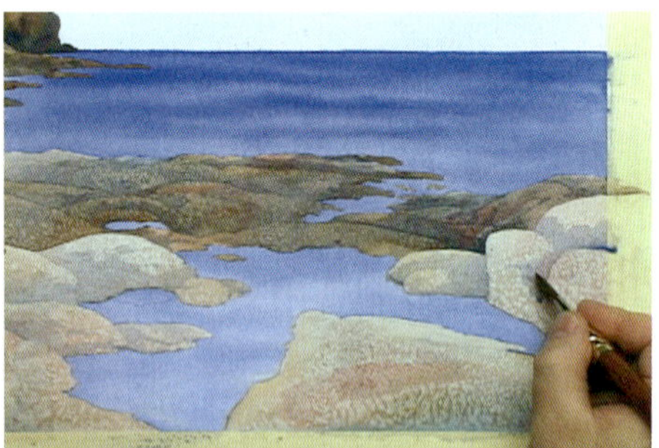

This first shading step was not intended to define individual rocks—that would come in the following steps—so I tried to focus on defining the general subsections of the rocks.

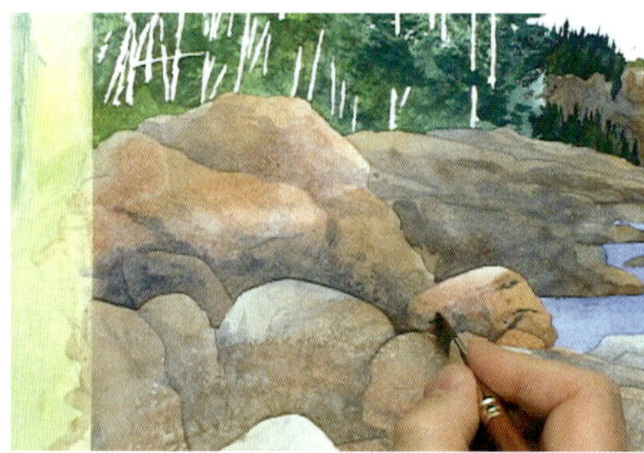

**Step 18:** After the first shading step had dried, I continued with the same color and brush to define some of the individual rock shapes within the previous subsections. I tended to shade within the previously shaded areas.

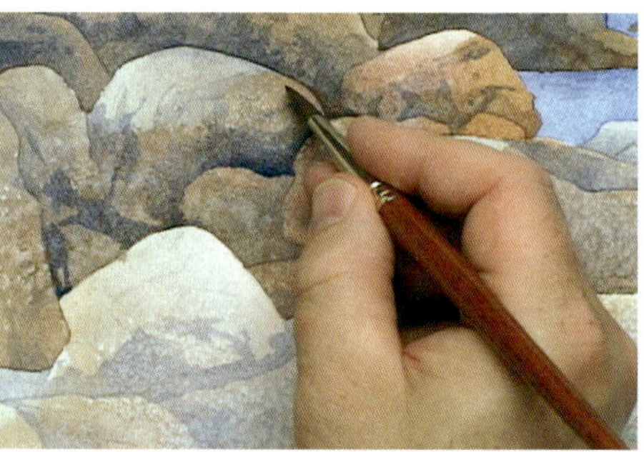

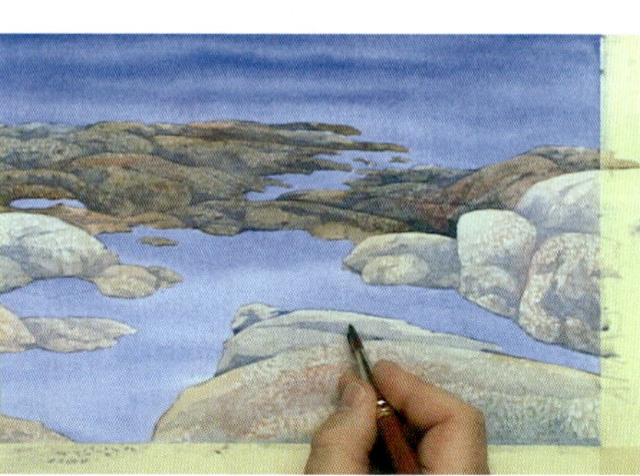

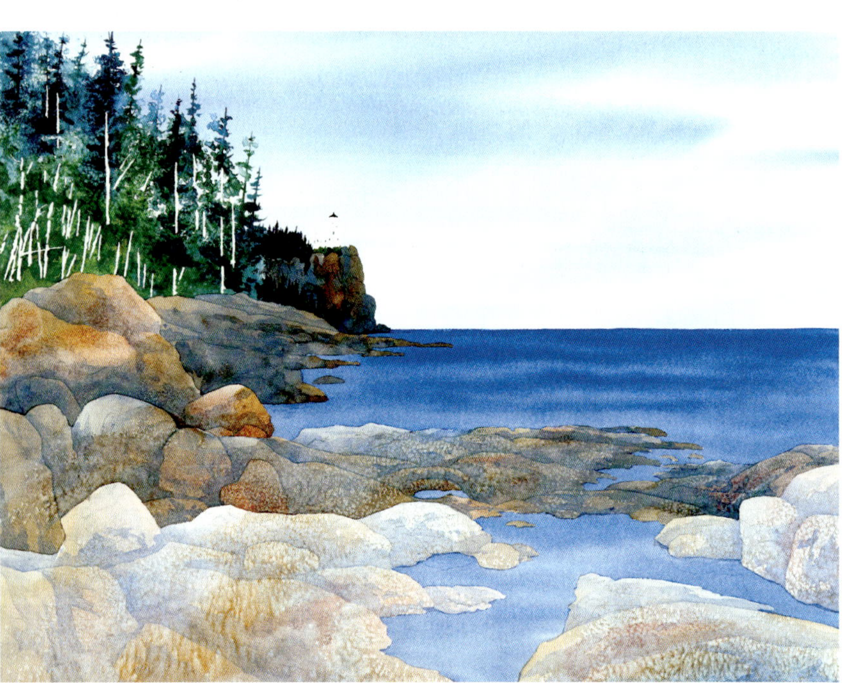

Throughout my progressive rock shading steps, I tended to shade within the previously shaded areas. I did not want to entirely cover the rocks with shade details and lose the impact of the underlying rock base colors.

I used care to not apply the shade details too darkly—particularly the first shade steps. Every ensuing shade step added to the value of the previous shade, so the shade details could easily get too dark. In this case, it was more effective to keep the shade details relatively subtle.

When portions of the rock's pencil sketch became too difficult to see—after adding these various layers of paint—I simply re-drew them right over the paint.

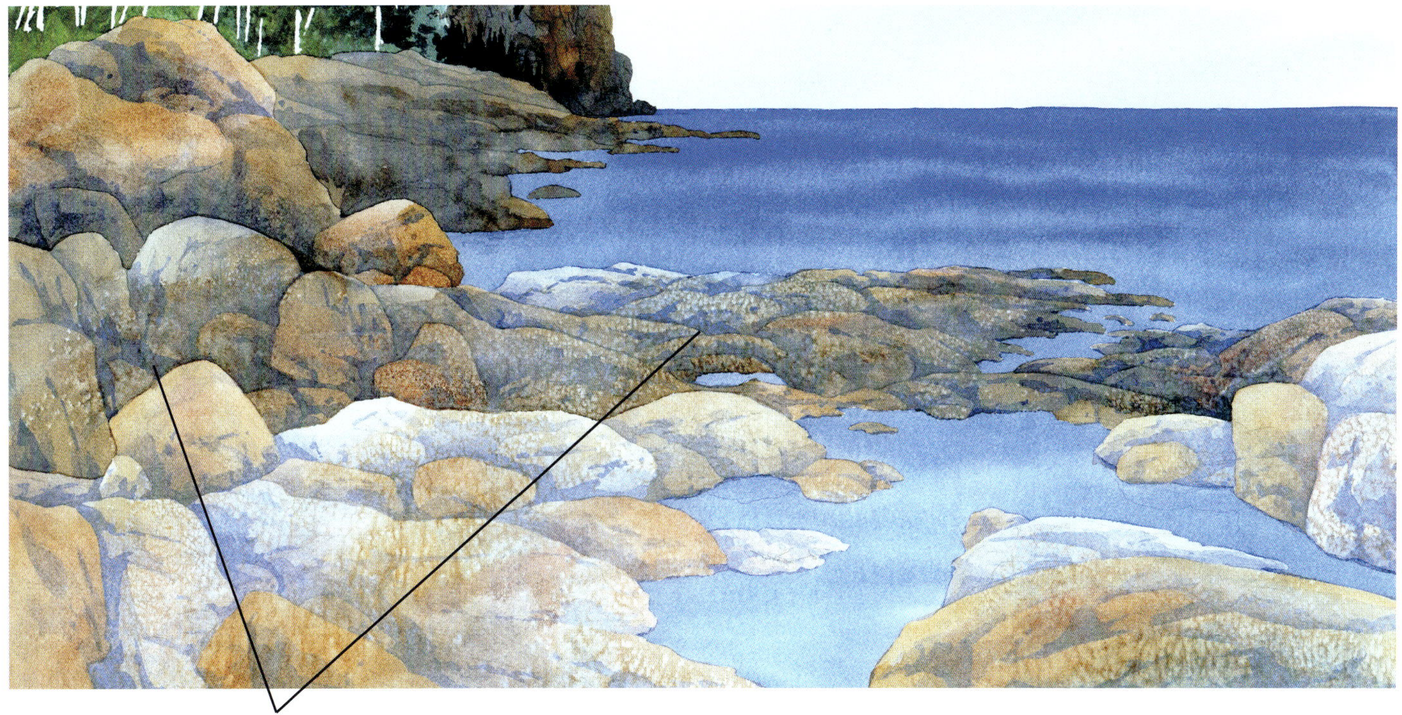

Even though the shade details were applied as relatively light values, they effectively darkened as they were layered over one another. The values of transparent watercolors are cumulative.

It is easy to overdo shade details. I wanted to provide just enough visual information so that the viewer could determine that these were, indeed, rocks. But, much was left to the viewer's imagination, as well.

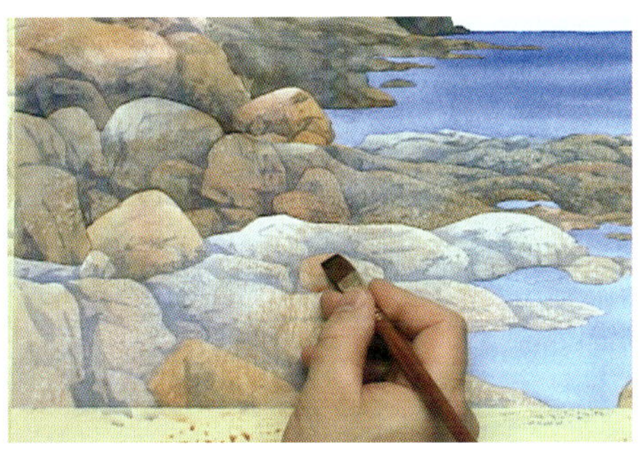

**Step 19:** After studying the shoreline rocks, I determined that they needed a bit more variety. So, with a lean mix of Burnt Sienna, I enhanced the color on a few select rock shapes.

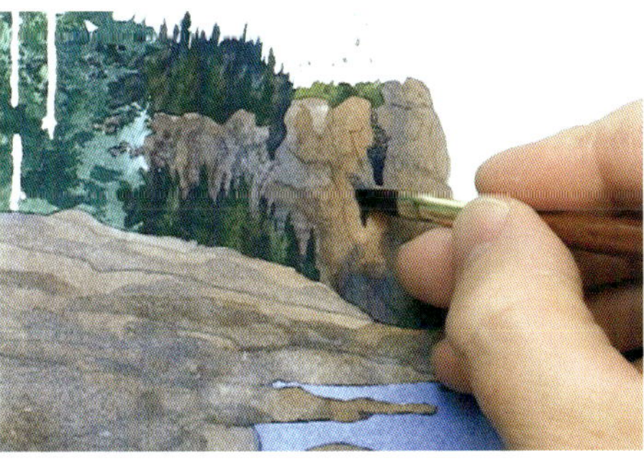

**Step 20:** I continued to paint in rock shade details with Ultramarine Blue. With a 1/4" flat brush, I worked in some shade details on the distant cliff.

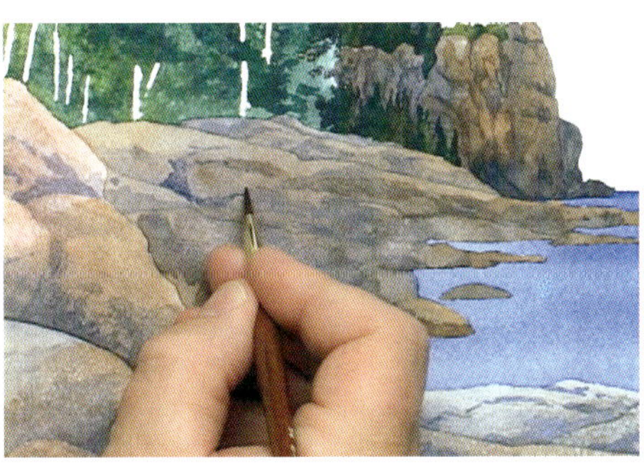

Working forward with this smaller brush, I continued to paint in shade details—generally shading within the previously shaded areas.

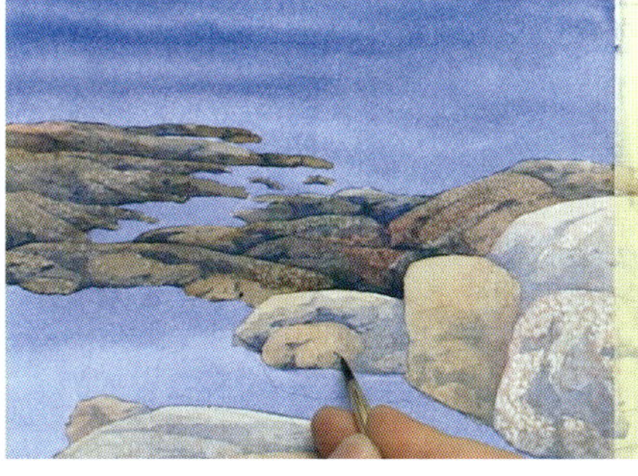

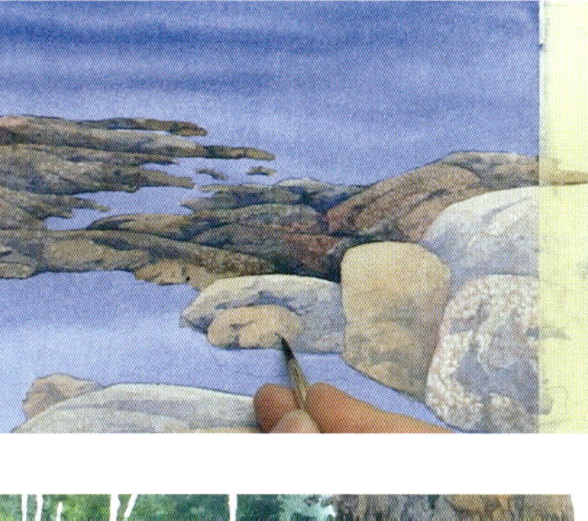

**Step 21:** Then, switching to a #6 rigger brush with a slightly richer mix of Ultramarine Blue, I painted in even finer shade details. On this step, however, I occasionally worked outside of the previously shaded area with an extended crack or crevice shape.

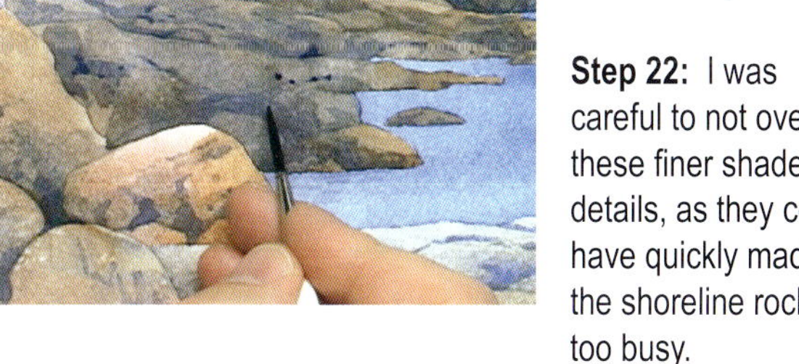

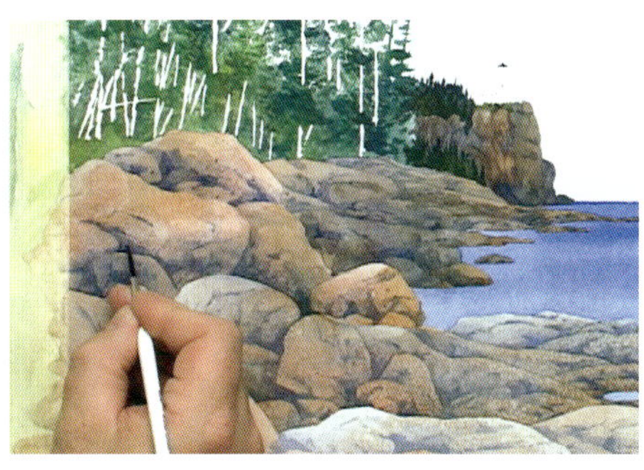

**Step 22:** I was careful to not overdo these finer shade details, as they could have quickly made the shoreline rocks too busy.

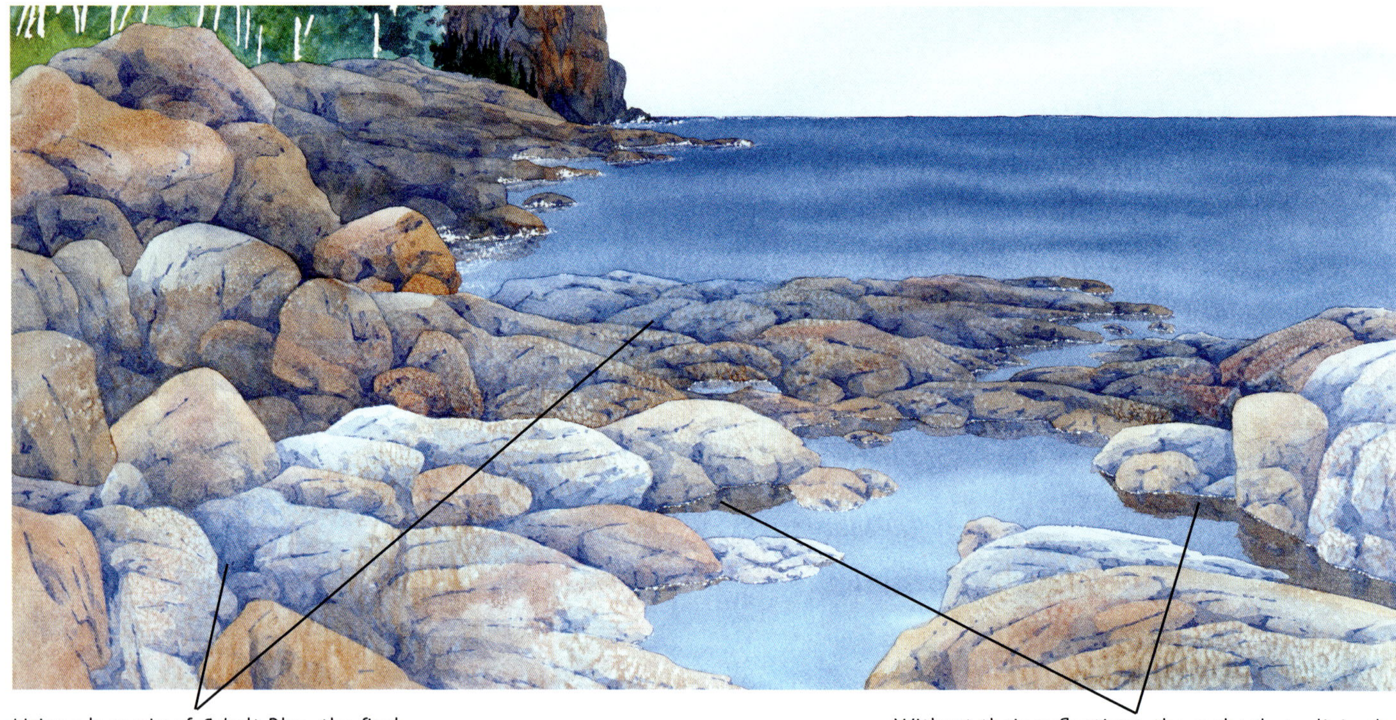

Using a lean mix of Cobalt Blue, the final step of shading was a very subtle one.

Without their reflections, the rocks that adjoined the pool of water appeared to be floating.

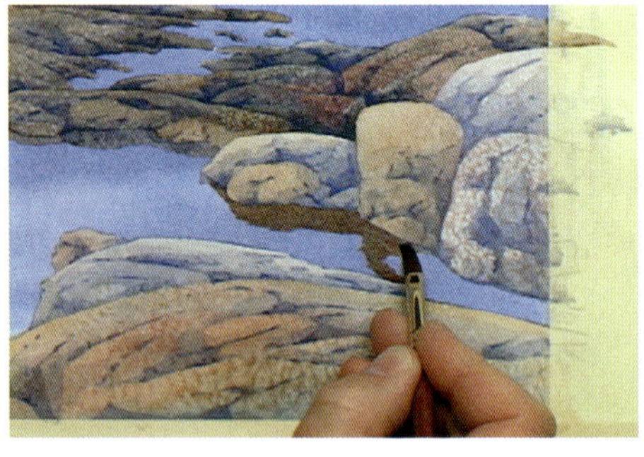

**Step 23:** Next, with a mix of Burnt Sienna and Ultramarine Blue—using a 1/4" flat brush—I painted rock reflections into the pool of water in the foreground. I applied these as a slightly darker value.

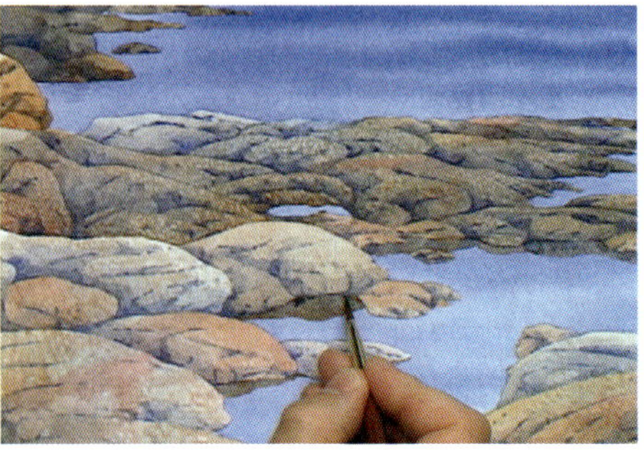

As they dried, I mimicked some of the shade details from above, using Ultramarine Blue. Since this was a reflection, it was actually preferable to have these shade details blend (blur) into the underlying wet paint.

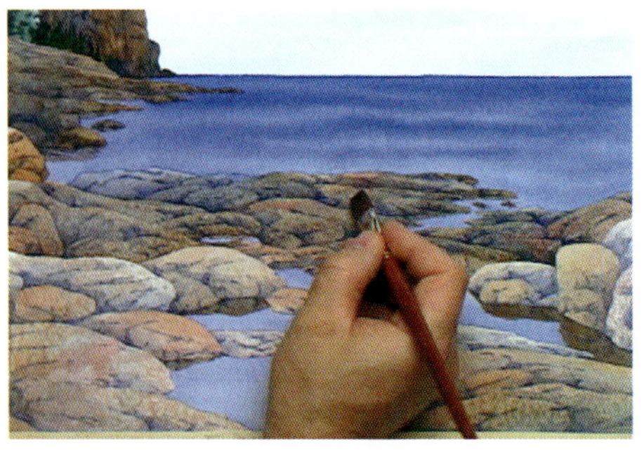

**Step 24:** With a lean mix of Cobalt Blue and a 1/2" flat brush, I painted in subtle shades to further separate and distinguish groups of rocks.

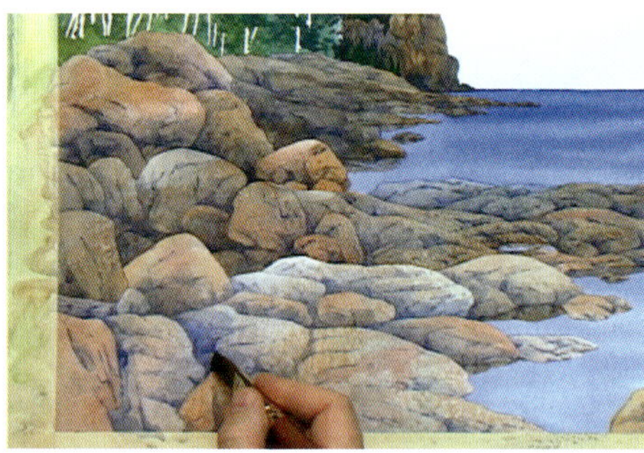

(Step 24 continued)

This additional shading helped provide the rocks with even more depth and dimension.

**Step 25:** Using a single-edged razor blade, I scraped water light reflection marks along the perimeter of the pool. These provided yet another clue that the rocks were not floating in the pool of water.

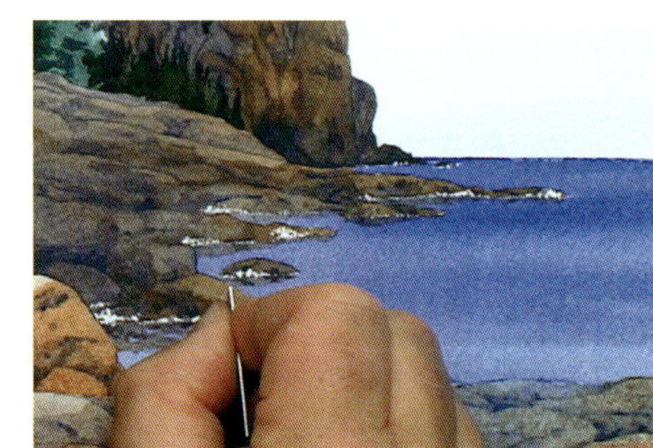

**Step 26:** With the same razor I scraped in the white water that the lake swells caused to gently break against the distant rocks.

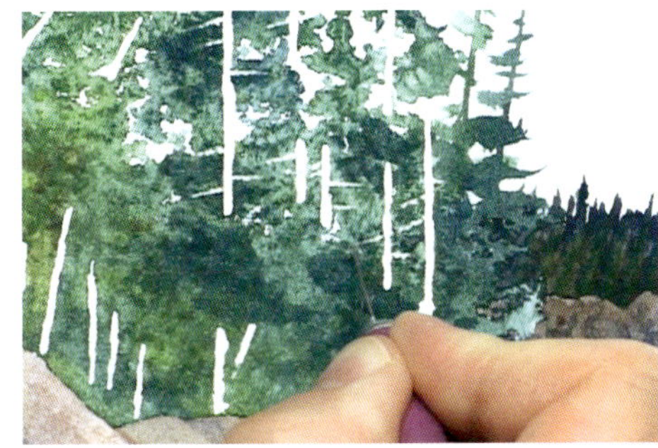

**Step 27:** With an exacto-knife, I scraped branches off of the previously masked trunks of both the birch trees and pine/fir trees.

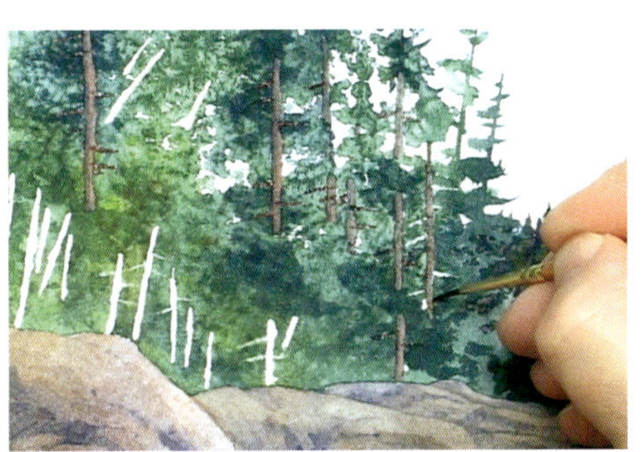

**Step 28:** Using a mix of Brown Madder and Phthalo Blue—and a range of round brushes between a #1 and a #2/0—I painted the visible trunks and branches of the pine/fir trees.

Then, with the same round brushes, but with Payne's Gray, I painted in the dark birch tree markings. These did not require great detail as they were relatively far from the viewer. Again with the exacto-knife, I lightly scraped and lightened the uplight side of the tree trunks.

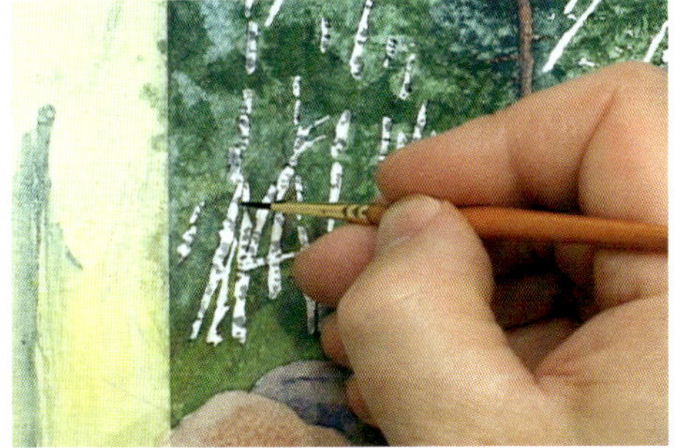

**Step 29:** Continuing with small round brushes, I shaded the downlight side of these trees with a thin mix of Cobalt Blue.

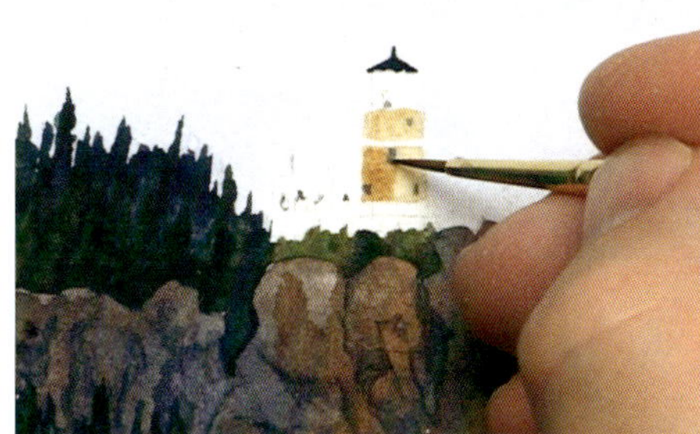

**Step 30:** Next, with Yellow Ochre, Payne's Gray, and a #1 and a #0 round brush, I carefully painted the lighthouse.

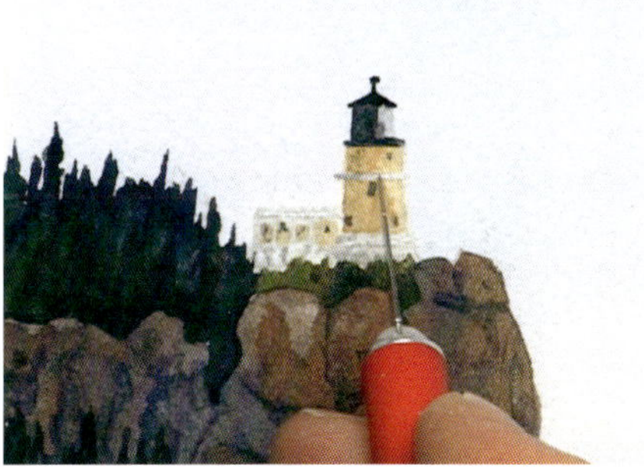

With an exacto-knife, I cleaned up some of the structure's white trimmings. Then I subtly shaded its downlight side with a lean mix of Cobalt Blue.

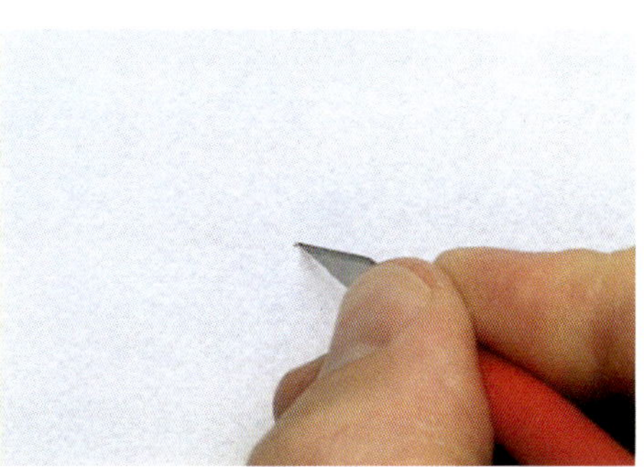

**Step 31:** Finally, I completed the painting by carefully "picking" at the small dots of paint that had accidentally landed in the sky area. Picking into the white of the paper, lessens the impact of the offending dot of color without unduly disturbing the underlying sky wash.

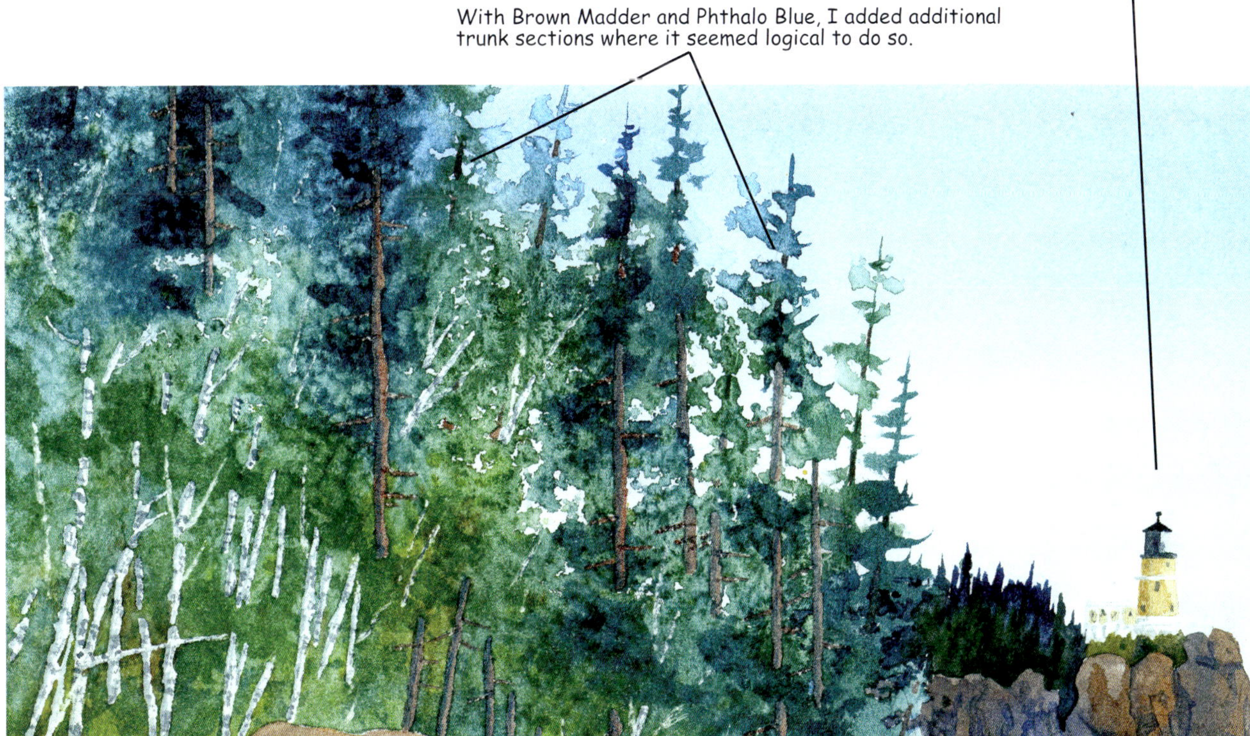

I provided just enough detail on the distant lighthouse to make it recognizable. As this is an actual place and a well known lighthouse, I did not take any liberties regarding its colors, shape or placement on the cliff.

With Brown Madder and Phthalo Blue, I added additional trunk sections where it seemed logical to do so.

# About The Author/Artist

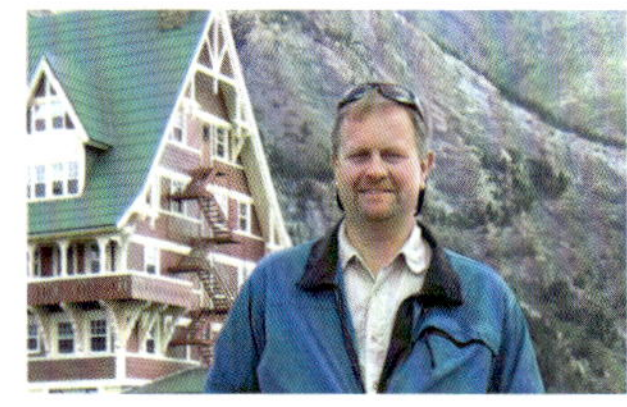

Through his art, Gary attempts to enrich the viewer's appreciation of the wild. His watercolor paintings strive to capture the ambiance of wilderness. While photography can record a precise—"at that moment"—visual image of nature, Gary believes that a painter must reach beyond this to acquire some semblance of the actual spirit of nature. In short, he believes that a painter must bring it alive! This pursuit—to bring wilderness alive through watercolors—is his passion and challenge as an artist!

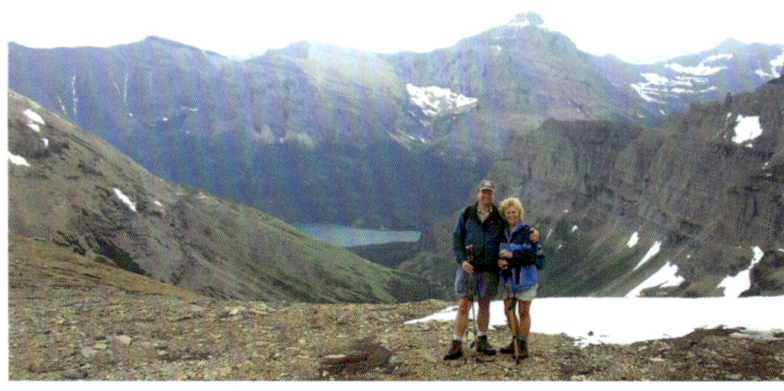

With a primary theme of mountains, wilderness lands and shorelines, Gary travels extensively in his quest to collect painting materials and find new paths to explore. In truth, he enjoys the "going to" as much as the painting process itself. As an avid outdoors enthusiast, he hikes, skis, sails, and kayaks through the landscapes that he paints.

Although educated at the University of Minnesota with a liberal arts degree, Gary is essentially self-taught as a watercolor painter—save an occasional painting workshop. He was actually a law-school-bound-political-science-major who abruptly took a sharp turn on the "road of life," shortly after graduation, to pursue his true interest and passion of painting. Gary has never regretted this move (nor has he created any noticeable vacuum in the legal world!).

Over the years, he has achieved numerous painting awards, including 7 acceptances into the prestigious "Top 100" National Park painting collections of the National Park Academy of the Arts. Many articles about his work have appeared in *Watercolor*, *The Artist's Magazine*, and *Watercolor Magic*. Recently, his work has been published in the books, *Searching For The Artist Within* and *Art From The Parks*. Gary's artwork has been collected and has been commissioned by some well-known corporations, such as US West, Georgia Pacific, Federated Insurance, and General Mills.

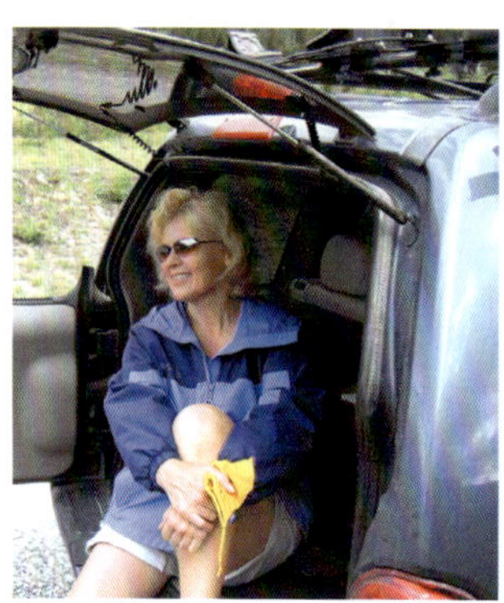

In 2004, he and his wife, Marlene, began producing a series of how-to-paint television programs for Public Television. These are distributed nationally by American Public Television and are presented by their home state's MontanaPBS.

When not "in the field," Gary and his wife, Marlene, reside near Montana's beautiful Flathead Lake and the "Crown Of The Continent," Glacier National Park.

Gary is a "signature member" of the National Watercolor Society.

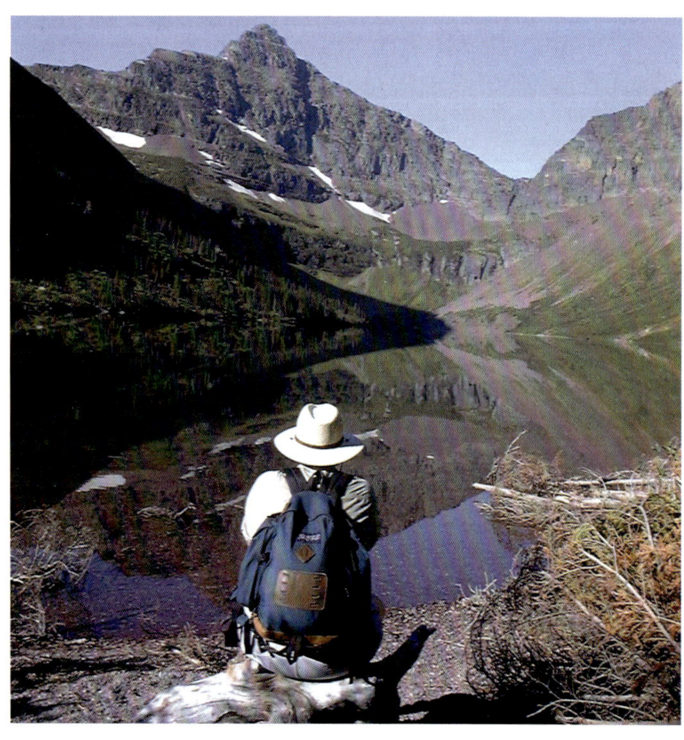